GRAMSCI'S POLITICAL THOUGHT

Hegemony, Consciousness, and
the Revolutionary Process

by
JOSEPH V. FEMIA

CLARENDON PRESS · OXFORD
1987

Oxford University Press, Walton Street, Oxford OX2 6DP

Oxford New York Toronto
Delhi Bombay Calcutta Madras Karachi
Petaling Jaya Singapore Hong Kong Tokyo
Nairobi Dar es Salaam Cape Town
Melbourne Auckland

and associated companies in
Beirut Berlin Ibadan Nicosia

Oxford is a trade mark of Oxford University Press

Published in the United States
by Oxford University Press, New York

British Library Cataloguing in Publication Data
Femia, Joseph V.
Gramsci's political thought: hegemony,
consciousness and the revolutionary process.
1. Gramsci, Antonio
I. Title
320.5'315'0924   HX288.G7
ISBN 0-19-827543-9

Library of Congress Cataloging in Publication Data
Data available

Printed in Great Britain
at Oxford University Printing House, Oxford
by David Stanford
Printer to the University

To

MY MOTHER,

and to the memory of

MY FATHER

Preface

Translations of passages from Gramsci quoted in the course of this book are my own. This does not imply serious dissatisfaction with existing English translations, which are generally reliable. The problem is that *most* of his writings have not yet been translated. For reasons of consistency in the rendering of Gramsci's terms and style, it was best, I decided, to work from the Italian original even when an English translation was available. Nevertheless, I have consulted, and in many cases benefited from, the English translations mentioned in the Bibliography. My debt to them is here gratefully recorded. As regards terminology in the *Quaderni*, the reader should be forewarned that Gramsci (probably because of prison censorship) tended to use the neutral word 'group' when he apparently meant 'class' in its Marxist sense. The former word, however, is not always meant as a euphemism for the latter. Whenever they appear in a quotation from the *Notebooks*, I translate *gruppo* and *gruppi* literally and leave it up to the reader to sort out Gramsci's meaning in the particular instance.

The primary research for this study was completed before the appearance of Valentino Gerratana's critical edition of the *Quaderni del Carcere* in 1975. Citations in the text are consequently given with reference to the original Einaudi edition, which—it should be observed—has in no way been superseded by the new one. By grouping together notes on related subjects, the old edition has the merit of imposing a thematic structure on Gramsci's fragmentary and disordered work. In so doing, it of course obscures the subtle development of his thought between 1929 and 1935, the period when he penned the *Quaderni*. But how significant was this development? No one has managed to show that Gramsci's ideas changed in any important or relevant ways during these years. Gerratana presents the notes in the order in which they were written and not according to topic headings. Indeed, his edition even reproduces preliminary drafts which Gramsci himself deleted! While this meticulous chronological approach certainly allows us to follow the rhythm of Gramsci's thought processes, it hardly enhances our comprehension of his *ideas themselves*. And it suffers from the disadvantage of rendering the reading of the entire work much more difficult and disorienting. For all these reasons, the original edition will, I think, remain the standard one. (Details of the works cited in this Preface may be found in the Bibliography.)

Turning now to acknowledgements, I should first point out that this study is a revised version of my Doctoral thesis, written for Oxford University and completed in the spring of 1979. I wish to express my deep gratitude to Leszek Kolakowski, my friend and academic supervisor, who—over a period of seven years—patiently read the thesis in draft form and provided invaluable advice, encouragement and criticism. Steven Lukes and Charles Taylor were scrupulous and generous examiners, whose acute observations stimulated me to amend parts of the manuscript. My debt to them is considerable. My thanks are also due to Sir Isaiah Berlin, who first prompted me to write about Gramsci and was kind enough to comment on some preliminary chapters—even though he had no formal responsibility for my supervision. At early stages in my research, I benefited from the criticisms and suggestions of a number of scholars who have themselves written on Gramsci—Martin Clark, Giuliano Procacci, Alistair Davidson, and Alessandro Pizzorno. The last two were especially helpful, as they read my 'exploratory' papers and kept me from travelling down some blind alleys. I must also thank the officials of the Gramsci Institute in Rome for allowing me (during the summers of 1973 and 1974) to use the excellent library housed there. Signora Elsa Fubini was particularly kind in supplying me with exhaustive and up-to-date bibliographical information. I am indebted to Nuffield College, which, by awarding me a studentship and travel grants, made this study possible. Finally, I am profoundly grateful to my wife, Josephine, for her assistance and infinite patience—and for putting up with Gramsci for so many years.

Earlier versions of some of the material in this book have appeared in the form of three articles by the author: 'Hegemony and Consciousness in the Thought of Antonio Gramsci', *Political*

Studies, XXIII (March 1975), pp. 29–48; 'Gramsci, the Via Italiana, and the Classical Marxist-Leninist Approach to Revolution', *Government and Opposition*, 14 (Winter 1979), pp. 66–95; and 'The Gramsci Phenomenon: Some Reflections', *Political Studies*, XXVII (September 1979), pp. 472–83.

Joseph V. Femia
December 1980

Contents

Abbreviations

Brief Biographical Sketch of Gramsci

1891—Born at Ales in Sardinia. Fourth son of a minor public official.

1911—Awarded scholarship at University of Turin and begins studies there. Specializes in linguistics.

1914—Starts to contribute to the Socialist newspaper, *Il Grido del Popolo*.

1915—Partly because of poor health, breaks off university studies.

1916—Begins to write a regular column for the Piedmont edition of *Avanti!*, the main Socialist Party newspaper.

1917—Becomes a leading figure in the Turin branch of the PSI.

1919—Co-founder and editor of *L'Ordine Nuovo*. Takes an active role in the Turin factory council movement.

1921—Becomes Central Committee Member of new Italian Communist Party, founded at Livorno in January.

1922—June. Arrives in Moscow as Italian Representative on the Comintern Executive. While there, meets Giulia Schucht, who becomes his wife.

1923—December. Sent by Communist International to Vienna, from where he tried to revive the Italian Party, torn by factional strife over the 'United Front' policy.

1924—May. Returns to Italy after being elected Deputy in Veneto constituency. Soon becomes Secretary General of the PCI.

1926—November. Arrested by Fascist regime.

1928—June. Condemned to twenty years' imprisonment.

1935—August. Transferred, for reasons of ill health, to a special clinic in Rome.

1937—April. Dies of brain haemorrhage.

CHAPTER 1

Introduction and Preview

> Marx has not written a catechism, he is not a
> messiah who left a string of parables laden with
> categorical imperatives, of absolute, indisputable
> norms outside the categories of time and space. The
> only categorical imperative, the only norm is:
> 'Workers of the world unite.'
>
> (Antonio Gramsci, 'Il Nostro Marx',
> *Il Grido del Popolo*, 4 May 1918)

I

THOUGH SCARCELY available to non-Italian readers before
the 1960s, the writings of Antonio Gramsci have had a global
impact. There is now almost universal agreement that he ranks
as one of the most innovative and important Marxist thinkers of
this century. In the words of an eminent Italian scholar, 'If we
except the great protagonists of the Soviet revolution, there is
no personality in the history of the workers' movement whose
person and work have aroused greater interest than Gramsci's.'[1]
The Sardinian's theoretical originality revolves around his
attempts to establish human subjectivity as a core element of
Marxism. In the classical Marxist tradition, of course, objective
material conditions were given pride of place; consciousness (in
all its manifestations) was conceptualized as the automatic
reflection of 'deeper' economic and social processes. It was
Gramsci's intention, by contrast, to accord it an independent
and creative role within the framework of historical materialism: he reformulated the doctrine in such a way as to allow room
for both the influence of ideas and the powerful effect of human
will. The problem of consciousness consituted his focal point—
how does it relate to the material world, what are its effects, how
can it be changed? Along with Lukács and Korsch, Gramsci
was one of the founders of *le marxisme occidental*—the revolt

against the orthodox tendency to interpret the historical development of society solely in terms of the production of material objects. Impressed by the categories of idealist philosophy, these exponents of so-called 'Hegelian Marxism' or 'Marxist humanism' placed at the centre of their theoretical discussions the relationship between mental events and reality. By accentuating the role of cultural objects and spiritual factors in social development, Gramsci and his Central European counterparts broke with the mechanical determinism of the official doctrine and established a new way of conceiving Marx's patrimony. It is common to trace this disenchantment with positivist Marxism to a number of factors: the growth of reformism within the Western working class, the outbreak of the First World War (revealing as it did the fragility of proletarian internationalism), the failure of the socialist revolution to spread outside Russia, the crushing defeat of the post-war rebellions in Germany and Hungary, and the subsequent rise of popular right-wing movements. This series of psychological and physical defeats led to grave doubts about the theoretical foundation of revolutionary action. The march of events apparently demonstrated that Marx's 'scientific' hypotheses were wrong—though few believers could bring themselves to admit this in so many words. Even Lenin, whose explicit theoretical grounding always remained impeccably orthodox, *behaved* as if the 'dialectical laws of history' could not be altogether trusted. Marxism as a determinist theory of social development had greater appeal when the trend of events actually appeared to be leading towards revolution and it could be confidently asserted that 'history is on our side'. When the course of history revealed a less agreeable aspect, a 'subjective' interpretation of the doctrine came to the fore. As an Italian, Gramsci had additional reasons for rejecting 'scientific' Marxism. His Italy was a semi-developed country with deep internal differences between North and South, industrial areas and countryside, modern and ancient. It possessed a labouring mass at widely divergent stages of development in different parts of the country, a proletariat with a broad rural base, a large, essentially conservative peasantry, a preponderance of intellectuals in the working-class leadership, and a style of politics at once bombastic and conspiratorial, conditioned by centuries of fragmentation and foreign domination. Looming above this bewildering and contradictory set of circumstances was the massive spiritual and social power of the Catholic Church, sustained not only by transcendental premises but also by a vast army of clerics and functionaries. This was a country entirely ill suited to the confident, evolutionary, schematic brand of Marxism it had borrowed from Germany.

Gramsci's stress on cultural and intellectual factors underlies his celebrated doctrine of 'hegemony' (*egemonia*), or ideological ascendancy. He saw in a way that no previous Marxist had done that the rule of one class or group over the rest of society does not depend on material power alone; in modern times, at least, the dominant class must establish its own moral, political and cultural values as conventional norms of practical behaviour. This is the essential idea embodied in 'hegemony', widely accepted as 'the basic theoretical point of departure for Gramsci's Marxism',[2] the 'central nucleus of his conceptual system'.[3] On the assumption that hegemony provides the analytical scheme around which the component parts of Gramsci's mature thought are built, this study will focus on this concept in order to reconstruct his leading ideas and theories. Since the theme of hegemony does not emerge as an integral part of the Sardinian's analysis until his period of incarceration (1926 to 1937), we shall deal mainly with his *Prison Notebooks* (*Quaderni del Carcere*), which doubtless constitute his most impressive contribution to Marxist thought. The earlier writings (almost entirely consisting of newspaper articles, editorials, book reviews and short political pronouncements)[4] will be discussed only when doing so will somehow illuminate the basic ideas advanced in the *Quaderni*—i.e. help to (1) trace their formation, (2) set them in their intellectual context, (3) bring out their full meaning, (4) explain why they have been misinterpreted. My refusal to view Gramsci's work as a unified corpus will not find favour in all quarters. Massimo Salvadori, a respected authority on Gramsci, echoes many when he claims 'that Gramsci's work, from his youthful writings to those composed in prison, is unitary like very few others' and 'that the *Quaderni*, taken as a whole, do not represent a qualitatively new thematic compared with the elaborations completed before 1926'. Rather, the *Notebooks* 'reflect, in substance, a theoretical systematization of the problems that arose during the period of his directly political activity'.[5] While this interpretation undeniably possesses a grain of truth, it tends to blind commentators to the revisions and developments in Gramsci's thinking, thus giving rise—as we shall see—to a number of misunderstandings about the nature of his message. Partly the result of changing conditions in the real world, this process of intellectual maturation will receive lengthy treatment in the course of our study, but for now let us briefly outline its basic form.

Without risk of distortion, we can discern four distinct phases in Gramsci's political life and thought—phases which represent different theoretical priorities and responses to the political world. The initial one, spanning the period 1914 to 1919, comprised the formative years of his intellectual and political evolution. While Gramsci, at this stage, was a fiery and intransigent socialist revolutionary, his philosophical orientation was more idealist than Marxist. In these years he was under the spell of Benedetto Croce, the great neo-Hegelian philosopher who was widely revered (and feared) as the 'God-father' of the Italian intellectual scene. Gramsci's articles and reviews during this period (most of which appeared in the socialist newspapers, *Avanti!* and *Il Grido del Popolo*) express a deep concern with the cultural and spiritual conditions of revolution, together with a messianic desire to inculcate the proper consciousness into the workers through intense educational activity. To this end, he delivered lectures, ran study circles and conducted seminars on literary and philosophical topics.

The second phase covers the dramatic months of the *biennio rosso* of 1919–20, an epoch punctuated by mass strikes and factory occupations. In May of 1919 Gramsci and a small group of Marxist intellectuals started *L'Ordine Nuovo*, a journal designed to give theoretical expression and practical direction to the increasingly militant struggles of the North Italian workers. Using *Ordine Nuovo* as his vehicle, Gramsci—with the aid of his colleagues—worked out his well-known factory council theory, with its anti-centralist, anti-bureaucratic bias. At this juncture, his philosophical idealism yielded to a more recognizably Marxist (though hardly orthodox) position concerning the role of the economic structure. Also, we witness two further, closely related changes in his approach: (1) more emphasis on the *self*-education of the workers, and (2) a greater personal commitment to concrete political organization. Class consciousness, he now believed, would arise as a spontaneous product of the workers' 'conciliar' activity. The task of the revolutionary party, therefore, should be not to tutor the proletariat but to promote the formation of the *consigli di fabbrica*. It is essential to realize that, in Gramsci's eyes, the Italian revolution was *actual* during this period. 'Today Italy can be compared', he wrote, 'to the Russia of Kerensky.'[6]

The years of 1921 to 1926, from the founding of the PCI to Gramsci's arrest and imprisonment, mark the third phase of his career. During this time, he gradually came to see the process of revolution as a much slower one than had seemed to be the case in the heady atmosphere of the *biennio rosso*. With the humiliating collapse of the council movement, it became plain that the autonomous activity of the masses was by no means sufficient for the overthrow of capitalism. In consequence, Gramsci turned his attention to the party and its vanguard role. Much of his energy in this period was devoted to everyday organizational problems and factional turmoil within the PCI and the Comintern. Indeed, he spent much of 1922–3 in Moscow, and by 1924 he assumed (with the blessing of the Russians) leadership of the Italian Party. Not surprisingly, his writings during these years, directed as they were to the concrete exigencies of political strategy and tactics, displayed little theoretical boldness. The Gramsci of 1921–6 might be described as a loyal, but not uncritical, Bolshevik.

Last (but certainly not least) there is the period of confinement in a number of Fascist prisons. Soon after his arrest Gramsci planned an immense labour of research and meditation, designed to set his active political experiences within a wider historical and philosophical framework. Despite appalling obstacles (see below), he went on to execute a great part of his self-assigned task. Between 1929 and 1935, he filled 32 notebooks with close to 3,000 pages of handwritten notes, covering a vast range of topics. In these now famous notebooks—a monument to intellectual tenacity and heroism—Gramsci evolved themes, interests, principles and concepts which were barely visible, if not entirely absent, in his previous writings. Why this change? The composition of the *Quaderni* corresponded to a new stage of development in the working-class struggle—one engendering profound pessimism. By the early 1930s, the myth of imminent world revolution had been exposed for what it truly was. If even the worst depression in capitalist history had not impelled the proletariat to rise up against its oppressors, then clearly a *ripensamento* was in order. Obviously, the 'bourgeois' system possessed sources of stability whose vitality had been obscured by the false optimism that had pervaded Comintern thinking. Since revolution was not just round the corner, inherited Marxist categories and formulae had to be revised and adapted to existing, unpalatable facts. More than any other Marxist, Gramsci realized this need for a fundamental reinterpretation of the standard doctrines, and his concept of hegemony—along with its surrounding theory—arose out of this concern. What the *Notebooks* attempt to do, then, is to readapt the Marxian 'weapons of criticism', to construct a new theoretical-strategic paradigm applicable to the conditions of mature capitalism. Gramsci the young agitator and activist becomes Gramsci the mature scholar.

No doubt we can detect some unity transcending the shifts in his theoretical and political perspective. Certain themes and fundamental attitudes *did* persist throughout his career. Above all, he consistently stressed the active, 'voluntarist' side of Marxist theory, in contrast to the fatalistic reliance on objective economic forces and immutable 'scientific' laws. The necessity for the masses to acquire a critical consciousness, the need for cultural and ideological battle, was, in varying degrees, an enduring preoccupation of his thought. He never deviated from his desire to give Marxism a sound philosophical foundation, capable of restoring the subjective dimension and placing human actors at the centre of the revolutionary process. The *Quaderni*, to be sure, often reflect a theoretical elaboration of insights, intuitions and historical observations contained in his earlier output. With some exceptions, the ideas in the *Notebooks* were either intimated or affirmed, in some shape or form, in his youthful writings. But none of this entitles us to deny the twists and turns of his thought or to assert, as does Cammett, that hegemony 'is the unifying idea of Gramsci's life'.[7] What could this mean? The word itself is not actually integrated into

Gramsci's theoretical vocabulary until 1926, when—in his essay on the *Quistione meridionale*—he refers to the 'hegemony of the proletariat' as 'the social basis of the proletarian dictatorship'.[8] True, most of the basic ingredients of the concept were palpably present in earlier works—in particular, the notion that successful political revolution must be complemented by a transformation in the spirit of the age. We can accept, moreover, that a concept may be implicit in a body of theory even though the theorist in question does not mention it explicitly. For example, a writer may *employ the concept* of alienation *without actually using the term*. In making this assertion, we can invoke the authority of Gramsci himself, who deplored, 'the confusion of questions of terminology with questions of substance'[9] Nevertheless, any particular concept receives its *full* meaning only in relation to the entire conceptual structure in which it is embedded, in relation to all its dimensions. Theoretical ensembles must be considered in their unity, and not as agglomerations of discrete, self-sufficient elements which might be torn from their context without altering their significance. The ideas set out in the *Notebooks* are the *defining context* of hegemony, and (as we shall see more clearly and fully in ensuing chapters) these were in crucial respects different from Gramsci's earlier ideas.

Gramsci's prison focus on hegemony, on the moral and cultural legitimation of political rule, enabled him to furnish novel (if sometimes oblique) solutions to three problems which have plagued Marxist thought and behaviour for well over half a century. First, why the gap between Marxist theory and proletarian practice? In other words, why have Western industrial workers not taken the path set out for them by Marxism—why have they not become the gravediggers of capitalism? Second, how do we close this gap—by what means can a revolutionary party increase its support and eventually attain power in the highly developed societies of the West? The third broad question is this: why does socialist practice not fit Marxist theory? Or, why have extant 'Marxist' societies not succeeded in establishing the 'realm of freedom' envisaged by Marx and Engels? The primary purpose of this study will be to explore and evaluate Gramsci's answers (direct and indirect) to these perplexing questions. But doing so raises preliminary (and formidable) problems of interpretation, which will now be considered.

II

Despite the huge and ever-growing pile of secondary literature, there remains to this day remarkably little general agreement about what Gramsci really said. His work has called into existence an army of interpreters whose unceasing labours have buried them beneath a mountain of commentary which has obscured the texts themselves. Commentators have emended, conjectured, transposed, elided and inserted with an energy and diversity that can leave the reader the impression of hopeless confusion. Just how does one deal with a thinker who has been variously described as a dialectical materialist and a subjective idealist, a Stalinist totalitarian and a mild democratic socialist, an intransigent revolutionary and a prophet of peaceful evolution?[10] Controversy continues amidst uncertainties and muddles—many of which must be attributed to the *politically inspired* content of much of the literature, especially in Italy. Debates on Gramsci are not always reducible to a simple confrontation of different exegeses: the gist of the interpretative disputes is frequently partisan and polemical, with the result that bias prevails over dispassionate study and historical understanding. All great men attract legends and misinterpretation, and all too often what they thought and wrote is ignored or distorted, as disciples (or enemies) impose their own subjective preconceptions on the object of investigation. Gramsci has perhaps suffered more than any Marxist writer since Marx from partial, politically motivated interpretations, by supporters and opponents alike. What matters most to some commentators is the advantage they could win for their political positions by arguing for a particular concept of his objectives. As a result, Gramsci's authority, as we shall see, has been called upon in support of an often incompatible range of theoretical opinions and practical policies. Those who disagree with the opinions or policies so justified often confuse them with Gramsci's own ideas and attack him accordingly, or else reinterpret his ideas in conformity with their own personal preferences. And so there develops a vicious circle of misunderstanding and distortion, with Gramsci being dragged hither and thither, his thought enclosed within a number of mutually exclusive formulae. The PCI bears much of the responsibility for this sorry state of affairs. The prestigious figure of Gramsci was, immediately following his death, converted into an official ideological symbol of the Party, invoked to justify every nuance of Party behaviour.

Unfortunately, his writings *do* provide texts to support a wide variety of interpretations. For one thing, since his ideas altered over time, his thought can appear quite different depending on which phase is stressed. Hence the need to bear in mind the *evolution* of his ideas. But even if we confine ourselves to the *Notebooks*, we encounter enough ambiguity to permit diverse readings. Let us not dwell on the minor inconvenience caused by Gramsci's frequent use of code words (e.g. Marxism becomes 'the philosophy of praxis') in order to circumvent prison censorship. For all its awkwardness, this code is fairly transparent and presents no real obstacles to understanding the *Quaderni*. Other obstacles abound, however. We are confronted with an unfinished work, replete with elliptical passages, disorders, apparent contradictions, cryptic utterances, sly asides, esoteric allusions, aborted observations, unassimilated 'rough' facts, and seemingly endless digressions—a monumental labyrinth of often opaque and undeveloped ideas. Sometimes Gramsci was merely suggesting projects for future study or raising questions for which he provided tentative or equivocal solutions, if any. Rarely do his arguments or essays reach final draft form. Mostly we have a collection of raw materials and fragmentary discussions which—for all their suggestiveness and originality—are never quite fused into an organic totality. There is ample space here for a 'battle of citations', with each commentator able to unearth what *appears* to be written confirmation of his position. What ambiguity there is, it must be underlined, does not stem from unnecessarily obscure language or convoluted prose or a fondness for intangible abstractions, but from the simple fact that the *Notebooks* constitute a work *in itinere*—notes and jottings intended for the author alone, not for publication. Small wonder that when the first volumes were published in the late 1940s, Croce dismissed them as 'roughly sketched and tentative thoughts, self-questionings, conjectures and doubts . . . [devoid of] that power of synthesis which discriminates, builds and integrates into a whole'.[11] While this dismissal has been superseded by history, Croce's complaint is not without foundation.

The incomplete state of the *Quaderni* is lamentable, but easily explicable by the distressing conditions under which he laboured. In the first place, his prison governors exhibited, to borrow Giuseppe Fiori's apt phrase, 'a well developed bureaucratic taste for refusal and minor harassment'.[12] Gramsci had much trouble in acquiring the books and journals he needed to pursue his studies; many were consistently denied him. Add to this his incredibly numerous physical ailments—hypertension, angina, tuberculosis, Pott's disease, to mention but a few—which rendered his life in Fascist gaols a constant struggle against physical pain and emotional despair. He literally rotted away in prison, and this made it difficult for him to concentrate or work systematically. Many of his vivid, intensely moving letters from prison testify to his physical and psychological torment. They are studded with references to his 'acute agony', 'nervous tension', 'enervation', and 'physical deterioration'.[13] In a communication of 1932, he tells his wife, Julca: 'I live miserably, barely at all, an animal or even vegetable existence'.[14] Gramsci finally expired at the relatively young age of 46, just after his release from prison. The great work he was preparing could never attain its final form.

Since Gramsci bequeathed no 'finished' intellectual legacy, no extended and systematic piece of theoretical writing, and since, furthermore, he was a highly committed, active political combatant, attempts to find universal content in his thought or to restructure it into an architectonic whole are especially vulnerable to methodological censure. Indeed, the need for a strict historicist approach to his writings, the need to dissolve his thought into the world of political actuality, has been a dominant theme amongst PCI leaders and theoreticians ever since his martyrdom established him as the patron saint of the Italian revolutionary movement. From 1937 right up until his own death, Togliatti dismissed any attempt to view Gramsci as an original thinker, as an independent seeker of new truths, as a reflective scholar in any way detached from the world of affairs. Togliatti's Gramsci was, on the contrary, a staunch Leninist, a loyal steadfast Bolshevik, a maker of revolution, a politician for whom ideas were nothing unless made practical. At the first conference of Gramsci studies in 1958, Togliatti proclaimed that Gramsci's writings, in so far as they were valuable, could only be examined in 'the knowledge of the concrete moments of his action' for to these 'concrete moments . . . adhere every general formulation and affirmation'. All Gramsci's thoughts were directed to one goal: to provide 'a guide to revolutionary action'. Even the prison notes did not constitute a 'detached reflection' on the struggles of the preceding years, but rather a 'continuation of these struggles'. Gramsci's work, then, presented not timeless formulae and was not susceptible to abstract systematization.[15]

In the years after Togliatti's demise, PCI spokesmen were somewhat reticent about asserting that Gramsci was doing nothing more than applying (or adapting) the Leninist model to Italian circumstances; Togliatti's methodological strictures, however, continued to be reiterated. Amendola, writing in 1967, argued that 'Gramsci's writings are *always* . . . those of a political militant who never surrenders and always resolves the attainment of political ends. . . . Present, therefore, in his writings are exigencies imposed by disciplinary ties, by practical motives of expediency, and by necessary concessions not only to the general line of the party, but also to formulations more or less obligatory in a specific moment'. It follows that '. . . Gramsci's writings . . . [must] always be related to the concrete circumstances in which he found himself acting, to the problems posed in that moment'. Scattered remarks cannot be detached from their practical context and inflated into coherent doctrines.[16]

While this picture of Gramsci as essentially a man of action obviously contains a large element of truth, it is nevertheless exaggerated and, ironically, ahistorical; for it ignores the more disinterested, meditative side of his character that emerged during his incarceration. To be sure, the articles and documents he wrote as an active militant in, first, the Socialist Party and, after 1921, the Communist Party were closely bound up with specific circumstances, events, and objectives. Because these pieces were mostly designed as weapons, their theoretical content is often secondary, usually implicit, and always difficult to extract from the minute details of political controversy. Gramsci's thought in these years shifts between the theoretical and the practical: the same piece may be viewed, simultaneously, as an act of political persuasion (or polemic) or as an incident in the pursuit of understanding. But if we are to identify this latter component, to isolate it from the transitory and the exaggerated, we must do so by a process of historical reconstruction. Abstractly to juxtapose aphorisms culled from these writings is to risk grave misrepresentation. It is, moreover, to misunderstand the nature and functions of political rhetoric, to gloss over the distortions and simplifications indulged in by all political activists, who must at once persuade, arouse, and attack.

Gramsci was, however, more than an activist. His *Prison Notebooks* were by and large directed to a much higher level of abstraction than were his earlier articles and tracts. Four months after being arrested in 1926, he strongly suggested, in a letter to his sister-in-law, that his interests were no longer immediately political (in the narrow sense):

> I am spurred on . . . by this idea: that I ought to do something *für ewig*,[17] to use Goethe's complex conception, . . . In short, I would like to work intensively and systematically, according to a pre-established plan, on certain subjects which could absorb me totally and give focus and direction to my inner life.

He was contemplating at least four possible projects: (1) research into Italian intellectuals, their origins, their groupings in relation to cultural trends, and their various modes of thought; (2) a study of comparative linguistics; (3) a study of Pirandello's plays and the transformation of Italian theatrical taste that Pirandello represented and helped to bring about; (4) an essay on popular taste in literature.[18] While Gramsci later changed his plan of work, the tone of this letter, along with its selection of topics, clearly reflects a desire for some measure of scholarly detachment. Indeed, he had little choice in the matter, as his imprisonment effectively isolated him from political life. It is difficult, in either the *Quaderni* or the *Lettere*, to find references to current events or political activity: Stalinism, popular frontism, Nazism—these phenomena form only a shadowy presence. In a number of letters he expressed sorrow over 'being cut off from the life of society'.[19] While in prison, he had virtually no contact with his former political associates, most of whom were in exile or themselves incarcerated. His news of developments within the Party and the International was sparse, taking the form of belated and summary accounts. If Gramsci's *Notebooks* are embedded in a concrete context, it is that of the political universe within which he operated *prior* to his arrest.

In the end, the main lines of investigation pursued by Gramsci in his *Quaderni* are: the historical analysis of past cultural movements and trends, especially in Italy; a critique of Croce's philosophy; his (Gramsci's) battle against mechanistic and fatalistic deformations of Marxism; and his ideas on the construction of the new proletarian society. Even a cursory reading of these *Notebooks* is sufficient to indicate that Gramsci was dealing with issues and proposing hypotheses of a universal nature, transcending both national boundaries and the hum of concrete politics. Many of the topics he discussed, such as the nature of man, the role of ideas in history, the relationship between philosophy and politics, and the ontological status of the external world, represent traditional philosophical concerns. It is hardly surprising that in one revealing passage, he passionately calls for a 'renewal of the philosophy of praxis [Marxism] . . . which has become progressively *"vulgarized"* *because of the necessities of immediate, practical life*', so that it can solve the task of creating a new civilization, possessing 'the classical character of the cultures of Ancient Greece and the Italian Renaissance'.[20]

It is of course true that all Gramsci's prison reflections are directed ultimately towards one over-arching goal—the construction of a morally integrated socialist society. Gramsci's *Quaderni* were by no means divorced from his general revolutionary concerns; they are not the product of ivory-towered, purely contemplative musing. Indeed, much of his speculation and observation revolves around specific, empirical problems of contemporary relevance. But every political theorist is to some extent *engagé* and every work of political thought is to some extent a tract for the time. Political theory—whether it focuses on description or evaluation or both—must necessarily consist of abstraction and extrapolation from concrete examples and actual behaviour. The boundaries and substance of the subject matter are in large part determined by the practices of the existing society; that is, what the political thinker says is influenced by the problems agitating his society; his statements and propositions are, in Cassirer's phrase, 'abbreviations of reality'. Certainly, if he wishes to gain the attention of his contemporaries, he must direct himself to their problems and accept the terms of debate imposed by their concerns. And most political theorists *are* interested in the implementation of their theories: Machiavelli, Grotius, Locke, Rousseau, Saint-Simon, Marx, and others have all addressed their work to a particular person or group.

To sum up, the issues that concerned Gramsci in prison, his approach to his subject matter, the types of arguments he used, the nature of his hypotheses, the broad scope of his insights—all these enable us to classify him as a bona-fide political thinker and not merely as a polemicist or pamphleteer or activist.

The reader will, I hope, permit me a parenthesis here about why Togliatti and later PCI spokesmen have felt compelled to ignore the foregoing considerations. As is well known, the Party, since the war, has been widely praised and blamed (depending on one's angle of vision) for its flexibility, for its willingness to adjust to changing circumstances and to come to terms with capitalism's vexing powers of regeneration. The logical corollary of such a policy is to eschew firm commitments to *specific* formulations and prescriptions. In other words, the vaguer the contours of the doctrine, the better. To emphasize the intimate nexus between Gramsci's thought and practice, such that his ideas cannot be extracted from the matrix which generated them, permits the Party to free itself from the confines of any of his *particular* teachings.

But what are his teachings? We have come full circle to the problem of interpretation. Since the *Notebooks* have no clearly articulated structure, the reader must unravel and reassemble the threads of the various arguments as they occur in different parts. In searching for the essential lines of Gramsci's position, it is constantly necessary to sift the chaff from the grain, to extract the deeper intuitions and main ideas from the mass of raw details and otiose digressions. Eventually a general design becomes visible. Although the *Quaderni* are far from systematic, they do not lack an underlying coherence. Certain guiding themes make the whole more or less intelligible: (a) the nature of power in advanced capitalist regimes; (b) the methods whereby this power can be undermined; (c) the character of the new proletarian civilization; (d) the relationship between the material and spiritual sides of existence. Gramsci's thoughts on these themes group themselves round his concept of hegemony—the unifying or organizing principle which enables us to clarify the links between his propositions and generally bring his fragmentary notes into focus. This exercise can only be pushed so far: the doctrines enunciated in the *Notebooks*, it is plain, tend to resist tidy formulation; the commentator must frequently accept incoherence or engage in surmise. Still, in teasing out Gramsci's ideas, I shall necessarily have to impose an artificial pattern on his disjointed notes, thus raising them to a much higher level of organization than they ever in fact reached; and to do so is to invite condemnation not only from the ghost of Togliatti but also from the increasingly influential 'revisionist' school of intellectual history, which complains about the prevailing abstractness and lack of historicity in the recovery of the meaning of past ideas. John Dunn states the essence of their grievance succinctly enough:

The history of thought as it is characteristically written is not a history of men battling to achieve a coherent ordering of their experience. It is, rather, a history of fictions—of rationalist constructs out of the thought processes of individuals, not of plausible abridgements of these thought processes. It consists . . . not of plausible accounts of how men thought but of more or less painful attempts to elaborate their ideas to a degree of formal intellectual articulation which there is no evidence that they ever attained. Because of these features, it is often extremely unclear whether the history of ideas is the history of anything which ever did actually exist in the past.[21]

The argument is impressive in its scope and worth exploring in some detail: it is not simply that the utterances of this or that political thinker—say Gramsci—cannot be properly understood unless located in their unfolding historical context; it is that the connection between an adequate philosophical account of notions held by *all* writers in the past and an accurate historical account of these notions is an exceedingly intimate one. For, the argument runs, thinking is not directed towards the construction of closed formal games but towards problem solving. As Quentin Skinner puts it, any 'statement . . . is inescapably the embodiment of a particular intention, on a particular occasion addressed to the solution of a particular problem, and thus specific to its situation in a way that it can only be naïve to try to transcend'.[22] There are no 'timeless truths' or 'perennial questions'. Thus the phenomena of political thought must be treated as historical phenomena, even as historical events, as things happening in a context which defines the kind of events they were. The problem of interpretation is always the problem of 'closing the context'; and 'what closes the context in actuality is the intention (and, more broadly, the experiences) of the speaker'[23]—phenomena to be disclosed through detailed analysis of historical conditions.

The 'revisionist' position, of course, is not entirely original. The belief that a true understanding of any intellectual product and an adequate assessment of its value are to be garnered through considering it in terms of the place it occupied and the role it played within the process of development enjoys a distinguished ancestry—which can be traced in the thought of, among others, Vico, the German historicists, Marx and Gramsci himself. If not pressed too far, this view can yield valuable insights (as I shall argue below). But one detects in the writings of Dunn, Skinner, and others like them more than a hint of the sort of determinism which considers the relationship between linguistic acts and their setting such that the act derives from—or is reducible to—the setting. In their desire to deal with the uniquely historical questions of what the author *intended* to say and what circumstances occasioned his reflections, the 'revisionists' neglect another crucial, closely related question: how far is the meaning or value of any set of ideas irreducibly infected by the conditions of its birth? Notwithstanding their disclaimers, they come perilously close to mistaking the origins of a statement for its logical status. Involved here are two different types of questions, requiring different kinds of explanation and verificatory procedures. This is not to say that the two types of enterprise are completely unrelated; it is only to insist that the relationship can never be one of identity. Moreover, the extent to which they are related depends on individual cases. Some works are more historically specific than others (e.g. Burke's *Reflections on the Revolution in France* and Lenin's *What is to be Done?*). On the other hand, there are works, such as Rosseau's *Social Contract*, which do not intrinsically appear to be so specifically occasional. Gramsci's *Quaderni* perhaps lie somewhere in between. The revisionists never consider these differences and their implications.

To speak plainly, this new methodological puritanism renders futile any investigation of the theoretical or conceptual validity of past bodies of thought. To follow literally the instructions of the 'revisionists' would be to consign Gramsci to some gallery of respected ancestors. Needless to say, thinkers develop their ideas in a determinate historical context and with particular purposes in mind; but it on no account follows that these ideas cannot transcend their origins. As Isaiah Berlin so rightly observes:

If the ideas and the basic terminology of Aristotle or the Stoics or Pascal or Newton or Hume or Kant did not possess a capacity for independent life, for surviving translation, and, indeed, transplantation, not without, at times, some change of meaning, into the language of very disparate cultures, long after their own worlds had passed away, they would by now, at best, have found an honourable resting place beside the writings of the Aristotelians of Padua or Christian Wolff, major influences in their day, in some museum of historical antiquities.[24]

While Gramsci himself espoused historicism (see Chapter 3), he, too, readily conceded that an intellectual enterprise was capable of transcending its social precipitants; but the extent to which it did so could only be established by empirical investigation:

The question arises whether a theoretical 'truth' discovered in correspondence with a specific practice can be generalized and deemed universal. . . . The proof of its universality consists precisely in that which it can become: (1) a stimulus to know better the concrete reality of a situation different from the one in which it was discovered (and this is the prime measure of its fecundity); (2) when it has stimulated and helped this better understanding of concrete reality, it incorporates itself into this reality as if it were originally an expression of it.[25]

(Gramsci does not here specify precisely what he means by 'universal'.) Elsewhere he pointed out that the 'intrinsic value' of certain ideas or concepts, like natural rights, was '*limited*' by their historicity, 'but *not negated*'.[26] Gramsci, it is clear, did not wish to dissolve theory into historical practice; between the two there was unity but no identity.

An insistence on historicity is one thing; an *a priori* determination to fossilize all past thought quite another. If understood in a 'hard' sense, the revisionist thesis is crippling, implausible, and fully capable of creating more mischief than the disease of hyper-abstraction it is designed to cure; if understood in a 'soft' sense (and there are passages where Dunn and Skinner retreat to safer terrain), it is rather banal, though perhaps a useful antidote to the more extreme ahistorical methodologies. Ideas are not born in a vacuum. If the historian of political thought is truly concerned with understanding and accurate representation of past ideas, then a purely textual approach will not do. Biographical and other contextual considerations can help to reveal the unstated (and perhaps unconscious) premises, the intellectual paradigms, underlying expressed arguments, and thus better enable us to resolve the ambiguities of those arguments or to assess their relative status within a given corpus of work. John Plamenatz, in his introduction to *Man and Society*, denies that 'to understand what a man is saying, we must know why he is saying it'. Instead, 'We need only understand the sense in which he is using his words'.[27] But there are occasions when one cannot know what a theorist means by certain words or propositions unless one knows, at least in a broad sense, what he is doing; viz., the identification of his arguments is often contingent upon a broad understanding of his purposes. Take a thinker like Gramsci, whose writings are often oblique, puzzling, and conditioned by a fear of censorship. It is hard to see how we could comprehend or evaluate his *Quaderni* without knowledge of his previous political experience as a revolutionary—the class struggle in Turin, the formation of the Italian Communist Party, the rise and consolidation of Fascism, the strategic debates within the PCI. Only in light of such knowledge can much of what he says be placed in perspective or made intelligible. Speaking generally, in order to identify and analyse properly the ideas of a political thinker, especially one who is unsystematic, we must usually know something of his private world, as well as of the social and political conditions and controversies of his time and place. As noted earlier, no political thinker is wholly severed from the practices and interrelationships of his society, which, in some measure, must impinge upon the form and content of his thought. But the revisionists go too far. They speak as if all political thought consists of a series of disconnected statements for ever bound in a straitjacket of *particular* experiences and *particular* intentions. But the historian of ideas is usually interested in works that (a) are fairly cohèrent, and (b) transcend, in some critical sense, spatio-temporal exigencies. In these cases, it is sufficient to know the *general* purposes and experience of the author.

The revisionists are led astray, I would argue, by their failure to grasp the range of reasons why we might want to study past ideas about society. They assume that our interest must be solely historical, that we must endeavour either to ascertain precisely 'what X *really* said (meant)' at any given time, or to trace the genesis and evolution of his ideas. They need to be reminded that the examination of political thought is 'not so much a venture into antiquarianism as a form of political education'.[28] Our interests may be less historical than con-temporary. We may deem the work of a past theorist valuable because it suggests concepts, models, or approaches that we may wish to incorporate into present theorizing; or we may find that studying the history of political thought can enrich con-temporary theory in a less direct manner, by showing the failures and successes of other minds grappling with problems similar to ours, or by revealing theoretical resemblances and linear continuities and how these relate to conceptions of the world or to general historical circumstances. Thus, even if the thoughts of our predecessors can supply no immediate answers, analysis of these thoughts can help us to construct our own arguments, in so far as it alerts us to certain sorts of errors, suggests potentially fruitful lines of inquiry, and provides us with a more profound understanding of the concepts we employ. Finally, a work of political thought may, in a much less tangible sense, help to expose the nature of our present predicament, much as a good novel might enhance our knowledge of human psychology and behaviour.

The revisionists seem to ignore the truism that the inter-action of men engaged in moral and social activities presents problems which preserve a considerable degree of continuity from one age to another. '. . . the past is never wholly super-seded; it is constantly being recaptured at the very moment that human thought is seemingly preoccupied with the unique problems of its own time'.[29] The *central* features of our social experience are invariant and omnipresent. However differently they may be defined in particular cultures or epochs, certain basic categories—order, change, authority, security, good and bad, happiness, efficiency, truth and falsehood—are indispensable components of political language in any society which reflects on its common experience.

When the intellectual historian confronts the works of past thinkers, his approach is, indeed, often artificial: he stresses themes to which they only assigned a subordinate role; he imputes to them coherent answers to questions they never even posed to themselves; he draws analogies between their thoughts and those of other writers unknown to them. Unless absolute historical accuracy is the only criterion, such strategies are entirely valid. Sometimes it is more appropriate (and useful) to bring into relief the value and implications of 'what X apparently said or suggested' rather than to attempt to divine, through laborious, and often futile, attention to historical detail, 'what X *really meant*'. The worth of a theory need not be confined to what its author saw in it or intended by it—or to the specific problems that occupied his attention. To argue otherwise is to obscure the important *educative* task of intellectual history.

My own interest in Gramsci is far from antiquarian. His *Quaderni*, I believe, contain observations, insights and hypotheses of *contemporary* resonance. In the history of political thought, genius does not always assume the form of unprecedented originality. Mostly, it consists of modifying and combining existing ideas to form a new whole. What is original in the result is not any one component element, but the apportionment of emphasis among the various parts, so that they are bound together in a unique way. Gramsci's originality must be understood in this sense. By viewing social experience from a slightly different angle than the prevailing Marxist one, he unfastened established ways of thinking and fashioned a new synthesis, appropriate to the conditions of advanced capitalism. Whether this synthesis fully withstands the test of critical scrutiny is another matter. The ensuing study is both expository and critical. It will aim not only to deepen our understanding of Gramsci's mature thought but also to form judgements about its value. Readers should not, however, expect a complete survey of the prison writings. Using 'hegemony' as its point of departure, this study will attempt to excavate the *leading*, most pregnant *philosophical* and *political* ideas embedded in those writings. (Gramsci's remarks, for example, on literary criticism and popular tastes in literature will receive scant attention.)

In the following chapter, we shall look at the concept of hegemony—explore its range of meaning, reveal its nuances, highlight its ambiguities, draw out its implications, and explain its novelty within the Marxist framework. Next (in Chapter 3), the concept's underlying theoretical and philosophical assumptions will be examined. How does Gramsci view the relationship between the economic base and the superstructure of society? What are his epistemological premises? How does he conceive the nature of reality itself? All his political thinking, I hope to show in the course of this work, is inextricably intertwined with his answers to these questions. Chapter 4 will discuss his theory of the revolutionary party, the agency entrusted with the task of formulating and building the new proletarian hegemony. How does he picture its (the party's) internal structure and operations? Its relationship with the masses? Chapter 5 sets out Gramsci's rather sketchy ideas about the future society and considers the vexed question, prominent in the secondary literature, whether 'hegemony' constitutes a justification for bureaucratic collectivism and totalitarian thought control. Having disposed of this problem, we examine (in Chapter 6) the extent to which Gramsci's hegemonic strategy is compatible with the so-called 'Italian Road to Socialism', which aims for a peaceful, constitutional transition to the 'realm of freedom'. What exactly are the strategic consequences of the doctrine of hegemony? The study concludes with a systematic assessment of Gramsci's mature thought. To what fruitful insights and explanations does it lead? Does it in fact provide satisfactory solutions to the theoretical and practical problems that trouble contemporary Marxism?

Along the way some attempt will be made to evaluate the often contrasting interpretations of Gramsci's legacy. Since these interpretations have, in a sense, taken precedence over the Sardinian's actual writings, it would be unwise to ignore them in a study of this length. The plethora of myths and misunderstandings must be identified and eliminated. Gramsci, we shall see, barely resembles some of the portraits painted in the secondary literature. In his basic theoretical assumptions, he was neither an orthodox dialectical materialist nor a neo-idealist. In his political thinking, he was neither a crypto-Stalinist nor a quasi-revisionist. Neither was he merely adapting the Leninist schema to new conditions. The Gramsci who will emerge from these pages is a creative revolutionary Marxist, who breathed new life into the doctrine of historical materialism, and posed the possibility of an alternative, more humane and diversified form of communism.

CHAPTER 2

The Concept of Hegemony

Certainly the philosophy of praxis is realized in the concrete study of past history and in the contemporary activity of creating new history. But a theory of history and politics can be made, for even if the facts are always singular and changeable in the flux of historical movement, the concepts can (and must) be theorized. . . .

Gramsci, *MS*, p. 126

THE CONCEPT of hegemony needs considerable amplification and analysis before we can see at all clearly how it is to be applied or what claims it makes. In spite of the voluminous literature on Gramsci, remarkably little attention has been devoted to identifying the precise meaning (or meanings) he assigned to what is, arguably, the key concept of his mature writings. Consequently, the concept's nuances, along with its theoretical potentialities, have been obscured if not completely disregarded. Treatment and use of hegemony is generally marred by conceptual vagueness; it has become one of those fashionable political catchwords which is often invoked but seldom properly defined or submitted to close scrutiny. Whenever certain Marxist analysts come across a situation involving (what they deem to be) the ideological predominance of a particular group or class, the term 'hegemony' is immediately adopted—as if the notion of 'ideological predominance' were itself free of ambiguity.[1] This lack of rigour tends to preclude a full appreciation of Gramsci's efforts to enrich Marxist theory and practice with a sophisticated analysis of mass psychology. What follows is an attempt to reveal the complexities and implications of his scattered and fragmentary exposition of hegemony. In this chapter it is my intention: (a) to elucidate the various forms and functions of the concept, (b) to specify how it links up with Gramsci's theory of the revolutionary process, and (c) to show in what respects 'hegemony' represented an innovation within the Marxist tradition.

I. *General Definition*

Starting from a traditional dichotomy—characteristic of Italian political thought from Machiavelli to Pareto—between 'force and consent', Gramsci states that the supremacy of a social group or class manifests itself in two different ways: 'domination' (*dominio*), or coercion, and 'intellectual and moral leadership' (*direzione intellettuale e morale*).[2] This latter type of supremacy constitutes hegemony.[3] Social control, in other words, takes two basic forms: besides influencing behaviour and choice *externally*, through rewards and punishments, it also affects them internally, by moulding personal convictions into a replica of prevailing norms. Such 'internal control' is based on hegemony, which refers to an order in which a common social-moral language is spoken, in which one concept of reality is dominant, informing with its spirit all modes of thought and behaviour.[4] It follows that hegemony is the predominance obtained by *consent* rather than force of one class or group over other classes. And whereas 'domination' is realized, essentially, through the coercive machinery of the state, 'intellectual and moral leadership' is objectified in, and mainly exercised through, 'civil society', the ensemble of educational, religious and associational institutions.[5] Hegemony is attained through the myriad ways in which the institutions of civil society operate to shape, directly or indirectly, the cognitive and affective structures whereby men perceive and evaluate problematic social reality. Moreover, this ideological superiority must have solid economic roots: 'if hegemony is ethico-political, it must also be economic, it must also have its foundation in the decisive function that the leading group exercises in the decisive nucleus of economic activity'.[6]

In his *Quaderni* Gramsci credits Lenin with the 'theorization and realization' of hegemony and calls this 'a great metaphysical event' as well as Lenin's 'major theoretical contribution to the philosophy of praxis'.[7] This attribution is somewhat enigmatic. Lenin did use the word—or its nearest Russian equivalent (*gegemoniya*)—in various writings, most notably *Two*

Tactics of Social Democracy, when discussing how the proletariat, because of the weakness of the Russian capitalist class, should assume a leading, or hegemonic role in the bourgeois-democratic struggle against Tsarist absolutism. But hegemony in this context has a purely instrumental, strategic significance: the key *cultural* emphasis the word conveys in Gramsci's usage has no place in Lenin's theory of revolution. Also, the Russian never extended the term, as did Gramsci, to the phenomenon of bourgeois supremacy or rule in a stable capitalist society.[8] An intriguing solution to the puzzle is suggested by Luciano Gruppi in his book, *Il Concetto di egemonia nel pensiero di Antonio Gramsci*: 'What does Gramsci mean when he speaks of hegemony with reference to Lenin? Gramsci understands the dictatorship of the proletariat.'[9] There is some textual justification for this interpretation. Gramsci, after all, applauds Lenin's 'realization' of hegemony and does, at one point in his notebooks, explicitly use the term as the equivalent of intellectual and moral leadership *plus* political domination: 'The "normal" exercise of hegemony on the now classical terrain of the parliamentary regime is characterized by the combination of force and consent which balance each other in various ways. . . .'[10] Gramsci was not entirely consistent; but from this meagre evidence, Gruppi infers too much, proclaiming, in a well-known article, that: 'For Gramsci the concept of hegemony *normally* includes those of "leadership" and "domination" together.'[11]

This intepretation is both unjustified and unjustifiable. When Gramsci refers to hegemony in his *Quaderni*, it is almost invariably clear from the context that he conceives it purely in terms of ideological leadership, and that he wishes to counterpose it to the moment of force.[12] Even when he speaks of 'political hegemony' or 'political leadership' (*direzione*), he undoubtedly means the *consensual aspect* of political control.[13] In his desire to portray Gramsci as a staunch Leninist, Gruppi has blurred a crucial dimension of his thought. Gramsci's usual—and decidedly unLeninist—use of hegemony is well brought out in a now famous letter he wrote to his sister-in-law from prison in 1931. Here he distinguishes between 'political society (or dictatorship, or coercive apparatus, for the purpose of assimilating the popular masses to the type of production and economy of a given period)' and 'civil society (or hegemony of a social group over the entire national society exercised through so-called private organizations, such as the Church, the trade unions, the school, etc.)'.[14] Gramsci's deference to Lenin, his hesitancy to admit his departure from strict Leninism, his modesty about the extent of his own contribution, betokened his profound respect for the Bolshevik's practical achievements and status as a patron saint of revolution.

II. *Civil Society/Political Society*

At the foundation of his analysis, Gramsci employed yet another time-honoured dichotomy in political thought—that between civil society and political society. The distinction is usually associated with Hegel's *Philosophy of Right*, but its origins can be found in the writings of the French and English philosophers, politicians, and economists of the seventeenth and eighteenth centuries who first discovered and investigated 'society' as a special, independent realm of knowledge and activity. The concept of society was the fruit of a long process of intellectual elaboration. All the same, Gramsci claimed that his definition of civil society was taken from Hegel.[15] If so, then his interpretation of the German philosopher was, at least in this respect, rather idiosyncratic; for Hegel clearly understood by civil society the complex of commercial and industrial life, the totality of economic instruments and relations, together with the public services needed to maintain order within them (e.g. civil courts, police). Gramsci, by contrast, identified civil society with the *ideological* superstructure, the institutions and technical instruments that create and diffuse modes of thought. He was perhaps inspired by those passages in *The Philosophy of Right* where Hegel included in the realm of civil society the corporations, or trade associations, which, through their educative functions, mediate between the anarchic particularism of civil society and the integrated, universal aspect of social life embodied in the state. Whatever his motive, Gramsci departed not only from Hegelian usage but also from Marx's equation of civil society with the material substructure (i.e. the structure of economic relations).[16] What Gramsci did, then, was to use traditional terminology in order to highlight an important, though generally neglected, theoretical distinction within the Marxist conception of superstructure, a distinction whose relevance for explaining the structure of power and dynamics of revolution he wished to illuminate.

Thus, Gramsci's division of the superstructure into two realms, and his concomitant distinction between hegemony and domination, signal an attempt to construct a theory of the superstructure, which, before Gramsci, constituted a glaring lacuna in Marxist thought.[17] This inadequacy was rooted in the historical peculiarities of the doctrine. Marx himself concentrated most of his mature efforts on the study of economic processes. After his death, most of his followers erroneously attributed an influence to the different social spheres in proportion to the treatment accorded them in his published writings. This error was facilitated by the standard interpretation of Marx's well-known claims on the relationship between the domain of material production and the superstructure. If the economic life of society is solely and wholly responsible for the character and development of other spheres, the activities which go on in the latter can be safely ignored or, if need be, deduced. Marxism from the start was preoccupied with the economic base to the virtual exclusion of the superstructure. By the early thirties, it became patently obvious that this approach was deficient. Capitalism showed no signs of succumbing to its 'insoluble contradictions' and history had not 'taken care of itself'. The stage was set for systematic thought about the superstructure, and Gramsci took up the challenge.

Before proceeding any further, some additional points about his dichotomy between political and civil society should be made. To begin with, the distinction is essentially analytical, a convenient device designed to aid understanding; in reality Gramsci recognized an interpenetration between the two spheres. For example: 'the State, when it wants to initiate an unpopular action or policy, creates in advance a suitable, or appropriate, public opinion; that is, it organizes and centralizes certain elements of civil society'.[18] In this connection, Gramsci discusses the manipulative potential of radio and the yellow press, which may or may not have *direct* ties with the government. The crucial point, to his mind, is that governments can often mobilize the support of the mass media and other ideological instruments, partly because the various élites, political or otherwise, share similar world-views and life-styles, and partly because the institutions of civil society, whether or not they are directly controlled by the state, must operate within a legal framework of rules and regulations. Indeed, Gramsci takes note of the tendency towards *increasing* state intervention in civil society, especially in the realm of culture (libraries, theatres, museums, etc.) and education.[19]

Moreover, as Gramsci indicates, the *functions* of the two moments of the superstructure overlap to some extent. Political society *in itself*, he suggests in a couple of brief passages, exercises a limited hegemonic role. The elaborate structure of liberal democracy (e.g. parliaments, courts, elections, etc.), by creating a façade of freedom and popular control, and by educating men in the ways of bourgeois politics, conditions them to accept the status quo willingly.[20] While Gramsci only alludes to this function and hardly gives it much weight, we should not be misled by the stark simplicity of his definition of political society as the 'apparatus of state coercion which legally assures the discipline of those groups which do not consent'.[21] Conversely, certain hegemonic institutions of civil society, such as political parties and organized religion, are transmuted, in specific historical situations and periods, into constituent components of the state apparatus.[22] And, needless to say, all organs of civil society coerce those non-conformists and rebels who come under their particular jurisdictions.

This close collaboration, this ambiguous line between civil and political society, is translated in the *Quaderni* into a broad definition of the state, comprehending all institutions which, whether formally public or private, enable the dominant social group to exercise power. (Confusingly, Gramsci retains the more conventional, narrow conception of the state as political society). At various points, he defines the state in the following manner:

State = political society + civil society, that is hegemony armoured by coercion.[23]

State in the integral sense: dictatorship + hegemony.[24]

[The State is] the entire complex of political and theoretical activity by which the ruling classes not only justify and maintain their domination but also succeed in obtaining the active consent of the governed.[25]

For Gramsci, then, the critical superstructural distinction is not so much civil/political or private/public as hegemony/domination; and individual societies can be analysed in terms of the balance between, and specific manifestations of, these two types of social control.

III. *Hegemony and Taylorism-Fordism*

Thus far we have discussed hegemony as a superstructural phenomenon, whose essential centre of radiation is 'civil society'. But in a disjointed and somewhat inconclusive set of prison notes headed 'Americanism and Fordism', Gramsci seems to be saying something rather different. In these long overlooked pages, whose importance has recently been alleged by a number of commentators,[26] he explores the technocratic and corporatist tendencies at work in advanced capitalism. In particular, he is concerned to examine the significance of 'Taylorism' as a method used by American capitalists to subordinate the workers to machine specialization and the 'cult of efficiency'. Frederick Taylor, whose system is expounded in *The Principles of Scientific Management* (1911), constructed an integrated body of principles for the purpose of maximizing efficiency within the labour process. His whole theory, it is fair to say, was based on the conception of man as a highly specialized machine, whose internal mechanisms could be precisely adapted to the needs of modern industry. 'Taylorism' can be encapsulated in three propositions: (1) the worker must be confined to a particular and minute task within the productive process; (2) he must develop automatic and mechanical attitudes (or reactions) to his work; there is to be, as Gramsci notes, no 'active participation of intelligence, fantasy and initiative on the part of the worker';[27] he becomes, in effect, an appendage of the productive apparatus; and (3) there must be an emphasis on *individual* monetary incentives, with the aim of breaking down the spirit of solidarity in the work force—which spirit, so the argument runs, lowers the general standard of performance.[28] According to Gramsci, Taylor's ideas form the basis of 'Americanism' or 'Fordism', the ideology of the advanced sectors of American industry. The chief goals of this ideology, Gramsci points out, are to rationalize production and create 'a new type of man suited to the new type of work'.[29]

America, he believed, enjoys a 'preliminary condition' which facilitates the implementation of 'Fordism':

This condition could be termed 'a rational demographic composition' and consists in the fact that there do not exist numerous classes without an essential function in the world of production; that is, purely parasitic classes. European 'tradition', European 'civilization' is, on the contrary, characterized precisely by the existence of such classes, created by the 'richness' and 'complexity' of past history, which has left behind a heap of passive sedimentations, as evidenced by the saturation and fossilization of state officials and intellectuals, of clergy and landowners, of predatory commerce and the [professional] army. . . .

Since America has no feudal past, she is relatively free of these 'parasitic' ('idle and useless') residues, whose presence has hindered the development of European industry and commerce.[30] The absence of this incubus has enabled the United States to organize production on rational lines and to dispense relatively high wages—at least in certain industries. To some extent, then, America has realized the 'Taylorist' project: she has apparently suppressed the critical faculties of the workers, undermined their natural tendency towards collective organization, and—so to speak—'bought them off'. It follows that in the USA, 'hegemony is born in the factory' and requires for its exercise only a 'minimal quantity' of ideological intermediaries.[31] None the less, Gramsci did think that *some* ideological mediation was necessary—hence his stress on how the Puritan ethic was manipulated to legitimate the behaviour (abstention from alcohol and 'disorderly' sexual activity) necessary for rationalized production techniques. (Maximum efficiency is of course impossible when workers dissipate their energies.)[32] Also, we must ask ourselves, how seriously did Gramsci take these new developments within capitalism? Did he, for example, actually believe, like Marcuse, that the rhythm of work in semi-automated factories could degrade men into stupefied automatons?[33] The answer is no. The total mechanization of labour, reasons Gramsci, 'does not spell the spiritual death of man'. Once the worker adapts to the new conditions, his brain, 'far from being mummified, achieves a state of complete freedom'. Because of the routine nature of his task, the worker acquires *greater* opportunities for thinking; and 'the fact that he gets no immmediate satisfaction from his work and realizes that [the capitalists] want to reduce him to a trained gorilla, can lead him into a train of thought that is hardly conformist'.[34] Neither can high wages serve as a long-run instrument of hegemony, for it is a 'transitory form of remuneration', which 'will disappear along with the enormous profits' as modern techniques of production become more widely diffused.[35] 'Fordism', as a mechanism of winning consent, was therefore geographically limited and historically doomed. For Gramsci, hegemony emanated primarily, if not entirely, from the organs of civil society; it could have no firm or lasting basis in the economic structure of capitalism, which—as we shall see—he regarded as a decadent, essentially inefficient mode of production.

IV. *Hegemony and the Marxist Definition of Power*

Disillusioned by the failure of the revolution to spread beyond Russia, Gramsci came to view hegemony as the most important face of power, the 'normal' form of control in any post-feudal society, and, in particular, the strength of bourgeois rule in advanced capitalist society, where material force is resorted to on a large scale only in periods of exceptional crisis. The proletariat, in other words, wear their chains willingly. Condemned to perceive reality through the conceptual spectacles of the ruling class, they are unable to recognize the nature or extent of their own servitude. Thus, he redefined the Marxist view of power in bourgeois society in more comprehensive terms. The idea that human society depends on voluntary agreement by its members to associate for the achievement of common goods, and upon the voluntary acceptance of mutual obligations and common arrangements is one of great antiquity. What was original about the concept of hegemony was its incorporation of this ancient proposition into a Marxist theory of class domination. For Marxists, dwelling on their apocalyptic vision, had invariably pictured capitalist society as little more than a battleground of irreconcilable forces and warring classes.

It is true that Gramsci's conception harks back to the passage in *The German Ideology* where Marx and Engels declare that:

In every epoch the ideas of the ruling class are the ruling ideas, that is, the class that is the ruling *material* power of society is at the same time its ruling *intellectual* power. The class having the means of material production, has also control over the means of intellectual production, so that it also controls, generally speaking, the ideas of those who lack the means of intellectual production.[36]

This assertion, which was reiterated in the *Communist Manifesto*,[37] is consonant with Marx's famous dictum, expressed in his essay on Hegel's *Philosophy of Right*, that 'religion is the opium of the people'. Marx and Engels plainly conceded the possibility that the ruling class could perpetuate its rule by controlling the means of legitimation and enshrining its definitions in the major institutional orders. Still, the founders of the 'philosophy of praxis' gravely underestimated the depth and pervasiveness of so-called 'false consciousness'. In the very same work quoted above, they inform us that, for the proletarians, 'such theoretical notions [bourgeois ideology] do not exist'. If the working class ever did adhere to these notions, they 'have now long been dissolved by circumstances'.[38] These circumstances are made explicit in the *Manifesto*:

. . . modern industrial labour, modern subjection to capital, the same in England as in France, in America as in Germany, has stripped him [the proletarian] of every trace of national character. Law, morality, religion, are to him so many bourgeois prejudices behind which lurk in ambush just as many bourgeois interests.[39]

The workers, on this argument, have come to inhabit a world where bourgeois culture—its norms and values, ideals and beliefs—is irrelevant, and where new forms have emerged in its stead. Commenting on the class structure of nineteenth-century England, Engels remarks that the proletariat has become a 'race wholly apart' from the middle classes. 'The workers speak other dialects, have other thoughts and ideas, other customs and moral principles, a different religion, and other politics than those of the bourgeoisie.'[40]

Attendant upon this radical cultural divergence is open hostility, manifest in a wage struggle Marx describes as 'a veritable civil war'.[41] For Marx and Engels, as for all Marxists before Gramsci, conflict, not consensus, permeates the system: 'Our epoch, the epoch of the *bourgeoisie* possesses this distinctive feature: it has simplified the class antagonism. Society as a whole is more and more splitting up into two great hostile camps, into two great classes directly facing each other: Bourgeoisie and Proletariat.'[42] Indeed, every social order based on a division of labour is, according to this view, necessarily a conflictual system: a class divided society is inevitably a society rife with turmoil. The problem of order, therefore, is typically solved by force or the threat of sanctions. The repressive function that Marxism characteristically assigns to state power arises logically out of the requirements of a set of social arrangements whose very persistence is always at stake. The state is a weapon, regularly and systematically used, because the internal threat to the system is continually manifesting itself in violent ways. Power is the key variable in this model of society: men do what is expected of them largely, if not wholly, because they are compelled to do so by those who monopolize the means of coercion. If they do not comply, they are threatened with or made to suffer some sort of punishment or deprivation.

It might be argued, with some plausibility, that Lenin did not accept the foregoing model, that all his thinking was conditioned by a fundamental despair over the proletariat's inherent tendency towards submissiveness, towards acceptance of the essentials of the existing order. To be sure, in his most memorable (and quoted) pamphlet, he puts forward the following argument:

There is much talk of spontaneity. But the *spontaneous* development of the working-class movement leads to its subordination to bourgeois ideology; . . . for the spontaneous working-class movement is trade unionism, . . . and trade unionism means the ideological enslavement of the workers by the bourgeoisie.[43]

In other words, the exigencies of survival and day-to-day practicalities restrict mental (or ideological) development, and subordinate even the unwilling and rebellious to the logic and norms of the system. Revolutionary consciousness is not the natural product of the life experience of the working people. This observation is widely regarded as epitomizing Lenin's theoretical contribution to Marxism. It is not generally realized, however, that the pessimism of *What is to be Done?*—a work produced in 1902—accords ill with certain of his earlier and later writings, which articulate the conventional Marxist optimism about the subversive propensities of the proletariat. During the course of the revolutionary events of 1905, for example, we find him suggesting that 'the working class is instinctively, spontaneously social-democratic', a view he still maintained some years later when reviewing this period in retrospect.[44]

Of course, we must be chary about what inferences we draw from Lenin's pamphlets and articles. His writings are always difficult to assess because of their engaged and rhetorical character, their intimate connection with concrete political activity, with specific controversies, events, and circumstances. Much more than Gramsci, Lenin was an activist first and a theoretician second. It is usually forgotten that *What is to be done?* was a polemic produced as part of an internal debate within the Russian Social-Democratic Party. Lenin later insisted that 'it is false to consider the contents of the pamphlet outside of its connections with this task'.[45] In addition, he was concerned, in this work, with the status of trade unions within Tsarist Russia rather than within capitalism generally.

The point to be emphasized is that Lenin made no clear-cut attempt to deviate from the classical Marxist analysis of capitalist society, at least not on a theoretical level. And regardless of whether he consistently (or 'really') believed that the proletariat is spontaneously disposed to mere 'trade unionism', he was constant throughout his career in his interpretation of the bourgeois order as essentially coercive. Capitalist democracy was 'the dictatorship of the bourgeoisie', shot through with coercion and violence: '*the more highly developed a democracy is, the more imminent are pogroms or civil war in connection with any profound political divergence which is dangerous to the bourgeoisie*'.[46] Conflict between oppressors and oppressed, Lenin believed, is endemic in the capitalist order; trade unionist or 'economist' tendencies can only divert, and possibly temper, this ubiquitous and bitter confrontation; they cannot eliminate it, or transform a society riddled with internal contradictions into an integrated whole.

But, in this *Quaderni*, Gramsci stresses that class conflict is not just channelled by generally accepted norms: it is effectively neutralized. To his mind, the present, antagonistic social reality can be upheld *only* if the antagonisms contained in it are hidden from view. Prior to social life, beneath it, enveloping it, is an underlying consensus. As far back as 1919, long before he developed his concept of hegemony, he devoted considerable theoretical attention to how trade unions and socialist parties, by working within the categories of bourgeois democracy, come to accept the very presuppositions of its operation.[47] Writing from prison some years later, he completely dismissed these traditional working-class institutions as mere 'instruments of political order', fully incorporated into the capitalist regime. Under their tutelage, class conflict becomes domesticated and degenerates into a desire for marginally higher wages. This illusory conflict is consensus in disguise, and only serves to strengthen bourgeois hegemony by obscuring its true character.[48] For Lenin, trade unionism was a sign of poor strategy; for Gramsci, it was both a mechanism and symptom of cultural integration.

To conclude this section, Gramsci seized upon an idea marginal (or, at most, incipient) in earlier Marxist thought, developed its possibilities, and gave it a central place in his own thought. In so doing, he rerouted Marxist analysis to the long-neglected—and hopelessly unscientific—territory of ideas, values, and beliefs. More specifically, he uncovered what was to become a major theme of the second generation of Hegelian Marxists (i.e. the Frankfurt School): the process of internalization of bourgeois relations and the consequent diminution of revolutionary possibilities. But before we can accept hegemony as a useful tool of analysis, it must receive much further clarification.

V. *Consent, Consensus, Hegemony: a Conceptual Analysis*

At this point, two crucial, difficult, and closely related problems present themselves. Hegemonic rule is rule through 'consent' (*consenso*), but what exactly does Gramsci mean by this notoriously vague concept? That is to say, what sort of conforming behaviour does he have in mind? And if hegemony involves some measure of societal consensus, what aspects of the social order must be included in this agreement?

Consent, like many terms of political theory, is capable of a multitude of ambiguities and meanings, and it might prevent confusion to say a few words about its history and current usage. Some notion of consent as describing the relation of subjects with their government has been present throughout virtually the whole history of political speculation. Historically the idea has functioned within a theory of political obligation: since its inception, the concept of consent has been proposed as a ground or foundation of the right to exercise political authority, and as a moral limit on the extent and nature of that authority. For example, in ancient Rome, 'the great jurists of the Digest recognized one, and only one, source of political authority in the Empire, that is, the Roman people, and the emperors themselves, as late as Justinian, acknowledged this as the true theory'.[49] But the individualist overtones which the concept came to acquire in seventeenth-century contract theory were not present in either classical or mediaeval thought. Pre-modern notions of consent had nothing to do with individual acceptance by each and every human being; nor did they entail express choice or deliberate authorization. They simply affirmed that the authority of the ruler somehow flows, at least in part, from the fact that his subjects—understood as a corporate community, transcending individual preferences—allow or acknowledge it. Such a view of consent was appropriate to an organic conception of society, infused with the idea that every man has his appointed status and function in a natural hierarchy, and that problems of political ethics are problems not of rights but rather of the duties a man owes to his community, his people, his lord, his king, his Church, or his God, by virtue of his role in the universal order. This model of society could not survive in the face of an advancing individualism, expressing itself theologically in protestantism, economically in mercantile capitalism, and politically and philosophically in the theory of natural rights and social contract. In this latter doctrine consent came to be understood primarily as (a) a deliberate and voluntary act on the part of individuals, and (b) as the *only* ground of political authority. Nothing could make any man a subject of a commonwealth, wrote Locke, 'but his actually entering into it by positive Engagement, and express Promise and Compact'.[50] The inconvenience of this view is clear enough, and succeeding centuries witnessed a reversion back to the collectivist sense of consent among those who did not abandon the term altogether. In contemporary political

thought, 'consent of the governed' has been refashioned to take account of the weaknesses of the earlier liberal definition and to express a new demand. No longer does it refer merely to the necessary ground of the general right of governments to exercise authority, but also to the continuing processes—e.g. representative government, freedom of speech and association—by which, it is thought, governments are made responsive to the demands of the governed. 'Consent' has come to indicate the *manner* in which individual citizens ought to be involved directly or indirectly in the activity of governing, the manner, that is, in which political society should be organized and constituted. Thus, the concept has taken on a burden of meaning absent from the minds of contract theorists and, in the process, has ceased to refer to a mental disposition of agreement. Plamenatz, for example, asserts that 'where there is an established process of election to an office, then, *provided the election is free*, anyone who takes part in the process consents to the authority of whoever is elected to the office'.[51] Whether or not an individual citizen *in fact* consents is no longer considered relevant; 'consent' emerges as an immanent principle of procedural 'correctness': 'the consent which is a necessary condition of political obligation . . . is rather the maintenance of a *method*, which leaves open to every sane, non-criminal adult the opportunity to discuss, criticize, and vote for or against the government'.[52]

'Consent', then, has come to be regarded as specifying the nature or *raison d'être* of the whole system of familiar democratic institutions. In its absorption into modern liberal ideology, the concept has tended to acquire a restricted, somewhat arbitrary connotation. Used in this narrow fashion it becomes useless in throwing light on the structure and working of political societies. In any case consent would not seem to be a useful specification of a democratic regime, whose important qualities could be better (and less perversely) defined in a different manner.

When Gramsci speaks of consent, he refers to a *psychological* state, involving some kind of acceptance—not necessarily explicit—of the socio-political order or of certain vital aspects of that order. Gone are the moral and prescriptive connotations which traditionally have been attached to the term: his conception of consent is purely descriptive, referring to an empirical, if not directly observable, fact. Thus, a hegemonic order need not incorporate liberal institutions and practices; indeed, it may be totalitarian in the strictest sense. To Gramsci, the contemporary liberal assumption that a people without the opportunity to express opposition or dissent cannot truly be said to consent would seem most curious. But, assuming that consent refers to a mental disposition, there are weaker and stronger, more passive and more active senses and forms of it. In order to elucidate Gramsci's meaning, it would be useful, first, to map out what sorts of political and social conforming behaviour might plausibly be said to be connected with the idea of consent.

Needless to say, conforming behaviour which is similar in its external manifestations may be the expression of very different attitudes, which can be grouped into three broad categories. First, one may conform because of the fear of the consequences of non-conformity, which may produce punitive deprivations or inflictions, including the loss of honour or self-esteem. This is conformity through coercion, or fear of sanctions—acquiescence under duress. Second, one may conform because one habitually pursues certain goals in certain ways in response to external stimuli. Thus, a man adheres to certain patterns of behaviour not because he consciously values them but because he has seldom entered situations in which the possibility of their rejection or modification has arisen. Conformity in this sense is a matter of unreflecting participation in an established form of activity.

Now there is no great linguistic impropriety in classifying 'forced' compliance or unconscious adherence as consent; Gramsci, however, did not include them in his definition of consent. As we shall see more clearly in a moment, hegemony is instead characterized by a third type of conformity: that arising from some degree of *conscious attachment* to, or *agreement* with, certain core elements of the society. This type of assenting behaviour, which may or may not relate to a perceived interest, is bound up with the concept of 'legitimacy', with a belief that the demands for conformity are more or less justified and proper. Gramsci does not specify exactly what kind of consensus (consensus with regard to what?) defines a situation of hegemony. His vagueness on this matter is shared by later consensus theorists, working within the Parsonian tradition in sociology and political science. Many recent critics of consensus theory have noted how its proponents experience enormous difficulty in isolating the objects of agreement they deem necessary for the maintenance of social cohesion. The now platitudinous phrase, 'consensus over fundamentals', comes perilously close to being a vacuous tautology. Certainly, there must always be consensus on linguistic and other norms involving symbolic communication, or else no society could possibly exist. Consensus in this sense has little explanatory value; but Gramsci meant much more than this. His concept of hegemony embodied a hypothesis that within a stable social order, there must be a substratum of agreement so powerful that it can counteract the division and disruptive forces arising from conflicting interests. And this agreement must be in relation to specific *objects*—persons, beliefs, values, institutions or whatever. Not included in hegemony are other types of unity or solidarity not forged around common objects, such as the intense bonds of affection and loyalty that may be present among the members of a family or kinship group, or the 'consciousness of kind' that some social theorists have spoken about in connection with social and national solidarities. While it is impossible to be precise about what objects of consensus Gramsci had in mind, he seemed, by contextual implication, to regard agreement on what Edward Shils has called 'the centre' to be the essence of hegemony—at least in modern industrial society. The 'centre', on Shils's definition, includes cognitive propositions and moral standards about the societal distribution of benefits and about the worth of institutions of authority and order by which this distribution is brought about, changed, or maintained. Consensus must focus on the allocation of scarce goods, the permissible range of disagreement, and the institutions through which decisions about such allocations are made—that is, on the values, norms, perceptions and beliefs that support and define the structures of central authority.[53] In Aristotle's metaphor, all men either sound the same note or else different notes in the same key.

But consent through voluntary agreement can vary in intensity. On one extreme, it can flow from a profound sense of obligation, from wholesale internalization of dominant values and definitions; on the other, from their very partial assimilation, from an uneasy feeling that the status quo, while shamefully iniquitous, is nevertheless the only viable form of society. Yet Gramsci, as we shall see, is far from clear about which band or bands of the continuum he is talking.

There is perhaps a fourth possible type of conformity, which can be called *pragmatic acceptance*. Such acceptance occupies a central place in exchange theory, now enjoying currency among sociologists. One conforms, on this theory, because it is convenient, because this is the way to insure the reciprocal conduct of others, which is a necessary condition of success in achieving one's own goals, among them, the pursuit of wealth, material security, power, prestige, social acceptance, love, and so on. An individual consents, then, because he perceives no realistic alternative—i.e. no other alternative which does not run the risk of diminishing or eliminating his satisfactions. The basic assumption here is that, in a condition of scarcity and interdependence, it is simply imprudent not to behave in certain socially accepted ways; conformity arises out of the existential conditions that make social units interdependent.

This type of conformity, I would maintain, can be subsumed under one or another of our previous categories. In the first place, it is logically impossible to define a *social* interest independently of an ideological system. The definition of such interests must have reference to goals, and goals are not chosen randomly or 'objectively' but in terms of a hierarchy of values and beliefs. Against this, it might be argued that the desire to increase or preserve one's material benefits is indeed an objective interest, and one, moreover, which goes a long way towards explaining social conformity. But the desire to seek after the fleshpots of the consumer society is itself a value, irreducible to any timeless, absolute human needs. It *is* reasonable to designate as objective interests a certain class of *natural* needs in as much as they involve our biological preservation. Thus, if a potential non-conformist is threatened with severe deprivation, such as dire poverty or death, it is unquestionably in his interest to comply. Such an extreme situation, however, can be fitted into a coercion model. But what about situations where our biological interests are only mildly or marginally threatened, and where invocation of the coercion model would be inappropriate? For instance, in this age of the welfare state, it would be odd (though not implausible) to say that anyone in Britain is being coerced into remaining at any *particular* job; yet even a short spell on subsistence level unemployment insurance can threaten one's health or vitality, if it leads to significant changes in diet or living conditions. In a wide range of cases, then, to avoid unemployment is surely a biological interest. Is it not therefore an objective interest? A less complex issue, such as the problem of air pollution, might prove instructive here. *Ceteris paribus*, a low level of air pollution can categorically be said to be in everyone's interest; but the *ceteris paribus* clause is critical, for a rational man might be willing to risk breathing bad air in exchange for, say, the economic benefits of having the local factory operating at a level of maximum efficiency. In any given situation, whether or not it is in my interest to breathe pure air will depend upon the nature of my objectives. For the dangers of air pollution are not normally so severe or definite that they must be avoided at all costs in all circumstances. The same can be said for the dangers of temporary unemployment, at least in advanced societies. One might reasonably trade off *some* physical deprivation for extra psychic satisfactions. Speaking generally, the greater the number of realistic alternatives (and in complex, liberal societies, these are likely to be many), the more the definition of interests is determined in reference to values and beliefs, to ideological presuppositions. These premises may themselves deviate from social conventions, but it is with *conforming* behaviour that we are concerned. If an individual's perceived interests mesh with those of the rest of the community, then it is most likely that his perception will be based upon consensual principles. Ideological consensus, especially when it is firmly rooted, is bound to assume the guise of a collective pursuit of rational interests. But we should not forget that the very definition of what is 'rational' or 'pragmatic' itself conceals evaluative propositions as well as a particular cognitive framework. To speak of prudential consent *simpliciter* is not only conceptually inadequate; it also diverts attention from a vital question about social interaction, a question central to Gramsci's concept of hegemony: namely, *why* do men define their interests as they do.

The distinctions made here between different modes of conformity are analytic and hence easily drawn. But it is not all that easy in actual circumstances to determine, for example, where compliance originating in voluntary agreement ends and where compliance deriving from constraint begins. On cases that fall near the margins, clear demarcation is impossible. Different types of conformity flow imperceptibly into their neighbours. In any event, it is not our purpose here to quibble over marginal possibilities, but only to distinguish Gramsci's conception of consent from other conceivable ways of defining the term. But even if we define consent as conscious agreement over principles and practices, it is, as has been noted, a condition compounded of attitudes and motives capable of ranging over many different shades of quality and degrees of intensity. This is not merely an academic point: social stability will depend in large part on the *depth* of societal consensus. Gramsci's actual words on the subject are ambiguous (though only superficially so) and merit more attention than they have hitherto received.

At times, Gramsci implies that consent in a hegemonic situation takes the form of active commitment, based on a deeply held view that the superior position of the ruling group is legitimate. For example, he characterizes hegemony as the 'spontaneous consent given by the great masses of the population to the general direction imposed on social life by the dominant fundamental group, consent "historically" caused by the prestige (and therefore by the trust) accruing to the dominant group because of its position and function in the world of production'.[54] Elsewhere he suggests that those who are consenting must somehow be truly convinced that the interests of the dominant group are those of society at large, that the hegemonic group stands for a proper social order in which all men are justly looked after: 'The fact of hegemony undoubtedly presupposes that account be taken of the interests ... of the groups over which hegemony is to be exercised ... that the leading group make sacrifices of an economic-corporate kind.'[55] Evidence such as this leads one widely read commentator, Giuseppe Tamburrano, to claim that consent, as understood by Gramsci, is an 'expression ... of intellectual and moral direction through which the masses feel permanently tied to the ideology and political leadership of the State as the expression of their beliefs and aspirations'.[56]

This interpretation, I think, captures only a part of Gramsci's meaning. For in those passages where he is most explicit about the nature of mass consciousness in bourgeois society, his concept of hegemony takes on a richer, more penetrating character. In the chapter of the prison notebooks entitled 'Relation Between Science, Religion, and Common Sense', Gramsci focuses on the superficiality of consent within the capitalist system, by drawing attention to the frequent incompatibility between a man's conscious thoughts and the unconscious values implicit in his action:

. . . is it not often the case that there is a contradiction between one's intellectual affirmation and one's mode of conduct? Which then is the real conception of the world: that logically affirmed as an intellectual act? Or that which emerges from the real activity of each man, which is implicit in his behaviour?[57]

Gramsci goes on to answer these questions by suggesting a distinction between 'true' and 'false' consciousness:

. . . this contrast between thought and action . . . cannot but be the expression of profounder contrasts of a social historical order. It signifies that the relevant social group [the working classes] has its own conception of the world, even if only embryonic; a conception which manifests itself in action, but occasionally, by fits and starts— when, that is, the group is acting as an organic totality. But this same group has, for reasons of submission and intellectual subordination, adopted a conception which is not its own but is borrowed from another group. . . .[58]

A few pages later he elaborates on these points:

The active man-in-the-mass has a practical activity, but has no clear theoretical consciousness of this activity. . . . One might almost say that he has two theoretical consciousnesses (or one contradictory consciousness): one which is implicit in his activity and which truly unites him with all his fellow-workers in the practical transformation of reality; and one, superficially explicit or verbal, which he has inherited from the past and uncritically accepted. But this 'verbal' conception is not without consequences. It binds together a specific social group, it influences moral conduct and the direction of will, in a manner more or less powerful, but often powerful enough to produce a situation in which the contradictory character of consciousness does not permit of any action, any decision or any choice and produces a condition of moral and political passivity.[59]

Consent, then, becomes essentially passive. It emerges not so much because the masses profoundly regard the social order as an expression of their aspirations as because they lack the conceptual tools, the 'clear theoretical consciousness', which would enable them effectively to comprehend and act on their discontent—discontent manifest in the activity which unites them 'in the practical transformation of reality'. Presumably this would include all forms of collective worker action—bargaining, strikes, riots, factory takeovers. Because it is devoid of overall direction or purpose, this action is sporadic and ineffective. The 'active man-in-the-mass' lacks the means with which to formulate the radical alternative 'implicit in his activity'. On the one hand, his education has never provided him with the ability to manipulate abstract symbols, to think clearly and systematically; on the other, all the institutional mechanisms through which perception is shaped—the schools, the Church, the conventional political parties, the mass media, even the trade unions—in one way or another play into the hands of the ruling groups. The very framework for his analysis of the existing system is fixed by the dominant ideology.[60] In this respect, language itself serves a hegemonic function. Gramsci displays interest in how its subtle connotations freeze perception and conception, thus facilitating the acceptance of conventional assumptions and impeding the expression of heretical ideas. Trained in linguistics and aware of its latest discoveries, he recognized that every culture discloses and guides its system of values and its general cognitions in its language: '. . . every language contains the elements of a conception of the world'.[61] Mental activity will depend on the character of the available vocabulary; if abstractions like 'democracy' and 'liberty' are identified with existing institutions, this will present a barrier to the diffusion of alternative images of society. So, all things considered, while the workers may be dissatisfied, while they may sense the contradiction between the positive official definition of reality and the starkness of their own subordination, they are unable even to locate the source of their discontent, still less remedy it.

The masses, Gramsci seems to be saying, are confined within the boundaries of the dominant world-view, a divergent, loosely adjusted patchwork of ideas and outlooks, which, despite its heterogeneity, unambiguously serves the interests of the powerful, by mystifying power relations, by justifying various forms of sacrifice and deprivation, by inducing fatalism and passivity, and by narrowing mental horizons. Such social conflict as exists is limited in both intensity and scope: there is general acceptance of means for adjudicating labour and other disputes, and large sectors of the established system enjoy immunity from political attention. The reigning ideology moulds desires, values and expectations in a way that stabilizes an inegalitarian system.

What overall picture emerges of the nature of mass consent in advanced capitalist society? It is well summarized in Gramsci's felicitous phrase, 'contradictory consciousness'. The thinking of the common man is neither coherent nor consistent over time; it is instead 'disjointed and episodic':[62] elements of intellectual and moral approbation coexist in unsteady equilibrium with elements of apathy, resignation, and even hostility. To be more schematic, on a general and abstract plane, the 'active-man-in-the-mass' expresses a great deal of agreement with, or at least passive acceptance of, the dominant conception of the world (if in a naïve, common-sensical form); but on the situational level, he reveals not outright dissensus but nevertheless a reduced level of commitment to the 'bourgeois' ethos, because it is often inappropriate to the realities of his class position.

This account of mass consciousness is meant to be paradigmatic. Gramsci of course understood that reality is far more complex and differentiated. Clearly, the states of mind associated with different types of compliance—fear, habit, indifference, acquiescence, positive attachment—are interwoven in different ways in the social personalities of individuals. Some men are more successfully socialized than others, who may be at the margins of the dominant consensus or even outside it. In Gramsci's conception, where a man falls on the continuum between absolute commitment and total rejection is intimately related to his socio-economic conditions. Those who experience pain from the existing distribution of income, power, and status, though often sharing much of the consensual pattern of belief, also have contrary inclinations. A society which unjustly inflicts the distress of exclusion or deprivation cannot wholly succeed in assimilating into its affirmative consensus those whom it mistreats.

Gramsci's description of popular consciousness in modern bourgeois society is, in principle, empirically testable; and in later pages, we shall assess it in the light of recent survey studies. But his conceptualization of 'contradictory consciousness' also possesses a rationalist, specifically Marxist component, which is not susceptible to survey techniques. In Gramsci's eyes manifestations of lower-class discontent are not simply random, empirical data open to a wide variety of interpretation. On the contrary, these expressions of deviance fit into a pattern: they have an objective, intrinsically subversive meaning and incarnate an embryonic revolutionary ideology. What is more, Gramsci posits that the ideology the masses adhere to on a general level is 'false', not only because it is historically regressive but also because it reflects the interests and experience of the ruling classes. A man's 'real' conception of the world should not be sought in his verbal affirmations; it is implicitly revealed in his practical activity.

Beset by contradictions and sustained by deception, bourgeois hegemony is characterized by equivocal consent—at least as far as the majority is concerned. But this shallow form of hegemony does not exhaust all the possibilities, for hegemonic situations differ in intensity, and the degree of variation is rooted in the dynamics of historical development. It is rarely noticed that Gramsci speaks of three different levels, or types, of hegemony. (Hence the apparent inconsistency in his definition of consent.) In a paradigm case, which we can call *integral hegemony*, mass affiliation would approach unqualified commitment. The society would exhibit a substantial degree of 'moral and intellectual unity', issuing in an 'organic' (to use the Gramscian idiom) relationship between rulers and ruled, a relationship without contradictions and antagonisms on either a social or an ethical level. Such a stable situation, however, can persist only in those historical periods when well organized, widespread opposition is absent or discredited and when the ruling class performs a progressive function in the productive process, when it 'really causes the entire society to move forward, not merely satisfying its own existential requirements but continuously enlarging its social framework for the conquest of ever new spheres of economic and productive activity'.[63] Gramsci singles out post-revolutionary France as a close his-

torical approximation to the ideal type and as a proper model
for the proletariat to emulate in its struggle to build an *ordine
nuovo*. By attending to the aspirations and enlisting the energies
of 'the great popular masses', the Jacobins 'created the bourgeois State, turned the bourgeoisie into the leading, hegemonic
class of the nation; that is, gave the new State a permanent
basis, and created the compact modern French nation'.[64]

But in modern capitalist society, Gramsci claims, bourgeois
economic dominance, whether or not it faces serious challenge,
has become outmoded: no longer is it capable of representing,
or furthering, everyone's interest. Neither is it capable of com-
manding unequivocal allegiance from the non-élite: 'as soon as
the dominant group has exhausted its function, the ideological
bloc tends to decay'.[65] Thus, the potential for social disintegration is ever-present: conflict lurks just beneath the surface. In
spite of the numerous achievements of the system, the needs,
inclinations, and mentality of the masses are not truly in
harmony with the dominant ideas. Though widespread, cultural and political integration is fragile; such a situation might
be called *decadent hegemony*.

The third and lowest form of hegemony—let us label it
minimal hegemony—prevailed in Italy from the period of unification until (roughly) the turn of the century. This type of
hegemony rests on the ideological unity of the economic, political
and intellectual élites along with 'aversion to any intervention
of the popular masses in State life'.[66] The dominant economic
groups do not 'accord their interests and aspirations with the
interests and aspirations of other classes'.[67] Rather, they maintain their rule through *trasformismo*, the practice of incor-
porating the leaders—cultural, political, social, economic—of
potentially hostile groups into the élite network, the result being
'the formation of an ever broader ruling class'.[68] The inducements used may range from mere flattery to offers of employment in administration to the granting of substantial power in
decision-making. Because of *trasformismo*, 'the popular masses'
of the Italian nation 'were decapitated, not absorbed into the
ambit of the new State'.[69] For them the institutions of the liberal
state were either nothing but names, distant and irrelevant, or
else alien and coercive forces. The seeds of this disaffection were
sown during the Risorgimento, when the dominant Moderate

Party (which represented the company bosses, rich farmers, estate managers and entrepreneurs) succeeded in unifying the country politically but failed to establish an ideological bond between itself and the common people, over whom it (or the groups it spoke for) exercised 'the function of "domination" and not "leadership": dictatorship without hegemony'.[70] Strictly speaking, the hegemony of the Moderates extended only to other sections of their own bourgeois class; in particular to the forces associated with the Republican *Partito d'Azione*, the Party of Mazzini and Garibaldi, whose deference to the premises of the liberal order impoverished and ultimately neutralized its radicalism.[71] Whatever its pretensions, the Risorgimento never managed to reach down to the masses and construct a truly national community. To quote Gramsci's bitter condemnation: 'They said that they were aiming at the creation of a modern State in Italy, and they in fact produced a bastard.'[72] The illegitimate offspring was most unhealthy, an unbalanced and corrupt—if economically progressive—society, founded on widespread passivity and the spectre of violent repression. 'Hegemonic activity' (Gramsci's own words) did exist, but it was confined to the upper and middle classes, and as such 'became merely an aspect of the function of domination'.[73] What the Risorgimento and its aftermath amounted to was a 'passive revolution', a process of modernization presided over by the established élites, who used the 'revolutionary' changes to maintain their supremacy and consolidate the extant order.[74] This supremacy, as we have seen, rested upon a narrow consensual foundation. Yet, because popular leaders were assimilated into the system, and because the masses themselves did not possess the cultural sophistication to fit their grievances into anything resembling a coherent framework, social discontent, while prevalent, lacked any direction whatsoever. Alternating with lengthy periods of sullen acquiescence, disruption did not move beyond what Hobsbawm has called 'primitive rebellion',[75] pre-political and chaotic, contained by existing categories of thought and behaviour, incapable of being directed into reformist or revolutionary channels, and doomed to total failure. Such rebellion was based on '"generic" hatred', which was '"semi-feudal" rather than modern in character'.[76] Thus, in a very negative sense, the people were subject to the 'intellectual and moral hegemony' of the ruling groups; but it was an exceedingly weak hegemony, marked by a low level of integration.[77]

This concept of integration lies at the heart of hegemony, and, for Gramsci, serves to distinguish the ancient and mediaeval from the modern state. The following passage furnishes much insight into what a hegemonic order is not:

In the ancient and mediaeval State alike, centralization, both political-territorial and social (and one is a function of the other), was minimal. The State was, in a certain sense, a mechanical bloc of social groups, often of different races: within the sphere of political-military compression, exercised in acute forms only occasionally, the subaltern groups had a life of their own, their own institutions, etc., and sometimes these institutions took on State functions, which made the State a federation of social groups with separate functions not organized for a common purpose.[78]

Thus Gramsci wished to dispense with the organic metaphor so commonly applied to ancient and mediaeval societies. It is far more fruitful, he believed, to view them as mechanical assemblages of distinct units, characterized by an absence of interdependence in the critical sphere of economic activity. What such societies represent is a primitive form of state, where the links between what people actually experience and the larger social, economic, and political framework are remote and indirect.[79] (On this conception, post-Risorgimento Italy was semi-mediaeval.) Social order stems mainly from inertia, from habit and indifference, not from consensus. The system is rigid: there is little or no contact and mobility between the dominant and subordinate groups.

But the bourgeois state, as the first modern state, 'substitutes for the mechanical bloc of social groups their subordination to the active hegemony of the directive and dominant group, thus abolishing certain outmoded autonomies, which are, however, reborn in other forms, as parties, trade unions, cultural associations'.[80] These allegedly autonomous institutions incorporate the masses into the structure of bourgeois rule, which, for all its subtleties and apparent pluralism, is more or less total:

The revolution which the bourgeois class has brought into the conception of law, and therefore into the function of the State, consists especially in the will to conform. . . . The previous dominant classes were essentially conservative in the sense that they did not tend to allow an organic passage from the other classes into their own; i.e. to enlarge their class sphere 'technically' and ideologically; their conception was that of a closed caste. The bourgeois class poses itself as an organism in continuous movement, capable of absorbing the entire society, assimilating it to its own cultural and economic level. The entire function of the State has been transformed; the State has become an 'educator'. . . .[81]

In place of the vulgar caricature of liberalism—offered by both romantic conservatives and socialists—as an atomistic doctrine, seeking to dissolve the solidarities of social relationships and to replace them by the unfettered individual, the masterless man, Gramsci presents a view of the doctrine, and its bearers, as deeply informed by a spirit of common life and social union. Thus, the modern state (assuming that it is functioning properly) transcends the particularism of the 'economic-corporate phase'; it is a state in the real sense, enjoying the 'consent of the governed', however superficial this consent may be.[82]

VI. *War of Manœuvre/War of Position*

Hegemony, as Gramsci understood it, was not just a tool of historical and social analysis; it was also a guiding concept for political practice. His ideas on integration enabled him to add a new dimension to the Marxist theory of revolution, thus superseding its aridities but, at the same time, introducing a whole new set of problems.

The United Front policy of 1922 pointed to the need to formulate new approaches to the socialist revolution, owing to the notable difference in development between pre-1917 Russia and Western European countries. No one spoke of *deviating* from the Russian model (which remained the unquestioned paradigm of revolutionary practice), only of adhering to it in more resolute and imaginative ways. Gramsci first deals with the problem theoretically in a letter of 1924, where he discusses the strength of superstructural forms 'created by the greater development of capitalism', which 'render the action of the masses slower and more prudent and therefore demand of the revolutionary party a strategy and tactics much more complex and vigorous than those used by the Bolsheviks in the period between March and November of 1917'. Refurbishing one feature of the old *L'Ordine*

Nuovo theory of 1919–20, he focuses on how the development of capitalism has created 'a worker aristocracy with its adjuncts of trade union bureaucracy and social-democratic groupings'.[83] In directives to the central committee of the PCI in July of 1925 and August of 1926, he pressed these themes yet again.[84] A few years later, in his *Quaderni*, he wove the pessimistic strands of these communications into a full-blown revision of the sacred texts.

To clarify his argument, Gramsci compares political struggle to military conflict, prudently warning, however, that the comparison must be taken with a 'pinch of salt', as a mere 'stimulus to thought', since confrontation in the political sphere is 'enormously more complex' than war between nations.[85] Yet parallels are evident. In their reflections on armed hostilities among 'the more industrially and socially advanced States', modern military experts have proclaimed the centrality of the 'war of position' (protracted trench warfare) and relegated the 'war of movement', or 'war of manœuvre' (rapid frontal assault on the adversary's base) to a subsidiary role. The latter has been 'reduced to more of a tactical than a strategic function'. 'The same reduction', Gramsci counsels, 'must take place in the art and science of politics'. The reasons for this 'reduction' are then elaborated:

In the most advanced States . . . civil society has become a very complex structure, one which is resistant to the catastrophic irruptions caused by immediate economic factors (crises, depressions, etc.). The superstructures of civil society are like the trench-systems of modern warfare. In war it would sometimes happen that a dogged artillery attack seemed to have destroyed the enemy's whole defensive system, whereas in fact it had only destroyed the outer perimeter; and at the moment of their advance and attack the assailants would find themselves confronted by a line of defence which was still effective. This is what happens in politics during the great economic crises.[86]

To put it less picturesquely, the dominant ideology in modern capitalist societies is highly institutionalized and widely internalized. It follows that a concentration on frontal attack, on direct assault against the bourgeois state ('war of movement' or 'war of manœuvre') can result only in disappointment and defeat. Gramsci associates this futile strategy with Trotsky's formula of 'permanent revolution', and consigns it to:

an historical period in which the great mass political parties and the great economic trade unions did not yet exist, and society was still, so to speak, in a state of fluidity in many aspects: greater backwardness of the countryside, and almost complete monopoly of political-state power [*efficienza*] by a few cities or even by a single one (Paris in the case of France); a relatively simple state apparatus, and greater autonomy of civil society from state activity; . . . greater autonomy of the national economies from the economic relations of the world market, etc.[87]

From this catalogue we can infer three historical trends which, for Gramsci, complicate rather than further the revolutionary process: rapid economic development, increased centralization, and the growth of popular participation. So the optimism of Marxist thinking had been misplaced. The march of industry, according to him, leads not to certain revolution but to the *integration* of the masses into the capitalist system, as the agencies of socialization become more and more sophisticated and ubiquitous. What is needed in such circumstances is a 'war of position' on the cultural front. This strategy requires steady penetration and subversion of the complex and multiple mechanisms of ideological diffusion. The point of the struggle is to conquer one after another all the agencies of civil society (e.g. the schools, the universities, the publishing houses, the mass media, the trade unions). In the absence of a prior 'revolution of the spirit', a seizure of state power would prove transitory if not disastrous. It would be a matter of destroying only the 'outer perimeter' of the capitalist system of defence. The momentarily triumphant revolutionary forces would find themselves facing a largely hostile population, still confined within the mental universe of the bourgeoisie. Attention must therefore be directed to the inner redoubt of civil society, to the dissemination of radical ideas about man and society—in short, to the creation of a proletarian counter-hegemony. Before revolutionizing class and political relations Communists must revolutionize man himself, his way of thinking and feeling. Gramsci expresses some doubt as to whether this mental transformation can be *fully* achieved before the demolition of the capitalist state apparatus; in two passages he admits that the new Marxist regime will need to employ legal punishments (and rewards) in order 'to eradicate certain customs and attitudes and encourage others'.[88] Despite this qualification his message emerges with clarity: in modern capitalist society a 'reversal of hegemony' is a precondition of successful revolution. But it is not simply a matter of substituting one hegemony for another. The principle of hegemony must itself be transformed—from a principle that mystifies the social situation to one that exposes exploitation and supersedes it.

What Gramsci's proposals amounted to, in effect, was the abandonment of the hallowed Bolshevik model. He placed much emphasis on a distinction between the 'organic' and 'conjunctural' dimensions of revolutionary change.[89] The former refers to a gradual shift in the balance of social and cultural forces, and corresponds to the 'war of position'. The latter refers to the realm of contingency, to the momentary period of crisis in which political forces contend for state power; it is the arena of political combat, of military confrontation, roughly equivalent to the 'war of movement'. Imprisoned by their scientific categories, Marxist revolutionaries had taken the 'organic' component for granted and focused their energies on the 'conjunctural', thus abandoning themselves to the momentary practicalities of economic and political struggle. They saw no need for a genuine cultural confrontation with the bourgeoisie. Gramsci was advocating a reversal of emphasis. Value conflicts could no longer be dismissed as illusory or unimportant. On the contrary, one of the movement's first tasks, according to the Sardinian, was to discredit or refute the 'cornerstones' of the dominant value-system—i.e. its 'great philosophical syntheses'. 'It is necessary', he wrote:

to strike against the most eminent of one's adversaries . . . A new science [in this case, Marxism] proves its efficacy and vitality when it shows that it is capable of confronting the great champions of the tendencies opposed to it, when it either resolves, in its own way, the vital questions they have posed or demonstrates, peremptorily, that such questions are false.[90]

The 'battle of ideas' was to be waged at all levels—including the highest. Marxists could no longer afford to remain encased in their 'economist' shells.

In light of all this, we can attempt to make sense of his vaguely formulated (though often cited) thesis, propounded in his discussion of the Risorgimento, that 'a social group can, and indeed must, already exercise leadership [i.e. be hegemonic] before winning governmental power (this is one of the principal conditions for the very conquest of such power)'.[91] In the passage in question, Gramsci makes no attempt to qualify or restrict the application of this 'methodological criterion'. But understood as a universal hypothesis, it would seem, on its face, to be contradicted by the Russian revolution, prior to which, as he himself noted, the 'war of position', the struggle for cultural supremacy, received scant attention.[92] He does not seem to recognize a problem here and, in a famous passage, justifies Lenin's strategy by underlining the significant differences between East and West:

In Russia the State was everything and civil society was primitive and amorphous; in the West there was a proper relation between the State and civil society, and when the State trembled a robust structure of civil society was at once revealed. The State was merely an outer trench, behind which there stood a powerful chain of fortresses and casemates, more or less numerous from one State to the next.[93]

The Bolsheviks, it appears, did not need to exercise intellectual and moral leadership in pre-revolutionary Russia because they were operating in an ideological vacuum. The various peoples within the Empire clung to beliefs of autochthonous origins and were in no way integrated into the regime's scale of values. But where does this leave Gramsci's thesis about the universal necessity of hegemonic activity as a preliminary to the conquest of power? Given the nature of the *Quaderni*, we would be foolish to expect absolute consistency. If we come across apparent contradictions, perhaps we should resist the temptation to collect debating points and instead attempt to sort out the origins of these contradictions or to trace them back to a more fundamental unity. In any case, Gramsci's overall position is, I think, clear enough: that in *post-feudal orders*, in societies on the road to social integration, 'there can and must be hegemonic activity even before the rise to power, and that one should not count only on the material force which power gives in order to exercise an effective supremacy'.[94] Just how much hegemony is needed will vary in accordance with the degree of social integration, with the sturdiness of civil society. In the conditions of advanced capitalist society, for instance, the hegemony of the proletariat would have to be self-conscious, widespread, and deeply-rooted. But all this is very general and leaves open the thorny questions of concrete analysis and application. As Gramsci says, 'an accurate reconnaissance of each individual country' is required.[95] Identifying the foci and levels of strength of the various hegemonic orders, and specifying suitable lines of attack, are problems for empirical study. Implicit here is the need for a complex, differentiated analysis of the revolutionary process and of the strategies appropriate to it. Gramsci does not himself cast this insight in the form of a testable hypothesis, but he does mark out the necessary analytic path for students (and advocates) of social change and revolution, by suggesting models and areas for future research.

Thus, there are not simply two grand strategies: one, the 'war of movement', appropriate to a non-organic, neo-feudal society; the other, the 'war of position', appropriate to a situation of advanced social development. The gradations of social integration, Gramsci seems to believe, can be arranged, like consent, along a continuum; an infinite range of strategies is therefore possible. Yet, for purposes of simplicity, we can focus on the areas near the two poles of the continuum. On one extreme, where civil society is 'primitive and amorphous', revolution can be viewed as a technical-military operation, depending less on the empirical consciousness of the masses than on the deployment and structural relations of forces. This would be, in Stanley Moore's classification, a 'minority revolution'. On the other extreme, where civil society is healthy, a prolonged ideological struggle is a necessary precondition. On this conception of revolution (what Moore labels a 'majority revolution'), the state apparatus is finally left isolated and helpless, its ideological and institutional supports eroded. Revolution takes the form not of sudden destruction but of gradual dissolution.[96]

The major premise of Gramsci's theory of revolution is that objective material interests are not automatically or inevitably translated into class consciousness. In contrast to the mainstream of Marxist analysis, Gramsci understood that responses are invariably culturally conditioned, that political action—even in the long run—cannot be conceived as an 'objective' calculation of costs and benefits, for the very definition of what constitutes costs and benefits necessarily presupposes some framework of values and categories which does not itself merely reflect 'external reality'. That is to say, political and social preferences do not simply arise from the facts of economic struggle; they reflect a man's assumptions about how society is and should be run, and in capitalist society, Gramsci claimed, these mediating assumptions are largely set by the ruling classes through their highly developed mechanisms of political socialization.

Left to their own devices, then, the masses in western countries are powerless to overcome their intellectual and moral subordination. The long and ardous process of demystification requires an external agency:

Critical self-consciousness means, historically and politically, the creation of an intellectual élite. A human mass does not 'distinguish' itself, does not become independent, 'for itself', without, in a broad sense, organizing itself; and there is no organization without . . . organizers and leaders.[97]

Thus, Gramsci's concept of hegemony provides the basis for a theory of the revolutionary party. For it falls upon an organized élite of professional revolutionaries and communist intellectuals to instil in the masses the 'critical self-consciousness' which will enable them to overthrow the existing order and develop a morally integrated society based on proletarian, collective principles.

The nature of this task will be discussed in later chapters. What interests us here is Gramsci's belief that the proletarian revolution is not inherent in the historical process, but just one conceivable outcome among others, dependent on the existence of sufficient organization, energy, and imagination to overcome the integrative tendencies of modern society. Before Gramsci, Marxists from Marx onwards approached each crisis in capitalism with the certainty that *this time* the proletariat would become class conscious, that is, come to view its social being as embedded in the necessary structural antagonisms of capitalist society. Revolutionary consciousness was regarded as unproblematical, a natural outgrowth of tensions and disruptions occurring during a period of systemic collapse. Even Lenin retained the *theoretical* baggage of inevitability, though his practice and strategic injunctions belied it.

It is, I believe, reasonable to affirm that, before Gramsci, *no* Marxist thinker had been sufficiently sensitive to the historical impact of ideologies and consciousness; none saw any point in delving into the intricacies of mass psychology. It has become fashionable in some circles to play down the fatalistic element in Marx's own thought and instead stress the rather tentative role he assigned to superstructural factors. Some commentators deny that Marx was putting forward an inexorable law of history or that he viewed the communist future as the necessary culmination of historical development. To quote Lichtheim,

the 'relentless onward march of civilization' is a Comtean, not a Marxian, postulate. If the second generation of his followers understood Marx to have expounded a kind of universal optimism, they thoroughly misunderstood the meaning and temper of his message. . . . Like every commitment [Marxism] carries with it the implied possibility of failure. Were it otherwise there would be no sense in speaking of 'tasks' confronting the movement.[98]

No doubt, in Marx's theory, neither institutions nor men function as inert, passive victims of history's inner logic. But the fact that consciousness is active is not to be equated to a contention that it can counteract either the dynamics of production or the predestined course of history. The distinguishing question, of course, is whether the action is in harmony with the system of production and its immanent tendencies or is able to obstruct or recast them. Marx's 'true' position on this is not easily recoverable. Like most interesting thinkers, he took insufficient pains to make himself understood, thus leaving room for considerable controversy over the meaning of the concepts and laws he enunciated. Pareto once likened Marx's statements to bats: you can see in them something that looks like a mouse and something that appears like a bird. But mouse-like interpretations of Marx, which attempt to defend him by minimizing his now embarrassing 'scientific' image, cannot bear the full weight of the textual evidence; nor, if taken far enough, do they do justice to his originality. He was of course willing to qualify his views in the light of political events or new data, but such changes never led to changes in his overall perspective.

Marx stated quite plainly—and often enough—that the working class would, through its own efforts and perceptions, attain a fully developed consciousness of its situation and aims, that the everyday struggle for survival in class society was the school for revolution. In other words, the proletariat is a class whose conditions of life, whose experience at work and elsewhere, whose common struggles and discussions, will sooner or later bring them to an understanding of their state and what must be done to transform it. Some major features of Marx's view of class consciousness are summarized in the following passage from *The Holy Family*:

. . . because the conditions of life of the proletariat bring all the conditions of present society into a most inhuman focus, because man is lost in the proletariat but at the same time has won a theoretical awareness of that loss and is driven to revolt against this inhumanity by urgent, patent, and absolutely compelling *need* (the practical expression of *necessity*)—therefore the proletariat can and must emancipate itself. . . . Its aim and historical action is prescribed, irrevocably and obviously, in its own situation in life as well as in the entire organization of contemporary civil society.[99]

In the *Communist Manifesto*, Marx casts this process in a more sociological mould:

The advance of industry, whose involuntary promoter is the bourgeoisie, replaces the isolation of the labourers, due to competition, by their revolutionary combination, due to association. The development of modern industry, therefore, cuts from under its feet the very foundation on which the bourgeoisie produces and appropriates products. What the bourgeoisie therefore produces, above all, is its own grave-diggers. Its fall and the victory of the proletariat are equally inevitable.[100]

To be more specific, the evolution of industrial capitalism both furnishes the preconditions of collective organization, by herding workers together in large numbers, and creates the deprivation which spurs them to combination. This unity develops consciousness of conflicting interests and trains workers in methods of struggle. The limited economic achievements of their unions lead workers to adopt political forms of action, and ultimately to challenge directly the whole structure of class domination. And so, 'The knell of capitalist private property sounds. The expropriators are expropriated ... capitalist production begets, with the inexorability of a law of Nature, its own negation.'[101]

For Marx, then, the growth of revolutionary consciousness is an inevitable concomitant of the very economic contradictions that generate the downfall of capitalism. The philosophical basis of this argument is given blunt expression in *The German Ideology*, where he and his partner observe that:

The phantoms formed in the human brain, too, are necessary sublimations of man's material life-process which is empirically verifiable and connected with material premises. Morality, religion, metaphysics, and all the rest of ideology and their corresponding forms of consciousness no longer seem to be independent. They have no history or development. Rather, men who develop their material production and their material relationships alter their thinking and the products of their thinking along with their real existence. Consciousness does not determine life, but life determines consciousness.[102]

Thus, conscious activity is an ideological reflex of the primary process whereby men organize their relationship to nature and to each other. Yet, as is well known, Marx anticipated Lenin (who never reconciled his mechanistic materialism with his theory of the party) in speaking of the need for an enlightened vanguard to systematize and promulgate the revolutionary theory at first only implicit in mass consciousness. On the one hand, then, Marx felt quite certain that the contradictions engendered by capitalism would inevitably lead to class consciousness; on the other hand, he attributed to political action and to his own scientific theory of history a major role in bringing about the result. In his own eyes this difficulty was resolved because such subjective elements as revolutionary science and political activism were themselves necessary by-products of the structural deficiencies inherent in capitalism. While Marx obviously realizes that no revolution can be made without some sort of prior change in proletarian consciousness, he consistently denies that this change has any independent causal significance. But, in the final analysis, he (and his later disciples) failed to supply a convincing account of the theoretical link between determining conditions and determined response; he (and they) did not correctly estimate the real gap between 'objective' and subjective interests.

Here again, as with the analysis of bourgeois rule, the concept of hegemony advances us beyond the categories of classical Marxism. But Gramsci's theory of class consciousness cannot be fully understood in isolation from his theory of social causation. What, if any, are the underlying conditions for the emergence of a new culture, a new mode of thought and being? To what extent was Gramsci a voluntarist? What role did he assign to the economic infrastructure? To these (and related) questions, we now turn.

CHAPTER 3

Base and Superstructure: the Role of Consciousness

The canons of historical materialism are valid only *post-factum*, to study and comprehend the events of the past; they ought not to become a mortgage on the present and future.

(Gramsci, 'La critica critica', *Il Grido del Popolo*, 12 January 1918)

I. *The Neo-Idealist Interpretation*

MUCH ITALIAN discussion of Gramsci has centred on the fundamental question of his status as a Marxist writer. Prima facie, his preoccupation with hegemony, with intellectual and spiritual supremacy, does seem to situate him in the idealist camp. For was he not, after all, speaking in terms of the autonomy of ideas? Was it not a common idealist tendency to interpret all cultures and epochs as expressions of a distinctive *Geist*, or ethos, that gradually penetrates institutions and belief systems until its various forms are exhausted and a new *Geist* replaces it? The idea that revolution can be conducted in the realm of thought, that liberation can be attained through philosophy, was always considered a Young Hegelian heresy. If, according to Marxism, the course of history is shaped by the determined action of material conditions operating in conformity to immutable laws independent of human will, then how could Gramsci, with his denial of historical inevitability and stress on the *subjective* dimension of human experience, possibly be a Marxist? Not surprisingly, it has been the view of many that, in the Sardinian's writings, a quasi-idealist voluntarism replaces historical and economic determinism. On this interpretation, Gramsci does not, like Marx, stand speculative idealism on its feet; he merely injects into the doctrine some

Marxist ingredients. What *really* counts, for him, is 'will' and consciousness, the world of the intellect, of sentiments and passions. This way of looking at Gramsci is fortified by his apparent aversion for serious infra-structural analysis. For the purely economic theories of Marx and his later disciples, Gramsci showed neither sustained interest nor profound understanding. Trained in philosophy, literature and linguistics, he was in no position to confront the theoretical problems of Marxism from the point of view of an economist. But how can any genuine Marxist theorist—it is asked—ignore what is generally regarded as the bedrock of the system—inquiry into the 'laws of motion' of capitalist economy?

Many commentators have underlined the affinities between Gramsci's approach and that of Benedetto Croce, who, in the manner of a cultural pontiff, dominated Italian intellectual life on both the political Right and Left during Gramsci's formative years. Paradoxically, they say, the earnest Communist Party leader never escaped from the philosophical shadow cast by the Grand Old Man of Italian liberalism. This reading of Gramsci as Crocean traces its lineage back to 1933, when Umberto Calosso, a former aquaintance of the Sardinian, raised eyebrows with his claim that Gramsci had always been an idealist philosopher in the Italian tradition.[1] In 1947 (before the publication of the *Quaderni*) this line of interpretation received impetus from none other than Croce himself, who asserted that Gramsci's *Lettere dal Carcere* showed him to be 'one of us', a philosopher in the speculative, anti-positivist tradition, who recognized the value of idealist categories, displayed a lively appreciation of high culture, and took a broad view of historical development.[2]

The thesis that Gramsci was a Crocean *tout court* gave way, after the publication of the first volume of notes, to a more refined view of his place in the indigenous philosophical tradition. This volume, which contained a series of essays and brief comments on both Marxist theory and Croce's philosophy, made it plain that the mature Gramsci regarded Croce as a doctrinal opponent. But the neo-idealist interpretation, now suitably modified to take account of new evidence, refused to die and even prospered. The most important post-war spokesmen for this perspective were Guido Morpurgo-Tagliabue[3] and

Giampiero Carocci.[4] Both were keen to emphasize Gramsci's traditional intellectual bearing, his 'objectivity', and therefore played down the significance of his pre-prison political involvement. Whereas for previous Marxists the purpose of theory was to guide practice, the Gramsci of the notebooks, they argued, was interested in cultural themes and formal philosophical problems solely for their own sake.[5] Gramsci thus emerged as something of a post-Marxist, a 'Crocean of the Left', who affirmed 'the autonomy of particular spiritual activities'.[6] While acknowledging that Croce was 'the adversary against whom Gramsci battled each day for mastery of himself', Morpurgo-Tagliabue, for example, still maintained that the Sardinian endeavoured to rethink Marxism in terms of Crocean philosophy, thus purging the first of its shallow materialism and the second of its speculative vices: 'Among Croceans he is a Marxist and among Marxists a Crocean.' In other words, Gramsci used Croce, his imaginary interlocutor from 1929 to 1935, 'to correct Marx', to eliminate the economic bias from his social and historical analysis.[7]

Since such interpretations constituted a serious challenge to the Communist orthodoxy that Gramsci was a straightforward Leninist, they were subjected to vehement condemnation by Party theoreticians.[8] The chief objections were three. First, the PCI pointed to the methodological inadequacy of interpreting Gramsci's writings abstractly, in isolation from the specific historical context which renders them intelligible. His theoretical reflections, it was contended, could not be separated from his activity as a militant and Party leader. Gramsci was a political revolutionary, not a contemplative intellectual, and all his texts must be examined in this light. Second, the neo-idealist interpretation rested on a definitional mistake. Failing to comprehend the breadth and flexibility of Marxist theory, observers like Morpurgo-Tagliabue wrongly assumed that the narrow, determinist version which incurred Gramsci's wrath was Marxism itself. Third, it was asserted that all attempts to present the Sardinian as a disciple of Croce neglected the importance of those passages where he (Gramsci) utterly rejected the abstract, speculative qualities of the latter's thought.

Although these criticisms exaggerated Gramsci's devotion to the Leninist perspective, they constituted powerful, effective arguments against the tendency to read him as a 'post-Marxist'. In particular, the Party was justified in objecting to the idealist notion that Gramsci could be considered *sub specie aeternitatis*, viewed as a purely abstract thinker grappling with the eternal problems of humanity and not as a committed political analyst, seeking to develop theoretical weapons for the proletarian struggle. It is absurd to 'historicize' Gramsci's ideas into oblivion; but it is equally unreasonable to proclaim, without any real historical evidence, that the most prominent spokesman for Leninism in Italy was suddenly transmogrified into an ivory-towered intellectual, more Crocean than Marxist in his philosophical orientation.

The PCI theoreticians did seem to have the better of the argument and throughout the 1950s, there arose no significant challenges to the orthodox line on Gramsci. The neo-idealist interpretation appeared to be dead and buried.[9] In 1963, however, it was resurrected in spectacular fashion by Giuseppe Tamburrano, a Socialist Party activist.[10] He argued that Gramsci did not so much *embrace* Croceanism as attempt to retranslate it into concrete historical terms. Thus the purely speculative component of idealism, dealing with the movement of abstract ideas, was jettisoned by him in favour of a more realistic approach. Gramsci reduces 'what is real to man, not separate from his world but immersed and a participant in it . . .'.[11] Still, in the final reckoning, Tamburrano's Gramsci turns out to be something of a subjective idealist, albeit of a Marxist variety. The central theme of the notebooks is the re-emphasis on man as the maker of his own history rather than as a reflection of structural determinants: 'History, says Gramsci, is the will of men who act on nature in order to change their world, to effect their goals, to satisfy their needs.'[12] Human action transcends objective conditions through free creation; indeed, the objective world is no more than man's 'consciousness of the existence of these conditions'.[13] Gramsci, according to Tamburrano, 'places the primary accent on the subject rather than on the object'. His theory stresses 'the predominance of "ought-to-be" over being, of idea over fact, of innovative action over external conditions'.[14] Thus Gramsci's subjectivism 'expunges from the philosophy of praxis all determinism whatsoever'.[15] For Tamburrano's Gramsci, building socialism is, *in fine*, simply a matter of winning men's minds. In effect, his *real* adversary is 'not Croce but vulgar Marxism'.[16]

The detail and sophistication of Tamburrano's analysis rendered it pretty much immune to the criticisms levelled at the earlier version of the neo-idealist thesis. Eschewing all attempts to picture Gramsci as an Olympian thinker, he readily affirmed that the Sardinian always remained an ardent *Marxist activist*, who wished to focus attention on real historical movements and struggles. Gramsci's Croceanism, on this account, consists not in any fascination with abstract ideas or rarefied philosophical questions, but in his emphasis on the subject rather than the object as the primary maker of social change, in his refusal to recognize the existence of any objectivity that cannot be overcome through conscious praxis. The *materialist* aspect of historical materialism virtually drops out. Gramsci emerges as a 'realist' neo-Crocean, a Marxist working within a voluntarist, subjectivist, idealist framework, totally opposed to any form of economic determinism.

The PCI did not manage a convincing reply to Tamburrano and the essential points of his interpretation took firm root, remaining very much alive (and widely accepted) to this day.[17] But the past decade or so has witnessed the emergence of yet another variant of the neo-idealist reading. On the whole, the commentators mentioned thus far expressed sympathy for what they deemed to be Gramsci's 'revision' of orthodox Marxism. They viewed his *œuvre* as a commendable attempt to expand the range of a doctrine which had become unduly narrow and mechanical. In recent years, however, theorists on the 'Trotskyist' Left have denounced Gramsci's 'idealism' as a pernicious Right-wing deviation, closely linked with the 'reformist' sins of the Italian Communist Party. These theorists fail to see how any serious Marxist-Leninist perspective can be reconciled with Gramsci's 'culturalist' and 'voluntarist' bias. In drawing a philosophical transfusion from the Italian neo-Hegelians, Gramsci, they say, contracted an extreme case of subjective idealism.[18] One critic even calls him 'the last of the great ideologists of the Italian democratic tradition'.[19]

Enough has been said to indicate the importance of the 'neo-Crocean', 'voluntarist', 'subjectivist', 'idealist' interpretations of Gramsci. In this chapter, I shall question the validity of such readings, which—I believe—fail to comprehend how historical materialism can incorporate a crucial role for consciousness without losing, in the process, the essential economic core that constitutes its uniqueness. It was Gramsci's achievement to fashion just such a synthesis. Scrutiny of his philosophical and theoretical assumptions will reveal a firm materialist basis for the concept of hegemony. Nowhere in the *Quaderni* does Gramsci embark on a sustained exposition and analysis of his basic ideas. To some extent, the tenor of his doctrines must be inferred from scattered observations. However, he comes closest to a systematic discussion of the principles underlying his own approach to Marxism in those sections of the *Notebooks* where he undertakes extensive critiques of, on the one hand, Bukharin's *The Theory of Historical Materialism, a Manual of Popular Sociology* (Popular Manual—*Saggio popolare*—in Gramsci's prison code), and, on the other, Croce's brand of speculative philosophy.[20] This chapter will therefore rely heavily, though not entirely, on these two critiques for evidence of Gramsci's position.

II. *The Attack on Bukharin and Orthodox Marxism*

As the historical situation progressively frustrated the expectations of nineteenth-century Marxism, many socialists sought a kind of fatalistic deliverance in the quest for scientific certainty. Obviously influenced by the growing prestige of the natural sciences, and the increasing preoccupation with scientific methodology in all spheres, Marxists came to define their doctrine as a comprehensive science of society, which all but obliterated even the minimal voluntarist component discernible in Marx's own writings. All 'subjective' elements, including politics, philosophy, culture, and psychology, were excluded from serious consideration by the mania for scientific rigour. While it would be unfair to ignore its 'maverick and contentious' side,[21] Bukharin's *Popular Manual* (by and large) mirrored this dominant intellectual current within Marxism, a current which included the German School around Kautsky and the Russian School started by Plekhanov. The Bolshevik thinker was the expositor and inheritor of a materialist, determinist tradition which flourished as much in social-democratic circles as within the Communist movement, and whose influence has survived to this day. The historical importance of the *Popular Manual* should not be underestimated. The book established Bukharin, despite his subsequent disgrace, as the foremost Soviet systematizer of Marxism in the 1920s. Against this background, Gramsci's demolition of the *Saggio popolare* presents itself as much more than a critique of Bukharin; it is also a vehicle through which Gramsci expresses his contempt for the crude positivism and vulgar materialism of all 'orthodox' Marxism, the main tenets of which I shall now sketch out. Despite particular internal disagreements, there emerges a familiar general picture.

The 'scientific' Marxists claimed to be faithful disciples of Marx's teaching, but in fact it is in the writings of Engels that we find the first systematic *exposé* of their outlook, which combined four basic elements: (a) a positivist epistemology, (b) a dialectical variant of metaphysical naturalism, (c) rigid economic determinism, and (d) a quasi-Darwinian evolutionary history.

According to their theory of knowledge, man's conceptual apparatus constantly endeavours to copy ever more accurately the external world, which is regarded as a pre-existent model independent of this effort. Man's knowledge consists of 'reflections', or abstract pictures of actual objects and processes. These mirror images may be 'correct' or 'distorted' but in either case they only translate what takes place in the 'real', primary world of 'given' things. Conceptual categories therefore serve no independent cognitive function; they evolve through sensate perception, thus enabling them better to imitate the external world's properties and relations. The theory, it can be seen, denies the active contribution of the mind.

In this schema, all knowledge begins with matter—which is accorded ontological priority. Since all existence is material, the human mind itself is nothing more than matter, and thought is merely a chemical secretion within the brain. Mental events—values, goals, purposes, ideas—are ultimately reducible to arrangements of molecules, to physiological processes which, in turn, reflect external stimuli. Of course, *dialectical* materialism is not to be confused with what Marxists call the 'metaphysical materialism' of early 'bourgeois' philosophers, like Hobbes and Holbach. These thinkers viewed the universe as a huge machine, proceeding in a perpetual cycle of the same processes. The world, they believed, consisted of permanent and stable things or particles with definite, fixed properties such as position, mass and velocity. It was a central point of this philosophy to view nature as *immutable*. In whatever way nature itself might have come into being, once present it remained as it was as long as it continued to exist. All development was denied. For the dialectical materialists, however, the universe is not static but dynamic—in a continuous process of transformation and development. The driving force is to be found within the material processes themselves, in the internal contradictions that operate in every process of nature and society. Development proceeds through the struggle of mutually exclusive, opposite tendencies in all phenomena. The dialectical motion of matter comprehends all changes and processes in the universe from mere change of place to thinking.

If man is but a link in the material chain, an object in nature—no more, no less, then 'our subjective thought and the objective world are subject to the same laws'.[22] Human behaviour can be adequately accounted for by verifiable physical hypotheses. Man cannot, through his free will, control his own destiny. It is only his ignorance of the natural causes of his action that makes him suppose himself in some sense different from the falling stone. In the final analysis, everything in life occurs as it does as a result of unalterable processes of nature; human choice, individual or social, is subject to causes that fully determine it—it is merely an exemplification and verification of physical laws. Historical materialism is therefore a specific application of a general materialist ontology to historical phenomena. Human history, in this view, becomes natural history, and the movement of social and economic life follows a series of laws of the same character as those of natural science. In Bukharin's words, 'Society and its evolution are as much subject to natural law as is everything else in the universe'.[23] The dialectical necessity that governs nature, in other words, *ipso facto* governs the development of civilization. History is a process obeying discoverable evolutionary laws of universal applicability. Impelled by the irresistible logic of technological advance and class struggle, it follows an inexorable pattern, leading to conclusions independent of human designs and actions, consciousness and intentions. The study of history, then, is an exact science, from which the advent of socialism can be predicted with all but mathematical certainty. And so there arose the unshakable conviction that, whatever the present difficulties or setbacks, the stars in their courses were promoting the socialist cause.

It follows from this 'scientism' that the totality of society and history can be explained in the language of the physical sciences, in terms of mechanical causality: the material forces of production *cause* certain types of class relations, which *cause* certain types of conflict, which *cause* certain types of institutional development, and so on. The assumption is that society is a closed system, whose internal processes can be analysed as if they were those of a biological organism. Knowledge of the physical world becomes the paradigm of all valid knowledge. Social science— the study of society and its evolution—is treated as involving simply the extension of the presuppositions and methods of the natural sciences to human beings. Marxism is thus turned into a global, scientific sociology, a tightly integrated system of general laws and propositions, purporting to provide a detailed cognitive map of the past, present and future. If, for Marx, the 'materialist inversion' of Hegel's philosophy aimed at the termination of speculative system building, for his followers— like Bukharin—it entailed the construction of a materialist edifice as systematic, *a priori* and all-encompassing as Hegel's own. Certainly, while the evolutionary scheme owes much to Darwin, the appeal to immutable, 'inner, hidden' dialectical laws, beyond the reach of human volition, recalls Hegel's 'cunning of reason', the providential design working through individuals subordinated to its purposes.

Mainly through his assault on the *Popular Manual*, Gramsci rejected nearly every principle and assumption of this scientific Marxism. In exposing what he took to be gross mystifications, he sought to return to the spirit of Marx himself, thus liberating the philosophy of praxis from the degenerate theoretical tendency that developed after its founder's death. In Gramsci's estimation, Bukharin and his ilk had burdened the doctrine with a cumbersome metaphysical apparatus that spelled the death of both critical thought and effective practical action. For the ill-starred Bolshevik theorist, with his 'ptolemaic conception of the world',[24] Gramsci reserved special contempt. Bukharin, he took trouble to demonstrate, was a purveyor of pseudo-scientific mumbo-jumbo, a theoretical charlatan, lost beyond rescue in a realm of intellectual darkness. The *Popular Manual* constituted an 'infantile deviation'[25] of the worst kind, 'chaotic and indistinct' in conception,[26] 'disconnected and disjointed' in execution,[27] 'nebulous and vague' in its use of concepts,[28] 'superficial and sophistic' in its argumentation,[29] and 'puerile and ingenuous' in its search for dogmatic certainty.[30] In this torrent of anti-Bukharin invective, reminiscent of the fierce and celebrated polemics of the Renaissance, Gramsci concentrates his hostility towards the 'so-called orthodox tendency'.[31] Here we shall discuss only those criticisms which apply to orthodox Marxism in general and not just to Bukharin's sometimes idiosyncratic formulation of it.

Underlying Gramsci's entire critique was his desire to restore the possibility of conscious, creative human activity in the historical process. On the most fundamental level, he took issue with the passive materialism of the scientific Marxists. For Gramsci the human mind is neither a mere network of physical components and processes nor an inert receptacle of sense impressions; it is an active, transforming agency:

Man does not enter into relations with nature just by being himself part of nature, but actively, by means of work and technique. Furthermore these relations are not mechanical. They are active and conscious.[32]

Reality must not be construed as pure objective datum, external to man; it 'does not exist on its own, in and for itself, but in an historical relationship with the men who modify it, etc.'[33] Thus the picture of reality sketched by everyday perception, the world we know by means of our senses and reason, is—in some measure—a product of immanent mental categories, a human creation, not an imitation, since both the linguistic and scientific division of the world into particular objects corresponds not to some pre-existent natural classification which the mind registers through the operation of the senses, but to 'qualities that man has distinguished because of his practical interests'.[34] Human thought, then, cannot be reduced to a 'receptive' activity; there is a dialectical interdependence between 'being' and 'thinking'. After Kant and Hegel had pointed to the creative role of the mind in shaping the world of experience present to the individual consciousness, the naïve sensationalism of the orthodox Marxists seemed to Gramsci a giant step backwards.[35]

He used as his authority on these issues the testimony of Marx's *Theses on Feuerbach*, to which he referred repeatedly in his *Quaderni* in order to prove that Marx posits as the most important factor in history not brute matter but thinking, feeling *man*.[36] To be sure, in his critique of Feuerbach (and French materialism) Marx denounced the dualism of mind and matter, mental activity and external reality, which regarded consciousness as nothing but a 'reflection' of the material conditions of man's existence:

The chief defect of all previous materialism (including that of Feuerbach) is that things (*Gegenstand*), reality, the sensible world, are conceived only in the form of *objects* (*Objekt*) *of observation*, but not as *human sense activity*, not as *practical activity*, not subjectively.[37]

Marx, it seems, argues for a constant reciprocity between the subject (man in society) and the 'object' (the material world)— an interaction manifested in *praxis*. The 'objective' world, on this conception, is not wholly precedent to consciousness. Although it (the 'objective' world) conditions man's activity, it is at the same time shaped and transformed by this activity, which strives to subordinate it to practical human needs.

Armed with the *Theses on Feuerbach*, Gramsci felt confident to reject 'the dogmatic presupposition that historical materialism is traditional materialism slightly revised and corrected'. He deplores the 'philosophical dilettantism' of those who confuse questions of terminology with questions of substance. It may be that Marx labelled his theory 'materialist', but we should not infer from this appellation, as many do, that his 'materialism' had anything in common with the philosophical materialism of the Enlightenment: 'Identity of terms does not signify identity of concepts.'[38] No doubt Marx found some 'instrumental value' in philosophical materialism, but this mechanistic doctrine never became an integral part of his *Weltanschauung*. Indeed, the philosophy of praxis must be understood as a theoretical breakthrough, a 'completely self-sufficient and autonomous structure of thought', not simply as the highest development of a materialist philosophy whose origins are traceable to the primitive, metaphysical doctrines of the ancient Greeks.[39] It is legitimate for Marxism to *use* other forms of thought but these must be digested and synthesized 'at a higher level of development'.[40] (What he seems to have in mind here is some sort of dialectical supersession, or *dépassement*, of a Hegelian kind. This attitude towards past philosophies will take on added importance when we examine his relationship to Croce and idealism.) Gramsci does appear to be correct in his assertion that Marx, when he took over the dialectic from Hegel, had no intention of substituting an abstract 'material' for an abstract 'idea'.[41] The 'being' that determines consciousness in Marx's famous aphorism does not comprise pure material but the instruments and relations of economic activity, i.e. phenomena shot through with conscious human activity. In his philippic against Bukharin, Gramsci hammers the point home with considerable force:

It is evident that, for the philosophy of praxis, 'matter' should be understood neither in the meaning that it has acquired in the natural sciences . . . nor in any of the meanings that arise out of the various materialist metaphysics. The various physical (chemical, mechanical, etc.) properties of matter . . . should be considered, but only in so far as they become a productive 'economic element'. Matter as such is therefore not our concern but how it is socially and historically organized for production . . . the philosophy of praxis does not study a machine in order to know and to establish the atomic structure of its materials or the physcial-chemical-mechanical properties of its natural components . . . but only to the extent that it is a moment of the material forces of production, is an object of property of determinate social forces, and expresses a social relation which in turn corresponds to a determinate historical period.[42]

His insistence that the world of objects is not, in any straightforward sense, prior to the world of consciousness manifests itself, on a more practical level, in a rejection of the positivist dogma (accepted by Marxists and non-Marxists alike) that the subject matter of social and natural scientific disciplines is a realm of objective facts, logically separate from the values of the investigator and capable of being described in a wholly neutral way. It is impossible, he believes, to follow the exact configurations of observed experience. Empirical data possess no intrinsic significance. Bare 'facts' acquire meaning only when ascertained and organized in the frame of a theory, which cannot itself be derived from the facts to be explained. The analysis of reality must be filtered through *a priori* theoretical assumptions—a set of categories and a hierarchy of values:

An investigation into a series of facts to discover the relations between them presupposes a 'concept' that permits one to distinguish that series of facts from other possible ones. How can there occur a choice of facts to be adduced as proof of the truth of one's own assumptions if one does not possess a pre-existent criterion of choice? But what will this criterion of choice be, if not something superior to each single fact under investigation? An intuition, a conception, which must be regarded as having a complex history, a process that is to be connected with the whole process of the development of culture.[43]

Contrary to the beliefs of the 'self-styled "orthodox" adherents of the philosophy of praxis',[44] in no sphere can knowledge be likened to a photographic plate that reproduces the picture it receives, for our images of reality are, in part, artificial creations, tied to culturally determined presuppositions. Even natural science 'does not present itself as a bare objective notion; it always comes forth clothed by an ideology, and concretely science is the union of objective fact with a hypothesis or system of hypotheses that transcend the mere objective fact'.[45] The physical scientist, like his counterparts in the humanities, can observe phenomena only through the media of prior categories and questions which are themselves bound up with philosophical speculation and practical preferences.

If, as Gramsci argued, human consciousness has an independent and creative role to play, then those, like Bukharin, who seek in the material structure of society the efficient cause of all social behaviour are absurdly mistaken:

The claim (presented as an essential postulate of historical materialism) that every fluctuation of politics and ideology can be presented and explained as an immediate expression of the structure must be contested theoretically as primitive infantilism.[46]

Gramsci offers a couple of examples by way of illustration. He notes, for instance, that the French Revolution 'did not happen as the result of immediate mechanical causes; namely, the impoverishment of the social group which had an interest in breaking the equilibrium and which did in fact break it'. On the contrary, it 'happened in the context of conflicts on a higher plane than the immediate world of the economy, conflicts bound up with class "prestige" (future economic interests), and an exacerbation of sentiments of independence, autonony and power'. Economic issues were a 'partial aspect' and it would be a mistake to view the revolution solely in their terms.[47] In some cases, says Gramsci, cultural conflicts seem almost totally un-related to economic movements. He cites the dispute between Roman and Byzantine churches on the theological issue of the procession of the Holy Spirit. 'It would be ridiculous', he con-tends, 'to look in the structure of the European East for the affirmation that it proceeds only from the Father, and in that of the West for the affirmation that it proceeds from the Father and the Son.' Rather, this conflict was 'connected with sec-tarian and organizational necessities', which—it is argued—often account for political and ideological activity.[48] Indeed, Marxist determinism, with its mania for explaining everything by recourse to a 'final cause', is itself a 'manifestation of the "search for God"', simply 'old fashioned metaphysics' in modern non-theological guise.[49] Gramsci, therefore, ridicules all attempts to conceive the superstructure as a mere reflection of the means of production and exchange. Far from being a realm of 'appearance' or 'illusion', which must be reduced to hidden economic conflict, the superstructure is 'a reality . . . objective and operative', for it is the terrain on which men gain consciousness of their social position and tasks.[50] Thus, the relationship between the structure and the superstructure is 'necessarily interactive and reciprocal'.[51] (The precise character of this reciprocity will be explored in Section V, where I shall try to set out Gramsci's alternative to the 'de-generate' form of historical materialism which so upset him.) In order to make his point vivid, Gramsci uses an intriguing analogy with the female body. When discussing a woman's attractions one would never say that her skin or her breasts (superstructure) were unimportant illusions and that the *real* source of her charms, her *real* beauty, lay in her skeleton (base). What makes a man become infatuated with a woman, what stirs him to court her or fight for her or defend her, is not her skeleton, but the 'superstructural' features attached to her skeleton—though it is understood that her bone structure will, to some extent, account for her facial beauty, grace of movement and so on.[52]

Last but not least, we turn to Gramsci's ringing denunciation of all attempts to convert Marxism into a scientific sociology—a denunciation closely linked with his stress on the importance of superstructural activity. Such attempts, he explains, rest on a 'quasi-fetishism' which insists on natural science as the pattern to which all other forms of intellectual activity should conform.[53] 'It must be established', Gramsci writes, 'that every research has its own specific method.' Consequently, to think that one can advance the progress of a particular discipline 'by applying to it a standard method, chosen because it has given good results in another field of research to which it was naturally suited, is a strange misunderstanding which has little to do with science'.[54] Gramsci, in opposition to Bukharin, posits a cleavage between the domain of natural science and the world of human activity, so that the categories of the former cannot be applied to the latter. There is an irreducible difference between, on the one hand, the explanatory resources available to us in our dealings with natural phenomena and, on the other, those modes of understanding specifically adapted to the realm of human actions. The central categories of interpretation of human behaviour are in principle different from those used in explaining facts about plants or animals, because such behaviour, in both its individual and collective forms, is not wholly susceptible to quantitative treatment. However true it may be that human action exhibits regularities of occurrence in situations of a certain type, and however much the analyst may be able to produce hypotheses concerning these regularities, it is not the case that we can *fully* explain human behaviour by referring to hypotheses of this kind. For civilization is 'rationality and irrationality, free will and necessity, it is "life itself"'.[55] The greater part of our common experience must be understood in terms of purposes, motives, acts of will, thoughts, hopes, fears, desires and so forth. These enable us to distinguish human beings from the rest of nature. That is to say, problems of meaning and purpose are central to human relations, and cannot be dealt with using the same procedures by which natural science explains the movement of a piece of matter. Thus, to restrict our

knowledge to those features of men which they share with the
non-human world, and, in consequence, to try to explain
human behaviour in mechanistic terms is to misconstrue the
distinctive characteristics of the human condition. As Gramsci
declares roundly, 'if one excludes all voluntarist elements . . .
one mutilates reality itself'.[56] If man can be clearly distinguished from the physical world by his possession of independent powers of reason, subjective elements must always be
central rather than peripheral to social science inquiry. Social
life must be understood, in large part, through the various
concepts and categories, the modes of feeling and expression,
embodied in concrete institutional behaviour. Social analysis
involves not simply—not even mainly—the methodical application of technical rules and procedures but also the inner
perception of understanding, the recovery of subjective meanings and conscious intentions.

It follows that social change (and historical development)
cannot be explained by reference to a formal system of causal
laws, beyond human intervention.[57] Marxists who spend their
time building neat, universally applicable systems of thought
ultimately mystify rather than illuminate history. To begin
with, by viewing all facts as particular instances of abstract
laws, they ignore the unique patterns and arrangements that
emerge through the variations in social development: 'The
experience upon which the philosophy of praxis is based cannot
be schematized; it is history itself in all its infinite variety and
multiplicity.' Although the characteristics of a particular social
structure or historical epoch may closely resemble something
that has occurred before or after it, its totality must in some
sense be *sui generis*. Because their successful application depends
upon recurrence and repetition of phenomena, cut-and-dried
formulae and scientific techniques must, by definition, fail to
embrace complex, contradictory and changing situations. Thus
the Bukharins of this world, who long for 'a mechanical formula'
which holds 'the whole of history in its grasp', are incapable of
comprehending 'particular facts in their unique individuality'.[58]
Yet again the Bolshevik shows himself to be a prisoner of
metaphysics, if this term is understood in the sense of 'any
systematic formulation put forward as an extra-historical truth,
as an abstract universal outside of time and space'.[59] Indeed,

his aversion for social and historical variability, his undeviating search for uniformity, for objective laws is 'a baroque form of Platonic idealism, since these abstract laws bear a strange resemblance to Plato's pure ideas, which are the essence of real, terrestrial facts'.[60]

Those who seek to provide a schematic description of historical and social facts according to criteria derived from the natural sciences also distort reality by falsely claiming the ability to 'predict' future events. Given the mediation of human consciousness, Gramsci informs us, neither Marxism nor any other theory is in a position to derive laws of human evolution similar to the scientific prediction that the oak tree will develop out of the acorn.[61] It is impossible to predict any determinate outcomes because outcomes depend on human decisions, which are not themselves determined by their antecedent conditions. Marxism could predict with the accuracy of the natural sciences only if human beings were absolutely passive, for their behaviour could then be quantified and subsumed under a systematic body of statements embodying precise correlations. But such is obviously not the case. History is about 'opposing forces in continuous movement, which are never reducible to fixed quantities, because within them quantity is continually becoming quality'.[62] What Gramsci means by this Hegelian terminology is simply that the 'nuts and bolts' of economic and practical activity are constantly being transformed by ideational elements, whose movement and development cannot be isolated and measured under controlled laboratory conditions.[63] To put the point more simply, the future is '"non-existent" and therefore unknowable by definition'. All we can do is to 'predict' the tendencies of present practice:

In reality one 'foresees' only to the extent that one acts, to the extent that one applies a voluntary *effort* and therefore contributes concretely to the 'foreseen' result. Prediction is thus revealed not as a scientific act of knowledge, but as the abstract expression of the effort made.[64]

In other words, 'prediction' is bound up with the penetration of political will into the factuality of the given. It is impossible to separate prognoses from the acts by which they are fulfilled.

For Gramsci, the essence of Marxism (and the dialectic) is

not to be found in Bukharin's 'blind clash of physical forces'; it
resides, rather, in the dialectical, or reciprocal, relationship
between human will and material reality, superstructure and
base, theory and practice. Understood in this sense the Marxian
dialectic tends against the establishment of universally applicable, evolutionary laws of social development. But Gramsci's
rejection of 'objective laws of historical development similar in
character to natural laws'[65] does not mean that he denies the
existence of regular, repeatable connections that can be encapsulated in general formulations. On the contrary, it is 'useful
and interesting' to 'build up an empirical compilation of practical observations', to systematize and classify observations and
to establish probabilistic social uniformities: '. . . a theory of
history and politics can be made, for even if the facts are always
singular and changeable in the flux of historical movement, the
concepts can (and must) be theorized'. The construction of
models, general principles, and laws of tendency can establish
significant correlations, provide fruitful descriptions, clarify
issues and identify general lines of development.[66] The formulation of concepts and *limited* causal laws based on empirical
analysis constitutes, to Gramsci's mind, one of the dividing
lines between the Marxist approach and the ancient, outmoded
metaphysical approach. In a couple of interesting sections he
attributes this scientific (in a broad sense) aspect of Marxist
methodology to the innovations of the classical economists, in
particular David Ricardo, who suggested a new way of thinking
about society and life. In observing and describing the inter-
relations of the major factors of the productive process, he
established 'the formal logical principle of the "law of tendency",
which leads to the scientific explanation of the economy, of *homo
economicus*, and of "determined market"'. The philosophy of
praxis 'has universalized Ricardo's discoveries, extending them,
in measured form, to the whole of history'.[67] That is, Marx
sought in historical (and social) development a 'regularity', a
certain 'rationality', *relatively* independent of individual choices.
And these ideas he took not from the natural sciences but from
political economy, especially from Ricardo's perception that
specific forces operate with a certain 'automatism', thus allowing some degree of certainty about the consequences of individual initiatives. But, Gramsci hastens to point out, this search

for regularity 'is not a matter of "discovering" a metaphysical law of "determinism", nor even of establishing a "general" law of causality'.[68]

Gramsci's criticism of the purveyors of such laws is not only theoretical but also practical. Most important, they encouraged, with their iron-clad predictions, a complacent, do-nothing fatalism—'a mental laziness and a superficiality in political programmes'.[69] By transferring political initiative and responsibility from self-conscious human beings to structural entities and abstract forces, the mechanistic Marxists transformed theory into an academic project, remote from political practice. If everything will turn out right, no matter what you do, if salvation comes through grace and not works, then why bother to man the barricades or in any way expend revolutionary energy? Again, Gramsci returns to the analogy between orthodox Marxism and theology. The 'assured rationality of history', we are told, 'becomes a substitute for predestination, for Providence'. The deterministic, fatalistic Marxism of Bukharin and his crowd is 'rather like religion or a stupefying drug'.[70] Gramsci's remarks did seem to have a sound historical basis. One of the fundamental oddities of Second International Marxism was the yawning chasm between its revolutionary pronouncements and doctrines, on the one hand, and its manifestly reformist policies and actions, on the other. It was during the hey-day of the Second International that Gramsci began his relentless polemic against the 'pocket-geniuses' (*genialoidi*),[71] those who wait around with hands in pockets for the contradictions of capitalism to generate revolution. Before Bukharin, his chief target on this front was the maximalist strand of Italian Marxism, ranging from Serrati in the Socialist centre to Bordiga on the extreme Communist Left.

Gramsci was willing to concede that, at an early stage of the struggle, mechanical determinism may have been necessary in order to dispel doubts about the future:

When you do not have the initiative in the struggle and the struggle itself comes therefore to be identified with a series of defeats, mechanical determinism becomes a formidable force of moral resistance, of cohesion and of patient and obstinate perseverance.[72]

To illustrate his point, Gramsci refers to early Christianity.

Faith in a secure future, in the immortality of the soul destined to eternal joy, was the solid foundation that enabled the religion to survive initial setbacks. Free from doubts, and certain that a superior force was supporting him in the struggle, the early Christian was ready to stand firm in the face of any adversity. But when the time comes to seize the initiative, to turn the proletariat into an historical protagonist, determinism—especially if embraced by the revolutionary élite—becomes a hindrance, leading to the passive capitulation before objective conditions.[73]

Gramsci also believed that the sheer intellectual vulgarity of mechanistic Marxism undermined its practical efficacy. Once again he was willing to grant an historical dimension: any mass, or popular, doctrine assumes 'uncouth and even superstitious forms' in the early stages of its dissemination. Protestantism, for example, was for a couple of centuries all but sterile in the field of study, criticism and philosophy. In the words of Erasmus: 'Where Luther enters, civilization disappears.' But this very sterility helped the new religion to attain 'popular penetration', in contrast to the much more intellectually robust Renaissance, which always remained a movement of élite circles.[74] However, the time has come to rescue Marxism from its intellectual degeneracy, which has emasculated Marx's teachings, blunted their critical edge, and limited the analytical basis for action.[75] Effective action requires meticulous study of concrete, particular events and situations, and such investigation is undermined by fanatical devotion to mechanical categories and standardized methods, whose effect is to blot out historical variability. A fascination for the natural scientific method—which method rests on a search for the general, the abstract, the formal—dooms the social analyst to an otiose dogmatism, by excluding from his consideration the *specific* traditions and class configurations at work in any given society. These cannot be derived from a set of universally valid propositions. To be sure, Marx himself never tried to give a universal definition to all social formations; rather, he emphasized the unique features and special laws of different historical societies. It was no wonder to Gramsci that when the 'pocket geniuses' did act, they were capable of little more than defiant posturing, grandiose gestures signifying nothing.

To summarize this section, we can say that historical materialism was, for Gramsci, a set of concepts comprising tools of analysis, a method of examining social situations, *not* a rigid framework of absolute laws and principles. It was essential to realize, he thought, that men are able to influence events for good or evil through their freely held ideals and convictions. Since man is a creative being capable of shaping historical reality, social phenomena can be rendered intelligible neither by a system of analytical laws nor by recourse to purely economic explanations. Certain idealist themes and arguments are indeed visible in Gramsci's polemic against orthodox Marxism. The attack on the positivist faith in an integrated natural science of all there is, the stress on imaginative understanding in the appreciation of historical change, the focus on conceptual or symbolic structures, the elevation of human consciousness (the subjective element) as a crucial factor in social life, the desire to present reality not in its abstract moments but in the full course of its unique flesh and blood activity—all these provide plenty of ammunition for the familiar tendency to interpret Gramsci as a Crocean (or neo-Hegelian). Let us now turn to a close examination of Gramsci's relationship to Croce and other strands of idealist thought.

III. *Gramsci, Croce and Idealism*

By way of preliminaries, it would be useful to sketch out the essential points of Croce's doctrines, which cast a spell over a whole generation of Italian intellectuals. But a word of caution is in order. Beyond a certain point it is difficult to attribute a definite view to Croce with any degree of assurance. A brilliant and seductive stylist, sometimes praised as the greatest master of Italian prose since Manzoni, he had a tendency to gloss over intellectual obscurities and difficulties with graceful phrases. When we subject his philosophical musings to careful analytical scrutiny, we find that too many matters are left hanging in the air, too many questions unanswered, too much conceptual incoherence unresolved. With this caveat in mind we can now attempt a rough reconstruction of his basic ideas.

In Croce's idealist world-view, reality is the self-expression of 'spirit' (or 'mind'), and there is no reality which is not spirit. He makes this point with considerable force in the second section of his *Logic*:

. . . if being is conceived as external to the human spirit, and knowledge as separable from its object, so much so that the object could be without being known, it is evident that the existence of the object becomes a datum, or something placed before the spirit, given to the spirit, extraneous to it. . . . But all the philosophy which we are now developing demonstrates that there is nothing external to the spirit, and therefore there are no data confronting it. These very conceptions of something external, mechanical, natural, have shown themselves to be conceptions, not of external data, but of data furnished to the spirit by itself. Spirit creates the so-called external something. . . .[76]

Given his porous terminology and opaque style of argumentation, it is difficult to elucidate, in the space available, the *precise* limits and character of Croce's philosophical idealism. (In any case, the characterization of Gramsci as a Crocean does not refer to what Croce manifestly *said* or *meant*, but to vague entities known as 'Croceanism' and 'neo-Hegelianism'.) Even such a distinguished student of his thought as H. Wildon Carr is reduced to conjecture:

Does [Croce's philosophy of spirit] only insist that thoughts about things are thoughts and not things, and that there is no passage from thoughts about things to things, no means of escape from a subjective world of knowledge to an objective world of independent reality? Is it only *esse* is *percipi* once again? Or is it the doctrine that mind makes nature? . . . In some form Croce would, *I suppose*, acknowledge the truth of all these maxims, but he means something more and something different from anything which finds expression in them. He means that every form which reality assumes or can assume for us has its ground within mind. There is not and there cannot be a reality which is not mind.[77]

Broadly, what Croce seems to mean is this: all in our human experience which enables us to classify, divide and relate, all which enables men to form a scheme or diagram of immediate experience, is mental. What is left of experience when all mental elements are removed? Nothing. The apparent independent existence of a material substratum is but a delusion, born of practical needs. In Croce's vision, the status of objects is equivocal and he, in effect, denies the objectivity of the natural world: '. . . nature has been shown as a moment and a product of the spirit itself'.[78] If there is anything outside human concepts, external to the human spirit, it can only be a meaningless chaos, a shadowy limiting concept, to which mind has not yet given form; hence it lacks concrete reality, for the formless is nothing; it is literally inconceivable. All reality, therefore, is mental activity. But it does not appear that Croce wanted to reduce things to products of the *individual* mind. The productive subject, if I read him correctly, is not the finite mind but some supra-individual mind.

These ontological premises formed the basis of his conception of human history. Taking from Hegel the idea of a philosophical history, Croce depicted historical evolution as the dialectical unfolding of a quasi-deity called 'spirit'. But this 'deity' was not transcendent, not 'above the world' in the traditional theological sense; it was, rather, the collective, evolving human consciousness.[79] In the manner of all idealism, Croce assumed that historical progress was preceded and guided by a progress of thought: the primary determinants of social life were values, beliefs and outlooks. In other words, he believed, with his illustrious German predecessor, that it was the development of man's spirit, the human soul, that provided the key to historical understanding. Hence in Croce's discussions of history the cultural ('ethico-political') element occupies a predominant place and we find only passing allusions to material conditions or concrete social structures of any kind. Still, he retained a sense of the *particular* and the *contingent* in historical change, which led him to dismiss, as a theological remnant, Hegel's *a priori* concept of the movement of history towards predestined goals. For Croce, there was no providential principle whose operations were immanent within the course of events and determined its overall direction. It was impossible, he maintained (at least in his earlier writings), to discover the meaning or pattern of historical reality as a whole—past, present and future. The 'absurd desire' to create a universal history could only result in the creation of 'theological or naturalistic fictions'.[80] And yet, while he admitted no foreordained plans of historical development, no providential design, he did—in his later historical writings—see the evolution of civilization as perpetual progress, in which spirit, through the development of philosophy, becomes self-conscious and therefore free. Perhaps in contradiction of his original historiographic programme, he came to share with Hegel the belief that history was the history of freedom, and that each successive stage in its development was marked by a further realization of man's potential for liberty.[81] History, then, was a 'rational' process, wherein even apparent evil had a positive role to play. In Croce's dialectic of the spirit, injustice, tyranny and the like are necessary ingredients. The existing world is the best of all possible worlds because it is a product of human rationality, a projection of the spirit—God come down to earth.

Croce's professed belief that there could be no universal history was logically tied to his denial of the existence of a universal philosophy. In his wish to expunge every trace of transcendence and metaphysics from philosophy, he espoused the doctrine of historicism, which may be defined by the formula, *veritas et virtus filiae temporis*—truth and values are daughters of time, daughters of history. Hamlet's epigram to the effect that 'there is nothing either good or bad but thinking makes it so' expresses the point in a nutshell. Values or ideas or theoretical concepts are not inherent in the constitution of the universe: on the contrary, they are expressive of nothing but our historically conditioned needs and choices. Moral standards and conceptual categories, according to Croce, correspond to specific societies and cultural periods. There are no eternal human predicaments, no unalterable goals of humanity, no fixed principles, no tran-historical truths or absolute values. The problems that philosophy confronts are therefore not abstract derivations from previous philosophical thought, but puzzles proposed by actual historical processes. Moreover, since there are no mysteries of the universe to be unveiled or riddles of existence to be solved, philosophy, in Croce's opinion, should view itself as a science of order and arrangement, seeking to classify the moments of the spirit's development.[82] Hence the much lamented *formalism* of Croce's philosophy. Preoccupied as he was with fitting the various phases of experience into the appropriate schema or framework, he became entangled in a web of mind-boggling abstractions, which belied his claim to apprehend the life of the mind in its concreteness.

If there can be neither a universal history nor a universal philosophy, if there is no extra-human reality—no transcendent Gods, no Absolutes, no objective historical laws to govern human life; then men must take upon their own shoulders the whole responsibility for creating their reality, their values and world. Here we have the essence of Croce's immanentism. History is generated neither by the theologians' self-sufficient Lord of the Universe nor by the speculative unfolding of a transcendent Idea nor by the mechanistic evolution of material forces. *Man* is the protagonist.[83]

To the young Italian intellectuals before 1914, Croce's philosophy gave a sense of moral purpose to life and history, and thus represented a refreshing departure from the triumphant positivism that dominated the latter half of the nineteenth century. 'Not since Goethe', writes H. S. Hughes of Croce, 'had any single individual dominated so completely the culture of a single major European country'.[84] Gramsci, like others of his generation, was swept into the camp of Crocean thought. It is undeniable that he discovered Marxism through the theoretical lens of idealism and that the 'idealist' interpretation of his legacy can be supported by going back to his juvenilia. Even Togliatti has conceded that in the writings of the youthful Gramsci, 'elements of the idealist dialectic still prevail'.[85] The Sardinian himself acknowledged this while in prison. Reflecting, in his *Quaderni*, on his early years as a Torinese activist, he admitted that he had been 'rather Crocean in tendency'.[86] In a prison letter to Tatiana, he noted that, in those early years, he was 'to some degree part of the movement of moral and intellectual reform initiated in Italy by Benedetto Croce'.[87] Central to this movement was a certain moralism, anchored in a fervent belief that men are responsible for their own actions and make their own history. In 1908 Croce himself identified the origin of the 'rebirth' of idealism in the need for a spiritual 'concept of life and of reality'—a need left unfulfilled by a scientific, positivist orthodoxy which ignored men's deepest urges.[88] The point was to develop a total 'man-centred' vision of life, to satisfy those very needs expressed by religion—namely commitment, purpose, inner peace and community. These Italian trends must be viewed against the background of a marked change in the European intellectual landscape. During the decade of the 1890s, there developed an increasingly pervasive revolt against positivism and all its works. Boundless faith in the primacy of sense perception and in the infallibility of empirical procedures, it was felt, had caused men to overlook intangible but nevertheless central features of the human condition. In the eyes of the anti-positivists the consequences were pathological: an unmistakable cultural sterility and spiritual restlessness. If the idealist remedy was initially associated with the Right, it soon spread to socialist circles.

The theme of spiritual renewal through a socialist vision was diffused in Italian culture by Georges Sorel, who was far more interested in the death of a decadent bourgeois culture than in the destruction of capitalist economic organization. Determined to link socialism to the themes of romantic and idealist philosophy, Sorel stressed the voluntarist and ethical aspects of the movement. In his *Reflections on Violence*, for example, he criticized the notion of historical inevitability and argued that socialism was primarily a *moral* doctrine, aiming for a new type of human virtue powerful enough to purify a rotten society. He refused to regard the normal objects of socialist politics—higher wages, better working conditions, transfer of economic power— as ultimately significant. The primary purpose of revolt was to lift the workers above the moral decadence of bourgeois society, to achieve 'heroism', 'grandeur', and ethical integrity, not more spacious dwellings or ampler leisure or greater material comforts. The main problem of capitalism, he declared with the fervour of a religious prophet, was not so much inequality and exploitation as hypocrisy and mediocrity. Sorel's hatred for the schematic, determinist conceptions of orthodox Marxism was of a piece with his 'culturalist' emphasis. For the idea that social science could lay bare the laws of history was rooted in the reduction of culture to nature. The Frenchman, on the other hand, always insisted on the autonomy of the human will, the ability of man to shape his environment. In large part because of Sorel's powerful impact, it was not considered extraordinary, in the early years of the century, for Italians to combine socialism with the essential themes of Croce's anti-positivist philosophy (e.g. stress on human creativity, belief that man is more than a material creature, a passion for ethical rejuvenation), even though the great man himself chose (until 1910 at least) to stand outside partisan politics.[89] It was just such a combination that characterized Gramsci's early writings.

The Sardinian's admiration for Croce stretched back to his schooldays, when he was an avid reader of *La Voce*, a cultural-cum-political journal opposed to every form of positivism, materialism and industrialism. The chief theme of the journal, to which Croce was a frequent contributor, was that men can change the world by understanding themselves and their situation, by daring and creation, by imposing their wills.[90] Gramsci's attachment to Crocean, voluntarist ideas was later strengthened at the University of Turin, where nearly all the teachers he heard or met were active combatants in the war against positivism. Whatever their political affiliations, they preached the humanist doctrine that men were responsible for shaping their own destinies. Some, who were active in Socialist circles, encouraged their students to take the new philosophy of idealism and personal ethical responsibility into the Socialist movement and the working class.[91] After some initial resistance, based on his provincial, Sardinian nationalism, the young Gramsci followed their advice and joined the PSI in July of 1913. By late 1915 he was writing regular columns for the Party newspapers *Avanti!* and *Il Grido del Popolo*. Although the PSI professed commitment to the ideas of Marx and Engels, Gramsci, in his writings before 1918, devoted little space to Marxist ideas. Rather, his articles were permeated by tenets characteristic of the idealist revival—that thought is paramount in history, that change for the better can be effected by strength of mind alone, that the conditions of life are man's own creation, and that socialism constitutes, essentially, a moral yearning for a noble future, where men will discover the spiritual wholeness denied by bourgeois society. For example, in his first important article, entitled 'Socialism and Culture', he delivered a blistering attack on all forms of materialist determinism:

Man is above all spirit, that is, he is a product of history, not nature . . . only by degrees, layer by layer, has humanity acquired knowledge of its own value. . . . And this knowledge has been formed not under the brute stimulus of physiological necessity, but through *intelligent reflection*.[92]

In the same piece he calls for a redemption of society from corrupt ('weak and colourless') values and an intensification of moral life. It is crucial, he says, 'to be master of oneself, to distinguish oneself, to liberate oneself from a state of chaos, to exist as an element of order—but of one's own order and one's own discipline in striving for an ideal'. In May of 1916, Gramsci continued this Sorelian theme by identifying socialism with religious myth:

Socialism is precisely the religion that must overwhelm Christianity. [Socialism is] Religion in the sense that it too is a faith with its mystics and rituals; religion, because it has substituted for the consciousness of the transcendental God of the Catholics, the faith in man and in his great strengths as a unique spiritual reality.[93]

Around this time Gramsci found two new intellectual heroes, the Frenchman Charles Péguy and the Swiss Romain Rolland, both of whom advanced similar views to those of Croce and Sorel, but with a literary rather than philosophical bias. Péguy's appeal lay in his vibrant faith in the future and in his iron-willed commitment to the cause of the common man, even at the expense of his own artistic personality.

I am re-reading a book which I love so much, Charles Péguy's *Notre jeunesse*, and I became drunk on that mystical religious sense of socialism, of justice, which pervades it through and through.[94]

Like all Gramsci's favourite writers, Rolland too preached how men could find an immanent nobility in themselves which would enable them to overcome obstacles—'the murderous forces of nature, confused desires, dark thoughts'—and create a new and better life.[95]

Gramsci's early idealism received clear expression in *La Città futura*, a short treatise published in newspaper format by the Socialist Youth Federation of Piedmont on 11 February 1917.[96] Prepared and edited entirely by Gramsci, this work may be regarded as a summary and synthesis of his ideas and political experiences up to that point. In it we find a number of articles by Gramsci himself as well as some excerpts from Salvemini, Croce and Armando Carlini, a follower of Gentile's 'actualist' philosophy.[97] The treatise discloses an avid espousal of idealism in general and Croce in particular, whom the young militant pronounced 'the greatest thinker in Europe at this moment'.[98] The main themes that emerge are: (1) the irresistible power of man's collective will, (2) complete opposition to the scientific and determinist conceptions of history that dominated Italian socialism, (3) emphasis on personal moral responsibility, and (4) a deep concern with the cultural and philosophical aspects of socialism. All positivist modes of thought were rejected in favour of Hegelian categories. For example, Gramsci argued that socialists should fight for *ideals* rather than concrete proposals, the main ideal being '*the opportunity for all citizens to realize an integral human personality*'. This is the 'concrete universal', the inspirational guide of socialism. The moment of revolutionary rupture, then, is identified with the victory of a new order of values.[99] The class struggle must be waged primarily on the level of ideas. In keeping with this focus on the realm of consciousness, Gramsci cried out for more aggressive and imaginative political action. Socialism, he feared, was falling prey to pedantic bookworms and passive political functionaries, all bewitched by a view of history as an uncontrollable natural phenomenon: 'Life for them is like an avalanche seen from afar in its irresistible descent.' For Gramsci, there were no forces outside men (and their wills) which made life what it was; there were no unbreakable 'laws': 'For natural laws, the fatalism of pseudo-scientists, has been substituted the tenacious will of men'.[100] The intimate connection between Gramsci's theorizing and actual political imperatives is here evident. Just as his concept of hegemony was inspired by the failure of Marxist revolution in practice, so his youthful attacks on the fatalism of 'scientific' Marxism were animated by a political motive—his fierce conviction that positive, creative action could, in the given historical situation, bear revolutionary fruit. It did not escape his notice that scientific veneration for the 'laws of motion' of society had led to distaste for the rigours of revolution.

Gramsci was already being castigated, within the Party, for 'Bergsonian voluntarism'[101] when he stunned his comrades with what appeared to be a direct and fundamental attack on the 'Bible' of the Second International, Marx's *Capital*. His famous article, 'The Revolution Against "Capital"', first appeared as an editorial in *Avanti!* on 24 November 1917. Its basic argument was simple enough: in one historic episode the Bolshevik Revolution dramatically repudiated the mythical powers of economic determinism. The Revolution was 'against'

Capital in so far as Marx's grand work attempted to demonstrate the fatal necessity of bourgeois development:

Events have exploded the critical schema according to which the
history of Russia would unfold in line with the canons of historical
materialism. The Bolsheviks reject Karl Marx; they affirm, backed by
the testimony of explicit actions and successful conquests, that the
canons of historical materialism are not so iron-clad as might be (and
has been) thought.

Revolution, then, is subject to no determinist timetable. It was
Lenin's insight to understand that the conditions for socialism
are ideal and moral, and that the various stages of development
need only be realized 'in thought'. But while the Bolsheviks 'are
not "Marxists"', in that they 'have not employed the works of
the Master to compile a rigid doctrine of dogmatic propositions', they nevertheless accept the 'invigorating' part of Marx's
thought, the 'eternal' part, which 'represents the continuation
of Italian and German idealism, which in the case of Marx was
contaminated by positivist and naturalist encrustations'. What
is the 'eternal' element? That which 'postulates as the dominant
factor in history not raw economic facts but man, men in
societies, men who interact with one another . . . and develop
through these contacts (civilization) a collective, social will;
men who come to understand economic facts, judge them and
adapt them to their will, so that this will becomes the motive
force of the economy, the moulder of objective reality'.[102]
Gramsci may have been an admirer of Marx, but his admiration
was highly selective.

Clearly, any commentator who wishes to portray Gramsci as
some kind of idealist will find no shortage of quotations in his
early articles and editorials. But the commentator will do so at
the expense of being blatantly ahistorical, for Gramsci's position undoubtedly changed over the years. In some prison notes
explicitly dealing with the problem of how to study past thinkers
but implicitly autobiographical, Gramsci strongly suggests that
his youthful writings reflected a lack of intellectual maturity:

It is a common observation among all scholars, from personal experience, that any new theory studied with 'heroic frenzy' . . . for a
certain period, especially if one is young, attracts the student of its
own accord and takes possession of his whole personality, only to be

limited by the next theory studied, until such a time as a critical equilibrium is established and one learns to study deeply but without succumbing immediately to the fascination of the system or the author under study. These observations are all the more valid the more the thinker in question is impetuous, has a polemical character and is lacking in *esprit de système*, or when one is dealing with a personality in whom theoretical and practical activity are indissolubly interwoven, with an intellect in a process of continual creation and perpetual movement. . . .

Gramsci therefore counsels that the historian of ideas devote serious attention to the intellectual history of the thinker in question 'in order to identify those elements which were to become stable and "permanent"; that is, those which were taken over as his own thought, distinct from and superior to the "material" which he had studied earlier and which served as a stimulus to him'.[103] This latter material, Gramsci adds, should be discarded by the historian. In a prison reference to *La Città futura*, he is much more explicit about the limitations of his early thought. His approach to Croce in those days, he admits, was 'primitive and most certainly inadequate, since at that time the concept of unity of theory and practice, philosophy and politics was not clear in my mind . . . '.[104]

While it is difficult to locate any 'epistemological break' in Gramsci's thought, it is plain that by 1919, idealist themes no longer enjoyed pride of place. On the contrary, he began to take a serious interest in those material conditions that *prevent* men from directing their lives in accordance with their ideals. Escaping from the philosophical wonderland that in his youth had held him captive, he began to express conventional Marxist ideas about the crucial importance of the economic substructure. In discussing the role of the Party, for instance, he maintains:

Communist society can be conceived only as a 'natural' formation inherent in the means of production and exchange; and the revolution may be conceived as the act of historical recognition of the 'naturalness' of this formation. The revolutionary process therefore identifies itself . . . as a spontaneous movement of the labouring masses, determined by the clash of contradictions inherent . . . in a regime of capitalist property.[105]

It is easier to discover this shift of emphasis than to explain it.

One possible catalyst in Gramsci's 'conversion' may have been the work of Antonio Labriola, the leading Italian theoretical Marxist at the turn of the century, who brought to Marxism traces of his earlier Hegelianism. In 1916 or 1917 Gramsci embarked on a careful reading of Labriola's writings, which he recommended warmly to his friends and colleagues.[106] It was Labriola, in fact, who introduced Marxist theory into Italy; yet he was something of a recluse and his impact, even on Italian culture, was curiously limited.[107] Although he left no real disciples, intent on continuing his work, it is arguable that many of the theoretical innovations attributed to Gramsci (or Lukács) were prefigured by this distant, rather haughty Neapolitan. Consequently a brief excursion into his thought should prove both interesting and illuminating.

Labriola's contribution resided in his brave (though not entirely consistent) rejection of crude positivist Marxism at a time when such a rejection was far from fashionable. His lonesome crusade can be summarized in four basic points. First, he set himself against a simple reductive reconstruction of historical and social events. Economic explanations were never sufficient. In particular, it was necessary to examine ideologies, which could not be dismissed as 'simple artifice' or 'pure illusion'. States of mind, 'those forms of inner life to which . . . we give the name of imagination, intellect, reason, thought etc.', play a significant role in historical change and conservation.[108] Labriola wanted to study societies (and their evolution) in all their complexity. That events came about precisely as they did and that they took on certain forms, that they were clothed in certain vestments and painted in certain colours—these specific elements were not mere trifles to be ignored. True to his Hegelian upbringing, he always embraced the proposition that a given society or sequence of events must be understood in its unique individuality and not just regarded as an instance of a type. True comprehension requires a grasp of the 'picturesque whole', not simply the economic skeleton.[109] The second major aspect of Labriola's reformulation of Marxism was his attack on the fatalism inherent in naturalistic materialism. It is absurd to regard human history as a straightforward prolongation of nature. Historical materialism 'was not and is not designed to be the rebellion of the material man against the ideal man'. It follows that 'there is no foundation for that opinion which tends to the negation of every volition . . .'. Men are not 'marionettes, whose threads are held and moved, no longer by Providence but by economic categories'. All that has happened in history is 'the work of man' not of 'the logic of things'.[110] The third basic aspect of his polemic against the dogmatic sclerosis of official Marxism flows from the second: a denunciation of the 'fanatics' who attempt to turn historical materialism into 'a new philosophy of systematic history'. Marxism 'cannot represent the whole history of the human race in a unified perspective'; it cannot 'pretend to be the intellectual vision of a great plan or of a design', whereby all events—past, present, and future—are fit into a universal, predetermined model. Only 'careless persons' wish 'to possess, once for all, summed up in a few propositions, the whole of knowledge, and to be able with one single key to penetrate all the secrets of life'.[111] Finally, Labriola was perhaps the only Second International thinker who, between Marx's death in 1883 and the Great War in 1914, called for an original and distinctive Marxist philosophy of life, or *Weltanschauung*. In reducing the obstacles which 'the fantastic projections of the emotions, passions, fears and hopes pile in the way of free thought', philosophical reflection, properly conceived, 'serves, as Spinoza himself would say, to vanquish *imaginationem et ignorantiam*' and impart unity or coherence to the results of our experience.[112] Intellectual mediation—'a supreme effort of thought, with the aim of triumphing over the multi-form spectacle of immediate experience to reduce its elements into a genetic series'—is seen as the decisive theoretical task.[113] In this connection, he criticized Engels for having unnecessarily downplayed the philosophical dimension.[114]

For their time, Labriola's criticisms were very bold indeed, and it would be unfair to consider Gramsci's demolition of orthodox Marxism in isolation from them. Yet the Neapolitan was not entirely consistent and failed to take his insights to their logical conclusions. For example, whereas Gramsci denied the possibility of predicting the future, Labriola retained a notion of historical inevitability, at least regarding the genesis of the classless society. Scientific socialism, he writes:

. . . affirms the coming of communist production, not as a postulate, nor as the aim of a free volition, but as the result of the *processus* immanent in history . . . the premise of this prevision is in the actual conditions of present capitalist production . . . a moment *will come*, when in one fashion or another, with the elimination in every form of private rent, interest, profit, the production will pass over to the collectivist association, that is to say, will become communistic.[115]

On the question of free will, he equivocates. Notwithstanding his aversion for fatalism, he states time and time again that 'being' *determines* 'consciousness'[116] and, in passages, takes pains to gainsay that the historical process is the product of 'acts and free and voluntary thought'.[117] While Labriola was blessed with a judicious, electic mind, full of lively ideas and suggestions, his attempt to synthesize spiritualism and naturalism was, in the final analysis, neither forceful nor convincing. Right up to his death in 1904, he was beset by 'lingering theoretical doubts concerning many fundamental questions'.[118] Labriola may have ridiculed the positivists as 'embarrassing guests'[119] at the Marxist party, but in the end we must agree with the historian of Italian Marxism who concludes:

Both from a political and theoretical point of view, and notwithstanding the greater degree of critical perspective in his interpretation of Marxism with respect to that of his contemporaries (Kautsky included), Labriola is a Marxist of the Second International, who does not transcend the limitations of the *positivism* that dominated the theoreticians of that generation.[120]

Still, Gramsci was obviously impressed with his predecessor's critique of *rigid* determinism, contempt for simple solutions or first principles, refined historical sense, and feeling for the moral, educative aspects of socialism. In Labriola's work Gramsci encountered the possibility of reconciling some form of economic determinism with a rejection of vulgar materialism and paralysing fatalism. Whether or not his reading of Labriola in any significant way accounted for his gravitation towards conventional Marxist principles remains a matter of conjecture.[121] What *is* beyond doubt is that the *Quaderni* lavish praise on Italy's first major Marxist theorist. Indeed, Gramsci bemoans the widespread ignorance of his work, expressing the wish that it be brought back into circulation as part of the struggle for a superior proletarian culture.[122]

Though the erosion of Gramsci's philosophical idealism began while he was still a young PSI militant, his wrestling match with Croce did not begin in earnest until after his imprisonment. His own prison critique he regarded as but the first step to a more systematic and complete 'Anti-Croce', which 'in the modern cultural atmosphere would have the meaning and importance that the *Anti-Dühring* had for the generation preceding the world war'. Gramsci seemed to have some improbably grandiose project in mind: '. . . it would be worth the trouble for an entire group of men to devote ten years of activity to this endeavour [the Anti-Croce]'.[123] But this seemingly monomaniacal desire for a relentless destruction of Croce's *œuvre* did not mean that the mature Gramsci judged his erstwhile mentor's thought as valueless. Quite the contrary. Spirited though his polemic was, he accorded Croce's ideas a certain *limited* validity.

Gramsci's enduring goal was to raise Marxism to the highest level attained by contemporary philosophy, so that it could furnish a proper philosophical foundation for a 'superior' mass culture. If the philosophy of praxis, a doctrine vulgarized 'because of the necessities of immediate practical life', was going to produce a 'new moral and intellectual order', there was a need for refinement of ideological weapons, for subtler elaboration of concepts and arguments.[124] Such could only emerge out of a sustained dialogue with opposing world views. Given its intellectual sophistication and unique insights, the philosophy of spirit in general, and Crocean thought in particular, could provide the 'premise' for the 'renewal' of Marxism, for its deepening and enrichment.[125] Put simply, Gramsci believed that the intellectual poverty of orthodox Marxism could be combated through infusions of idealism. What exactly did the older Gramsci find attractive and useful in Croce's system? First, Croce had the merit of presenting definitive arguments against metaphysics (in the sense of an ahistorical objective reality); in his attack on all forms of transcendence, he perceived the essential connection between philosophy and history (i.e. philosophy arises out of specific practical problems; it resolves 'problems presented by the development of the historical process').[126] Philosophical reflection is not, to Croce's mind, concerned with a noumenal reality beyond the phenomenal world of ordinary fact and historical events. The critique of transcendence was also a critique of theology, and Croce deserves credit, says Gramsci, for undermining the claims of Catholicism, by demonstrating that modern man 'can live without "mythological religion"'.[127] In an era when Marxism tended to view itself as a quasi-religious dogma, comprising universal principles, unchallenged myths and eternal verities, the insights of historicism could offer a vaulable corrective, according to Gramsci. Closely related to Croce's denial of transcendence was his repudiation of all determinism. This, too, found favour with Gramsci. Because of the creative and autonomous role of man's self-consciousness, the unfolding of history could not, Croce affirmed, be encapsulated in closed and definitive systems.[128] His emphasis on the centrality of human consciousness was manifest, on a deeper level, in his conceptualization of mental activity as a creative, not a receptive or ordering process. Gramsci, as we have seen, always retained something of the idealist conviction that knowing is by no means a simple relation between the mind and an object independent of mind; it is an active process. Finally, Croce's focus on the active human subject led him to draw attention to 'the importance of facts of culture and thought in the development of history'. Herein lay the antidote to dreary economism. In Gramsci's opinion, the doctrine of 'ethico-political history'— which concentrates on the *vita morale* of mankind, the whole area of human aspirations, as expressed in art, religion, ethics and political principles—should be 'used as an "empirical canon" of historical research, always to be kept in mind in the examination of historical development, if one wishes to write integral history, and not partial or extrinsic history'.[129]

But the partial assimilation of certain aspects of Croce's thought into Gramsci's own world-view should not be confused with anything resembling wholesale adoption. His Marxism was in principle open and stressed the need to learn from one's ideological enemies:

In scientific discussion, as one supposes that the interest is the search for truth and the progress of science, he demonstrates himself more advanced who takes the point of view that his adversary can express an exigency that must be incorporated, even if as a subordinate moment, in his own construction. To understand and evaluate

realistically the positions and reasons of the adversary (and sometimes the adversary is all past thought) means precisely to be
liberated from the prison of ideologies (in the worst sense, of blind
ideological fanaticism). . . .[130]

Of course, when we learn from our enemies, they do not cease to
be our enemies. Gramsci's 'Anti-Croce' essentially involved
standing Croce on his proverbial feet, i.e. bringing his dialectic
down to earth: '. . . it is necessary to perform on Croce's philosophical conception the same reduction that the first theorists of
the philosophy of praxis [Marx and Engels] performed on the
Hegelian conception'.[131] To be sure, anyone who reads the
pages that the young Marx dedicated to the criticism of Hegel's
speculative philosophy will find frequent parallels in Gramsci's
critique of Italy's answer to Hegel.

'The opposition between croceanism and the philosophy of
praxis', Gramsci announces, 'is to be sought in the speculative
character of croceanism'.[132] Croce takes every opportunity to
assert that he has eliminated all traces of transcendence, any
scent of metaphysics, from his philosophy; but such claims are
ultimately hollow. Despite its pretensions to immanence, 'the
philosophy of Croce remains a "speculative" philosophy and in
this there is more than a trace of transcendence and theology; it
is all transcendence and theology'.[133] He is so tangled up in the
language of speculative philosophy that he cannot escape from
its inherent logic. His unification of philosophy and history is
illusory, and the transcendent element he tries to purge comes
creeping back in the form of rarefied abstractions. Adrift in a sea
of naked concepts, Croce creates a dialectic of the ideal, not of
the real. He concentrates on the speculative expression of the
movement of history, on the movement of 'mind' with itself. By
separating human thought from real 'flesh and blood' man, he
turns it into an independent, semi-mystical subject. For him, it
is not the *concrete* individual who thinks, but the 'spirit' which
thinks itself *through* man. But, Gramsci complains, if history is
merely the record of the human spirit, then material reality is
dissolved into philosophy and man disappears into a heaven of
ideal values and abstract categories.[134] If Bukharin's chief fault
was to enervate the historical struggle by downgrading conscious choice, Croce's was to lose man in the 'spirit' or the
'Idea'. By reducing man and his reality to thought, the

Neapolitan ignores man as a sensual, active physical being. The biological analogy used against the Bolshevik theorist is now directed, with a new twist, against Croce. Certainly, a body with its flesh torn off (*scuoiato*) would no longer resemble a true human being, but neither would a body ' "boned" and devoid of a skeleton' (if such can be imagined) approximate to a recognizable member of the human species. 'Croce's history', says Gramsci, 'presents "boned" figures, lacking skeletal structure and possessed of flaccid, feeble flesh.'[135] Not an appealing piece of imagery, perhaps, but the point is made. While Bukharin ignores the flesh (superstructure) of history, Croce ignores its bones, its skeleton (sub-structure).[136] History, the Sardinian insists, is not the outward manifestation of 'spirit'; on the contrary, 'spirit' is a metaphysician's metaphor for the intellectual form taken by *concrete social labour*. True, Croce introduces the notion of an active subject but it is an idealized subject. While he may deny that philosophy is a refuge from time and appearance, his conception of 'spirit' or 'mind' appears to be an 'up-dated version of the old concept of "human nature"', of 'man-in-general', a meta-historical, metaphysical essence, removed from objective conditions.[137] Gramsci wants to place man at the centre of the philosophy of praxis, but *real* man who inhabits actual history, not man as an abstract category, as an hypostatized 'spirit'. It is imperative to descend from the speculative to the factual, from the heights of the Croce-Hegelian 'Idea' to the world of practical activity. The trouble with Croce is that, in his infatuation with concepts, he forgets that they must be formulated in close connection with a determinate order of things:

If it is necessary, in the perennial flux of events, to establish concepts, without which reality could not be understood, it is necessary also . . . to establish and remember that reality in movement and the concept of reality, while they can be distinguished logically, must be conceived historically as an inseparable unity. Otherwise there will happen what has happened to Croce, for whom history becomes a formal history, a history of concepts and in the final analysis, a history of intellectuals.[138]

History is thus reduced, willy-nilly, to an arbitrary schema. To avoid this, ideas must be studied (and developed) in relation to the social patterns in which they are embedded. History, then, is no longer a history of concepts but of men who think and act on the basis of their physical needs, in the context of their concrete environment—the relative sophistication of their material instruments, their social organization and so on. Indeed, history 'is a continuous struggle of individuals and groups to change that which exists in any given moment'.[139] For Croce, in contrast, real contradictions and struggles are perceived only through the theories that reflect them. It is once again a history of man who walks on his head, not his feet. Croce's refusal to come to terms with real conflict is reflected in his historiography. His history of Italy, for example, begins in 1871, when the tumults of unification were over, and his history of Europe starts in 1815, with the ending of the Revolutionary and Napoleanic upheavals. This enables him 'to leave out of consideration the moment of struggle, the moment in which opposing forces develop, gather momentum, and confront each other'.[140] In Croce's account, significant conflicts seem to exist only in university seminars or in the pages of scholarly journals. In this respect, he represents a 'step backwards' from Hegel, whose thought is conditioned by the 'immediate and vital experiences of an historical period intense with struggle, with misery'. Hegel, at least, made some attempt to identify 'doing and thinking'; he saw the dialectic between 'the two moments of life and of thought, materialism and spiritualism', even though his final synthesis was partial and unsuccessful: 'man walking on his head'. Croce and his disciples, however, 'have destroyed this unity' and returned to purely spiritualist systems.[141]

So Croce cannot remain faithful to his programme of 'historicizing' ideas, of relating them to particular historical conditions, since he fails to understand that ideas emanate not from some ethereal universal man but from physical creatures engaging in practical struggles. Oblivious to the dynamic relationship between the process of thinking and the real material world, and intent on locating all reality in man's head, he is unable to perceive philosophy for what it is: the reflection and elaboration of the socio-historical processes through which men confront and control nature. It follows that he can only pay lip service to the task of linking philosophy to its specific historical setting. If the socio-political order is expressive of ideal orientations, then the main source of dynamism in society must be found in conflicts of ideas. The logic of the argument leads, notwithstanding Croce's disclaimers, to the notion that systems of thought emanate from other systems of thought, rather than from the aspirations of men living in society and following a definite praxis. In the last analysis, he loses sight of the historicist principle that 'ideas are not born of other ideas, philosophies of other philosophies; they are an ever renewed expression of real historical development'.[142] For conclusive proof of the inconsistency of Croce's immanentism, we need look no further, argues Gramsci, than his conception of history as the story of liberty. Whereas a rigorous immanentism would view liberty as 'nothing but a conceptual envelope, useful only for the real nucleus that each social group encloses within it', Croce speaks of this protean concept as if its meaning were both transparent and universally valid.[143] Only the philosophy of praxis, Gramsci claims, represents pure immanentism; it alone is 'purged of any speculative aroma and reduced to pure history or historicity'; it alone is 'liberated from every residue of transcendence and theology'.[144] And this is so because Marxism, unlike Croce's philosophy of spirit, established the historicity of philosophy with close examination of concrete historical conflicts, 'not with vague principles'.[145]

Like his polemic against Bukharin, Gramsci's dissection of Croce's thought focuses not only on its theoretical inadequacy but also on its practical bankruptcy. Gramsci considered Croce's thought to be an ideological weapon of the bourgeoisie and Croce himself the unwitting, but none the less effective mouthpiece of a corrupt, repressive capitalist order. In a letter of 6 June 1932, Gramsci goes so far as to call his adversary 'the most potent mechanism that the dominant group now possesses for "bending" new forces to serve its own vital interests, both immediate and future ones'.[146] In his role as guardian of the established set up and dispenser of conservative theology, Croce functions as 'a sort of lay Pope'.[147] Once we divest his philosophy of 'the brilliant grandeur' attributed to it as 'a serene and impartial system of thought, placing itself above all the miseries and contingencies of daily life', then we can 'reduce it to its real role as *immediate political ideology*'.[148] Croce may think that he is constructing a 'pure' philosophy or a 'pure' history, but in reality he is offering 'instruments of practical action' to the dominant class.[149] To be more specific, Gramsci links Croceanism to the moderate liberalism of the 'Risorgimento' and to the 'transformist' tradition of Italian politics. By transposing the concrete reality of social conflict to the misty level of ideas, and by exalting liberty in its bourgeois manifestation as the culmination of historical development, Croce's philosophy ends up expounding the 'truths' of the ruling class and conferring on them an absolute significance. On a more mundane plane, Croce's élitist approach to the philosophical enterprise itself is, in Gramsci's view, conservative in its implications. Croce takes a 'Renaissance view' of intellectual life, regarding it as the domain of detached intellectuals carrying out missions assigned to them by the Spirit. Hence his hypocritical belief that religion—though nothing more than a tissue of myth and fantasy—should be propagated amongst the masses to fulfil their spiritual needs, but that the cultivated minority should be above such things.[150]

To summarize this section, we can say (a) that the works of the youthful Gramsci were heavily impregnated with the language and thought of idealism, (b) that his writings from 1919 reveal a more orthodox Marxist position, and (c) that his prison critique of Croce was both fundamental and remindful of Marx's materialist de-mystification of Hegel. It is true that Gramsci attributes, in his *Quaderni*, an importance to Croce out of all proportion to his philosophy's worth. It is also undeniable that Gramsci retains a favourable attitude to certain ideas put forward by his former idol, adopts some of his preoccupations and terminology, and claims to have found in him a revivifying philosophy for the Marxist movement. But Gramsci's open-minded approach should not blind us to the basic hostility infusing all notebooks devoted to his famous predecessor.

IV. *Science and the Objectivity of the External World*

The foregoing arguments have, it is hoped, gone some way towards disproving the 'idealist' reading of Gramsci, but our case is not yet concluded. On the basis of two very brief (but widely cited) essays composed by Gramsci in prison ('Science and "Scientific" Ideologies' and 'The So-called "Reality of the External World"'), some commentators maintain that

Gramsci—his critique of Croce notwithstanding—espouses the idealist thesis according to which the reality of things is possible only through thought and therefore material itself is a fiction. To Salamini, for example, Gramsci denies 'the objective dimension of natural and social processes'; and Orfei concludes, after an examination of the above passages, that the Sardinian's attachment to historical materialism was 'not a matter of theory but of sentiment and passion'.[151] Just what does Gramsci say to prompt such interpretations?

In criticizing Bukharin's naïve realism—which conceives 'reality in itself' as prior to cognition—Gramsci asserts that reality exists and is intelligible only in relation with human activity: 'reality does not exist on its own, in and for itself, but only in historical relationship with the men who modify it, etc.'[152] The world is not given as an object of contemplation, a world we have not made, waiting to be known. If it is given, it is given as a world in part constructed out of our own doings and makings, our language, our tools, our instruments, our experiments. The world as we know it, in other words, is not cognitively innocent. What exists appears to human beings in a particular way and is by them classified, interpreted, categorized and described in a particular manner. Our faculties and capacities do partly determine the world as it appears. Indeed, for Gramsci, to talk of the world as it is 'in itself', of a nature or reality independent of man and outside of history, is to talk nonsense. For to speak intelligibly of an extra-historical or extra-human objectivity, one would have to develop an understandable concept of it, but this is impossible. To conceive of something means we must attribute to that something properties by which it can be differentiated from the rest of the world as an individual object. But it is beyond the realm of possibility to comprehend the properties of anything before one is able to describe these properties with existing names and concepts, in which case the object has *already been touched by human decision*: its perception has already been filtered through man's conceptual apparatus. Thus a reality unrelated to man, preceding human consciousness, is, strictly speaking, *inconceivable*. To suggest otherwise is to suggest the absurd: that one can perceive without the employment of any particular mode of perception and describe without the use of any particular descriptive vocabulary. This is 'nothing but a paradox'.[153] It is Gramsci's conviction, then, that nature, when abstracted from conscious human purposes, is meaningless and irrelevant. Prior to becoming operative under the stimulus of human action, nature is 'nothing' to man, for it is not part of his intelligible reality.[154] So 'when one affirms that a reality would exist even if man did not', Gramsci concludes, 'one is either speaking metaphorically or falling prey to a form of mysticism. We know reality only in relation to man ...'.[155] The sole observer capable of making pronouncements about an extra-human objectivity would be one who could judge the world from 'the standpoint of the cosmos itself'—viz., God.[156] It is therefore no accident, to Gramsci, that the origin of the belief in an objective reality, untouched by man, is religious. For all religions proclaim that 'the world, nature, the universe was created by God, before the creation of man, and therefore man found the world already made, catalogued and defined once and for all'.[157] (Once more Bukharin stands accused of crypto-theological 'mysticism'.)

It is legitimate to speak of an objective reality but only if it is understood that 'Objective always means "humanly objective", which corresponds exactly to ... "universal subjective"'. One must have 'recourse to history and to man in order to demonstrate objective reality'.[158] Gramsci seems here to be making two claims. First, that the world of phenomena, of objects, necessarily bears the imprint of the organizational power of generic (i.e. collective and historical) man; in the objective given there is always present the project of human action. The second claim is this: that 'one affirms as ... objective reality, that reality which is verified by all men, which is independent of every viewpoint that is merely particular or group oriented'.[159] Or again, 'Man knows objectively in so far as knowledge is real for the entire human race'.[160] Objectivity, it would seem, is identical (or closely associated) with intersubjective consensus. The sciences furnish the paradigm here: 'Up to now experimental science has provided the terrain on which such a cultural unity has attained its furthest extension. ... It is the most objectified and concretely universalized subjectivity.'[161] To put the point in a more prosaic fashion, scientific theories are objectively 'true' in so far as they are universally accepted as valid—and this universal acceptance will only be forthcoming if the theories in question are *effective*, if they satisfy human needs, if they enable us satisfactorily to control and adapt to our environment. There is no point in saying that a scientific theory could be objectively true regardless of its practical consequences and acceptance, because such a judgement presupposes the inhuman ability to observe reality from 'the standpoint of the cosmos itself'. In all cases, then, objectivity must be understood in relation to the human spirit: objectivity is always a humanized objectivity; 'subjective' and 'objective' are not antithetical. The external world, in brief, is accessible to man only in its humanized form. As Leszek Kolakowski puts the same idea in a discussion of human cognition, 'in all the universe man cannot find a well so deep that, leaning over it, he does not discover at the bottom his own face'.[162]

These epistemological propositions led Gramsci into a *certain* relativization of the natural sciences. As we saw earlier, even in this sphere, commonly associated with rigorous inductive procedures, he believed that the 'simple' observation of fact entailed an element of creativity, a projection into the world of our (or the scientist's) evaluations and preconceptions. When we probe the foundations of scientific activity, we uncover a whole nest of antecedent assumptions. All our observations are dependent upon prior hypotheses, which in turn rest upon a particular theoretical paradigm, serving to establish what are to count as facts, what are to count as problems worthy of investigation and what are to count as their solutions. Such presuppositions, furthermore, are inseparable from a practical persuasion, itself bound up with 'culture, a conception of the world'. So Gramsci not only recognizes the humanist, creative character of science ('All science is tied to needs, to life, to the activity of man'; it involves a 'relation between man and reality'), he also argues that the scientific enterprise is inextricably intertwined with ideological warfare: 'In reality even science is a superstructure'; this can be demonstrated 'by the fact that it has undergone whole periods of eclipse', when it was obscured by the ideology of 'religion, which claimed to absorb science itself'.[163] Witness the way 'the authority of Aristotle and the Bible' exercised a constricting effect on scientific progress. If, for example, we look at speculation on the origin of springs, writes Gramsci, we find that the scientific community produced 'a succession of the most arbitrary and bizarre theories, straining to reconcile the Bible and Aristotle with the experimental observations'. While such debilitating authority was finally expelled from the scientific field, was this not 'due to the general progress of modern society'? (as opposed to the inherent logic of scientific inquiry itself).[164] If 'all scientific hypotheses and opinions are superstructures', indissolubly linked with practical exigencies, then we must accept that scientific propositions, even in their present, advanced state, are not at all definitive and peremptory. Gramsci considers modern atomic theory and asks, rhetorically, if it is 'established once and for all'. The answer, for him, is obvious: 'What scientist would dare make such an assertion? Might it not rather be simply a scientific hypothesis which may be superseded, that is, absorbed into a broader and more comprehensive theory?'[165] It is therefore impossible to escape the conclusion, Gramsci declares, that 'even science is a historical development, a movement in continuous development'. If it were not, 'science would cease to exist as such—as research, as new experiments—and scientific activity would be reduced to public dissemination of what has already been discovered'.[166]

These remarks on nature, reality, and science can be misleading if read hastily. Gramsci, it is true, did not regard reality (or nature) as a mere objective datum, external to man; but neither did he assume that the object of human consciousness was itself illusory or created by some hypostatized 'spirit'. Since it is common in the history of political theory for a writer to slant his position so as to sharpen its contrasts with that of his adversary, it is risky to fasten on isolated aphorisms or statements. Some attempt must be made to peel off the layers of polemical exaggeration and discover the fundamental line of thought. Let us remember that Gramsci, in the passages cited above, was attacking Bukharin (and dialectical materialism in general) for accepting the 'objective reality of the external world' in its *most trivial and uncritical form*.[167] Criticism of one extreme does not entail acceptance of the opposite extreme. To combat the positivist notion that the prevailing social and scientific order is based on a natural determinism, independent of any human contribution, is not tantamount to upholding the idealist doctrine that the natural and social worlds are *simply* constructions of mind. As for the more drastic forms of subjective idealism, like Berkeley's, which hold that the individual human mind knows only its own ideas as distinct from extramentally existing things, Gramsci dismisses them as 'bizarre' and 'fantastic'.[168] But elsewhere he makes it clear that *no* idealism is immune from the sin of solipsism. In discussing the nature of philosophical activity, Gramsci asks: 'What does "creative" mean? Should it mean that the external world is created by thought? But what thought and whose? One can fall into solipsism, and in fact *every form of idealism necessarily does fall into solipsism.*'[169] Presumably because, in the final analysis, no idealism can consistently admit of objective necessity.

Gramsci's terminology, in his consideration of the external world, is obviously influenced by idealism, but close inspection indicates that, in fact, he is denying not the *existence* of a nature prior to the human spirit, only the *relevance* or *intelligibility* of such a natural order: 'We *know* reality only in relation to man.'[170] It is one thing to hold that nature is *significant* solely in terms of human activity; it is quite another to assert, with Croce, that nature is a *creation* of human activity.[171] For the Sardinian, the crucial point is not that 'nature in itself' exists or does not exist, but simply that there is no sense in speaking of it, for an 'objective' reality unrelated to man is 'unthinkable', in the sense that it provides us with no object of reflection. This, according to him, is merely a tautology: a statement necessarily true by virtue of the structure of language itself. Thus, the question whether there exists some reality of nature even when men have not yet interacted with it is—strictly speaking—a false question. Nevertheless (and here he appears to contradict himself), it is a question Gramsci does not *entirely* avoid. When he does broach it, the answer he gives is far from idealist. It *is* possible, he declares, to think of 'something real' beyond our present consciousness, 'something still unknown, which will however be known one day when the "physical" and intellectual instruments of mankind are more perfect. . . . We are then making an historical prediction which consists simply in an act of thought that projects into the future a process of development similar to that which has taken place from the past to the present.' That part of nature which still escapes human know-

ledge, which is not yet mastered by man, is neither the unknowable Kantian 'noumenon' nor a realm about which we can
make definitive statements; it is simply a limiting concept—
what is momentarily unknown.[172] In another passage he refers
to it as 'an empirical "non-knowledge", which does not exclude
its knowability'.[173] Elsewhere, Gramsci is more emphatic in
affirming the reality of abstract natural forces and laws before
man turns his attention to them: 'As an abstract natural force,
electricity existed even before its reduction to a productive
force, but it was not historically operative and was just a subject
of hypothetical discourse in natural history. (Earlier still it was
historical "nothingness", because no one took any interest in it
or even was aware of it).'[174] Gramsci's position can perhaps be
clarified by an historical example.[175] A valid insight of idealism,
in his account, was the belief that we cannot attest to the
existence of what we do not know. To say otherwise is to lapse
either into theology or crude materialist metaphysics—itself a
variation of theology. A European living in the year 1000 not
only did not know America; for him the continent *did not exist* in
any meaningful sense. It was 'historical nothingness'. It would
therefore have been absurd for him to believe in what he did not
positively know, or, as the geographers at that time did, to
explain hypothetically or fancifully the world beyond Hercules'
pillars. The error of idealism, on the other hand, consists in
claiming that the reality 'thought' is the *whole* of reality. In
terms of the example, the fact that America existed in the year
1000, even if nobody knew anything about it, exposes the fallacy
of those who ruled out the existence of a world beyond the straits
of Gibralter. Hence the claim that there always exists something ('empirical "non-knowledge"') that we do not yet perceive. It is, in other words, legitimate to assert the existence of
an external world divorced from the human subject if—and
only if—in so doing one is simply leaving open the possibility of
new experience.

Man, it can be seen, does not construct or organize his world
out of literal nothingness but out of pre-existing materials.
Gramsci never pretends that we can escape from the determination of nature and its laws. This emerges clearly enough in his
elaboration of pedagogical principles, where he acknowledges
'the primal and fundamental fact that there exist objective,

intractable laws to which man must adapt himself if he is to master them in his turn . . . work cannot be realized in all its power of expansion and productivity without an exact and realistic knowledge of natural laws'.[176] There is, then, a material substratum, an external world of law-governed phenomena, whose existence does not depend on mind. Human freedom *vis-à-vis* the natural world is not the *negation* of necessity; it is the manipulation of necessity for human purposes. Nature, in sum, is not entirely amenable to human control; and man himself, with his flesh, blood, and brain tissue, is *part* of nature. So Gramsci rejects not only the materialistic monism that annuls the creative subjectivity of man; but also the spiritual monism that postulates the primacy of Spirit, making the real a mere fabrication of human thought:

> For the philosophy of praxis, being cannot be disjoined from thinking, man from nature, activity from material, subject from object; if one makes this detachment, one falls into one of the many forms of religion or nonsensical abstraction.[177]

There is a dialectic between man and reality which is a dialectic precisely to the extent that each term is defined and shaped in relation to the other. The ontology of the philosophy of praxis, says Gramsci, is neither materialist nor idealist; it is based on the 'identity of opposites in the concrete historical act; namely, concrete human activity connected indissolubly to a certain organized (historicized) matter, to nature transformed by man'.[178] Thus when Gramsci claims that 'reality does not exist on its own, in and for itself, but only in historical relationship with the men who modify it', he is by no means endorsing the ontological primacy of spirit over matter—he does not wish to reduce the latter to the former. In his view, the world of phenomena is subjective or mind-independent only in the sense that it embodies spiritual principles in such a way that the human mind can both encapsulate and find itself reflected in this world. Exactly what this means can be illustrated by Gramsci's comment on a famous example produced by Bertrand Russell in his defence of 'realism':

> What would North–South or East–West mean without man? They are real relationships, and yet they would not exist without man and without the development of civilization. East and West, it is evident,

are arbitrary and conventional, i.e. historical constructions, since outside of real history every point on the earth is East and West at the same time. . . . Nevertheless these references are real, they correspond to real facts, they allow one to travel by land and by sea, to arrive where one has decided to arrive, . . . to understand the objectivity of the external world.[179]

The 'objectivity of the external world', while it reflects (to some extent) conscious human purposes, nevertheless conditions men, imposing a concrete terrain of action to which they must adapt. The practical implications of this position exclude any possibility of 'voluntarism': 'the politician in action is a creator . . . but he neither creates out of nothing nor does he move in the emptiness of his dreams and wishes. His action is grounded in factual reality . . .'.[180] The will, for Gramsci, is not a spiritual-mythical principle; it is an aspiration constrained by (and arising from) a practical situation.

By now the reader may have noticed that Gramsci's views on these epistemological and ontological questions are remindful not of Croce but of the 'early' Marx, who also claimed, in the context of a critique of idealism, that the world we know is one we have in large part constructed. Gramsci composed his philosophical notes at the very time that the *Economic and Philosophical Manuscripts* were published (in German) in 1933, but he gave no sign of having read, or even heard of this work. It seems that Gramsci arrived independently at positions which Marx had worked out nearly a century before, though in some measure the Italian extrapolated these ideas from the *Theses on Feuerbach*.

Of course, there are some, like Louis Althusser, who *do* regard Marx's youthful philosophical 'problematic' as idealist in both tone and content; but idealism here is understood in an almost all-encompassing sense. Not surprisingly, Althusser is one of the sharpest critics of Gramsci's conception of science, which he views as pre-Marxist, Hegelian, and anti-scientific. If we wish fully to dispel the 'idealist' interpretation of Gramsci, it is worth answering this charge. For (let it be admitted) his remarks on science seem to express something of the *fin de siècle* pathos about the limitations of science—and this revolt against science was very much associated with idealist modes of thought. Gramsci, it will be recalled, declared scientific categories and theories to be superstructural and historically conditioned. For Althusser, however, we must distinguish between 'the relatively autonomous and peculiar history of scientific knowledge and the other modalities of historical existence (those of the ideological and politico-legal superstructures, and that of the economic structure)'. Science, he argues, must be viewed as an 'autonomous practice', independent of the vicissitudes of social structure and history. Althusser is concerned to discover an unimpeachable scientific knowledge lying beyond the flux of history, and this can hardly be achieved if the concepts of science are themselves historical and ideological, reflecting a particular set of circumstances and not eternally applicable. Gramsci, on this view, mistakenly dissolves science into historical praxis.[181] Though accurately reporting Gramsci's actual words, the founder of structuralist Marxism conveys the erroneous impression that the Sardinian was somehow agnostic or hostile towards the categories and procedures of science. Althusser tells us that he will only consider Gramsci's '*words* when I have confirmed that they have the function of "*organic*" *concepts*, concepts which really belong to his most profound philosophical problematic',[182] but does he (Althusser) consistently adhere to this commendable stricture? Does he not single out isolated phrases without regard for the 'profound philosophical problematic'? Certainly, Gramsci believed that any form of scientific analysis involves selection from an infinitely divisible profusion of data, and that such selection must be based on theoretical assumptions which are not themselves derivable from the observations to be explained. It is also true that, for him, scientific research was not ideologically pure, in as much as it could be (and had been) retarded or accelerated in diverse ways through the operation of superstructural elements. But *nowhere* does he say that the truth or falsehood of a scientific hypothesis will be determined by values or ideology. However provisional their status at any given time, and however much they may be connected with different definitions of reality, scientific theories, in Gramsci's conception, ultimately stand or fall by being publicly tested against potentially disconfirming evidence. The claim that certain kinds of social conditions were necessary for certain kinds of theoretical development does not imply relativism. Specific social conditions were of course propitious for the development of modern physical science, but the content of that science does not depend for its validity on any kind of social context. Questions of historical cause are not to be confused with questions of logical ground or empirical soundness. In so far as they are scientific, the laws of Newtonian physics, for example, do not depend for their scientificity on the historical destiny of capitalism. The scope, direction and procedures of scientific activity will at any given time be affected by the social or ideological setting, but the *validity* of the resultant theories will, in the final reckoning, depend upon their degree of correspondence with external forces. That this is Gramsci's viewpoint would seem to be confirmed by the following passage:

Science is, concretely, the union of objective fact with an hypothesis or system of hypotheses which transcend the mere objective fact. It is true, however, that in this area it is relatively easy to distinguish the objective component from the system of hypotheses, through a process of abstraction inherent in scientific methodology itself, such that it is possible to appropriate the one and reject the other. Here is the reason why a *social group may appropriate the science of another group without accepting its ideology*.[183]

Gramsci, of course, links the objectivity of science with universal acceptance of its findings (as distinct from congruence with 'external' reality), but this acceptance in turn depends upon whether or not the findings (or theories) *work* in practice. Gramsci's concept of science, as a matter of historical fact, is not all that different from that of Weber, who—as is well known—resolutely upheld the cognitive supremacy of the scientific method. Weber, too, thought that descriptions of natural phenomena had to be filtered through *a priori* assumptions, but he also recognized that when these assumptions blatantly conflict with the data of the external world, they must be discarded. While scientists do not, to his mind, discover an external reality, totally independent of the human mind, neither do they 'produce' scientific theories in the same way that ideologists produce theories of man and society. There is no reason to believe that Gramsci disagreed with this characterization of the scientific enterprise. If there is a difference, it is purely verbal. Indeed, his depiction of natural science is quite laudatory:

There can be no doubt that the rise of the experimental method separates two historical worlds, two epochs, and initiates the process of dissolution of theology and metaphysics, and the process of development of modern thought, whose consummation is the philosophy of praxis.

Science is emancipatory because it frees man from the fetters of old-fashioned metaphysics, thereby initiating 'a new form of active union between man and nature', a practical, non-fetishistic relationship, of which Marxism is the culmination.[184]

Compare this view with that of Croce, who deprecates the claims of natural science, by describing its laws as mere 'practical creation', 'arbitrary constructions', which 'do not furnish real knowledge'. The natural sciences 'are nothing but edifices of pseudo-concepts', of theoretical fictions constructed for essentially practical purposes. The law and order we 'discover' in nature is in some sense 'put there' by the theorizing mind.[185] Gramsci explicitly criticizes Croce (along with Gentile) for his scepticism towards the objective value of scientific knowledge and for undermining the cultural prestige of the scientific community in Italy.[186] So when Gramsci says that science is ideological, he does not use ideological in the derogatory Marxian sense of 'mystification' or 'illusion'; still less does he intend to question the solidity of the main conclusions of the physical sciences. Rather, he simply wants to place us on guard against inflated claims that science describes an absolute truth 'in itself'. Gramsci did not, like Lukàcs in *History and Class Consciousness*,[187] dismiss scientific knowledge as an ideological weapon of the bourgeoisie, as a particular form or expression of its world-vision. No, for Gramsci, natural science is a mechanism of liberation, indispensable for the realization of a better society. Althusser, of course, might still complain that a certain relativization of science remains. But if he believes that scientific truth depends purely on 'the way things are', if he really thinks that science arrives at 'Absolute Knowledge' determined from the point of view of a 'privileged present', then he is expressing an out-dated, pre-Kantian ideal that is generally rejected by both practitioners and philosphers of science.[188]

In sum, Gramsci by no means casts doubt on the reality of the natural sciences. Neither does he say that the human spirit creates the world *ex nihilo* or that 'to be' is the same thing as 'to be thought of' or that physical objects are only disguised forms of mind. He denies, too, that men are free to mould their world in accordance with their abstract wishes. If Gramsci is an idealist, it is only in the attenuated sense that, since Kant, 'we are all idealists'. But was Gramsci a bona-fide Marxist? Those who believe he betrayed the legacy of Marx and Engels will need further convincing. In the next section, I shall attempt to explain *how* Gramsci fits into the Marxist tradition.

V. *The Gramscian Synthesis*

Gramsci certainly characterized himself as a Marxist and his thought as 'materialism perfected by the work of idealist philosophy'.[189] Those who question the validity of this claim do so, perhaps, because they hold a rigid view of the nature of Marxism and its core doctrine, historical materialism. If this doctrine must necessarily rest upon *philosophical* materialism, then even Marx himself did not adhere to it, for he surely did not believe that social facts are reducible to physical facts. There is an unfortunate tendency to identify historical materialism with the more extreme, and often polemical or tentative, formulations it receives in certain writings of Marx and Engels. For our purposes, it is not necessary to enter into futile debate about 'what Marx *really* meant'. It is obvious enough that his historical writings were much less schematic and suggested a much broader (though undefined) conception than did his more systematic presentations of his theoretical position. The crucial task for us, at any rate, is not to divine Marx's obscure and probably vacillating intention, but to assess whether historical materialism loses its uniqueness and explanatory power if presented in a non-schematic form. Put another way, can the Marxist insistence on the primacy of economic factors accommodate a creative, non-epiphenomenal role for ideas and consciousness? I think so, and, what is more, I believe that in Gramsci's *Quaderni*, we can perceive the outline of a plausible and interesting synthesis.

For Gramsci, as for Marx before him, those who conceive of an abstract, timeless human nature are victims of delusion:

If we reflect on it, we can see that in putting the question 'what is man?' what we mean is: what can man become? . . . Man is a process and more precisely the process of his actions.

'Man', moreover, is to be conceived not as an individual limited to his own individuality but in a collective sense, 'as a series of active relationships' with other men and the natural world.[190] Man, understood as generic man, creates himself (and his institutions) throughout history, and he does so not 'out of nothing' or 'in the emptiness of his dreams and wishes' but in confrontation with the exigencies of nature 'by means of work and technique'.[191]

In this confrontation, man subdues, organizes and classifies the raw materials of nature in order to satisfy his material needs, so that the world of phenomena confronting us in everyday perception consists essentially in 'qualities that man has distinguished because of his practical interests (the construction of his economic life) . . .'.[192] Herein lies the metaphysical basis of historical materialism. Gramsci inherits from Marx the belief that material needs are primary in human evolution, not because men must eat to live but because the labour process directed to the satisfaction of these needs constitutes the substratum, indeed, the engine of history. The auto-genesis of man implies that, in satisfying his biological needs through his contact with nature, man also develops new material wants as well as the possibilities for their fulfilment. Human needs are thus historical, not naturalistic, and the never-ending dialectical pursuit of their creation and satisfaction underlies historical development.

Cognition, which is a factor in the assimilation of the natural world, cannot evade this determinism. Thought emerges as a function of practical behaviour, of how men produce. The world is differentiated not according to some natural classification but to the classification imposed by the practical need for orientation and mastery in one's environment. This quest for control of the environment involves more than the imposition of a linguistic structure on primal data; it also entails the development of scientific knowledge and technical mechanisms—in a word, technology—to harness and humanize the abstract forces of the natural world. While this technology, along with its structural embodiments, is ultimately a human creation, the purposeful outcome of man's as yet incomplete conquest of nature, it nevertheless possesses its own imperative and in specific historical situations becomes an 'external force which

crushes man, assimilates him to itself and renders him passive
. . .'.[193] In any event, it severely circumscribes human action.
When Gramsci cautions that political activity 'is grounded in
factual reality', the reality of which he speaks is ultimately
economic in origin. In his critique of Bukharin, for example, he
paraphrases two well-known propositions contained in Marx's
Preface to a Contribution to the Critique of Political Economy and
recommends that they be placed at the foundation of Marxist
analysis:

1. Mankind only poses for itself those tasks that it can resolve; . . . the
task itself only arises when the material conditions for its resolution
already exist or at least are in the process of formation. 2. A social
formation does not perish until all the productive forces it can accommodate have been developed; new and higher relations of production
do not take its place until the material conditons of these new relations
have grown up within the womb of the old society.[194]

This is no isolated quotation. In fact, Gramsci describes the
Preface, which contains the classic, summary statement of historical materialism, as 'the most important and authentic
source for a reconstruction of the philosophy of praxis'.[195] The
basic ideas of the *Preface*—in particular, the explanatory
priority of the productive forces—find an echo in many sections
of the *Quaderni*, but a few examples should suffice. In his explanation of 'Regularity and Necessity', he argues that the
'realization of the impulse of the collective will' presupposes
'the necessary and sufficient material conditions'.[196] When
discussing political parties, he writes:

On the basis of the level of development of the material forces of
production, there arise the various social groupings, each representing a function and occupying a specific position within production
itself. . . . By studying these fundamental data [material forces of
production], it is possible to assess whether, within a particular
society, there exist the necessary and sufficient conditions for its
transformation—that is, to check the degree of realism and practic-
ability of the different ideologies which have been born on its own
terrain. . . .[197]

He also claims that the dominant complex of bourgeois cultural
and political institutions 'corresponds to the requirements of
the development of the productive forces'.[198] The obvious im-

plication here is that the material base not only sets limits to historical change but also shapes the contours of the superstructure. This list of quotations could be lengthened still further.[199] Close inspection of the *Quaderni* thus indicates that Gramsci completely rejected the Crocean notion that values and beliefs constitute the primary determinants of social life. Neither can his theory be reduced to a facile interactionism, asserting merely that the economic realm must be given its due. Rather, priority is given to the productive forces (tools, machines, human skills, etc.), which operate with a certain 'automatism', i.e. a 'relative independence from individual choices and from arbitrary government intervention'.[200]

A qualification must be entered here. Gramsci, it would appear, believes only that *the basic trajectory of human history* is explained by the development of productive forces. *The specific course of any given society*, however, may vary in accordance with the dynamics of its own individual situation. There are, in other words, exceptions to the rule: backward countries may find themselves in a position to 'borrow' ideas and institutions from more technologically advanced zones. As he fully realized, both the Italian Risorgimento and the Russian Revolution did not so much liberate 'already developed economic forces from antiquated legal and political fetters' as 'create the general conditions that would allow these forces to arise and evolve on the model of other countries'.[201] Exogenous factors, such as 'the relation of international forces', can influence the sequence of events in a country, producing progressive change even where the internal material conditions for such change are 'scanty and inadequate'.[202] In these cases, the 'normal' base/superstructure relationship is inverted. But even under 'normal' conditions, according to Gramsci, superstructural forms do not passively reflect alterations occurring in the economic infrastructure. Remember, he represented the relationship between the two spheres as 'necessarily interactive and reciprocal'. While changes in the productive process may be of primary importance, the superstructure is by no means devoid of independent influence: 'At certain moments the automatic thrust due to the economic factor is slowed down, obstructed, or even momentarily broken down by traditional ideological elements.'[203] Though they are initially rationalizations of socio-economic pressures, organized illusions themselves become part of the objective social situation, part of the external world which precedes and conditions the behaviour of individuals. Ideologies come to be detached from the environment whence they took their birth and hold themselves above men as imperative rules and models: 'Ideologies are anything but arbitrary, they are real historical facts that must be combated and unmasked as instruments of domination.'[204] The conditions of the capitalist system, reasons Gramsci, unleash liberating forces; technology sets the premises for a new, freer system of social relationships, 'but it is not necessarily the case that these tendencies must be realized'.[205] As seen earlier, socialism for Gramsci (and here he deviates from Marx) was not the inevitable outcome of a natural order written into history. Economic facts in themselves are by no means *decisive*. They 'only create a terrain more favourable to the diffusion of certain modes of thought, and certain ways of posing and resolving questions concerning the entire subsequent development of national life'.[206] It follows that purposive ideological and political initiative 'is always necessary to liberate the economic thrust from the shackles of traditional policies'.[207] The changing forces of production generate new ideas which may or may not become the ruling ideas. If they do, then they will establish the emerging forces of production and the class or classes associated with them. Although men are rooted in an economic reality that circumscribes their free initiative, this objective world of fact is not to be passively registered; human intervention is decisive. Gramsci underlines this point with an implicit analogy to Machiavelli's opposition between *fortuna* (roughly—the natural force of circumstance) and *virtù*—the ability of the individual to act upon and mould the given world of circumstance. Instead of *fortuna*, Gramsci talks about 'chance', loosely defined as the concatentation of objective forces. If we 'intervene actively' in the operation of chance, we can 'render it, from our point of view, less "chance" or "nature" and more the effect of our activity and will'.[208] In his exploration of the relationship between the economic and superstructural spheres, Gramsci obviously wishes to make a distinction between 'underlying' and 'immediate' causes. A frequent error in historical analysis, he informs us, is not to grasp the correct relationship between the two types of cause. Thus one attempts:

to expound as immediately operative causes that are instead operative
indirectly, or else to affirm that the immediate causes are the only
efficient causes; in one case we have the mistake of economism or of
pedantic doctrinairism; in the other, the mistake of 'ideologism'; in
one case mechanical causes are overvalued; in the other, the voluntarist and individualist element is exalted.[209]

At this point, it is worth pausing to consider what Gramsci
actually means when he refers to 'automatism' or to 'the automatic thrust due to the economic factor'. Is this appropriate
phraseology for an implacable foe of mechanistic Marxism? Is
he suggesting that, in general, machines run men rather than
vice versa? Certainly he inveighs against Bukharin for imagin-
ing economic forces as an antecedent sphere, an isolated factor,
prior to any human mediation and divorced from social relations. Economic techniques, Gramsci insists, have human relations built into them; they do not exist in a void; they incorporate '"mental" instruments, philosophical knowledge'.[210]
While Gramsci grants that the material techniques of production are 'an active, propulsive force', he also declares that the
'concept of activity applied to these forces must not be confused
or even compared with activity in the physical or metaphysical
sense', for these forces become historically active only when
'dominated by man'.[211] But if productive forces represent the
organization of human will and consciousness, if it is impossible
to separate the physical reality of material instruments from the
human element, then how can Gramsci speak of the 'economic
factor' providing an 'automatic thrust' to historical development? This hypothetical objection, which has in fact been
raised against Marx by H. B. Acton and John Plamenatz,[212]
rests upon what I deem to be a *non-sequitur*: namely, because the
invention, introduction, and continued operation of the various
forces of production require thought, laws, and moral values
(all of which are superstructural by definition), it therefore
follows that these forces cannot in any sense determine the
superstructure. Because base and superstructure are not
separate processes, no causal relationship can be postulated.
The criticism can be represented symbolically as follows: A
cannot determine B because A and B are not conceptually

distinct, and an effect cannot be included in its cause. Implicit in this criticism is the fallacious assumption that structures created and perpetuated by a multitude of conscious, individual acts cannot develop some sort of internal logic, or institutional imperative, over and above these acts. The empiricism so ingrained in our Anglo-Saxon culture has always been inclined to understand social events as resulting from a totality of individual actions, but Marxism (along with other forms of 'holism') sees no problem in endowing collective agents with an unconscious purposefulness distinct from their individual members.[213] Marxism is surely right on this point. We simply cannot explain all that happens in society or history wholly in terms of facts about human individuals—their dispositions, beliefs, decisions, etc. Collective acts and phenomena do occur and cannot be analysed away into atomic constituents. In Gramsci's words, '. . . every social aggregate is something more (and different) from the sum of its components'.[214] Social interaction may have patterned consequences that none of the participants intended or foresaw. The independent conscious decisions of the various individuals in the system may produce a configuration of forces which confront each man compulsively. So productive forces which have intentionality built into them *can* be determining, in so far as they entail consequences and requirements that elude our control. In this case, *all* men's choices mould, and *each* man's choice is moulded by, the economic system. The basic point, for Gramsci, is that man allows himself to be enslaved by machines and processes which he himself has made, but which apear to him as natural forces, directing the way he organizes his social and political life.

But, as we have seen, human agents are not, according to Gramsci, merely the bearers of ineluctable forces; though men operate within structurally determined limits, they perform a creative and potentially autonomous role. Men in history, as he conceived it, are striving to realize their full potentialities,[215] and this effort is a struggle to escape from being the plaything of forces that seem at once mysterious and irresistible; that is, to attain mastery over these forces, to subjugate them, to make 'the passage from "objective to subjective", from "necessity to liberty"'. This transcendence of necessity is the moment of 'catharsis'.[216] The economic process comprises the realm of necessity: 'objective and independent of the will of men'.[217] It can, however, be transformed and incorporated into the realm of freedom by political action. This seems to have been Marx's viewpoint. He, too, envisaged a unique historical occurrence which would enable mankind to comprehend history as its own creative act. While the mature Marx more and more stressed historical necessity and processes operating independently of human volition, he never abandoned his youthful vision of a breakthrough in which man at last becomes sovereign over his circumstances.

Let me now briefly summarize Gramsci's position. Like all Marxists he regarded the economic struggle of man with nature as the moving force of history. The productive techniques, moreover, constitute the backbone of any given society. These material forces of production more or less follow their own inner logic of development and determine which sorts of class relations and superstructural elements can take hold in society. In certain historical periods, the components of the superstructure may be mutually contradictory (i.e. some operate to preserve the existing relations of production; others may be subversive). These discrepancies reflect the contradictory interests of economic classes. And finally, the superstructure can crucially react upon the base, mainly by accelerating or impeding the social changes implicit in technological advance. For example, relations of production which have become regressive (e.g. those of the capitalist system) can continue indefinitely because of the growth and persistence of supportive structures and, especially, ideologies. It is precisely at such a historical conjuncture that hegemony becomes decisive, either in maintaining or destroying the existing order, depending on which class ideology prevails.

Thus Gramsci does not deny the objectivity of material conditions; he gainsays only that the objective conditions for social transformations can be historically operative until subjectively perceived, and that such perception is not contingent:

. . . the existence of objective conditions . . . is not yet sufficient: it is necessary to 'know' them and know how to use them. And to want to use them.[218]

Effective human action is the consequence neither of pure will nor of inexorable forces, but of a particular kind of interaction between objective circumstances and the creative spirit of man.

To bring the nature of Gramsci's Marxism into sharper focus, it might be useful to outline four models of the relationship between the material base (forces of production) and consciousness. (It is to be kept in mind that theoretical models represent deliberate simplifications of reality, which help us to bring some important aspect or aspects of that reality into greater relief. There need be no claim that these models grasp all the complexities of the relationships they formalize.) Two can be considered non-Marxist; (a) *consciousness determines base* (the idealist view); and (b) *consciousness and base interact on a more or less equal basis* (the common-sense view). As I hope I have shown, Gramsci accepts neither of these models.

The two remaining models can be considered Marxian: (a) *base determines the form of consciousness* (classical, 'scientific' Marxism); and (b) *base determines what forms of consciousness are possible*. Gramsci fits into this latter category, which we might call 'open' Marxism. The economic base sets, in a strict manner, the range of possible outcomes, but free political and ideological activity is ultimately decisive in determining which alternative prevails. There is no automatic determination: only the creation of a more or less favourable atmosphere for the diffusion of a new ethos. The will, then, moves history but only in so far as it conforms to the needs constituted by extant economic conditions. This position may lack the precision of an empirically testable hypothesis, but it does manage to steer a middle course between the Scylla of absurdity ('production determines *everything*') and the Charybdis of banality ('everything influences everything else').

Gramsci definitely went further than Marx in seeing the impossibility of any precise correlation between economic circumstances and intellectual or political developments. For Marx, it will be recalled, capitalism, through its own internal contradictions, nurtures within itself the forces that impel it towards its inevitable downfall. The destiny of human history, so runs the argument, cannot be altered by the mere intervention of individuals governed by this or that ideal. If, as Gramsci believed, socialism was not inscribed in the logic of history, then it must be based on an ideal goal, on a vision of what 'ought-to-be'. The open and indefinite perspective of the 'ought-to-be' replaces the closed chain of determinism. As long as the relationship between man and reality is not a passive, scientific one, the dimension of 'ought-to-be' is intrinsic to politics. Existing economic discontent must be poured into a mould set by some hierarchy of values or else 'a new balance of forces' will not emerge.[219] Hence the need for a *neue Weltanschauung* to form the basis of a truly collective 'intellectual-moral' order. But Gramsci's call for an ethical infusion into Marxism was more than just instrumental; he was genuinely worried about the movement's philistine indifference to cultural problems. Scientific Marxism displayed little interest in intellectual or moral renewal; its energies were focused on the task of making a revolution in the name of particular class interests, a revolution whose prime purpose was the institution of more rational (non-contradictory) relations of production. Tolstoy's famous question, 'What shall we do and how shall we live?' was dismissed as a symptom of pre-scientific, utopian day-dreaming. The Sardinian, on the other hand, never deviated from his youthful tendency to portray Marxism as, essentially, a doctrine of regeneration and redemption, more concerned with the full development of all human faculties than with economic contradictions. If it is to succeed in its vast work of liberation, the philosophy of praxis 'must reach for the solution to more complex tasks than those proposed by the present development of the struggle; namely, for the creation of a new, integral culture, having the mass character of the Protestant Reformation and the French Enlightenment as well as the classical character of the cultures of ancient Greece and the Italian Renaissance'.[220] For Gramsci, then, Marxism was not simply an interpretative instrument, a tool of political action; it was also a general conception of the world. This being the case, neither political economy nor sociology could provide an adequate theoretical basis. His stress on the *qualitative* side of revolution caused him to revive Marx's young Hegelian pronouncement that the 'realization' of philosophy was the real aim of the proletariat. Marx himself later became more radical: philosophy could not be realized but only extirpated, for what it contained was not latent potential but distorted economics. The analyst who thinks his patient's fantastic dreams can come true has contracted his patient's neurosis. The real cure is to rearrange life so that the *need* for fantasy disappears. Philosophy is thus abandoned or superseded as part of the scientific project. Gramsci, however, refused to believe that Marx 'really' wished to *replace* philosophy with practical activity. Rather, Marx was only advancing a claim, 'in the face of "scholastic" philosophy, purely theoretical or contemplative, for a philosophy that produces an attendant morality'. Therefore, the '11th thesis [on Feuerbach]: "Philosophers have only interpreted the world in various ways; it is a matter now of changing it" cannot be interpreted as a repudiation of every sort of philosophy, but only as a statement of disgust for ivory-towered philosophers, and as an energetic affirmation of the unity of theory and practice.'[221] Philosophy was to 'culminate' in the sense of winning a mass backing and becoming a popular faith. Whatever the merits of this interpretation of Marx, Gramsci himself rejects not philosophy but the contemplative attitude. Politics will always possess a philosophical dimension, but philosophy should not take refuge in 'abstract universality outside of time and space', in some city of the mind. Such a withdrawal is based on a fundamental misunderstanding of the philosophical enterprise. Even in its most intellectualist forms (and regardless of whether its practitioners are aware of the fact), philosophy is both a reflection on the practical acts of men and itself a practical act (though not practical in the immediate sense).

Thus Gramsci points out the folly of Croce's rigid distinction between philosophy and ideology: the first, theoretical-speculative; the second, practical-instrumental. If there is a distinction it is only one of degree. Philosophy may operate on a higher level of abstraction, but ultimately it, like ideology, provides man with a theoretical grasp of his own functions and tasks. Philosophy must now come down to earth and *explicitly* accept its practical function; it must cease to be, as it was for Croce, a sterile juggling of abstract concepts; it must emerge from the shelter of learned journals and seminar rooms and actively 'lead the masses to concrete action, to the transformation of reality'.[222] The *true* philosopher is a 'politician', an active man who reflects upon and modifies his environment, and encourages others to do likewise:

For a mass of men to be led to think coherently . . . about the real present, is a 'philosophical' event, much more important and 'original' than the discovery by some philosophical 'genius' of a new truth which remains the property of small groups of intellectuals.[223]

From this standpoint, the realization of hegemony would represent 'a great philosophical advance as well as a politico-practical one'.[224] Whereas for Croce, philosophy is the Spirit's self-consciousness of itself as thought, Gramsci redefines philosophy as man's conception of himself and society. It is his intention to synthesize Robespierre and Kant, politics and philosophy in a dialectical unity. For Gramsci, every concrete action has theoretical/philosophical implications (exemplifies a mode of thought and furnishes the practical basis for further development of thought) and every philosophy must be concretized (provide norms and values for practical action) to have any significance. Herein lies the essence of his much discussed 'identity' of philosophy and politics. The aim of the new culture, then, 'is a philosophy which is also politics and a politics which is also philosophy'.[225]

Gramsci's depiction of Marxism as a popular reformation, as an affirmation of noble ideas, owes much to Sorel, whose influence on Gramsci was far from negligible. Yet Gramsci was no Sorelian, in that he dissociated himself from the Frenchman's anti-intellectualism and philosophical irrationalism. In Sorel's view, human masses could be organized for the attainment of specific purposes only by uniting them around some 'myth'—a formula, or series of images containing a large measure of illusion. Men, like nature, were driven by dark and mysterious forces, opaque to human reason. Contrary to Sorel, Gramsci laid great emphasis on the analytical and critical understanding; his *Quaderni* exalted neither the power of imagination nor the role of feeling and intuition. While the appeal to romantic heroism struck a responsive chord in the passionate young Torinese militant, it was less than alluring to the sober, experienced politician that Gramsci had become. Sorel sought to exploit men's illusions; the Italian hoped to dispel them, to cut through the mass of distortions and build a world of reason, purged of all superstition and mythology.[226]

One other possible misconception needs to be cleared away. Gramsci's promotion of an idealist ethic, his exhortation to humanize the world by realizing philosophy, is not to be con-

fused with any neo-Kantian belief that the goals of socialism
can somehow be deduced from a supra-historical ethic, binding
on all mankind.[227] On the surface, he does appear to endorse
Kant's dualism between *müssen* and *sollen*, 'is' and 'ought', but
his 'historicism' prevented him from appealing to absolute
moral standards or sets of values, whose desirability needed no
demonstration, being self-evident to all men with normal moral
vision. For Marxists like Max Adler and Otto Bauer, who
thought that the science of historical materialism had to be
supplemented by the transcendental ethics of Kant, Gramsci
expressed nothing but contempt. The so-called neo-Kantians,
he lamented, had transformed the doctrine into a sub-species of
speculative idealism.[228] Correctly understood, socialism is not
a derivation from fundamental laws of human nature; it is
essentially the expression of proletarian class interests, themselves the manifestation of concrete economic developments.
For Gramsci—as for Marx—judgements of value cannot be
sharply distinguished from those of fact. There is no non-
empirical, purely contemplative moral reason. Marxist morality
must have a 'scientific basis', which is to be sought 'in the
affirmation that "society does not pose for itself tasks the conditions for whose resolution do not already exist" . . .'.[229] Far
from being a traditional moral imperative, based on an eternal
model and divorced from changing historical conditions, the
'ought-to-be' is the projection of forms and principles inherent
in existing actuality. In the absence of forces that make for their
realization, 'ideals' are nothing but absurd fantasies. What
'ought-to-be' cannot be 'arbitrary . . . idle fancy, yearning,
day-dream'; it must be 'necessary', 'concrete', implicit within
the existing equilibrium of forces. When formulating aims and
goals for action, we should emulate Machiavelli, who remains
firmly on 'the terrain of actual reality'.[230] And it so happens
that, in terms of realizing the abstract potentialities of man,
within a co-operative community, the process of production
under capitalism affords better opportunities than ever before.
The 'ought-to-be' of socialism is immanent in—though not
guaranteed by—things 'as they are'.

VI. *Conclusion and Summary*

In Gramsci we encounter a Marxism strongly influenced by

traditional philosophical concerns and concepts. In contrast to the orthodox school, he was interested not only in the development of production and the relation of classes, but also in life-styles, ways of thinking and feeling, and the cultural formation of the masses. In addition, his conception of man as an autonomous being, as a creator of himself and the world, bears the stamp of the Italian philosophical tradition. Common in Renaissance humanism, this conception was powerfully formulated by Vico, who extended it into the foundation of an all-embracing, systematic philosophy of history and man. But there can be no doubt that the Italian thinker who bulked largest in Gramsci's intellectual formation was Benedetto Croce. Even the mature Gramsci employed the Crocean idiom, and this usage is emblematic of how the Neapolitan's ideas are woven into the *Quaderni*. The notion of ideological and spiritual rule through consent, the insistence on the relative autonomy of ideas, the hostility to philosophical materialism and so-called 'economism'—all these were learned primarily from Croce. Through his confrontation with Italy's leading Hegelian, Gramsci came to appreciate that every historical action presupposes a cultural framework, a complex organization of ends and means enclosed within a system of values. This insight, gained in his youth, always stood at the centre of his analysis, providing a foundation for his critique of mechanistic versions of Marxism. In the course of this polemic, he came perilously close to outright apostasy. Not only did he display more interest in politics and culture than in economic 'laws of motion', he also contradicted what is usually regarded as an essential axiom of the Marxist creed: the objective necessity of the socialist future. Bewitched by the 'rational kernel' of Hegel's dialectic, Marx and his disciples were led to view certain social developments as 'necessary' or 'inexorable'. Although the new materialism elevated science and the data of observation, an unacknowledged residue of Hegelian metaphysics underlay all talk of dialectical inevitability. It is ironic that in Gramsci, the unremitting foe of positivism, Marxism found a true guardian of its 'empirical conscience'. He vehemently denied the existence of an *a priori* dialectic which guaranteed the ultimate success of mankind's pilgrimage. To search for a pre-ordained design in history was to turn a deaf ear to the genuine voice of experience. Because of the unpredictable role of consciousness, of human will, history—in Gramsci's conception—was not a rational process whose dynamic structure was penetrable by the theorist. He therefore could not share Marx's faith that 'natural science will one day incorporate the science of man, just as the science of man will incorporate natural science; there will be a single science'.[231] But it would be mistaken, I have argued, to infer from Gramsci's marginal, perfunctory discussion of capitalism[232] and from his emphasis on the creative phase of human activity, that he strayed from the Marxist fold. Even in his heterodox version of the doctrine, the basis of the revolutionary process lies within the sphere of production: the complex pattern of human life is firmly embedded in the methods men use to satisfy their material wants. Nothing moves men except ideas and ideals—on this point Gramsci was adamant. But to be operative such ideas and ideals must fit the facts of existence. Following Marx, Gramsci attempts to bring ideological phenomena into some correlation with the material interests of the economic order. With his keen eye for rationalizations and fictions, he accepts the view that different ways of economic life incorporate different ways of classifying and interpreting the environment and human life. *In the last analysis*, then, history works itself out through the discontents of men afflicted with the contradictions that exist in the economic sphere. Any given hegemony must always be traced back to its material roots.

The burden of my argument is this: Gramsci, in his *Quaderni*, was far from denying the classical Marxist primacy of being over thought; he only wished to say that subject and object existed in an interactive relationship, manifested in *praxis*. Man is at once cause and effect, author and consequence of certain definite conditions. Once objectified, however, these conditions—especially their economic manifestation—preclude the possibility of *sovereign* choice. Men make their own world and their own history, but not as they please. They are weighed down by their own past constructions, which are in turn conditioned by the primal forces of nature. It was Gramsci's hope to develop a concept of Marxism equi-distant from both idealism and positivism. History is generated neither by the speculative unfolding of some transcendent 'spirit' nor by the evolution of material forces. In Gramsci's words:

The elements of Spinoza, Feuerbach, Hegel, French materialism, etc., are in no way essential parts of the philosophy of praxis, nor can that philosophy be reduced to those elements. . . . On the level of theory the philosophy of praxis cannot be confused with or reduced to any other philosophy. Its originality lies not only in its surpassing of previous philosophies but also and above all in its opening up a completely new road, renovating from head to toe the mode of conceiving philosophy itself.[233]

Orthodox Marxism, Gramsci stated repeatedly and with deep conviction, had obscured the essential element in Marx's own work, which was the dialectical relationship between subject and object in the historical process. There is a great deal of truth in this assertion. By insisting that men are capable of transforming their reality, the Sardinian came close to restating certain elements of the original Marxist conception—elements lost in the headlong rush to develop eternally valid systems of inexorable laws. Gramsci, it can be argued, took Marx's view of human action to its logical conclusion. For such action, according to Marx, was creative—an ability to transcend the givenness of the situation was intrinsic to consciousness as he employed the term. But the uncertainty and open-endedness implicit in this conception of human action would seem to contradict his unshakable belief that mankind could not ultimately fail in its task of liberation. In removing this theoretical incoherence, Gramsci constructed an original synthesis, infused with a moralism and (unspoken) pessimism which Marx himself eschewed. But *how* original is this synthesis? The affinities with Labriola have already been remarked. And what about Lukács? The influential *History and Class Consciousness* was, after all, published a decade before Gramsci wrote his prison notebooks. He and Lukács alike represent the post-war generation of Marxist thinkers, who developed a particular philosophical form of Marxism, inspired by the Hegelian tradition and hostile to the banalities of the orthodox school. In their mutual desire to introduce Hegelian categories into Marxist theory, the two thinkers staked out a number of similar positions. Both rejected the 'reflection' doctrine of cognition, instead assigning an active role to human consciousness in the construction of the external world; both wanted to dispense with vulgar materialism and arrive at a dialectic in which being and thinking were interdependent; both denied that Marxism was a science, comprising immutable laws, much like those which prevail in the processes of the physical world; both contrived to recast Marxism into a humanist social philosophy, stressing freedom, self-development and cultural renewal; both sought a philosophical transcendence of the existing order and believed that the decisive struggle would be fought out at the level of consciousness.

Nevertheless, a couple of points need to be made. First, the similarities between the two theorists should not be allowed to obscure their very real differences. Most important—whereas Gramsci categorically rejected the possibility of a comprehensive philosophy of history, Lukács thought that the historical process possessed an 'inner logic', which could be deciphered by speculative reasoning. In fact, he remained within the determinist framework, only now the inevitable course of historical development was formulated in terms of 'objective mind' rather than materialist terms. Although the dialectic of history was enacted on the 'existential' plane of will, not through the laws of the economic system, the working class was still driven by 'the absolutely imperious dictates' of its misery to rebel against the inhumanity of capitalism.[234]

It is also necessary to remind the reader that Gramsci was already articulating a quasi-Hegelian Leftism during the war years. It may be that, in this early phase of his thought, he was not yet a Marxist, but neither is it obvious that *History and Class Consciousness*, permeated as it was by the themes of German idealism and romanticism, constituted an authentically Marxist work. Lukács himself, in a later preface to the book, described its distinctive theses as an 'attempt to out-Hegel Hegel'.[235] Since I have no wish to indulge in the 'first-past-the-post' approach to intellectual history, suffice it to say that it is by no means unusual in the history of ideas to find two thinkers independently and almost contemporaneously hitting upon the same ideas. Neither Lukács nor Gramsci possesses any absolute claim to the title: founder of Hegelian Marxism. Both were bold innovators, who refused to believe that Marxism meant the uncritical exposition of sacred texts. They saw themselves as authentic Marxists, upholding a tradition of genuine as opposed to spurious Marxism. In the case of Gramsci, at least, this claim is well justified. Such, in essence, has been the argument of this chapter.

CHAPTER 4

The Revolutionary Party: Architect of the New Hegemony

> One should highlight the importance and signifi-
> cance which, in the modern world, political parties
> have in the elaboration and diffusion of conceptions
> of the world, because what they do, essentially, is to
> work out the ethics and the politics corresponding to
> these conceptions; that is, they function almost as
> historical 'laboratories' of these conceptions.
>
> Gramsci, *MS*, pp. 12–13

I. *The Intellectuals*

GIVEN THE importance that Gramsci attributed to the 'battle of ideas', his well-known emphasis on the role of intellectuals is hardly surprising. The fruit of his historical research was a firm belief that intellectuals are the group most responsible for social stability and change; it is they who sustain, modify, and alter the modes of thinking and behaviour of the masses. In Gramsci's conception of history, then, intellectuals are the purveyors of consciousness; but, as we have seen in the previous chapter, the form and content of this consciousness must be rooted in the world of production. The image of intellectuals as a social category independent of class is false and misleading:

Every social group born on the terrain of an essential function in the world of economic production creates together with itself . . . one or more strata of intellectuals which give it homogeneity and an aware-ness of its own function not only in the economic, but also in the social and political fields. The capitalist entrepreneur creates alongside himself the industrial technician, the specialist in political economy, the organizer of a new culture, of a new legal order, etc.[1]

Gramsci's highly original use of the term 'intellectual' needs elucidation. He decries the 'widespread error of method' which searches for the criterion of distinction between intellectuals and non-intellectuals in the 'intrinsic nature of intellectual activities'. What this error leads to is the classification of individuals according to the existence or non-existence of a cerebral component in their particular occupations or pursuits. But on this criterion, he argues, 'all men are intellectuals'. Gramsci does not follow Marx in recognizing a separation between mental and manual labour, for 'in any physical work, even the most mechanical and degraded, there exists a minimum of technical qualification, that is, a minimum of creative intellectual activity. . . . There is no human activity from which every form of intellectual participation can be excluded: *homo faber* cannot be separated from *homo sapiens*.'[2] Moreover, outside his occupation, each man carries on some form of intellectual pursuit. At the very least, 'he participates in a conception of the world, he has a conscious line of moral conduct, and therefore contributes to sustaining or to modifying a conception of the world . . .'.[3] Thus, intellectuals and other workers must be distinguished in terms of their 'immediate social function', in terms of whether 'their specific professional activity is weighted . . . towards intellectual elaboration or towards muscular-nervous effort'; and this is determined by 'the ensemble of the system of relations in which these activities . . . happen to be situated within the general complex of social relations'.[4] With this in mind, Gramsci defines intellectual in a broad sense to include all those who exercise directive or high level technical capacities in society, 'whether in the field of production, in that of culture or in that of politics-administration . . .'.[5] The category of intellectuals thus contains not only 'thinkers' but civil servants, political leaders, clerics, managers, technocrats, etc. Within this general category, he distinguishes between 'organic' and 'traditional' intellectuals. The former are fairly directly related to the economic and political structure, and are more closely tied to the class they represent, giving it 'homogeneity and awareness of its own function' on all levels of society.[6] The traditional group comprises: (a) the creative artists and scholars (the organizers of culture), who are traditionally regarded as intellectuals; and (b) the vestiges of organic intellectuals from previous social formations (e.g. ecclesiastics), who come to fuse with the artists and learned men on the basis of a common feeling that they are 'autonomous, independent of the dominant social group'.[7] Although Gramsci, as a good Marxist, rejects this claim, he does admit that intellectuals (the traditional type in particular) are not usually passive agents of the classes they serve or represent. Rather, the relationship is 'mediated in diverse ways by the entire social fabric, by the complex of superstructures . . .'.[8] While the traditional intellectuals do not necessarily share the world-view of the ruling group, they eventually effect a compromise with it, in part because of institutional pressures and financial inducements.[9] At any rate, consciously or not, they usually propagate ideas and ways of thinking that are essentially conservative in their implications.[10] Hence, though there may be no direct controls over what intellectuals may think or say, all ideas somehow serve the interests of one or another economic class, even if indirectly. But the only ideas capable of becoming generally accepted and institutionalized in social life are those which *both* serve the interests and *reflect the experience of* either the dominant group or the class that is 'rising' (i.e. the possessor of qualities best suited to cope with the newly emergent productive forces).

Gramsci, as we have seen, claims that *every* system of thought originates in a particular practice (though it may linger on in various guises long after its social precipitants have disappeared). In the last analysis, even the most refined forms of philosophical and scientific thought are but ways in which human beings confer intelligibility on their own economic or practical activity. Concrete experience is the essential raw material of human reflection. But (and this is of course central to his theory) the products of this reflection then proceed to modify the social reality from which they emerge. While world-visions are spun out by 'great' intellectuals, they are (if successful) transmitted throughout society by lesser intellectuals (teachers, political activists, journalists, priests, etc.) and eventually become embodied in 'common sense':

Every philosophical current leaves behind a sedimentation of 'common sense': this is the documentation of its historical effectiveness. . . . Common sense is not something rigid or immobile, but is continually transforming itself, enriching itself with scientific ideas and philosophical opinions that have entered everyday life.[11]

The intellectual underlabourers who propagate modes of thought generally work within an institutional context. The chief institution for elaborating and disseminating the new proletarian culture is the Communist Party, which Gramsci often refers to as a 'collective intellectual'.

II. *The Revolutionary Party: an Introduction*

Gramsci, in his *Quaderni*, constructed his theory of the party around an analogy with Machiavelli's *Prince*, which was intended to arouse and educate politically the Italian people. The analogy was not merely designed for rhetorical or literary effect. Given the anti-political bias of orthodox Marxism, he wanted to make a case for the distinctly political as a language of communication, a form of analysis, and an instrument of revolutionary change. In their desire to deduce everything from the 'basic' level of economics, Marxists had forgotten that 'man is essentially political'.[12] It was his concern for the political sphere (understood in a wide sense to include all superstructural activity)[13] that attracted Gramsci to Machiavelli, whose desire for the unity of sixteenth-century Italy encouraged him to look to the binding, collective potential of political action. In Gramsci's words, '. . . what Machiavelli does . . . is to bring everything back to politics, that is, to the art of governing men, of securing their permanent consent, and hence of founding "great states"'.[14] Just as Machiavelli endeavoured to free Italian politics from the dead weight of religion and traditional morality, so Gramsci wished to liberate Marxist thinking from the incubus of economic reductionism. For the Florentine, as for the Sardinian, politics was the realm of *virtú*, whereby men could attempt to dominate objective reality—to create a sense of community in the midst of chaos and fragmentation. Gramsci saw in Machiavelli both an intuition of the historical problem of his own epoch—the need for impassioned engagement in the building of a unified national culture—and the specification of suitable procedures and strategies for attaining this end. Machiavelli was, to him, the theoretician *par excellence* of the unitary modern state. When he calls his illustrious predecessor 'the first Italian Jacobin',[15] he is alluding to Machiavelli's attempt to weld together city and country into a national militia, to create in his Prince an agent of mass mobilization:

Any formation of a national-popular collective will is impossible, unless the great mass of peasant cultivators bursts simultaneously into political life. This was Machiavelli's intention through the reform of the militia, and this was achieved by the Jacobins in the French Revolution, . . .[16]

For Gramsci Jacobinism does not signify (as it does to some) extremely violent action by a minority, the exasperated voluntarism of a sectarian, authoritarian group (or leader) which tries to *force* a political situation. Rather, it primarily defines the class content of a political revolution, the vision of a subordinate class or classes aiming at historical maturity through the guidance of a democratically inspired élite, aware of the importance of the people, sensitive to their needs and wishes. Put simply, Jacobinism denotes strong leadership tied to a democratic mission.[17] It is significant that Gramsci stresses the populist, consensual side of Machiavelli's thought, rooted as it was in an understanding that the basis of politics was being broadened and that the factor of 'the people' would have to be taken into account in future reckonings. This interpretation of Machiavelli is quite evident in the intriguing passage where Gramsci remarks that 'Machiavelli's *Prince* could be studied as a historical exemplification of the Sorelian myth—i.e. of a political ideology presented neither as cold utopia nor as doctrinaire ratiocination, but rather as the creation of a concrete fantasy which acts on a dispersed and atomized people to arouse and organize its collective will'.[18] In the conditions of a complex society, however, neither a 'concrete fantasy' nor a 'doctrinaire', 'cold utopia' nor anything in between can be embodied in the person of a post-Renaissance *condottiere*, however progressive: 'In the modern world, only an immediate and imminent historico-political action, characterized by the necessity of rapid proceeding, is capable of being entrusted to a single individual.' Such action is not of course appropriate to the founding of 'new States and new national and social structures. . .'. It is therefore the party, not the 'historical figure', which must emerge as the champion of popular energies. What is needed in the era of bourgeois hegemony is a 'Modern Prince', which 'cannot be a real person, a concrete individual. It can only be an organism, a complex element of society in which a collective will, which has been partially recognized and affirmed in action, already begins to take shape. Historical development has already provided this organism, and it is the political [revolutionary] party—the first cell in which the germs of a collective will tending to become universal and total are gathered together.'[19]

A crucial phrase here is 'historical development'. Politics is not for Gramsci the ultimate demiurge of society, an illusion Marx thought specific to 'jurists and politicians'. The party must arise and affirm itself as a *historical necessity*, not as an arbitrary voluntarist construction. As I argued in the last chapter, the emphasis Gramsci places on the moment of critical intervention, on the initiative of the revolutionary subject, should not lead commentators to exaggerate his voluntarism. The party comes into being only when the proletariat has already begun to exhibit an embryonic consciousness of itself as an 'autonomous' class, to perceive dimly (perhaps subconsciously) that its own interests are potentially universal. And the development of this nascent consciousness is intimately related to concrete material changes. Politics, he maintains, 'is born on the "permanent and organic" terrain of economic life'.[20] It was Gramsci's view, perhaps attributable to his uncritical acceptance of Marxist economic categories, that 'the objective conditions for the proletarian revolution have existed in Europe for more than fifty years'.[21] Gramsci never abandoned the conventional Marxist theme—which he put forward insistently in his *Ordine Nuovo* writings[22]—that production for private profit is incapable of utilizing to the fullest the productive potential of the increasingly socialized forces of production. The revolutionary party, both the 'expression and most advanced part'[23] of the proletariat, must activate the smouldering, 'incurable structural contradictions'[24] of capitalism into manifest social tensions. The principal problem, then, is to know how best to use the political element, to 'make politics'. The revolutionary party undertakes the task of completing that transformation in the working class which is immanent in capitalist society itself. Some further, clarificatory remarks on this task are in order.

Like Lenin[25] before him, Gramsci believed that socialist truth must be brought to the working classes from 'outside'; it does not spontaneously emanate from the conditions of production or from the class struggle. 'In its initial stages, innovation cannot flow from the masses, if not through the channel of an élite in which the conception implicit in human activity has already become in a certain measure actual consciousness; coherent, sytematic, precise, and decisive will.'[26] The party, then, is the necessary mediating force which enables the masses to transcend their mystified condition. It is essential to recognize that this heavy emphasis on a revolutionary *avante garde* represents a departure from Marx's thought, for the latter developed no clear doctrine of the party. Given his concern for organization and his occasional references to an ill-defined vanguard, it is perhaps inaccurate to attribute to Marx a naïve 'spontaneism'—a belief that proletarian consciousness is brought about solely from within the structure of capitalism and thanks to it. But organization, to Marx, was purely a practical matter, a flexible and changing instrument, anchored in concrete circumstance and subject to the wishes of a mass constituency. Organization expresses the rhythm of the mass movement; it does not precede this movement, or anticipate its actions and objectives. As Marx asserts in the *Manifesto*, Communists 'do not set up any sectarian principles of their own, by which to shape and mould the proletarian movement'.[27] The party is merely the political form of the proletariat and constitutes its transitory mode of being: he consistently rejected any notion of a political arm distinct from the proletariat's immediate existence. In any case, such an institution would be redundant, for Marx did not view the emergence of revolutionary consciousness as primarily a process of education from above, but as the inevitable, if mediated, by-product of irreconcilable economic contradictions.

Gramsci's conceptualization of the determinants and content of mass consciousness in advanced capitalist society renders such an unstructured view of the party inadequate. For Gramsci, it will be remembered, economic factors exert no univocal or unavoidable influence—even in the long term. Bourgeois hegemony has taken its toll. In the ordinary man's consciousness, left to its own spontaneity and not yet self-critical, there coexist disparate elements, manifold and contradictory values and desires. While the expressed beliefs and general behaviour of the subaltern classes tend to be conformist, their effective needs and claims often spur them to actions more or less incompatible with the vision of life to which they have been educated. Hence, their 'true' consciousness is implicit in these deviant and irregular actions; it does not consist of the sum total of their verbal affirmations. But the key words here are 'implicit' and 'irregular'. The frequent contradiction between explicit world-view and behaviour, theory and practice, means that the unmediated activity of the masses cannot be fully conscious or coherent. It is 'disjointed': there are moments of revolt and moments of stagnation, futile rebellion and dumb passivity, extremism and opportunism. Spontaneous discontent is contained by the pre-existing categories of the dominant ideology. Gramsci would have dismissed as irrelevant arguments to the effect that revolution turns on the spontaneous development of the working class; for he believed that, in any event, pure spontaneity was a fiction, an anarchist delusion. 'Even in the most spontaneous movements . . . the elements of conscious leadership are merely invisible; they have left no ascertainable proof.'[28] Direction comes from somewhere, even if it is covert or concealed; and in the conditions of capitalist society that direction is likely to be bourgeois in origin. In this connection Gramsci attacks Sorel for not proposing the creation of a popular revolutionary will and for supposing, instead, that one already exists. This faith in spontaneity, apart from revealing an (acknowledged or hidden) determinism, 'leaves the collective will in the primitive and elementary phase of its initial formation'.[29]

True revolutionary action, therefore, must be firmly guided by a fully articulated conception of the world. The problem is to unify theory and practice, to render *explicit* that which is still only *implicit*, and which can only remain implicit in the absence of *external* intervention. The party must give coherence to the diffuse, often latent anger and despair of the toiling masses; it must deliver the dominated social groups 'from tumultuous chaos' so that they can become 'a political army organically predisposed'.[30] Within this army of the oppressed and the disinherited, the main attacking force is the industrial proletariat; its advance is to become 'the motor force of a universal expansion, of a development of all the "national" energies'. If the party succeeds in its task, the proletariat will effect the passage from a corporate, and hence purely subordinate, role of limited opposition to a hegemonic role of conscious action towards revolutionary goals.[31] What this requires is both the destruction of old norms and meanings and the creation of a new universe of ideas and values—one capable of providing the basis for *complete* human liberation. It is a matter of formulating not simply a novel vision of social and economic structures but an integrated and all-embracing *Weltanschauung*, a distinctively proletarian culture and ethic. Party activity must make total, as well as qualitative, the fundamental conflicts of class society; it must create an awareness that struggle on the economic and political front is related in a systematic way to intellectual and spiritual renewal. The party, then, affirms and creates the 'integral autonomy' of the subordinate classes, by providing them with a new conceptual framework, by effecting a 'total and molecular transformation of modes of thought and being'.[32] This, remember, is a precondition for political revolution. In summary, the mission of the party is to establish a new collective will, a new national and popular unity:

The Modern Prince must be and cannot but be the proclaimer and organizer of an intellectual and moral reform, which also means creating the grounds for a subsequent development of the national-popular collective will towards the accomplishment of a superior and total form of modern civilization.[33]

In his search for a unified culture, Gramsci frequently addressed himself to the Roman Church. He was, it seems, impressed by the organizational and ideological potency of Catholicism, and laid particular emphasis on the care taken by the Church, in all phases of its history, to prevent an excessive gap developing between the religion of the learned and that of the simple folk:

The strength of religions, and especially the Catholic Church, has consisted, and still consists, in the fact that they feel very strongly the need for doctrinal unity of the whole mass of the faithful, and strive to ensure that the higher intellectual stratum does not get separated from the lower.[34]

The 'Modern Prince', Gramsci suggests, should become a 'Marxist Church', in pursuit of a universal spiritual order. The party militants, on this analogy, would function as a priesthood, entrusted with the duty of creating and preserving 'doctrinal unity'.

In Gramsci, the educative function of the party acquires a 'total', or all-encompassing, dimension (and a quasi-religious fervour) that take it well beyond the Leninist assault on 'spontaneism' and 'tailism'. But before pursuing this and related lines of investigation, we must dispel a myth that has blurred and confused Gramsci's present-day image. Anyone vaguely familiar with Gramsci's life and times might object that the foregoing account is either inaccurate or grotesquely one-sided, because it ignores the critical role Gramsci assigned to the factory councils (*consigli di fabbrica*), especially in 1919–20, when he took a hand in organizing them throughout Turin. Consequently, a digression here on the genesis and evolution of Gramsci's 'consiliar' doctrine is advisable, both to forestall criticism and, incidentally, to underscore the folly of treating his writings as a unified whole.

III. *Gramsci and the Factory Councils*

The theoretical basis of the councils was worked out in the pages of *L'Ordine Nuovo*, a dissident socialist publication based in Turin, which Gramsci helped to found and edit. His chief collaborators in beginning the weekly review (in April 1919) were Angelo Tasca, Umberto Terracini, and Palmiro Togliatti— all of whom shared with Gramsci a youthful and intransigent contempt for reformism, impressive intellectual capacity,[35] and 'a vague passion for a vague proletarian culture'.[36] The initial concern of the 'ordinovista' nucleus was a refined discussion of the problems of developing a socialist culture (in the sense of theatre, art, and literature). This involved an abortive attempt to implant in Italy a version of the Russian 'Prolekult' movement organized by Lunacharsky, who maintained that the specifically cultural side of life must be regarded with the same seriousness as the other three branches of the labour movement—the political, economic, and co-operative. The first few issues of *L'Ordine Nuovo* proved to be no more than a renewed and unimaginative venture in the 'cultural messianism' that had informed Gramsci's earlier work as a journalist and activist. And once again cultural indoctrination failed to strike a responsive chord in the movement.[37] Gramsci was later to describe the early *L'Ordine Nuovo* as 'nothing but an anthology . . . of abstract culture, of abstract information, with a tendency towards hair-raising stories and well-intentioned wood-cuts'.[38]

By June 1919, all the collaborators but Tasca—who was deposed in an editorial *coup d'état* and proceeded to register a growing dissent—had found the 'slogan' which was to characterize *L'Ordine Nuovo*, namely, the idea of the factory councils as the Italian equivalent of the Soviets. High-flown discussion of aesthetic theory was made to yield place to the theme which became the hallmark of the journal and of the group that had coalesced around it.

The idea of soviets enjoyed currency throughout the Italian Left in this period, from the reformists at one extreme, to Bordiga, whose 'absentionist' journal published in Naples was entitled *Il Soviet*, at the other. But the *Ordine Nuovo* group distinguished itself in a number of ways. To begin with, it had a programme for the institutionalization of a soviet system, fought for this programme, and, to some extent, realized it, managing by 1920 to enroll the majority of the working men of Turin. But most important, the radical *Ordine Nuovo* conception of the role and practice of the councils brought the group into direct conflict with the rest of the Italian Left. This is not the place for a detailed description and analysis of the Turin factory councils or of the theoretical positions underpinning them. For our purposes it is sufficient to mention their basic features. First, they were, as their name indicates, based in the *factories* or *units of production*, and therefore differed from the Russian Soviets, which were territorial organizations. Second, the *consigli* were independent of the traditional working-class institutions, and, unlike these institutions, representative of *all* the workers in a given plant, through a mechanism of mandatory democracy. Third, the councils, partly through the work of subsidiary bodies such as 'factory schools', served two basic educative functions: (1) to prepare the workers for a seizure of power in the factory by providing them with technical and administrative training,[39] and (2) to convince them 'that it is in their interest to submit to a permanent discipline of culture, and to form a [correct] conception of the world and the complex and intricate system of human relations, economic and spiritual, that form the social life of the globe'.[40] The councils, then, became—at least in theory—the main vehicles of revolutionary education. Finally, and because of the aforementioned characteristics, the councils were depicted as the institution that would ultimately replace the bourgeois state as the organ of government. Gramsci and his colleagues (excluding Tasca, who wished to subordinate the councils to the trade unions) saw the *consigli* as embryos of the future socialist state, as the prototypical organs of the proletarian society, epitomising its production, organization, and spirit:

The factory council is the model of the proletarian State. All the problems inherent in the organization of the proletarian State are inherent in the organization of the council. In the one and in the other, the concept of the citizen declines and is replaced by the concept of the comrade; collaboration to produce wealth . . . multiplies the bonds of affection and brotherhood. Everyone is indispensable; everyone is at his post; and everyone has a function and a post. Even the most ignorant and backward of the workers, even the most vain and 'civil' of engineers eventually convinces himself of this truth in the experience of factory organization. Everyone eventually acquires a communist viewpoint through understanding the great step forward that the communist economy represents over the capitalist economy. The council is the most fitting organ of mutual education and development of the new social spirit that the proletariat has succeeded in expressing. . . . Working-class solidarity . . . in the council is positive, permanent, and incarnated in even the most trivial moments of industrial production. It is contained in the joyous awareness of being an organic whole, a homogenous and compact system that, by useful labour and disinterested production of social wealth, asserts its sovereignty, and realizes its power and its freedom as a creator of history.[41]

Others wished to locate the focus of worker organization in the trade union centres or in the Socialist Party. Gramsci, however, wanted the future society to emanate directly from the cells of the social body that were both rooted in the productive process and *truly representative*. More than once, he compared the 'voluntary' or 'private' nature of trade unions and parties with the 'representative' or 'public' character of councils. The former are adhered to by an explicit act of consent, which could at any moment be withdrawn. But in 'the factory councils, the worker participates by virtue of his role as producer, i.e. in consequence of his universal character, in consequence of his function and position in society' and not through an express act of consciousness.[42] The factory councils are founded on the permanent foundation of industrial production, and not on transitory facts like wages, votes, or the exigencies of conquering power. Further, Gramsci believed that both trade unions and socialist parties were ineradicably tainted by their origins in capitalist society and by their tendency to function in accordance with its logic. Traditional working-class institutions 'arise and develop on the terrain of liberal democracy' and are 'necessarily inherent in the bourgeois system and the capitalist structure'.[43] These institutions are dependent not on laws implicit in the life and historical experience of the working classes but on 'rules of the game' imposed on them by the proprietary classes with whom they compete;[44] hence, they will 'decay and corrode along with the system in which they find themselves incorporated'. Operating in the liberal arena, the Socialist Party, for instance, must aim to win a majority of votes 'by the method proper to democracy, by displaying before the electorate programmes as general as they are muddled, and by promising to realize them at any cost'.[45] Ideological coherence is sacrificed to parliamentary electioneering. Trade unions especially suffer because of the *intrinsically* corporatist, limited character of their goals, which leads workers to regard labour not as a 'process of production, but as a pure means of gain', a commodity to be bought and sold in the market place.[46] Far from being revolutionary, the trade unions actually perform an integrative function for the regime of private property.[47]

The factory council, by contrast, encourages the worker to regard himself as a producer, not as a mere wage-earner. The councils alone are capable of elevating the worker above his immediate, individual interests and providing him with the mental habits of a producer. The essence of capitalist rationalism is division between those who have the power of decision and those who must execute orders, a division which capitalism pictures as necessary and permanent. It is precisely in this area that the council, by fostering a system of 'dual power' on the shop floor, undermines the practice of capitalist production: 'The existence of the Councils', Gramsci tells us, 'gives the workers direct responsibility for production; it conduces them to better their labour; it establishes a conscious and voluntary discipline, and creates the psychology of the producer, of the creator of history'.[48] Through participation in council decision-making, the worker develops a feeling of interdependence with his fellow-producers as well as a consciousness of his own worth, of his ability to control his destiny. So the actual unfolding of the revolutionary process takes place not on the political level but 'underground, in the obscurity of the factory', where there exists a spontaneous unity between theory and practice.[49] The Council theory, in brief, rested on the notion of 'revolution from below', a molecular, spontaneous process occurring in the industrial structure. Ultimately, revolution would have to come through the self-conscious initiatives of the masses themselves, not through the directives of a vanguard party acting in their name.

The themes developed in *Ordine Nuovo* were not entirely original. Indeed, factory councils were a phenomenon common to most of Europe after 1916. In revolutionary Hungary, for example, Bela Kun had exhorted the masses to transform their labour unions into soviets embracing all workers—a notion endorsed, incidentally, by Lukács. Gramsci himself recognized that the theoretical and practical activity of the journal and its staff was only the application to Italy of concepts originated by Lenin (and incarnated—albeit briefly—in the victory of the Soviets in the Russian revolution), leavened with inspiration from the writings of the American syndicalist, Daniel de Leon,[50] the theorist of the Wobblies, and from the British shop stewards' movement.[51]

During the fifties, there was a great deal of controversy in Italy about whether the 'essential' Gramsci favoured the party or the councils as the chief form of working-class organization. Needless to say, the PCI and its theoreticians stressed the role of the party in Gramsci's thought and minimized the meaning of the council experience.[52] The councils were emphasized by Marxist intellectuals who challenged the Communist Party's centralism and advocated forms of workers' self-government. This position was especially prominent after the Hungarian revolt in 1956, when many disaffected intellectuals left the Party. The whole debate possessed an element of futility, for it is undeniable that Gramsci underlined the councils in his *Ordine Nuovo* period, and the party thereafter. But one of the most perplexing (and legitimate) interpretative problems confronting Gramsci scholarship centres on the *degree* of rupture or continuity between the consiliar theory and the Leninist preoccupation with the party that receives such clear expression in the *Quaderni*. The thesis of a sharp discontinuity has been expounded most forcefully by the *Manifesto* group, dissident Left intellectuals who were expelled by the PCI in 1969.[53] Moreover, they proclaim that 'what is alive' in Gramsci is his anti-Jacobin theory of 1919–20, his focus on the role of councils in raising mass consciousness, not the 'Stalinist' and 'élitist' view of the party that surfaced in his later writings. Thus, they revived the old debate about the 'essential' Gramsci; but as Davidson points out, for the *Manifesto* circle, 'this emphasis on the "anti-Jacobin" Gramsci is usually intended to be no more than taking a few "live" guides to action from a corpus of doctrine. . . . It is not intended as a résumé of an interpretation of the whole of his thought.'[54] Others who elevate the *Ordine Nuovo* theory actually claim that it permeates the totality of his writings. Caracciolo, for instance, declares that, at least until 1926 and arguably until his death, the consiliar theory remains 'at the centre of Gramsci's attention as an indispensable and irreplaceable element of his theory of revolution'.[55] Martinelli, too, sees 'a basic continuity between Gramsci's treatment of the two institutions' and suggests that in his later writings the 'Party maintains decision-making power and has co-ordinating and directive functions, but its power is *ultimately based on and must ultimately respond to* the network of councils'.[56] The difference, then, becomes merely one of degree. This, I believe, is to press the continuity argument too far and to gloss over how Gramsci's ideas changed and developed in response to changing political conditions. But, ironically, the notion of a 'radical break' also betrays an ahistorical reading of Gramsci, wrenching quotations arbitrarily from the sequence of events and pattern of intentions that help to explain their meaning and significance. If we place Gramsci's writings on the party and the councils in their proper historical context, and scrutinize them with an open mind, it seems clear that his basic orientation did change, but not as fundamentally as some might think.

When Gramsci was advocating the councils, Europe was riding the crest of a revolutionary wave. The idea that revolution was on the agenda was common to both sides in the class struggle between 1918 and 1920. The *Ordine Nuovo* movement was inspired by the example of a triumphant Russian revolution, which indicated that soviets could furnish the basis for a socialist state, and supported by the widespread conviction that the Italian social and political situation was objectively mature. Certainly, Italian capitalism was faltering and worker unrest— spurred on by rocketing inflation, high unemployment, and the threat of starvation—was at a high point. The period was characterized by a succession of riots, lock-outs, general strikes and local uprisings. Partly because of the experience of the Great War (the sacrifices it demanded, the false hopes it raised, the dislocations it engendered), the dominant hegemony had apparently disintegrated. Moreover, in Gramsci's home city of Turin, with its relatively homogeneous, skilled, and militant work force, spontaneous revolutionary energy took a well organized and fairly sophisticated form. The council movement might have been geographically isolated in Italy's 'motor-city', but, granted its restricted range, it enjoyed considerable success on the local level—success which may have blinded Gramsci to the limitations imposed by the general backwardness of the country.

It is not easy to define precisely the role that Gramsci wished to assign to the party in this period. One source of difficulty, which receives no close attention in the exegetical literature, is that Gramsci was speaking at different times in different contexts of *two separate parties*: one, the Socialist Party, with which he became increasingly disillusioned, and, the other, a projected Communist Party, purged of all reformists and rhetorical 'revolutionaries', which actually materialized only after the Livorno split in 1921. Another (related) problem is this: Gramsci, in his *Ordine Nuovo* articles and editorials, put forward a number of arguments at least prima facie inconsistent with one another—inconsistency that was an accurate expression of a confused and contradictory reality. It should be kept in mind that these writings, even though now gathered together in one volume, do not in any way resemble a systematic treatise. The very nature of Gramsci's position as an actively committed political commentator forced him to respond to the dazzling flux of events and circumstances; hence the ambiguities and anomalies. Whatever consistent arguments or universal content we might find must be abstracted from the minute particulars of the evolving situation.

Any attempt to sort out Gramsci's views in this period must take as its point of departure one indisputable historical fact: in the face of what seemed to be an objectively revolutionary situation, the PSI was remarkable for its timidity and ineffectiveness. Initially, Gramsci's theoretical response was to celebrate the revolutionary potential of the councils and to demote the party to a mere 'agent', a strategic and tactical adviser to the spontaneously burgeoning mass movement.[57] But by the spring of 1920 this argument was conjoined with an apparently contradictory call for a reconstituted party, resolutely *Communist*, fully in tune with the Third International, and capable of playing the decisive part in the revolutionary process. For example, in an important editorial, 'For a Renewal of the Socialist Party', which was presented as a report at the Socialist Party National Congress in late April, Gramsci informs all concerned that:

The existence of a cohesive and strongly disciplined Communist Party, which, through its factory, trade union and co-operative nuclei, co-ordinates and centralizes within its own executive committee all of the proletariat's revolutionary activity, is the *fundamental and indispensable condition* for attempting any Soviet experiment.[58]

This curious juxtaposition of two distinct, though perhaps reconcilable, positions manifests itself in confusing oscillations in Gramsci's published work throughout the spring and summer. One especially deserves mention. On 4 September 1920, Gramsci wrote in *Ordine Nuovo* that 'the Communist Party is the instrument and the historical form of the process of inner liberation. . . '.[59] The party, according to this piece, takes on the educative and directive functions previously attributed to the councils. The productive process of capitalism in crisis no longer generates *of itself* the 'inner liberation' of the industrial workers. Yet, on the following day, he published an article in *Avanti!* reviving all the main themes of the council doctrine and not once mentioning the party![60] The press of events simply did not allow Gramsci the luxury of working out a coherent synthesis of his faith in the councils and his new-found appreciation of the creative potential of a revolutionary party. The historical reasons for this new appreciation require some elaboration here.

It is worth while noting (and often overlooked) that the consiliar theory never involved a syndicalist celebration of pure spontaneity. In an article entitled 'Il partito e la rivoluzione', published on 27 December 1919, Gramsci asserts that the Socialist Party, in spite of its intrinsic weakness and diminished role, remains the sole guardian of the 'correct line'. Armed with superior discipline and knowledge of historical development, and enjoying a vantage point above transient interests, it is well equipped to delineate the strategy, tactics, and final goals of the class struggle. Gramsci was apparently of the opinion that the councils would eventually come around to accepting Party guidance after their period of self-education through praxis. The Socialist Party may be sullied by its origin in the capitalist sewer, and it may exhibit a resultant tendency towards bureaucratic immobilism; but Gramsci nevertheless cherishes the hope that the consiliar movement can obviate the dangers inherent in the situation by rooting the Party in the economic life of the masses.[61] This hope was dashed by the PSI's outright opposition to the Piedmont general strike in the spring of 1920, an industrial action called in sympathy with the metalworkers' strike in Turin.[62] On a superficial level, this latter strike was provoked by a dispute over daylight saving time and the subsequent dismissal of an entire 'Internal Commission'.[63] But the significance of these events was magnified by the explicit intention of *Confindustria*, the new nation-wide employers' federation, to suppress or crush the council movement, whose revolutionary objectives it was not prepared to tolerate.[64] What was really at stake was the employers' authority within the workshop, and both sides realized this. In effect, the Torinese workers were fighting for the preservation of their councils.

The aforementioned Socialist Party National Congress was held in Milan at the height of the action (19–21 April). Hostility to what was considered the impetuousness of the metalworkers and their supporters in the Turin Section was general, and a majority of delegates refused to authorize the extension of the strike beyond Piedmont. The strike was clearly doomed to ignominious defeat. In his report to the Congress, Gramsci bitterly denounced the Party for its political and organizational deficiencies, saying that it remained 'a mere parliamentary party which holds itself immobile within the narrow limits of bourgeois democracy'.[65] For this state of affairs, he blamed the presence of reformists and urged the creation of 'a homogeneous, cohesive party, with its own doctrine and tactics, and a rigid and implacable discipline'. Those who are 'not communist revolutionaries', he continued, 'must be eliminated from the Party'.[66] This report amounted to a rupture with the PSI as constituted.[67] By early September his language had assumed an even harsher tone: he talked about a new Communist Party 'arising from the ashes of the Socialist Parties' and dismissed the PSI as 'by no means different from the English Labour Party'.[68] Gramsci's disillusionment with the PSI, it would seem, was also coupled with doubts about at least one of the specific contentions embodied in the *Ordine Nuovo* theory— that revolution essentially comes 'from below'. We have already noted how, in his report to the PSI gathering, he stressed that 'a cohesive and strongly disciplined Communist Party' must centralize 'within its own executive committee all of the proletariat's revolutionary activity'. Likewise, in an article of 8 May 1920, he remarks that one reason for the defeat of the Torinese working class lay in the 'lack of revolutionary cohesion of the entire Italian proletariat'.[69] Gramsci seemed willing to concede the paramountcy of conscious co-ordination, to grant that revolution must in *some* sense come 'from above'. This accounts for his preoccupation, following the failure of the Piedmont strike, with transforming the Socialist Party into a more active revolutionary instrument. But, as mentioned earlier, he confused the issue by not concomitantly downgrading the factory councils from their pre-eminent position as the central educative institutions of the revolutionary process.[70] Perhaps we can summarize his stance as follows. In 1919 he believed the Party could be renewed from below by the construction of the councils, but the failure of the PSI to lend support to the metal-workers convinced him that only a radical reorganization of the Party could ensure the success of the councils.

Throughout this period, then, his theoretical judgement of political parties *as such* was never really negative. A worker party, properly constituted and functioning, would be a repository of true consciousness and a more or less active agent of liberation. Events soon led him to lay primary, almost exclusive, stress on this agency, at the expense of the councils.

The mood of the country remained tense during the summer of 1920. Having emasculated the council movement after their April victory, the industrialists seemed determined to smash the revolutionary pretensions of the workers once and for all. Finally the dam burst. There is no need here to probe the intricacies of the situation. A few remarks will suffice.[71] Factory occupations broke out in Milan at the end of August and quickly spread throughout the country. The movement assumed a scale and character which far exceeded anyone's expectations. It was now that the real impact of *Ordine Nuovo*'s ideas and agitation made itself felt, as factory councils sprang up everywhere. The country as a whole seemed to be verging on revolution. Even peasants in certain districts of Sicily and Lucania joined the act, by 'occupying' unexploited lands belonging to large estates. Lacking unity of purpose or adequate preparation, the PSI vacillated, making a few insurrectionary noises but finally deciding not to call for full-scale revolt. The Party's irresoluteness owed much to the determined moderation of the CGL (the major trade union federation), which, from the start, was anxious to reach a compromise solution. The unions did manage to negotiate a contract that extracted some generous 'bread and butter' concessions from the industrialists, but the question of worker participation was evaded, with the industrialists accepting it 'in principle'. A referendum of the workers participating in the occupations was held on 24 September, the contract was overwhelmingly endorsed, and the factories were returned to the employers. The council movement in Italy had collapsed; though the workers won a technical victory, the revolutionary phase of post-war Italy was effectively brought to a close. Gramsci's reaction to this setback was a ferocious Jacobinism:

. . . a revolutionary movement can only be founded on the proletarian vanguard and must be conducted without prior consultation, without the apparatus of representative assemblies. A revolution is like a war. It must be minutely prepared by a workers' general staff, just as a war is prepared by the general staff of the army. . . . The task of the proletarian vanguard is to keep the revolutionary spirit awake in the masses, to create the conditions in which the masses respond immediately to revolutionary slogans . . . no revolutionary movement will be decreed by a national workers' assembly: to convoke an assembly means to confess one's own lack of faith.[72]

The *Ordine Nuovo* group proceeded to sink its theoretical differences with Bordiga over the councils in order to participate in the creation of an Italian Communist Party, whose first leader was the ultra-Left-wing Neapolitan. In the face of defeat and growing fascist power, Gramsci abandoned the consiliar theory. It is true that, in his writings from 1921 until his incarceration in 1926, he still viewed worker councils as an instrument for mass mobilization and as a mechanism for keeping the Party in touch with its base, for protecting it from bureaucratic ossification.[73] But the councils were now absorbed into a qualitatively different framework; the propulsive force of the revolution was no longer the council but the Party. In August 1924, for instance, he described the Party as 'the sole instrument through which . . . the idea of the complete redemption of the workers is able to be actualized and realized'.[74] A year later he declared: 'The proletarian Party must not "follow" the masses, it must lead them.'[75] He came to view the soviet system more as a goal to be achieved from above than as a means to achieve a goal from below. Indeed, in the *Prison Notebooks*, there is no discussion of factory councils at all. While it is probably true that Gramsci came to consider his previous, more limited conception of the party inadequate under any circumstances, his shift was also a reaction to a new type of situation—a situation of worker demoralization, of apparent revolutionary reflux, where conscious direction necessarily becomes all-important. I say 'apparent' because Gramsci seemed to believe, along with other Italian Communists, that the *objective* conditions for revolution were still ripe, that revolution was still an immediate possibility—even after the Fascist takeover.[76] The problem, as they saw it, was one of organization, co-ordination, discipline, and direction—*from above*.

Thus, the catastrophic events of 1920 extinguished Gramsci's faith in the spontaneous revolutionary proclivities of the proletariat. In the years from 1921 to 1926, he devoted himself mainly to the internal organization and politics of the

PCI. Upon becoming Party leader in 1924, Gramsci undertook to 'Bolshevize' the PCI, which meant that in the manner of the CPSU, the Party was set on a monolithic footing, with its policy, personnel, and style of activity strictly subordinated to Moscow. Since the International was directed by the men who had participated in the Revolution of October, it was for him the indisputable guide: 'He who is independent of the Soviet Union is "independent" of the working class, and thus "dependent" on the bourgeois class.'[77] While there exists documentary evidence to attest that he was occasionally critical of Soviet leadership and fearful of Stalin's depredations,[78] it is undeniable that in these years Gramsci became more and more Bolshevik and Leninist. It is only in his *Quaderni*, however, that his theory of the party as the principal and indispensable agent of the revolutionary process is given clear theoretical justification. It is back to the *Quaderni* that we now turn.

IV. *The Modern Prince: Composition, Organization, Function*

Thus far in this chapter I have sought to show, first, that Gramsci, even at the height of his infatuation with factory councils, always believed that a vanguard party could have an important co-ordinative role to play, and second, that the abrupt end of the *biennio rosso* convinced him of the unsuitability and historical specificity of the consiliar theory he had so strenuously fought for. Yet it is simplistic to argue, as have Togliatti and his PCI followers, that the Gramsci of the *Notebooks* espoused a thorough-going Leninism.[79] Unlike Lenin, Gramsci was not utterly contemptuous of spontaneity; he did not call for a purely downward flow of direction—from vanguard to mass. Even after his effective renunciation of the *Ordine Nuovo* principles he became increasingly disenchanted with Bordiga's sectarian approach, which elevated ideological and organizational purity above the need to keep in close contact with the masses. In 1924 he wrote:

The error of the Party has been to accord priority in an abstract fashion to the problem of party organization. . . . It was believed, and it is still believed, that the revolution depends solely on the existence of such an apparatus. . . . The Party has not been conceived as the result of a dialectical process, in which the spontaneous movement of the revolutionary masses converges with the organizational and

directive will of the centre, but merely as something suspended in the air, which develops in itself and for itself, and which the masses will join when the situation is propitious and the crest of the revolutionary wave is at its peak, or else when the party centre decides to initiate an offensive and stoops to the level of the masses in order to stimulate them and lead them into action.[80]

Clearly, his belief in the wisdom of the ordinary people never wholly deserted him, even in the years when he behaved like an orthodox Bolshevik. But his concern for mass involvement in the formulation of Party policy became much more pronounced after his imprisonment (although he never revived the conciliar vision). The theory of the revolutionary party that emerges from the *Quaderni* will now be examined in some detail. What follows can be taken as a critique not only of the Togliatti interpretation but also of the *Manifesto* group assertion that Gramsci, in his *Notebooks*, portrayed the Prince as the *sole* interpreter of social reality and truth, that his doctrine detached the party from its social base and obliterated the dialectic between the class and its organizational expression.

Gramsci distinguishes 'three fundamental elements' in any historically significant, or (to use his terminology) 'historically necessary', political party. First, there is 'a diffuse element, composed of ordinary, average men, whose participation takes the form of discipline and loyalty rather than creative spirit or sophisticated organizational ability'.[81] Though Gramsci writes that 'every party is only the nomenclature for a class', he makes a distinction between the social group a party represents and the party itself, which is the group's 'most advanced element'.[82] In one place, he insists that the revolutionary party must be an 'organic fraction of the popular masses'—in other words, 'a vanguard, an élite'.[83] But, assuming these words are to be taken seriously, Gramsci does not construe the notion of 'vanguard' in strict Leninist terms, as excluding all but the most dedicated, self-conscious, and professional activists. For he says that the 'ordinary, average' members are a force only 'in so far as there is someone to centralize, organize, and discipline them'. In the absence of this latter element, 'they would disperse into an impotent diaspora and render themselves null and void'.[84] This brings us to the second element, the 'principle cohesive element', which 'makes effective and powerful a complex of forces which left to themselves would count for little or nothing'. He goes on to say that this section of the party, 'is endowed with great cohesive, centralizing, disciplinary and—indeed, this may be the basis for the others—innovative powers'.[85] It is the highest element, whose function is to create the ferment necessary to transform a social group into a 'political army organically predisposed'.[86] Gramsci underlines the need for imaginative leadership at the top levels when he asserts that 'in reality it is easier to form an army than to form commanders. So much is this true that an already existing army is destroyed if it loses its commanders while a united group of commanders, who are in agreement and have common aims, will not delay in forming an army even where none exists.'[87] Gramsci also postulates the need for 'an intermediate element' in political parties, 'which articulates the first element with the second and maintains contact between them, a contact not only physical, but moral and intellectual'.[88]

At this point, we should stress a major difference between Lenin's organizational model and that of Gramsci. As noted above, Lenin's vision of the revolutionary vanguard comprised only a very small sector of the proletariat. One can justifiably assume that Lenin's party would not have encompassed Gramsci's first element. Still, comparisons here can be misleading, as Gramsci did not intend to lay down rigid, universally applicable rules concerning the internal composition and organization of revolutionary parties. Flexibility is built into his theory and is brought into relief in his discussion and use of the 'theorem of fixed proportions'.[89]

Gramsci uses the theorem as a device to clarify his thought; recourse to it 'has only a schematic and metaphoric value' for the study of human groups and organizations. It cannot, in his view, be applied mechanically to social reality, 'since in human communities the qualitative element (or that of the technical and intellectual capacity of the individual components) is predominant, and this cannot be measured mathematically'.[90] A rough application, however, is revealing, and indicates that a party will become a durable political force, will exercise an 'organic' function as an articulator of popular demands and aspirations, to the extent that it realizes a proportional equilibrium of the 'three fundamental elements' that constitute it.

One commentator suggests that we can usefully translate Gramsci's application of the theorem to political parties into the image of a pyramid with three levels. There is an optimal quantity of mass for each level, which is determined by the existing relationship among the three levels.[91] Thus, 'each change in a single part necessitates a new equilibrium with the whole, . . .'.[92] But, how are we to know when a 'proportional equilibrium' exists in social, as opposed to geometric or scientific, reality? Assuming, as Gramsci does, that social relationships are not quantifiable, only one answer is possible: such an equilibrium exists when the organization or community in question is operating at maximum effectiveness. But 'effectiveness' is a criterion with little descriptive content. Moreover, there is a problem of circularity: 'equilibrium' is a precondition of 'effectiveness'; but the sole criterion for determining 'equilibrium' is 'effectiveness'. It would seem, then, that use of the theorem in this context is of little heuristic or operational value. Nevertheless, Gramsci's 'metaphoric' application of the theorem does drive one important point home. For he declares that 'each social group [class] has its own law of fixed proportions, which varies according to the level of culture, independence of mind, spirit of initiative, sense of responsibility, and degree of discipline of its most backward and peripheral members'.[93] If so, then one cannot specify the composition and structure of the party, or vanguard, that represents a class without taking account of the characteristics of that class, which are in turn conditioned by the social environment. What is controlling in Gramsci's argument is that the optimal size and internal organization of a political party must be determined in accordance with its surrounding social context. Implicit here is the acceptance of even a small conspiratorial organization within *certain limited* contexts (though in such cases the party might not yet be 'organic', i.e. truly representative of the class it claims to embody). But in all cases, the party must have a 'monolithic character' in the sense that it must be based on fundamental values and concerns that unite the leadership and rank and file.[94]

To sum up, Gramsci attempts to theorize an original, pragmatic fusion between the social-democratic conception of a mass party, all-embracing but short on theoretical rigour, and Lenin's élitism, which endeavours to restrict membership to those with a reasonably high level of 'scientific' understanding.

Another aspect of Gramsci's conception of the revolutionary party which distinguishes it from Lenin's is his acceptance of the traditional social-democratic notion of the party as a *state in miniature*.[95] The party anticipates, in its very being, the character of the collective future. (On this point Gramsci has travelled a great distance from the conciliar theory.) The party is more than an external political agent: it is less a force able to attain a result distinct from itself than a germ of this result. But Gramsci believes this to be true of all 'organic' political parties; and, consequently, he does not conceive of parties purely as organizations directed towards political activity (in the narrow sense). A party is, instead, the complex of cultural, social, and political institutions that serve a particular class and world-view. The following passage illustrates how Gramsci uses party in what might be considered a loose and idiosyncratic sense:

One can observe that in the modern world, in many countries, the organic and fundamental parties, for necessity of class struggle or for other reasons, have split into fractions, each of which assumes the name of 'party' and even of independent party. Often, therefore, the intellectual headquarters of the organic party belongs to none of these fractions and operates as if it were a directive force of its own, above the parties, and sometimes is even believed to be so by the public. One can study this function with greater precision if one starts from the point of view that a newspaper (or a group of newspapers), a journal (or group of journals) are also 'parties' or 'fractions of a party' or 'functions of a particular party'. Think of the function of *The Times* in England. . . .'[96]

Elsewhere, in speaking of the liberal 'party' in Italy after 1876, he refers to the 'party as general ideology, superior to the various, more immediate groupings', among which he includes the Popular Party, nationalism, 'a great part of socialism', the democratic radicals, and the conservatives.[97] This broad definition of party, as an ill-defined grouping of those with similar interests and a similar ideology, is not without significance for his conception of the revolutionary party and must guide our understanding of the latter. In other words, his remarks about the communist party must always be viewed in light of what he says about 'organic' parties in general. Definite consequences flow from this canon of interpretation. For, though some textual evidence might be adduced to the contrary, we can reasonably start from the presumption that Gramsci does not, in his prison notebooks, visualize the revolutionary party as an organ (1) subject to tight, singleminded discipline, admitting of no opposition, and (2) geared solely to the over-arching goal of conquering power. Two points are being made here: the first concerns discipline and homogeneity; the second, purpose or function. I shall take up the second point first.

If there was a fundamental change in Gramsci's political thought it consisted in his coming to adopt fully the Leninist belief that bourgeois ideology, in one form or another, 'spontaneously' imposes itself on the working class, simply because it has at its disposal immeasurably more methods of inculcation. While Lenin saw the solution to this problem in political agitation and propaganda, Gramsci conceived the solution in broad ethical and cultural terms. The revolutionary party should not merely lead the masses into battle; it should also endeavour to create and instil in them an all-embracing working-class consciousness. The important distinction, then, lies in the greater emphasis in Gramsci on the party as a moral force; it imparts not simply watered-down theory and tactical directives, but social and cultural values as well. Laying exclusive stress on the political-military struggle and on the task of seizing power, Lenin always regarded cultural activity as ancillary to politics—at least in the pre-revolutionary period. He envisaged the making of the new man *after* the revolution, whereas for Gramsci it was essentially a matter of making him *before* the revolution. This followed naturally from his insistence on building up a counter-hegemony of socialist ideas within the capitalist framework; the proletariat *cannot* make a revolution (in the West) until it has persuaded itself and the bulk of society at large that its vision of the universe is superior to that of the bourgeoisie. An underlying reason for Lenin's narrower conception of the party's role is that he was, to a certain extent, locked in the premises of Second International Marxism. Although willing to grant that the dominant ideology could canalize mass behaviour, he never believed that it could penetrate to the very core of this behaviour, transforming the social unit into a more or less integrated whole. His conception of mass psychology was quite primitive. That capitalist social relations automatically generated great class hostility was a proposition he never questioned and often upheld. The problem, to his mind, was one of raising perennial, pervasive, and unstructured social rebellion to the level of socialist revolution; and for this enterprise strategic guidance and an injection of diluted Marxist theory would suffice.

We come now to the question of homogeneity and discipline. When Gramsci states that the revolutionary party must be 'monolothic',[98] he understands this as monolithic only *in the final analysis*. Hard evidence for such an interpretation can be found in the chapter where he discusses what he means by democratic centralism, which he considers the proper solution to the problem of the relationship between leaders and mass membership. Democratic centralism must be:

. . . a 'centralism' in movement, so to speak; that is, a continual adaptation of the organization to the real movement, a blending of thrusts from below with orders from above, a continual insertion of elements flowing from the depths of the rank and file into the solid framework of the leadership apparatus, which ensures continuity and the regular accumulation of experience. Democratic centralism is 'organic' because it takes account of the movement, of the organic manner in which history reveals itself, and does not rigidify mechanically into bureaucracy; and because at the same time it takes account of that which is relatively stable and permanent. . . .'[99]

Gramsci wishes to extend the sort of relationship Lenin considered appropriate only within a small élite (and then only under certain conditions) to the entire movement. Indulging his fondness for apparently inappropriate analogies, Gramsci employs (within the space of a single paragraph) the images of both an organism and an orchestra to highlight the need for the active, direct participation of all members of the movement, 'even if this creates an appearance of tumult and disintegration'. A collective consciousness, he holds, 'is a living organism. It does not form until multiplicity is unified through the friction of individual atoms . . . an orchestra in rehearsal, every instrument rendering its own account, gives the most horrific impression of cacophony; and yet those experiments are the conditions of the orchestra living like one "instrument".'[100] To ignore these considerations is to risk the development of 'fetishism' where the party becomes 'a phantasmagoric entity . . . a species of autonomous divinity'.[101] In such a situation, democratic centralism has given way to its degenerate form—'bureaucratic centralism', where the leaders have turned into 'a narrow clique which tends to perpetuate its selfish privileges by controlling or even by prohibiting the birth of oppositional forces'.[102] Thus, the party becomes *ipso facto* 'regressive, . . . a police organ', which does not deserve the appellation of political party.[103] Was Gramsci referring to the USSR? To be sure, he does not mention Stalin in this context and casts his argument in a very general form. Still, there is one passage which indicates that he had Soviet Communism in mind. Noting that all ruling parties use force to protect the established order, he distinguishes between 'regressive' and 'progressive' exercises of this repressive function:

It is progressive when it tends to keep dispossessed reactionary forces within the bounds of legality and to raise the backward masses to the level of the new legality. It is regressive when it tends to restrain the living forces of history and to maintain an outdated, anti-historical legality that has become an empty shell.[104]

The reference to 'dispossessed reactionary forces' gives the game away. Gramsci's tolerance towards 'oppositional forces' stands in marked contrast to the views he expressed in the 1924–6 period, when he denounced factions as 'incompatible with the essence of the proletarian party' and even proposed the suppression of 'those who weaken the compactness of the party'.[105] We can only speculate about the reasons for his change of heart, but despair over Stalin's brutal way with 'the living forces of history' was, one surmises, prominent among them.

Other Marxist thinkers, like Luxemburg and Trotsky, had articulated a fear of bureaucracy in the revolutionary party, but Gramsci was the first to confront bureaucracy as a *universal* problem. In a manner similar to that of Michels, he perceived that bureaucracy has a natural tendency to rigidify, to become preoccupied with its own maintenance, and to impede the development of dynamic energies from below. He declares that 'one of the most important questions regarding the political party' is 'the capacity of the party to react against the spirit of custom, against the tendency to become mummified and anachronistic'. Continuing this line of argument, he refers to bureaucracy as 'the most dangerous hidebound and conservative force; if it ends up by constituting a compact body, which stands on its own and feels itself independent of the mass membership, the party becomes anachronistic, and in moments of acute crisis, it is emptied of its social content and remains as though suspended in mid-air'. The chief danger Gramsci has in mind is that of Right-wing mobilization of mass discontent during periods of economic crisis. In this connection, he mentions the impotence of German liberal and socialist parties in the face of Nazism,[106] but his words also apply, we can safey assume, to the rise of Italian Fascism.

Gramsci's aversion to 'bureaucratic centralism' did not of course lead him to deny or diminish the *centralist* component of democratic centralism. He simply wanted to make certain that his organizational principle remained 'an elastic formula . . ., which comes alive in so far as it is interpreted and continually adapted to necessity'. The practical application of Marxist theory must be 'experimental, and not the result of a rationalistic, deductive, abstract process—that is, one proper to pure intellectuals (or pure donkeys)'.[107] The party must strive towards unity, but this demands vigour, which in turn requires mass participation, a free and open confrontation of ideas, a constant process of critical research and political invention, and an appreciation of the complexity of different political situations. Democratic centralism must be liberated from the mechanical and schematic application of abstract formulae.

This openness to initiatives originating in the mass movement, this hostility to the imposition of timeless recipes, is remindful not of Lenin (the man who invented democratic centralism but gave it such a narrow reference) but of Marx. Lenin's ideas may have varied with circumstances, but from 1902 onwards, his conception of the party, as revealed in *both* his writings and his practice, displayed a certain consistency and eventually became the unchallenged model for International Bolshevism. According to this model (which, it must be underlined, does not square with *all* of Lenin's published statements), the revolutionary élite alone embodies the auto-negation of the proletariat, the transcendence of its immediacy. This élite alone has deciphered history's true meaning. Taking their cue (ironically) from Kautsky, Lenin and his followers reduced revolutionary consciousness to the science of an objectified reality, produced exclusively on the intellectual level. Because of its profound scientific knowledge, the Marxist vanguard represents the authentic proletarian world-view, irrespective of what the real, empirical proletariat may think. Indeed, their *actual* consciousness appears as an impediment, a primitive state to be overcome, and never as a source of theoretical reflection. In its omniscience, the revolutionary priesthood has the duty of galvanizing the working class, full of discontent but ideologically unreliable, into action. Lenin's notorious contempt for mass organization was the logical consequence of his belief that the aims and interests of the proletariat could (and must) be determined without that class having a say in the matter. The political arm of the proletariat was to be a 'bureaucratic' structure, 'built from the top downwards',[108] a tightly disciplined organization of professional revolutionaries, who— by virtue of their scientific expertise—would impart form to the formless masses. The party, in sum, was depicted as an exclusive sect, steeled by doctrinal certitude, distant from, and effectively indifferent to, the everyday life of the masses. For Marx, on the contrary, revolutionary science was not autonomous, conceived and defined independently of class praxis; it was not knowledge of an objectified world, purified of all subjectivity and separated from historical development. Marx, as we have seen, maintained no sharp opposition between the party, as the formulator of revolutionary consciousness, on the one hand, and the working class on the other. The truth the party represents and elaborates must be developed in dialectical connection with the life of the class and permanently subject to change and reformulation.

Similarly with Gramsci, the revolutionary intellectual, in relation to the proletariat, does not so much illuminate the path to revolution with the light of science as perform a mediating role between the social immediacy of the proletariat and scientific culture in the broadest sense. Practice must be seen as exercising an influence on theory, by posing new problems and by bringing into question some of the propositions of the theory. Underlying all his work was a desire to avoid the arid extremes of both élitism and 'spontaneism'. He attached great importance to a close relationship between the mass and the revolutionary élite, to a 'unity between spontaneity and conscious direction'.[109] The relationship between the 'intellectual strata and the popular masses' must be analogous to that between theory and practice.[110] The activity of the party is to be ceaselessly confronted with the experience of the workers. Marxist doctrine must be fused with the actual content of working people's consciousness. Ways must be found of reaching the masses in terms of *their* ideas, *their* aspirations, *their* reality. The desired result is 'a reciprocal relationship' in which 'every teacher is always a pupil and every pupil a teacher'.[111] While revolutionary consciousness, for Gramsci, is not something inherent in proletarian experience, neither is it something that is simply injected into the masses from without; rather, it is to be, in large measure, mobilized from 'within', by drawing upon and shaping the spontaneous impulses, insights, and energies of the masses themselves. Though the party may be a vanguard which expresses the development towards universality, it is not the possessor of scientific truth established *ab initio* and simply applied in various ways to different historical situations; it represents instead the mechanism for elaborating a type of truth which is continuously subject to self-criticism. The party's educative role is seen as concrete development not as the authoritarian imposition of an *a priori* schema, of a doctrinaire truth established in principle and valid for all time. There is no possibility of any pre-fixed conception independent of political struggle. The party theoreticians must '"translate" into theoretical language the elements of historical life. It is not reality which should be expected to conform to the abstract schema.'[112]

This is what Gramsci termed the historicity of Marxism. In his *Quaderni*, Gramsci uses Labriola's phrase 'philosophy of *praxis*' to characterize Marxism, not simply because of a prudent fear of prison censorship (in other passages he uses the much more compromising, 'historical materialism'); but because he conceives of Marxism as a conception founded on praxis, and it is in practice that its very assumptions are validated:

Mass adhesion or non-adhesion to an ideology is the real critical test of the rationality and historicity of modes of thought. Arbitrary constructions are more or less rapidly eliminated by historical competition, even if sometimes, through a combination of immediately favourable circumstances, they succeed in enjoying a certain popularity; whereas constructions which correspond to the needs of a complex and organic historical period, always impose themselves and prevail in the end, . . .[113]

The link between Gramsci's political thought and his basic philosophical doctrines is here evident. 'Objective always means "humanly objective", which corresponds exactly to . . . "universal subjective"'.[114] It is meaningless, in his opinion, to speculate about an 'external', 'objective' reality (be it transcendental or mechanical) whose truth is a matter independent of whether it is known or believed. Practice, then, is the only basis for moral and political evaluation. The proof of a body of thought lies in its becoming historically effective. Historically 'rational' or 'necessary' or 'real'[115] ideologies, or conceptions of the world, are theoretical formulations capable of penetrating deeply into men's practical lives, and hence of animating and inspiring an entire historical epoch, by providing men with rules of practical conduct. Gramsci opposes such ideologies to 'arbitrary' constructions by maintaining that the former 'have a validity which is "psychological"; they organize human masses, and form the terrain on which men move, acquire consciousness of their position, struggle, etc.'[116] He continually refers to Marx's *Theses on Feurbach* to document the necessity of a unity between theory and practice, which for him carries the implication that concepts and ideas have value only in so far as they are concretized. The validity of a political or ethical statement is, on this view, inseparable from, though not identifiable with, its communicative power: an assertion which convinces no one has no value.[117] Marxism's 'scientific' validity, argued Gramsci, consists in the historical functions it performs, not in its supposed capacity to discover the 'objective', 'extra-human' laws of history. This, he believed, was a salutary point to make in an era when the 'philosophy of praxis', due to the outpourings of people like Bukharin, had become 'a dogmatic system of eternal and absolute truths'.[118]

Within the Marxist framework, Gramsci's position was indeed quite radical. The philosophy of praxis, according to him, was not a scientific world-view in the sense in which Marxists employed the term, i.e. a world-view that reflected reality as it was, regardless of whether we knew it or not. It has been rightly said that Gramsci goes well beyond Marx in his relativization of historical materialism itself. Marx, it is true, did not picture the doctrine as an autonomous science, severed from the real activity of the masses. At the same time, he never doubted that the general validity of his theory was affirmed by scientific analysis of historical development, not by popular consent. Indeed, the possibility of mass rejection did not figure at all in Marx's optimistic perspective. Thus, he was able to ignore the relativistic implications of his second Thesis on Feurbach:

The question whether human thinking can pretend to objective truth is not a theoretical but a *practical* question. Man must prove the truth, i.e. the reality and power, the 'this-sidedness' of his thinking, in practice.[119]

Operating within different political circumstances, Gramsci was moved to raise this observation to a justification for 'absolute historicism, the absolute terrestrialness of thought',[120] which entails the claim that no theoretical system enjoys absolute, eternal validity. All, including Marxism, must be continually submitted to the test of emerging socio-historical conditions. Against those Marxists who longed for a world of fixed categories, a world freed from doubt, he insisted on a healthy scepticism: the philosophy of praxis, he contended, must entertain the possibility that it will be superseded or else fail to prove its 'rationality'.

One wonders how Gramsci could square his conception of socio-political truth with his professed faith in natural science. For a belief or doctrine which enjoys mass acceptance and meets certain psychological needs may none the less embody claims about the universe which are, from a scientific point of view, patently false. What concerns us here, however, is not the worth of his epistemological standpoint but its political implications. As I hope I have demonstrated, Gramsci's insistence on a 'reciprocal relationship' between mass and élite, his rejection of any notion of an omniscient vanguard, had solid philosophical foundations. To reiterate, he favours the formation of a revolutionary vanguard but it must be linked 'organically' to the popular masses if it is not to degenerate into a pseudo-aristocracy. How is this 'reciprocal relationship' or 'organic link' to be effected in practice? Gramsci never dealt with this problem consecutively or at length, but he did provide scattered, lamentably underdeveloped, indications. In his years as a PCI activist, he advocated a revised version of the councils, now no longer autonomous from the party, as one means of cementing such a relationship. Though he scarcely mentioned factory councils in his notebooks, he did make a favourable reference to the old *Ordine Nuovo* group's attitude towards spontaneity, thus suggesting that he still believed the councils could serve a positive, if subordinate, function.[121] He also addressed himself, in the *Quaderni*, to the possibilities of socialist publications, which could provide not only an alternative means of socialization but also a forum for the exchange of opinions and the airing of mass grievances.[122] But perhaps most important in producing a dialectical unity between mass and élite is the role of the 'organic' intellectuals. It is the party intellectuals who arise out of the proletariat, who are connected to it by familial and institutional attachments, who express its way of life—it is these individuals who will keep the party in touch with its roots.[123] Of course, the new-type intellectual must not be a mere brain-worker. Rather he should concern himself with 'active involvement in practical life, as constructor, organizer, permanent persuader . . .'.[124] If the aim of Marxism 'is a philosophy which is also politics and a politics which is also philosophy',[125] then the organic intellectuals of the proletariat are truly the harbingers of the noble future.

All in all, while the party is to be a disciplined, semi-élite and hierarchical organization (or system of organizations), it constantly strives to enlist mass support and activity and to solicit initiatives from below. We may conclude, with Davidson, that the 'displacement of the problem of revolution in the West from the party (theory) and the masses (practice) to the relations and links between them is what constitutes Gramsci's novelty . . .'[126]—at least with respect to his theory of the party. We might also note how this theory blends together insights from various sources. Croce's wish for cultural renewal is combined with Machiavelli's fascination for 'the political'; Sorel's theory of spontaneous proletarian morality with Lenin's practice of disciplined party leadership.

CHAPTER 5

Proletarian Hegemony and the Question of Authoritarianism

'The truth must always be respected, whatever consequence it may bring.'
Gramsci, 'La conferenza e la verità,
Avanti!, 19 February 1916

I. *Hegemony and Party Dictatorship: the PCI Line*

IF THE analysis in the foregoing chapter is essentially correct, if the theory of the revolutionary party implicit in Gramsci's *Quaderni* points to structures and procedures more democratic than those of the Leninist model, then it is reasonable to argue that Gramsci was aiming at an alternative path to the communist future, one avoiding the police-state methods generally associated with the phrase, 'dictatorship of the proletariat', a phrase absent from his prison vocabulary.[1] This line of argument seems especially persuasive when we consider the logic of his concept of hegemony, which cautions that revolution in the West must be *preceded* by a radical transformation in mass consciousness. Whatever its merits, however, such an interpretation of Gramsci's enterprise has not enjoyed universal acceptance; indeed, it has been common to view his doctrine of the party (and the theory of hegemony of which it is part and parcel) as strictly Leninist or even Stalinist. We have already noted that the orthodox PCI line, particularly during Togliatti's lifetime, has been to identify Gramsci with Lenin. What this has usually amounted to has been a purchase of revolutionary legitimation at the price of submerging Gramsci's originality. There is a historical dimension worth looking at here. The Party (not to mention Togliatti's reputation) acquired in the course of its development a vested interest in its Leninist heritage, the reinforcement of which required the enlistment of Gramsci's enormous prestige. Especially before the war, the Party's and Togliatti's futures depended upon the maintenance of strong ties with Moscow, and historical accuracy often suffered as a result. For instance, in the lengthy and rather mawkish appreciation which Togliatti wrote in the Party's journal following the death of Gramsci, he was concerned to stress the profound influence exerted on Gramsci's thinking by that of Stalin.[2] After the war, with the emergence of the Party's novel '*Via Italiana*' strategy, such gross distortion could be avoided, and it became possible (if not necessary) to depict Gramsci, more realistically, as a thinker and politician national in his inspiration and orientation, as the author of a 'new perspective of development, of redemption, and of resurrection for Italy'.[3] But the old identifications, while modified, could not easily be thrown overboard and still served a crucial legitimizing function. Indeed, the need for the Party constantly to reaffirm its Leninist bearing became perhaps even more pressing as it consorted with heresy in its pursuit of national and parliamentary policies.

In order—it could be argued—to divert attention from this manifest incompatibility between Party theory and practice, Togliatti resolutely suppressed Gramsci's intimations of an alternative mode of communism and construed 'hegemony' as a mere adjunct to the dictatorship of the proletariat: 'Is there for Gramsci a difference . . . between the terms hegemony and dictatorship? There is a difference but not one of substance.' For Togliatti's Gramsci, every state is a dictatorship and every dictatorship presupposes a minimal consensual element.[4] The prison notebooks, it would seem, tell us nothing that would disturb Lenin's present angle of repose. In an earlier piece, another Party writer confronted the obvious and awkward fact that the *Quaderni* repeatedly accentuate the moment of consent, but he attributed it, in cavalier fashion, to 'a series of practical reasons, not least among which was the necessity of coming to terms with prison censorship, . . .'.[5]

As the Italian Communists have moved towards their 'historic compromise' with the forces of Catholicism and liberal capitalism, the Soviet connection has become something of a liability. This factor, along with Togliatti's death, has made possible a more 'democratic' interpretation of Gramsci. To take

one example, Alessandro Natta, writing in the PCI's chief
cultural journal in 1971, declared that Gramsci went well
beyond Lenin, that 'the formula of war of position not only
signals a different timing, but a different strategic terrain, a
different vision of the revolution'. It is not simply a matter of
varying or correcting the Bolshevik model to suit new circumstances, for this would ignore the 'historicity' of socialist
strategy. Hegemony thus becomes, according to Natta, the
'capacity and will for democratic direction and national unity'.[6]

By adopting an historicist analysis of our own, and relating
Communist theoretical positions to concrete and changing
political imperatives, we could easily dismiss the 'hard line
Bolshevik' portrait of Gramsci as transparent mystification, of
little interest to serious scholarship. But the prominence enjoyed
by this or similar interpretations in the exegetical literature
produced by *opponents* of the PCI precludes any such dismissal.

II. *Gramsci as Stalinist Totalitarian*

It is worth stressing that, when PCI theoreticians minimized
the consensual, democratic element in Gramsci's thought, they
did not intend this as a condemnation—far from it. Others who
concentrate on the 'authoritarian' side of Gramsci are not so
complimentary: in fact, some accuse him of advocating a
totalitarianism so extreme that it would shame even his Fascist
tormentors. Roughly, those who represent Gramsci as, basically,
a 'Stalinist' tend to fall into two categories: (1) Trotskyists,
Bordiga revivalists, worker control enthusiasts and other theoreticians associated with the far (beyond the PCI) Left; and (2)
social democrats, liberals, and humanists of many varieties,
who, despite their obvious differences, are united by their
common spatial positioning to the right of the Communist
Party on the ideological continuum.

The ultra-Left critics cluster around a number of theoretical-
cum-polemical organs, including *Il Manifesto*, *Giovane critica*,
Quaderni piacentini, *Nuovo impegno*, and *Rivista storica del socialismo*.
If it is appropriate to venture a generalization about how
this heterogeneous collection of disaffected intellectuals view
Gramsci, we can say that they have been mainly concerned to
attack his alleged 'idealism' and 'revisionism', not his 'Stalinism'—though the latter form of criticism is often implicit and

sometimes quite explicit. In particular, the *Manifesto* group, a probable exception to our generalization, was preoccupied with the notion that Gramsci 'betrayed' the worker movement by substituting for his youthful infatuation with factory councils an authoritarian conception of party rule. But perhaps the most memorable and well-known 'Left' assault on Gramsci's so-called 'authoritarianism' was levelled by Stefano Merli in an influential article in *Giovane critica*. Merli, who can be viewed as a typical 'Left' critic, situates Gramsci unequivocally within the Stalinist framework, claiming to find in the Sardinian thinker a bureaucratic conception of power—an exaltation of party leaders and an undervaluation of the class, a denial of its 'personality as an aggregate collective'. Gramsci, continues Merli, was 'the translator, the founder in Italy, of Bolsheviza-tion, the instrument and animating impulse of the gigantic and international Stalinist operation'. Moreover, Gramsci's re-current condemnations of bureaucratic centralism were merely formal, an external façade of democracy, peripheral to his real intentions. All appearances to the contrary, then, Gramsci was guilty, in both word and deed, of 'bureaucratic-authoritarian paternalism', of subordinating the class to the whims of the party chieftains.[7]

It is hard to take seriously an argument which rejects Gramsci's very words as irrelevant to a proper understanding of his thought. Certainly Merli's interpretation would seem to be contradicted, or at least substantially weakened, by the evidence marshalled in the previous chapter. One can only repeat what Gramsci actually said: that bureaucratic centralism is a pathological condition which must be counterposed to demo-cratic (i.e. healthy) centralism, the free and, to some extent, spontaneous formation of a collective consciousness. In his *Quaderni*, Gramsci sets himself against any attempt to stifle or control oppositional forces within the movement; and it has often been claimed, with justification, that these remarks con-stituted a veiled criticism of the existing form of Soviet party. Why, then, has Merli (and those of like mind) so arbitrarily consigned Gramsci to the Stalinist dung-hill? The answer to this question certainly lies in his opposition, during his spell as PCI leader, to Bordiga and the ultra-Left in general. This hardly disposes of the matter, however, since Gramsci's 'Right' critics are not exactly distinguished by an uncritical enthusiasm for Bordiga or Trotsky. Though starting from different assumptions and proceeding along different logical paths, these commentators arrive at conclusions remarkably similar to those of the extra-parliamentary Left.

Those who censure Gramsci from the Right make a number of characteristic claims, which can be summarized as follows:

(1) Gramsci's thought is rent by an internal contradiction, by the conflict between his explicit recognition of the need for liberty and a 'totalitarian' element, impregnated with Stalinism, of party tutelage and censorship. As Aldo Garosci puts it in his widely read essay, 'Totalitarismo e storicismo nel pensiero di Antonio Gramsci', 'the tenor of [Gramsci's] philosophy and of his political programme has . . . a dual character: totalitarian-tyrannical and liberal'.[8] Hegemony, his central idea, is thus Janus-faced: on the one hand it requires autonomy of thought and expression, and on the other it subordinates all liberty to party *diktat*.[9]

(2) The tension between the two irreconcilable strands in Gramsci's thought ultimately resolves itself in favour of totalitarianism: in Gramsci's jargon, the moment of force comes to take precedence over the moment of consent. To quote Garosci again: 'In reality . . . the "hegemonic" moment is achieved . . . in the creation of a massive hierarchy.' In the final analysis, hegemony represents an 'element truly illiberal and theological' in Gramsci's thought, implying a closed society where intellectual, social, and political forces must submit to iron organization.[10] The 'nucleus of Gramsci's ideals' is, in a word, 'totalitarianism'.[11] Another respected commentator, Buzzi, is even more emphatic. In his eyes, Gramsci's ideas culminate in a justification for 'absolutism' and 'arbitrary totalitarianism'.[12] Turning to the literature in English, we find equally harsh judgements. While recognizing the ambiguities in Gramsci's thinking, Lichtheim asserts that, ultimately, the great martyr of Italian Communism 'went on to develop a doctrine more totalitarian than that of his gaolers . . .';[13] and in much the same key, H. Stuart Hughes downgrades hegemony to a 'euphemism . . . a totalitarian thought . . . clothed in liberal guise'.[14]

(3) The root of Gramsci's totalitarianism, the fatal flaw in his conception, lies in his entrusting the creation of the new society to an 'enlightened' élite, in his apotheosis of the party as the 'infallible head' of the worker movement.[15] On this view, hegemony, which purports to synthesize liberty and authority, becomes 'a weapon in the hands of the party-State, which desires to "mould" the masses to an ideology. . . . Since the subordinate social class is the carrier of universal truth, its hegemony, visible in the party-State, will thus always be incontestable, thereby justifying authoritarianism and totalitarianism. . . . In a conflict between authority and liberty, it is always authority, the party, that decides . . . .'[16] Rodolfo Mondolfo, Gramsci's most prominent socialist critic, puts the point succinctly: 'To place the "Prince" on the throne of popular veneration can only lead to totalitarianism.'[17] What finally emerges from Gramsci's prison notes on politics, the argument runs, is one overpowering and uncomfortable fact: the individual is nothing and the party everything. The constructive will, whose need Gramsci so passionately feels and affirms, is that of a resolute minority, a Jacobin/Bolshevik élite, not that of the proletariat. Confident of its rectitude and inspired by its mission, the party develops into the 'absolute historical subject excluding all rivalry', and consequently 'nullifies the autonomy of individuals'.[18] Gramsci's noblest sentiments succumb to the fundamental incompatibility between his avowed goal (socialism and the full development of individuality) and the means he elaborates for attaining that goal (the Modern Prince). Like Rousseau and Marx before him, this sincere preacher of human liberation is transmuted, by the uncompromising passion of his millenarian dream, into an exemplar of the totalitarian abyss.

Unlike their opposite numbers on the political spectrum, Gramsci's 'Right' critics generally have the merit of buttressing their arguments with textual evidence. Such testimony is not difficult to find. Scattered about Gramsci's *Quaderni* are passages which lend themselves to a 'totalitarian' interpretation. Gramsci himself was fond of pointing out that his own vision of the future was 'totalitarian' (though the meaning he ascribed to this term is rather unusual, as we shall see below). Gramsci's aim, it will be recalled, was the perfect unification of theory and practice, the elimination of social and intellectual disharmonies and contradictions—the creation of an 'integral hegemony' of the highest order. The party, as the supreme agency of integration, the concrete embodiment of the unity of theory and practice, must impose order on a latently, and sometimes manifestly, chaotic situation. As such, its politics must be 'totalitarian' and seek:

(1) to ensure that the members . . . find in [it] all the satisfactions that they previously found in a multiplicity of organizations; that is, to break all the ties that link these members to external cultural organisms; (2) to destroy all the other organizations, or to incorporate them in a system of which the party is the sole regulator.[19]

The party must be a 'religion', the focus of an 'absolute laicism'.[20] In discussing criteria for the new morality, Gramsci proclaims, in almost lyrical tones, that 'any given act is [to be] conceived as useful or as harmful, as virtuous or as wicked, only in so far as it has as its point of reference the Modern Prince itself, and helps to strengthen or oppose it. In men's consciences the Prince takes the place of the divinity or the categorical imperative . . .'.[21] That is to say, the party becomes the ultimate referent of existence: all aspects of life, every manner of endeavour, must defer to its will. Moreover, he hopes to see 'a new conformism', which 'will permit new possibilities for self-discipline, that is, freedom. . .'.[22] Liberty, Gramsci believed, does not primarily entail the availability of choice or the existence of an inviolate 'private space'; men are truly free when they act rationally, unencumbered by the bourgeois veil of ignorance and illusion, and when their ends fit into a harmonious, universal pattern.[23] Accordingly, when he discusses cultural freedom in the new society, he allows 'that individual initiatives might be disciplined and ordered in such a way that they must pass through the sieve of academies or cultural institutes of various kinds and only become public after having undergone a process of selection'.[24] Mondolfo correctly observes that Gramsci here seems to be justifying preventive censure— preliminary elimination of ideas uncongenial to the party.[25]

And then there are the élitist implications of his oft-quoted remark that 'in the masses . . . philosophy must be lived as faith'.[26] If so, say Gramsci's opponents, how can ordinary

people ever become the subject of history? Are they not condemned to remain the object of an intellectual priesthood
ordained to formulate their needs?[27] This image of élitism and
condescension is reinforced by an observation Gramsci makes
on the following page, when discussing methods for changing
public opinion: '. . . repetition is the best didactic means for
working on the popular mentality'. Is *this* mentality, it may be
asked, the raw material for 'a superior . . . form of modern
civilization'?[28] Neither is Gramsci's brief essay on 'State
Worship' likely to reassure his critics. 'For some social groups',
he writes, 'which before their ascent to autonomous state life
have not had a long period of independent cultural and moral
development . . . ., a period of state worship is necessary and
indeed advisable.'[29]

III. *Criticism*

It is my intention in what follows to defend a 'democratic'
interpretation of Gramsci; but, at the outset, I must concede
that he was no liberal—certainly not in the twentieth-century
sense (though I think it can be shown that he shared certain
liberal attitudes). To judge the rightness of acts on strict utilitarian criteria, to elevate an institution, and the collective,
above the individual, to equate freedom with self-discipline, to
wish to negate the multiplicity of social groupings and institutions by harnessing them to a common purpose—all this is to
depart from conventional liberalism in the most fundamental
way. But, as I shall argue, the alternative to liberalism is not
necessarily authoritarianism.

By way of preliminaries, certain misconceptions and
methodological weaknesses underlying the 'Stalinist' interpretation of Gramsci should be exposed. The first relates to
Gramsci's often misleading terminology, one example of which
merits our attention here. Let us look at his employment of the
word 'totalitarian'. While Gramsci does indeed call his doctrine
'totalitarian', he does not use this adjective in the now accepted
sense, which conjures up images of systematic repression—of
absolutism and despotism, fanatical statism and popular de-
gradation. For Gramsci, totalitarianism is more a matter of
cultural unity than of political organization: a world-view is
totalitarian if it is comprehensive, that is, capable of affecting

and integrating an 'entire society down to its deepest roots'.[30] Every philosophy (or ideology) is totalitarian in so far as it endeavours to provide an account, however disjointed and open-ended, of all reality. Using the term in this way, Gramsci views liberalism as totalitarian, for it has brought an intellectual and moral revolution to fruition and permeated all elements of life in Western society. Often, when he speaks of totalitarianism, he apparently thinks he is merely registering an inescapable reality of the highly integrated modern world ushered in by the bourgeoisie.[31]

However, Gramsci also uses 'totalitarianism' in ways which clearly distinguish it from liberalism, inasmuch as he conceives it not simply as a philosophical/cultural concept, but also as an institutional fact (denoting a system in which particularistic forms of organization disappear or are openly absorbed into one movement) and as a psychological fact (a single-minded, selfless devotion to the construction of a new way of life, immersion in the realm of the political, a complete assimilation of socialist ideas and behaviour). Such notions may be unsettling and dangerous, but *in themselves* they neither necessitate nor justify arbitrary despotism. It might be objected, with some plausibility, that a free society cannot impose a common purpose without degenerating into authoritarianism. But, while this may stand as an empirical likelihood it is hardly a logical entailment. We must take care to distinguish between a theory or an idea that is authoritarian *in principle* and one that is liable to authoritarian abuse *in practice*. Put another way, it is both fallacious and unhistorical to substitute for an author's thought the consequences that may be non-logically deduced from it.[32] Studies of Rousseau, Hegel, and Marx have in the past suffered from this fallacy, and there is no denying that it helps to nourish the 'Stalinist' interpretation of Gramsci. Still, it might further be objected that the desire to fit all social life into a single purpose is indeed absolutist *in principle*. Whether or not this is the case, I believe, depends on the precise nature of the common purpose. Gramsci's critics do not seem to understand that a call for social unity and discipline need not be construed as a demand for régimentation and suppression of all diversity. And, as I hope to show clearly in a moment, the proletarian hegemony which fired Gramsci's imagination was open, expansive, and critical. He perceived a connection between totalitarianism and despotism but thought it only *contingent*;[33] on the other hand, totalitarianism was, in his eyes, *necessarily* linked with (in fact a prerequisite of) genuine consent and self-autonomy, which could only be achieved when the burden of past cultures was shaken off and a true collective unity took root. In conclusion, then, a favourable disposition towards totalitarianism, on Gramsci's usage, by no means entails or implies approval of Stalinist or fascist methods.

In reflecting on Gramsci's sometimes singular use of language, one is reminded of a comment by Rousseau—whose intensely personal style also got him into trouble with his readers—in a letter to Madame d'Epinay: 'Learn my vocabulary better, my good friend, if you would have us understand each other. Believe me my terms rarely have the common meaning; . . .'[34] All major political thinkers, in varying degrees, push against the boundaries of existing linguistic material: they attempt to stretch language to express new ideas. Speaking more generally, in none of the protean concepts used in political discourse does an unambiguous meaning simply inhere, governed only by its degree of correspondence with some unchanging reality. No doubt these are truisms, but their implications are often lost on intellectual historians.

Historians of past ideas are also in the—not entirely avoidable—habit of wrenching quotations out of context in order to bolster their often one-sided preconceptions. Those who represent Gramsci as a totalitarian (in the pejorative sense) carry this practice to an unacceptable extreme. The rhetorical power of many of Gramsci's more memorable utterances obscures the fact that they were often only elliptical pronouncements (sometimes put forward hypothetically), reflecting his recognition of the need for leadership and organization. Such pronouncements must be assessed in the context both of the surrounding argument and of his expressed desire to dissociate himself from all forms of anarchism, 'spontaneism', and utopianism.

To some extent, the supposedly authoritarian strand in his thought points merely to his realism. Gramsci had a feeling for the moral dilemma of politics: he was painfully aware of the anguishing element in the political condition, and from Machiavelli learned that a political actor, even with the best of intentions, must be part beast in order to survive. To put the point more literally, no society, even the most liberal, has been free from élite domination and repression in some shape or form, and Gramsci did not shrink from the implications of this fact. To underline the ubiquity of power relationships, as we do here, is neither to suggest that all societies are equally repressive nor to sanction the more extreme manifestations of social control. It is only to make the obvious point that political discourse, under present conditions at any rate, must revolve around the types, limits, and purposes of social regulation, not its elimination. This being the case, to recoil with horror at any mention of social intervention which does not entirely square with the liberal catechism not only hints at intellectual dishonesty; it also hinders serious debate of some of the most vital questions facing a discordant and troubled world, where the old categories carry little conviction. The liberal solution to the intricate problem of how best to maintain individual autonomy and dignity, in a setting where social control is unavoidable, need not be the only one. That Gramsci, unlike most other Marxists, was sensitive to the subtle nuances of this problem is itself interesting. We should bear in mind that he was working within an intellectual ambience saturated with the 'findings' of élite theory—among them, the hideous effectiveness of manipulation, the widespread prevalence of ignorance and apathy, the dehumanizing effect of mass culture. Rather than ignore or simply reject these observations, Gramsci chose to accommodate them, to confront the arduous problem of *developing* the conditions of socialism.[35] And he began from the standpoint that a fundamental axiom of politics *as it then existed* was the distinction between rulers and ruled. All political thought, he maintained, had to be grounded in this concrete reality:

The first element [of politics] is that there really do exist rulers and ruled, leaders and led. The entire science and art of politics is based on this primordial and (in certain general conditions)[36] irreducible fact. . . . Given this fact, it will have to be considered how one can lead most effectively (given certain ends). . . .[37]

Examined in this light, his remarks to the effect that the masses can only experience philosophy as faith, lose all the sinister connotations attributed to them. Far from expressing a prefer-

ence for élitism, they suggest a realistic perception of an un-
desirable (and hopefully transitory) situation. To be sure,
immediately after he asserts that 'repetition is the best didactic
means for working on the popular mentality', he exhorts revolutionary intellectuals 'to work incessantly to raise the intellectual
level of evergrowing strata of the populace, . . . ' .[38]

Likewise, when firmly located in their textual context,
Gramsci's observations on state worship seem rather harmless.
Intended, perhaps, as a retrospective comment on the October
revolution, they can be understood as encompassing only those
underdeveloped countries, such as Russia, where revolution is
possible *before* the development of a proletarian hegemony. In
addition, he takes pains to stress that state worship 'must not be
abandoned to itself, must not, especially, become theoretical
fanaticism and come to be conceived as perpetual: it must be
criticized . . .'.[39]

A parallel observation can be made concerning his notes on
intellectual freedom. Just before he throws out the idea—very
tentatively, it should be noted—that a certain degree of preventive censorship might be desirable, he tells us that: 'It seems
necessary to leave the task of searching for new truths, and
better, more coherent, clearer formulations of these truths, to
the free initiative of individual scholars, even though they may
continually question the principles that seem most essential.'[40]
Once again, when read in the context of the argument in which
it is embedded, one of Gramsci's 'authoritarian' propositions is
balanced by a more emphatic libertarian one, and the overall
picture conveyed by his treatment of cultural freedom in this
section is that of a cautious thinker, sincerely grappling with the
enduring problem of adjusting individual expression with com-
munal needs. (Have not liberals, at one time or another, con-
templated or even favoured the suppression of points of view
considered disruptive or beyond the pale?)

Indeed, a careful and sympathetic reading of Gramsci,
especially one concerned more with the spirit than the letter of
his essentially provisional writings, would discern the workings
of a mind obsessed, not by authority and command, but by the
need for human liberation—economic, political, and, above all,
spiritual. Gramsci's critics do not weigh the evidence properly:
they do less than justice to the generally open, non-sectarian,

humane, and democratic thrust of his thought. Let me be more explicit.

Gramsci's discussion of the future society was vague and generalized. Like Marx, he was more interested in the process by which revolution would come about than in what society would look like after the revolution. None the less, Gramsci does provide some indications. Lying at the core of his thinking was the vision of a non-coercive society, which for him meant the disappearance of political society, with its 'authoritarian coercive interventions', and the emergence of 'civil society' as self-regulative.[41] The end he sought was always 'catharsis', the leap from the realm of necessity to the realm of freedom, which would witness the utmost flowering of human diversity.[42] Accordingly, it was his intention that eventually every man should develop his abilities to the point where he is capable of shaping his own destiny, of contributing actively to the decisions which affect his life. 'Is it preferable', Gramsci asks, 'to "think" uncritically . . . or is it preferable to elaborate one's own conception of the world consciously and critically . . . and in connection with the activity of one's own mind, to choose one's own sphere of activity, to participate actively in the production of world history, to be one's own ruler and not to accept passively and supinely the externality imprinted on one's own personality?'[43] Needless to say, his own answer is clear. Freedom, for him, is not just a matter of behaving 'rationally'; it is also a matter of self-determination and individual autonomy. Elsewhere he contrasts the philosophy of praxis with Catholicism, by emphasizing that the former 'does not aim to maintain the simple folk in their primitive philosophy of common sense but instead to lead them to a higher conception of life'. The goal should be the 'intellectual progress of the masses and not only of scarce intellectual groups'.[44] The new hegemony will be progressive only if it is freely accepted and understood by the common people. Uncritical acceptance is ruled out by definition:

. . . It is to be put in relief how the political development of the concept of hegemony represents great philosophical, as well as politico-practical, progress, because it necessarily involves and presupposes an intellectual unity and an ethics conforming to a conception of the real which has superseded common sense and become . . . *critical*.[45]

Gramsci's Marxist ideal of a society without external constraints, social divisions and popular ignorance may be chimerical and indicative of a residual eschatology; but it is hardly a regimented nightmare of tame uniformity; quite the opposite, it is a libertarian vision of a world of men directing their own lives and experimenting with a variety of cultural forms and styles. For a man who placed so much stress on cultural reformation, Gramsci was remarkably hesitant to speculate about the *details* of the new culture (in the sense of literature, painting, drama, etc.). This was a matter of principle. In this sphere, he said, we must rest content with 'outlines only, rough sketches, which can (and must) be revised at any moment'.[46] This is remindful of a famous article he penned in 1921, where he declared that the new culture is 'absolutely mysterious, absolutely characterized by the unforeseeable and the unexpected'. Yet in this same article, he did lay down some guiding principles, the most important being audacity and flexibility. The task of the new culture will be to 'destroy spiritual hierarchies, prejudices, idols, rigid traditions', and this 'means not fearing novelty and boldness'. Accordingly, he professed his admiration for Marinetti and the Futurists, who, through a variety of art forms, had called into question a whole range of entrenched values.[47] If it is objected, by an observer mindful of Gramsci's intellectual evolution, that no inferences about his mature thought can be drawn from an article written in 1921, we need only reply that his *Quaderni* abound with similar opinions.[48] For example, in his notes on 'Art and Culture' he makes plain his belief that political control of art is both reprehensible and futile in *any* form of society: 'Art is art, and not "willed" political propaganda'; it is an end in itself, which can only be subordinated to the wishes of political masters at the expense of becoming 'fictitious' and 'dull'. A work of art is a work of art not because of its political content but because of its aesthetic merits. And aesthetic quality will never flourish if politicians, Marxist or otherwise, try to suppress the 'personal, non-conformist' element that infuses all art worthy of the name.[49]

This line of thinking is of a piece with his aforementioned defence of free intellectual inquiry, even though it might enable men to 'question the very principles that seem most essential' to the revolution. Gramsci's apparent desire to preserve cultural freedom is echoed in another section of his *Notebooks*, where he applauds 'so-called "freedom of thought and of expression of thought (press and association)" because only where this political condition exists can there develop . . . a new type of philosopher . . . a "democratic philosopher"'. Through dynamic interaction with his environment, this 'new type' intellectual subjects himself to 'continual self-criticism', which facilitates an active and reciprocal relationship between the élites and the masses.[50]

A sceptic could argue that Gramsci's libertarian programme is relegated to a vague and distant future. True, Gramsci does not promise the immediate 'withering away' of political society; but neither does he, in his *Quaderni*, clearly delineate stages in the long march towards communism; and nothing he says about artistic and intellectual freedom remotely suggests that these values must be held in abeyance during some transitional dictatorship. On the contrary, there is sufficient evidence (much of which we have already touched upon in other contexts) to prove that, for him, free criticism and debate, experimentation and innovation, are values to be cherished in all circumstances.

Gramsci declaimed against the blind dogmatism—extolled as a virtue by many orthodox Marxists—which denies that one's enemy can possess even the slightest insight into the truth. When he pictures Marxism as 'a completely self-sufficient and autonomous structure of thought',[51] he does not mean that we should turn from rival ideas in undiluted hostility. At least some of these can be transvalued and incorporated into the emerging truth itself:

In scientific discussion, as one supposes that the interest is the search for truth and the progress of science, he demonstrates himself more advanced who takes the point of view that his adversary can express an exigency that must be incorporated, even if as a subordinate moment, in his own construction. To understand and evaluate realistically the positions and reasons of the adversary (and sometimes the adversary is all past thought) means precisely to be liberated from the prison of ideologies (in the worst sense, of blind ideological fantacism). . . .[52]

This profound detestation of sectarian extremism also surfaces in other parts of the *Notebooks*.[53] The growth of civilization, according to Gramsci, requires debate—and debate marred by intolerance or fanaticism is not debate but mystification. Gramsci was acutely aware of the many-sidedness of truth; he had an abiding respect for the awesome complexity of social reality. Hence his explicit rejection of the notion, canvassed by many Marxists at the time, that the party—as crystallized in its leadership—could constitute an 'infallible carrier of truth . . . illuminated by reason'.[54] It follows that Gramsci could, in a number of places, underscore the need for free and strenuous participation of the masses in the development of the collective will, itself 'a living organism', which 'does not form unless multiplicity is unified through the friction of individual atoms [people]'.[55] It was 'criminal', in his view, to assume—as did certain political leaders—that obedience should be 'automatic' or 'beyond question'.[56] As was observed earlier, Gramsci did not envisage the movement towards the goal of a free society as the authoritarian translation of a pre-fixed schema, of a doctrinaire truth justified *a priori* and eternally valid, but as the evolution of aims and strategies through political dialogue and confrontation. On his theory, let it be repeated, the validity of concepts and ideas can only be established in practice. Hostility to dogmatism is therefore built into his conception of truth.

All in all, we may agree with Salvadori's conclusion that: 'In substance, while he [Gramsci] theorizes the necessity of the absolute autonomy of Marxism . . . at the same time he insists on the principle that in the field of a real and not apparent conquest of minds, all must be obtained with the weapons of criticism, while nothing can be obtained by the criticism of weapons.'[57] Yet the first part of this citation should give pause to free-thinking people, and indicates the weakness of Gramsci's libertarian posture. Though he was, it is clear, inspired by the ideals of classical culture and liberal education,[58] he was also a revolutionary who championed a complete break with the past and an unqualified submergence into a political movement. There is, consequently, an underlying margin of ambiguity in his position on the boundaries of individual freedom, both within the present movement and in the post-revolutionary society. He is evasive about *where* he would impose the limits of dissent; and he sometimes seems extraordinarily preoccupied with the virtue of unity, on the one hand, and the dangers of anti-social behaviour and factionalism, on the other. In this connection, one need only refer to the colourful passage where he contrasts 'party spirit' to the 'mean, petty individualism, [characteristic of Italian social and political life] which is anyway an unruly satisfying of passing impulses . . . an animalistic element "admired by foreigners", like the behaviour of the inmates of a zoological garden'.[59]

Gramsci's lack of clarity and consistency on the question of dissent mirrors the ambiguity which resides in the concept of democratic centralism itself. The phrase, of course, embodies a recipe for combining the rewards of both free expression and disciplined centralization. But the latter value, with its requirement of unanimity, is in fact antithetical to the vigorous and untrammelled exercise of the former. To insist on unity is necessarily to discourage those regions of non-conformity within which alternative interpretations and viewpoints can flourish. It is no accident that, in practice, democratic centralism turns out to be much centralism and little or no democracy. The attitude of the 'democratic centralist' towards dissent of any kind must be, at best, uncertain.

Nevertheless, it remains my view that a democratic interpretation, suitably qualified, can legitimately be extracted from the prison notes. But at this point, a crucial issue, which has been latent throughout the preceding discussion, has finally reared its vexatious head: namely, what is to be understood by that coveted and much-abused adjective, 'democratic'? It could be argued that much of the 'Right' criticism of Gramsci's 'authoritarianism' stems from an inability to grasp the complexities of this and related issues. These commentators, even those with socialist leanings, seem to view Gramsci from inside a liberal-democratic paradigm—a paradigm which holds that democracy is to be equated with the formal procedures of contemporary western political systems. Confronted by such a desideratum, Gramsci is bound to seem undemocratic. But does this liberal concept of democracy exhaust all the possibilities? Traditionally, the democratic ideal has expressed a *radical* demand. The so-called 'classical' theories of democracy were multi-faceted and often equivocal, but they all envisaged widespread and continual popular participation in the political process, where all decisions would reflect the people's wishes. Central to this view—especially as put forward by Rousseau and John Stuart Mill—was that the general attainment of the ideal of a rational, active, informed democratic citizenry was essential to the realization of genuine political democracy, the purpose of which was the fulfilment of some characteristic human excellence. At bottom, the doctrine—or doctrines—constituted a critique of reality in terms of a vision of human nature and human possibilities, a yardstick by which the shortcomings of society could be appraised. In the past thirty years or so, influential liberal theorists from Joseph Schumpeter to Robert Dahl have rejected the 'classical' view on a number of grounds: it lacks operational and empirical content in large, complex societies; it erroneously presupposes that man is essentially a political animal; it demands an unrealistic level of rationality from ordinary people, who, according to survey evidence, fall far short of the traditional model of democratic citizen; it is positively dangerous, since its call for participation by the ignorant and the irrational could (if taken seriously) undermine the stability of contemporary society; and so on. In the face of a gap between ideal and reality, modern liberal thinkers have chosen, not to press for changes in reality, but to abandon the ideal—or, rather, so temporize it that it fades into existing reality, becoming a matter of multi-party competition and quinquennial visits to the polling booth. Thus, democracy has come to be identified, in both the popular and élite imagination, with the present *modus operandi* of western society. Charges of woolly-minded idealism, if not incipient totalitarianism, are levelled at those who reject such complacency and seek to rescue the old democratic values. There is no space here to rehearse all the objections raised against the new, conservative definition of democracy.[60] Suffice it to take two points from the critical literature: the 'new' democracy is based on (1) methodologically dubious empirical evidence and (2) *a priori* notions about human nature and human capacities. In no way have the traditional, radical ideas of democracy been 'refuted'. The assumption that democracy = contemporary liberal practices is, in a word, arbitrary. If, as an alternative, we define democracy in terms of effective participatory procedures, then we can discern the genuinely democratic element in Gramsci's thought.

Contrary to the impression conveyed by much of the secondary literature, Gramsci never ceased his search for new forms of popular participation, qualitatively different from those of liberal democracy. By no means did he abandon this theme along with his factory council theory. In his *Quaderni*, he affirms the possibility of 'a diverse solution, both from parliamentarism and from the bureaucratic [Stalinist?] regime, with a new type of representative regime'.[61] A passage from another chapter serves to illustrate what he means. Evidently, the new order would consist of soviets, which he praises as 'representative systems' where 'consent does not end at the moment of voting'. 'This consent', he continues,

is presumed to be permanently active, so much so that the people who give it may be considered as 'functionaries' of the state, and elections as a means of voluntary enrolment of state functionaries of a certain type—a means which in a certain sense must be related (on a different level) to the idea of *self-government*. Since the elections are held on the basis not of vague and indefinite programmes but of concrete, immediate tasks, he who gives his consent commits himself to do something more than the ordinary juridical citizen towards their realization—namely, to be a vanguard of active and responsible work.[62]

While this passage is not without its obscurities, it does, I think, underline the vital role of popular control (of both decision-making and execution) in Gramsci's conception of future society—not just the distant stateless society, but, if we read his intentions properly, the immediate post-revolutionary set up as well. Thus, Gramsci's ideal of self-determination is given institutional embodiment; it does not vanish into the clouds of pure metaphysics. An individual is truly free, on Gramsci's positive definition, only when he is engaged in '*self-government*', when he is obeying laws that are genuinely self-imposed, in the sense that he realistically participates in their formulation and execution. Freedom is the converse of powerlessness; democracy of élite rule. There is a Rousseauian element here. Man attains freedom, or self-autonomy, by co-operating with his fellows in a participatory community. Thus all the constraints, obligations and inhibitions of society are the very means by which freedom is attained.

With this in mind, we can make better sense of his superficially disturbing fusion of discipline and freedom. The former, he insists, is not 'a passive and supine acceptance of orders', a docile assenting to the propositions of authority, but rather:

the conscious and lucid assimilation of the directives to be accomplished. Discipline therefore does not annul the personality in an organic sense, but only limits licence and irresponsible impulsiveness. . . . Discipline therefore does not negate personality and freedom; the question of 'personality and freedom' is posed not by the fact of discipline itself, but by the origin of the power that lies behind the discipline. If this origin is 'democratic', if, that is, the authority is a specialized, technical function and not 'arbitrariness' or an external, extrinsic imposition, discipline is a necessary element of democratic order, of freedom.[63]

'Technical' authority is a somewhat enigmatic concept here, but in contrasting it to 'extrinsic imposition', Gramsci seems to identify it with the imperatives arising out of the existential conditions of social organization; and the discipline it enjoins is the discipline necessary for life to function smoothly in a complex industrial society. Authority must attain an expression that is impersonal, theoretical, and independent of the arbitrariness of individuals. It is 'democratic' authority because it is self-willed, the product of critical examination and acceptance, and—if we read the two preceding passages in conjunction—self-generated, through a system of 'permanent' participation and consent. Gramsci follows Marx and Engels in seeing no incompatibility between authority relationships and discipline, on the one hand, and complete self-autonomy, on the other.[64]

In a nutshell, we can represent Gramsci's doctrine as a justification for absolutism only if we look at it through the conceptual spectacles either of liberalism or of anarchism in some form or other. To be sure, he equivocates about where freedom ends and licence begins; he underestimates the need for formal guarantees on the civil rights he seems to favour; he wishes to absorb the plurality of social authorities and responsibilities into the unitary mould of the party. All this might lead even a socialist to conclude that he was insufficiently sensitive both to the ramifications of human diversity and to the temptations of power. In no society of any complexity has there ever been unanimity on fundamental principles, and if power does not always corrupt, it certainly breeds arrogance and suspicion.

Naïveté, however, is not authoritarianism. It would be a gross error to overlook the centrality in Gramsci's thought of persuasion, consent, free debate, and democratic participation. Gramscian men are not to suffer totalitarianism in the pejorative sense of a system which 'obliterates the distinction between private judgement and public control'.[65] They are not to be engulfed in an anonymous mass or merged into a quasi-mystical body-politic intent on destroying their individual identities.

IV. *Theory and Practice: Some Doubts*

Rather than dismiss Gramsci's theory of the party (and hegemony) as dictatorial in principle, it is perhaps more appropriate to contend that the interplay he envisaged between party and mass is operationally defective, that the distinction he made between a 'real' conception of the world, discernible at first only to an enlightened élite, and the world-view verbally affirmed has authoritarian implications in practice. Still, in the final analysis, his absolute historicism, his insistence on praxis as the only criterion of verification, prevented him from assuming a rigid dichotomy between what people *actually* desire and what they *ought to* desire, between expressed preferences and 'real' wants:

> . . . can modern theory [i.e. 'authentic' consciousness] be in opposition to the 'spontaneous' feelings of the masses? . . . It cannot be in opposition to them: between the two there is a 'quantitative' difference of degree, not one of quality.[66]

Thus Gramsci eschewed the doctrinaire élitism of other noted Marxist theorists in this century, such as Lenin and Marcuse.[67] But what are these 'spontaneous feelings' worthy of inclusion in the 'authentic' consciousness formulated by the party? To reiterate, in Gramsci's view, the ordinary man possesses a 'contradictory consciousness': his perceptions and evaluations of social life exhibit inconsistency and superficiality, which express the gap between the dominant interpretation of reality and his own objective situation. Lurking below the usually conforming surface are subversive beliefs and values, latent instincts of rebellion, which are sometimes translated into actual behaviour. Thus the actions and demands of workers and peasants, in so far as they deviate from conventional norms, form the raw material of an alternative culture. Gramsci has here hit upon a serious weakness in the liberal approach. For it is one thing to urge that people's preferences go unchallenged; it is quite another to determine the precise nature of these preferences. An individual's desires and opinions rarely if ever compose a fully formed, internally harmonious whole: they are almost always inconsistent and vague at the margin, and this raises the question of what is to count in their specification. What about deflected or subterranean wants and preferences that never reach the political arena in fully articulated form but nevertheless receive expression in a multitude of oblique, undirected ways. Silence and apathy may well be signs of contentment, but they may also disguise genuine grievances which have not yet been given precise form. Gramsci comprehended this ambiguity and took advantage of its theoretical and practical potential.

Also, implicit in Gramsci's open-minded approach to opposing doctrines is the possibility of revolutionary intellectuals building on those widely held components of the dominant ideology which, because of their incompatibility with the present order, foster the ambivalence and contradictions in the thought and behaviour of the masses. Gramsci was willing to concede that certain values were capable of pointing beyond the social order and social classes which produced them:

The ideas of equality, of fraternity, of liberty excite passions among those strata of men who see themselves neither equal, nor brothers of other men, nor free in their social interactions. Thus it happens that in every radical movement of the multitude, in one manner or another, in the mould of particular ideologies, these claims are put forward.[68]

The revolutionary could attempt to show how widespread discontent is partly due to this contradiction between the splendid ideals of the French revolution and the realities of the liberal-capitalist system. Thus the truly universal values advanced by the dominant hegemony, such as freedom and equality, can be purged of their mystifying encrustations and fit into a radical framework.

For Gramsci, then, the revolutionary party must evolve its strategy and aims in terms of the concrete context within which people move—institutions, traditions, common sense and so on. What is more, formulating the 'authentic' consciousness of the masses does not go beyond drawing out the theoretical implications of what they are *in fact* doing and saying; it is a matter of 'rendering practice more homogeneous, more coherent, and more efficient in all its elements. . .'.[69] The presumption is against arrogance, paternalism, and imposition; against what Bakunin stigmatized as 'government by professors'.

An obvious and valid objection presents itself here. Although the party élite must mould its ideology out of existing materials (empirically ascertainable inclinations, beliefs, aspirations, desires, concerns, and the like), the élite is nevertheless, on Gramsci's account, an *intellectual vanguard*, enjoying a privileged insight into social phenomena; and, as such, its elaboration of the 'real' ideology implicit in the actions of the masses will be filtered through its own Marxist lens. Gramsci unconsciously alludes to the resultant difficulty when he states that '*The Modern Prince* must contain a part dedicated to Jacobinism . . . an example of the concrete formation and operation of a collective will, which in at least some of its aspects was an original, *ex novo* creation'.[70] The last few words of this quotation suggest an important set of points. No piece or pattern of behaviour, no observable event, possesses an intrinsic, univocal meaning. Gramsci himself, in assailing the empiricist tradition, maintained that observation as such cannot be prior to theory as such, since some theory, or point of view, is presupposed by any observation. Thus, what he calls 'rational' theory cannot be fabricated out of the results of observation. To some extent, it must be invented: 'original creation', an imaginative 'leap', is logically necessary. Behaviour which Gramsci might consider a symptom of *embryonic revolutionary consciousness* might more plausibly be interpreted as a limited demand for a limited reform, as evidence of a *full-fledged trade union consciousness*. He would of course reply, in proper Marxist fashion, that the latter interpretation is superficial. But this is to beg the question, for the criteria of superficiality and authenticity do not inhere in the experience to be interpreted. They are given by a prior theoretical framework.

So there seems to be a Gordian knot in Gramsci's thought: on the one hand, praxis is decisive, and 'mass adhesion or non-adhesion to an ideology is the real critical test' of its rationality;[71] on the other, a man may not verbally (or practically) adhere to the 'real' ideology 'implicit in his [deviant] activity'.[72] Gramsci's relativism, such as it exists, appears to be at loggerheads with his Marxist distinction between essence and appearance, knowledge and opinion. The conflict may only be superficial, however, for Gramsci regards Marxist analysis itself as a set of hypotheses which must *eventually* be proved in practice—i.e. establish itself as the animating ideology of an epoch, as the scheme of thought most in line with the needs of the period. Marxism is, according to Gramsci, *both* theoretical insight *and* unverified hypothesis.

Yet the fact remains that the Gramscian programme involves more than simply putting people's disjointed thoughts (those expressed behaviourally as well as verbally) into systematic form; in the process of conceptualization, these thoughts must necessarily be altered—embellished, clarified, and tied together in such a way as to endow them with new meaning. This transformation, in effect, amounts to telling people what they *really* believe, or, more precisely, what they would believe if they could free themselves from delusive formulas and fully understand the logic of their situation. And, under certain conditions, this process of 'education' could degenerate into the rational few ordering the benighted many to believe (and act) as they should. Despite Gramsci's instructions and strictures, the perils of élitism would not be easily avoidable in practice. Still, without denying this authoritarian potential, it is reasonable to argue that if 'contradictory consciousness' is indeed prevalent in bourgeois society, if consensus is tempered by a residue of deviance, then Gramsci's conception of an authentic proletarian consciousness is not entirely lacking in empirical basis; it is not *merely* an élitist construction. On this count, Gramsci can be supported by recent empirical studies of mass beliefs and attitudes—which shall be examined in our concluding chapter.

V. *Conclusion*

Gramsci never really solved the problem of *who* would define the new world-view; nor did he manage to delineate clearly the appropriate region of human liberty. All his formulations are unsatisfactory to those who do not share his boundless faith in a dialectical interplay between a central authority and the aspirations of a mass movement. The apparent inconsistencies in his thinking on the topic—between his passion for unity and his almost Millsian commitment to free debate, his obsessive preoccupation with leadership and his passionate belief in self-autonomy—were never properly resolved in a higher synthesis. But the theoretical value and energizing effect of Gramsci's efforts should not be in doubt. Even though he did not succeed in enunciating a truly convincing non-authoritarian Marxism, he deserved credit for keeping the possibility alive, for attempting to fuse the humanitarian and practical sides of the doctrine, and for doing so precisely when Stalin was busy sundering the cause of socialist revolution from the humane instincts which had nurtured it. While the Soviet despot was torturing and killing people for (real or imagined) non-conformity, the Sardinian was describing the new socialist man as a 'modern Leonardo da Vinci', exhibiting 'strong personality and individual originality'.[73] Gramsci's work provides a stimulus and point of departure for all those who wish to explore the possibilities for a genuinely Western and democratic form of Marxian socialism. Does this mean, then, that Gramsci was a revisionist *a là* Bernstein? an advocate of a peaceful and parliamentary 'road'? Did his concept of hegemony underpin a reformist brand of socialism? Was he the ideological forerunner of the '*Via Italiana*'? It is to these questions that we now turn.

NB. Femia is not very happy with the non-hierarchical and potentially dominating tendencies in Gramsci. You changed his mind to some extent on these arguments.

CHAPTER 6

A Peaceful Road to Socialism?

... to beat one's head against the wall is to break
one's head and not the wall.

Gramsci (letter from prison)

GRAMSCI'S VISION of the revolutionary process, we have
seen, was far from Stalinist; indeed, with its concern for popular
participation and free discussion, it can be viewed as a more
democratic alternative to the *Leninist* model. The purity of
Gramsci's Leninism is also called into question by his conviction—discussed in Chapter 2—that the revolution in Western
Europe must deviate sharply from the strategic path taken by
the Bolsheviks in Russia. With characteristic disdain for old
and rigid formulae, Gramsci pointed to the crucial differences
between advanced capitalist countries and the Russian Empire
of 1917, and he attempted, in his *Quaderni*, to develop criteria of
orientation and action appropriate to modern circumstances.
What he offered was a new *What is to be done?* for the developed
West, a fundamental reassessment and revision of the accepted
Marxist approach to revolution. The nature of this enterprise
has prompted many—critics and admirers alike—to lay emphasis on the tie between Gramsci and Togliattism. Gramsci
put forward ideas, it is claimed, whose logic is manifest in the
'Italian (read "constitutional", "parliamentary", "democratic",
"pacific") road to socialism'. It is now casually assumed in
many circles that he was the ideological progenitor of what has
come to be known as Eurocommunism, the increasingly influential body of doctrines that purports to marry liberalism
and Marxism. In the following pages, this assumption, and
other related ones, will be closely examined and evaluated.

I. *A Via Occidentale*

At the outset, it would be useful to restate what Gramsci took to be the essential points of contrast between East and West—differences he illustrated through the use of elaborate military metaphors. As I noted above, the Russian revolutionary experience did not, to his mind, furnish an appropriate model for the West. For Lenin enjoyed certain advantages denied to his counterparts in less backward areas; he could adopt a strategy of rapid frontal assault (in Gramsci's idiom, 'war of manœuvre' or 'war of movement') because of the relative simplicity of the mechanisms of socialization in his society. What Gramsci called 'civil society' was, in Russia, 'primitive and amorphous', incapable of providing a unitary moral and intellectual indoctrination.[1] The Tsarist state was founded on ignorance, apathy, and repression, not on the voluntary consent of its subjects. In the absence of a complex articulation of civil society, of that bloc of ideological 'fortifications' which could absorb and contain discontent, the state machinery was the sole defence of the old order.[2] But in the West, the state is 'merely an outer trench' an advanced line of defence, behind which stands 'a powerful chain of fortresses'.[3] This 'chain of fortresses' comprises the pervasive and highly developed ensemble of civil society, which propagates the *Weltanschauung* of the bourgeois ruling class, its mode of living and thinking, its aspirations, morality and habits. The bourgeoisie has thus managed to establish its hegemony over the great masses of citizens, who now consent, with varying degrees of enthusiasm, to the liberal state of affairs. This hegemonic order makes bourgeois society 'resistant to the catastrophic irruptions caused by immediate economic factors (crises, depressions, etc.)'.[4] Hence, in the advanced capitalist zones, open warfare, the Bolshevik strategy of sudden and direct attack, or 'war of movement', must yield pride of place to a 'war of position', which is not aimed simply at the conquest of state power (the 'outer trench') but focuses on the gradual capture and possession of the 'powerful chain of fortresses' behind. An indispensable condition of permanent proletarian victory in the revolutionary struggle is, in Gramsci's words, a 'detachment of civil society from political society . . .', that is, the erosion of bourgeois ideological dominance and its replacement by a Marxist *counter*-hegemony, a turning of the popular mind to new principles.[5] Without this prior 'revolution of the spirit', any communist victory would be ephemeral. The final destruction of the old order is viewed by Gramsci as but a single moment in the vast historical modification of cultural and social forces, a shift that occurs beneath the surface of formal political institutions. The main confrontations, it can be seen, happen neither in the factories nor in the streets nor at the military bases but in the sphere of civil society. And because this sphere grows more sophisticated with the march of technology, ideological encounters with the ruling class take on added importance with advancing stages of capitalist development. Thus Gramsci abandoned the fashionable Marxist tenet of a catastrophic crisis that would permit the successful and lightning-like intervention of an organized revolutionary vanguard. On the contrary, the war against the system would be prolonged, 'complex, difficult' and call for 'exceptional qualities of patience and inventive spirit'.[6] The myth of imminent revolution, he believed, must be exposed as false and dangerous. Even capitalism's most severe depression had not led to revolution, and neither would any future economic crisis do so unless preceded by assiduous ideological preparation.

The reformist *potential* of the above strategy should be evident. In a critical prison note on Trotsky's internationalism, Gramsci reinforces the impression that he is laying the foundations for what later became the *Via Italiana*. 'Certainly the development is towards internationalism', he remarks, 'but the point of departure is "national" and it is necessary to start here.' In order to play a hegemonic role, a class (or its chief spokesmen) must be able to 'interpret' exactly a specific 'combination of national forces'. It must study the particular national situation, concrete conditions and circumstances, and from this study evolve a strategy to cultivate the seeds of revolution as they present themselves in the specific setting. The purpose is to alter the complex and often unique equilibrium of forces to the advantage of the working class. To use Gramsci's colourful phrase, the proletariat must 'nationalize itself'. In practice this means it must become the leading cultural and political force in a system of alliances, guiding 'social strata strictly national (intellectuals), and rather often those less than national, particularist and municipalist (the peasants)'. In Gramsci's schema these alliances are not simply temporary and instrumental, but organic; certain non-proletarian social elements must be fully incorporated into the movement, and the implication is that a set of intermediate objectives, of initial compromises, must be put on the agenda if these groups are to be absorbed into the revolutionary process.[7] Gramsci, in these passages, is continuing and developing a theme he first discussed in his 1926 essay on the *Southern Question*. There he posed the question of class alliances and argued that the proletariat could be victorious and guarantee the stability of its new order only in proportion as it won over the other exploited and disaffected classes to its cause—above all, the peasant class. This, of course, was good Leninism. Still, in the *Quaderni*, the objective of class alliances is seemingly infused with a spirit of restraint and 'nationalism' that, from a Bolshevik perspective, smacks of apostasy.

That Gramsci was, during his imprisonment, moving away from the precepts of Communist internationalism may also be (and has been) inferred from his attitude to the famous 'third period' of the Comintern, which began in 1928. The 'third period' was characterized by a new ultra-Left political line, imposed by Stalin—who was then engaged in a violent struggle with Bukharin—and formally ratified at the Sixth Congress. Its main premise was the prediction that capitalism was in its death-throes and that everywhere proletarian protest was becoming more and more revolutionary. Its principles included the notorious identity of fascism and social-democracy, the latter being viewed as merely another form of bourgeois rule. (This was the era of 'social fascism'.) It followed that there was no possibility of coalitions between Communists and other forces on the Left. With the 'United Front' unceremoniously relegated to the dustbin of history, utterly intransigent and independent Communist action became the order of the day. In the Italian context this policy was more than just sectarian; it reeked of absurdity. Mussolini and his henchmen had destroyed the organized working class: its channels of communication had been disrupted, and its leadership arrested, killed, driven into exile, or frightened into silence. What was left of the Italian revolutionary movement could take no effective action whatsoever without allies among the rural semi-proletariat and the anti-fascist middle classes. Not surprisingly, the exiled Communist Party was thrown into turmoil over whether or not to follow the new 'turn' of the International. Togliatti, who had been given the job of explaining and engineering the change, found many leaders and a considerable proportion of the rank and file opposed to his arguments. Showing no sign of his post-war independence from Moscow, he managed by March of 1930 to enlist the Party behind the Comintern policy, though at great cost to Party cohesion and morale. (Three prominent members of the Executive were expelled for combating the new line.) In keeping with Stalin's wishes, a revolutionary situation was declared to be present in Italy, and the dictatorship of the proletariat was hailed as the only permissible immediate goal of struggle. There could be no transitional liberal-democratic phase, since bourgeois democracy, in the final analysis, amounted to nothing more than police dictatorship.

Condemned to languish for twenty years in a Fascist prison cell, Gramsci was unimpressed with this analysis, and believed that a bourgeois-democratic solution was both a desirable and probable immediate alternative to Fascism. Our knowledge of his opinions concerning the Italian situation is derived primarily from the testimony of his prison comrades, notably Athos Lisa, who wrote a report for Party headquarters when he was released from Turi prison in 1933.[8] In 1930 Gramsci and his fellow Communist prisoners started a political education class, consisting of discussions held during their exercise hour together in the courtyard. According to Lisa, the aim of Gramsci's education programme was the formation of new non-sectarian cadres. Gramsci, it seems, wanted to 'create a nucleus of militants who would have the task of propagating a saner ideology within the Party'.[9] He criticized the tendency to 'talk revolution without having a precise notion of what has to be done to accomplish it, of the means which might attain the end'. Such an inclination left one 'unable to adapt methods to diverse historical situations'. Many Communists, he lamented, 'prefer words to political actions, or . . . confuse the one with the other'. With clear reference to the new Comintern line, Gramsci argued against abstract and mechanical positions, whose quasi-metaphysical rigidity he regarded as anti-Marxist. The misery brought about by Fascism could not by itself be the decisive factor in propelling the masses into revolution. Misery in itself could bring about only isolated revolts and uprisings. The tyranny of Fascism, mainly through its sheer brutality but also by dint of its persuasive emotional appeal, had profoundly disoriented the masses and weakened their combative power. Fascism had driven the proletariat and the entire Italian people into retrograde positions: they had, for the most part, lost the socialist spirit and, at best, longed for a return to the familiar banalities of liberal democracy. In the circumstances, direct passage from Fascism to the dictatorship of the proletariat was a utopian dream, for there would 'most likely' be a 'period of transition' between the present regime and proletarian triumph. 'Therefore, the Party must adapt its tactics to this eventuality without fear of appearing unrevolutionary.' To be specific, it was necessary 'for the Party to develop action in common with the other parties struggling against Fascism in Italy'. If it failed to form such alliances, 'the proletariat would have no hope of engaging in any serious revolutionary activity'. The Lisa document indicates that the strategy Gramsci proposed in the prison yard seminars went well beyond what he said in his sparse prison notes devoted to the subject of class alliances. For now he was advocating solidarity not only with the impoverished peasants and the alienated intellectuals, but also with the brooding, restless petit-bourgeoisie, including, for example, 'the lower ranks of the army officer stratum, discontented about lack of promotion, precarious conditions of existence, etc.'.[10] The purpose of this new system of alliances would be an intermediate one: the restoration of the freedoms destroyed by Fascism. Since the Party's immediate task was to promote and lead a broad, popular anti-Fascist movement, it was necessary to formulate policies and slogans capable of mobilizing all anti-Fascist forces behind such a movement, and this would necessitate bargaining, compromise and concessions. After the establishment of the new liberal regime, the proletariat could prepare for the final struggle. Taking advantage of the prestige and influence garnered during the anti-Fascist campaign, the Party would be in an excellent position to discredit its opponents, remove the fantastic veil of bourgeois ideology and construct a Marxist hegemony. The superficial affinity between Gramsci's proposals and the actual strategy adopted by Togliatti and the Party towards the end of the war is striking. In 1930, however, this strategy spelled defiance of official policy and generated much hostility among the prison comrades. In fact, Gramsci's educational programme lasted just a few weeks. The atmosphere had become thick with accusations and recriminations, some prisoners going so far as to assert that Gramsci had become an opportunist social-democrat, of Crocean flavour. Disgusted with the new dogmatism, he withdrew into monk-like isolation.[11] But those prison seminars, short-lived though they were, have provided plenty of ammunition for those who wish to depict Gramsci as an apostle of 'the parliamentary road to socialism'. We shall now go on to elucidate the various permutations of this belief, which is shared by a remarkably disparate collection of people: democratic socialists who hope to rescue Gramsci from the smear of Stalinism, extra parliamentary Leftists who want to condemn him for his 'revisionism', and PCI activists and intellectuals who seek to claim his posthumous support for their official policy. It should be pointed out that no one is seriously denying that the young pre-prison Gramsci was a dedicated, intransigent Bolshevik revolutionary.[12] His political articles and editorials, all written before his arrest, abound with comments like this: 'Every revolution . . . cannot but smash and destroy the entire existing system of social organization.'[13] It would therefore be pointless and misleading to defend Gramsci's revolutionary honour by referring to these early writings.[14] No, the Gramsci who is associated with the anti-Leninist, constitutional path to socialism is the incarcerated Gramsci, whose *ripensamento* of classical Marxist approaches to revolution brought him into conflict with the Party he had helped to found.

II. *The Democratic Socialist View*

Following upon the publication of Gramsci's *Quaderni*, certain segments of democratic socialist opinion in Italy felt inclined to revise their image of the man who once raged so bitterly at their PSI forebears. Indeed, it became fashionable on the moderate Left to read Gramsci in a 'European' or 'Western' key, to look at him as a partisan of 'humanism', of a democratic, anti-Stalinist approach to Marxism. Gramsci's true heirs, on this interpretation, were not the Communist Party leaders who kept invoking his name (Eurocommunism had not yet been invented and the PCI still used *all* the Leninist rhetoric) but the Socialists themselves, who were not prepared to jettison constitutional niceties in the march to the free society. The most important proponent of this democratic socialist interpretation is Giuseppe Tamburrano, who also—as we saw in Chapter 3—advocates a neo-Crocean view of Gramsci's philosophy. (Many commentators perceive a connection between Gramsci's 'idealism' and his 'gradualism'.) Tamburrano claims to discover a fundamental break in the Sardinian's political thinking. By 1926, so runs the argument, he had more or less become an orthodox Leninist, dedicated to the Bolshevization of the Italian Party. But his confinement and the triumph of Stalinism in the Third International conspired to change the course of his intellectual journey. Isolated from the world of politics, withdrawn from the concrete struggle, Gramsci had a chance to reflect on the course of the world revolutionary movement. By the late 1920s and early 1930s, three indisputable facts weighted heavily on his consciousness: (1) the brutal degeneration of the Soviet regime under Stalin; (2) the upsurge of European fascism, which had developed a real popular base; and (3) the impotence and disarray of the revolutionary Left, which was unable to take the initiative even during the worst depression capitalism had ever suffered. Now, Gramsci's pre-prison throught was premised on the imminence of revolution and acceptance of the Soviet Union as the main repository of revolutionary virtue. With the disintegration of these premises, his proposed solutions to the problems of socialist struggle were bound to change profoundly.[15] Hence we have the much talked about crisis in his political and theoretical stance, which led to the formulation of new themes and concepts. Gramsci, it is contended, came to elaborate a democratic stragegy, far removed from the model constituted by the October Revolution. The new strategy was based on the idea of hegemony. In the developed societies of the West, the struggle for socialism should be pursued on the level of a search for broad agreement, of alliances with manifold social groups, *not* on the level of a violent confrontation for the possession of state power. In support of his interpretation, Tamburrano underlines the anti-authoritarian strains in Gramsci's thought: his denunciation of 'bureaucratic centralism' and advocacy of vigorous internal party democracy, his evident regard for the virtues of free intellectual expression and debate, and his general attachment to humane cultural values, to mental and spiritual cultivation.[16] Gramsci's strategic model, concludes Tamburrano, is not simply different from Lenin's; it is antithetical to it. The doctrine of hegemony signifies 'the abandonment of the Bolshevik strategy' in favour of the '*democratic* conquest and the *democratic* maintenance of proletarian power'.[17] According to this way of looking at Gramsci, his *via occidentale* to socialism is more 'modern' and 'advanced' than Lenin's approach, which was appropriate only to under- or semi-developed countries, countries—like Russia—where feudal encrustations bulked large. Unlike some of his Socialist Party colleagues,[18] Tamburrano is careful not to turn Gramsci into a straightforward social-democrat. He concedes that Gramsci was contemptuous of the claims of parliamentary democracy and that the new theory of hegemony did not preclude the possibility of violent encounters.[19] But there is little doubt that, in his eyes, Gramsci's alternative strategy is essentially about the 'peaceful acquisition'[20] of power, a painless evolutionary transition to socialism, mainly brought about by the pressure of the electorate. Tamburrano's 'Nennian'[21] thesis was greeted by howls of protest from the PCI, which viewed it as a crude PSI attempt to purloin Gramsci's patrimony. Before long, however, the Communists were moderating their Leninist language, striving for collaboration with Catholic and liberal forces, and to a large extent accepting the Tamburrano picture of Gramsci—which they had once denounced as mere distortion.

III. *The Far Left View*

Under the heading of 'far Left' we include all those who, in the Italian context, can loosely be termed 'Trotskyist' or 'Bordighist'. Like their opposite numbers on the Right-wing of the socialist movement, they seek to locate Gramsci in an orbit fundamentally alien to Lenin and Leninism. The difference is that their counterposition of Gramsci and Lenin is rooted in a fundamental critique of the former not the latter. Some Left commentators are more careful and nuanced than others, but all generally see Gramsci's writings and pronouncements as a key factor in the reformist degeneration of Italian Communism. On this analysis, his alleged desertion of faith is manifest in three ways: (1) through his emphasis on 'war of position' he effectively forsook the idea of revolutionary insurrection, of cataclysm; (2) because of his preoccupation with the movement responsible for his incarceration, he came to regard the anti-Fascist struggle as more important than the anti-capitalist one; in his subsequent support for liberal restoration and 'organic' alliances with objective class enemies, he relinquished the idea of a drastic break with the past; and (3) he substituted a national for an international perspective; the notebooks were obsessively concerned with the Italian national experience, with a desire to 'complete' the Risorgimento task of national integration; this provincial 'culturalist' outlook, traceable to the Hegelian-Crocean derivation of his Marxism, is (in the words of one critic) 'the original sin of Gramscism'.[22] In sum, it is argued that the concepts, terminology, and strategies devised by Gramsci in prison were not proper to revolutionary Marxism.

For an elaboration of this critique, it is appropriate to turn once again to Stefano Merli, perhaps the best known and most interesting of Gramsci's Left-wing detractors. In the very same article where he accuses Gramsci of Stalinist tendencies, Merli launches a diatribe against the Sardinian's 'revisionism'.[23] According to this critique, Gramsci, notwithstanding evidence to the contrary, tended towards a fatuous theory of revolution 'through democratic stages'. With its stress on democratic alliances, major reforms, and widespread consensus, his position is reminiscent of the ideology of the Second International: the revolution will simply happen through a spontaneous development; it is not necessary actively to make revolution; it is sufficient for the moment to propose *intermediate* objectives and to concentrate on these exclusively. In faithful expectation of a better world to come, one devotes all one's attention to the existing system, to the manipulation of power relations within it. The result, Merli complains, is that one becomes imprisoned within the logic of the status quo, with the corollary that the fundamental objective fades from view and finally disappears into the distance. In other words, the revolution gets postponed till infinity. The strategy of patient compromise inexorably leads to the extinction of any revolutionary fervour; instead there develops an implicit assumption that structural trans-formation can be effected without a negation of historical continuity: 'In Gramsci the concept of revolutionary rupture is substituted by that of . . . *revolution without revolution.*'[24] In Merli's view, then, Gramsci refurbished the positivist, evolutionist, social-democratic myth of a qualitative change produced not by a revolutionary leap forward but purely through a series of quantitative changes, of piecemeal reforms within the bourgeois capitalist framework.

In essence, if not in detail, Merli's critique is fairly typical of the *genre*.[25] Some commentators, however, are careful to point out that Gramsci himself, despite the pernicious potential of his theories, sincerely detested reformism and all its works. Tito Perlini, for example, thinks it necessary to separate the objective logic of Gramsci's formulations from his subjective political stance. Perlini agrees with people like Merli and Tamburrano that the logical outcome of the 'war of position' strategy is a 'peaceful road' to socialism; that is, social-democracy in the classical sense of the term. From a *theoretical* point of view, Gramsci was no longer a communist revolutionary; but Perlini concedes that Gramsci 'could not foresee the depressing results' of his ideas, 'results which certainly, politically and morally, would have met his firm disapproval'.[26] So we have a curious situation in which Gramsci adhered theoretically to a social-democratic perspective 'without wanting to and without realizing it. . . . The Gramsci of the *Quaderni* hides from himself the basic fact of his effective renunciation of a revolutionary point of view'. He thus suffered from 'false consciousness'.[27]

IV. *The Communist Party View*

What is it about PCI policies that causes it to be condemned (or lauded) as revisionist? Towards the end of the last war, the Party embarked on a new course, which—despite occasional waverings, inconsistencies, and rhetorical retreats—has been pursued to the present day. Initially reflecting Stalin's desire to mollify the Allies by non-revolutionary policies in liberated areas, the new Party programme eschewed working-class militance and revolution in favour of a policy of national solidarity and renewal. The ostensible goal was to create a democratic regime of a 'new-type', which would overcome the limits of pre-Fascist democracy and allow for socialist transformations. In practice this has meant a twofold strategy designed: (1) to minimize class conflict by appealing to 'national' interests and proletarian 'responsibility', and (2) to gain the allegiance of the 'productive' sectors of the economy (the peasants and *ceti medi*) against the common monopolistic enemy. In Togliatti's words, the Party seeks a 'grand alliance of social forces belonging to different camps', extending from 'workers, hired hands, and peasant small-holders' to 'technicians and engineers . . . shopkeepers, small and medium entrepreneurs . . . and teachers, professors, artists, men of culture'.[28] Everyone but the speculators and big capitalists is fair game; and the assumption is that these diverse strata will not respond to Communist advances unless the Party endeavours to emerge from its ghetto and defend a wide variety of social and economic interests. Togliatti hammered home this point during the early days of liberation from Nazi occupation:

We are the party of the working class. . . . But the working class has never been foreign to the interests of the nation. . . . We can no longer be a small association of propagandists for the general ideas of communism and marxism.[29]

Later, in his polemic against the Chinese, he openly endorsed the legitimacy of the parliamentary system: 'Parliament is part of the political structure of a democratic society and can have a greater or lesser degree of representativeness and of democratic functionality.' He went on to insist that in Western Europe, a socialist solution must guarantee 'an ample system of political liberties and autonomies'.[30] It was Togliatti's aim, then, to establish the Party as a legitimate actor within the Italian political system, and to do this through the pursuit of an electoral and parliamentary strategy. Such a revisionist policy, divergent as it was from the Leninist catechism, could not always be stated with the utmost directness and consistency. Ever attentive to rumblings on his left, Togliatti usually tried to cloak his deviations in familiar Leninist rhetoric,[31] thus causing a certain amount of confusion. Since Togliatti's death, such casuistry has not been much in evidence; indeed, under Berlinguer's leadership the PCI has been at pains to establish its democratic uniqueness, even at the expense of playing down its Leninist past.[32]

Although called forth by circumstances, this post-war departure was justified by reference to old gods, particularly Gramsci, in order to maintain the continuity and cohesion of the movement. Gramsci, after his martyrdom, became the tutelary deity of the Party; its identity was (and still is) bound up with his memory. This being the case, the leadership has chosen to designate him as the original theoretician, the 'founding father', of its popular front type strategy. It was Gramsci, they say, who laid the groundwork for the *Via Italiana*, the germs of which are recognizable in his *Quaderni*. The Party claims to be travelling in his footsteps; from him it claims to inherit both the spirit and methods of struggle. This homage is enshrined in the Party's official doctrine. According to its statute, the PCI is 'animated and guided by the teachings and by the example of Gramsci'.[33] What exactly has it learned from him? Certain themes have been constantly reiterated in the Party's numerous publications and declarations. Gramsci understood, asserts the PCI, that the revolution in the West would be a long march requiring intermediate aims and strategies. He was alive to the need for class alliances, for caution and short-term compromises, for the construction of a national consensus around socialist values and principles. It is essentially in this way, we are told, that he foreshadows and sanctions the 'Italian Road'.

The tactic of ransacking Gramsci's utterances for *ex post facto* legitimation of Party policy was inaugurated by Togliatti at the end of the Second World War. In a much quoted speech at Naples on 29 April, 1945, he presented his former colleague and comrade as a staunch supporter of anti-Fascist solidarity, a prophet of national unity in the task of resistance and democratic renovation:

> The central idea of the political action of Gramsci was the idea of unity: unity of the working-class parties in the struggle for the defence of democratic institutions . . . unity of the working-class parties with the democratic forces which were beginning to organize . . . unity of the socialist working masses with the Catholic working masses of the city and countryside; unity of the workers; unity of workers and peasants; unity of workers of the arm with those of the mind, for the creation of a great bloc of national forces.[34]

This attempt to invest the 'Italian Road' ideology with Gramscian paternity is not to be confused with the democratic socialist interpretation outlined above. While this latter reading unequivocally distinguished Gramsci from Lenin, the official interpretation of the PCI, at least when Togliatti was alive, pretended that there was little difference between the two patron saints. On this view, the Party's adherence to Gramsci's teachings had nothing whatsoever to do with un-Leninist revisionism; it was simply a matter of applying Leninist ideas in the Italian context, of—so to speak—translating the Russian experience into Italian. Hence the polemical attitude towards commentators like Giolitti and Tamburrano who found in Gramsci a radically new 'occidentalist' approach to the problems of revolution.[35] It was pointed out in the previous chapter that, in the period since Togliatti's demise, the Party—or at least some of its spokesmen—has been more honest and forthcoming about the very real differences between Gramsci and Lenin. It is now accepted that Gramsci, though still *basically* a Leninist, propounded 'a different vision of the revolution', one emphasizing the need for broad popular acceptance, for consensus around a new culture.[36] It is also possible to detect, since 1964, a rather more circumspect attitude towards the relevance of Gramsci's teachings themselves, a greater openness about the ways in which the Party has *developed* or *elaborated* on his legacy. For example, a 1967 editorial in *Rinascita*, while dutifully proclaiming 'a substantial continuity of inspiration and direction' between Gramsci and the PCI, acknowledges that the Master's views have been slowly 'renovated and amplified'. It then suggests that greater account be taken of the 'historical context of Gramsci's thought, and of its limits, and of the objective and subjective transformations which have come about in these thirty years since his death'.[37] In other words, while Gramsci's ideas provide justification for the 'Italian Road', and constitute the foundation for all Party strategy, there can be no question of a mechanical application of these ideas, because, as another PCI thinker puts it, we are now on 'a new, more advanced, terrain'.[38] Still, the assumption seems to be, even in this cautious interpretation, that Gramsci—were he alive today— would approve of the Party's moderate and flexible line.[39]

V. *Discussion*

It is easier to sketch out the above positions than to evaluate them. There are two broad reasons for this. First, as should be abundantly clear by now, Gramsci's prison writings were neither well-defined nor devoid of ambiguity: theoretical gaps and uncertainties often cloud his formulations, and this allows for a multitude of plausible readings. Second, the various interpretations that view Gramsci as a precursor of the peaceful road to socialism are not themselves usually enunciated with any great precision. Slippery words such as 'reformist', 'revolutionary', 'gradualist', and 'democratic', though sometimes used in idiosyncratic ways, are bandied about as if their meanings were transparent. Neither is the cause of clarity served when analysts make odd distinctions between Gramsci's subjective commitment to total revolution, and the contrary *logical consequences* of his theory. It is no small task to assess an interpretation that one cannot entirely pin down, and the difficulty is compounded when the evidence is, by its very nature, fragmentary and incomplete. Yet Gramsci's prison notes on the nature of the revolution were not so unformed or ambiguous as to be beyond distortion. Careful examination of them in their historical context enables us to argue that the above interpretations, while not wholly false or implausible, are seriously defective and in some respects flatly contrary to Gramsci's expressed convictions. If the democratic road to socialism is simply a matter of repudiating minority revolution, willingness to compromise on immediate objectives, and a receptive attitude to interclass alliances, then Gramsci certainly favoured it. If, however, it implies disavowal of violence and insurrection, i.e. a commitment to gradual evolution through parliamentary channels (and this is the way we normally understand democratic socialism), then nothing that Gramsci actually says permits us to associate him with it. Conciliation and moderation are little evident in his theory; the Jacobinism he favours is a radical and intransigent attitude, involving implacable hostility to both the old order and its guardians. And he shows little doubt that this hostility must culminate in a violent contest which will permit no compromise and which will result in the annihilation of one of the protagonists. The theory and practice of the Third International had been thoroughly imbued with emphasis on the historical necessity of violence in the destruction and construction of states. The creation of a radically new order, after the smashing of the bourgeois state machine, was the touchstone of Comintern Marxism. Nowhere in his notebooks does Gramsci directly question these principles. Indeed, they do not figure prominently in his discourse at all, for he was mainly interested in pursuing new ideas, in particular the concept of hegemony, that had been overlooked in the tireless proclamation of the official litany. Now does this mean that Gramsci intended to nullify these classical revolutionary axioms of the Comintern tradition? Or was it that they formed for him an indisputable acquisition which no longer needed affirmation, a complex of assumptions that underpinned his new explorations? The evidence (both direct and indirect) would seem to support the latter alternative. It must be remembered that Gramsci was ever mindful of the prison censor's watchful eye, and that he was incarcerated for plotting to overthrow the state, a charge he vigorously denied. Under these circumstances, it was hardly likely that his writings would be preoccupied with the need for armed struggle, which all communists accepted as gospel anyway. Yet, scattered throughout his notebooks are passages that, in one way or another, indicate his acceptance of a violent, coercive phase of the revolutionary battle, when a fundamental and conclusive break with the past is effected.

Interpretations that view Gramsci as an apostle of a constitutional and 'gradual' path to socialism are often based on two fallacies: (1) the belief that the 'war of position' strategy and the 'war of manœuvre' are seen by him as mutually exclusive alternatives, and (2) the belief that support for intermediate objectives and class alliances signals an acceptance of historical continuity and an exclusion of revolutionary rupture. Each of these assumptions will be dealt with in turn.

Nothing that Gramsci writes about the 'war of position' suggests that the proletarian capture of power will be peaceful or parliamentary. In fact, in his *Quaderni*, he expresses nothing but contempt for the parliamentary system, regarding it as irredeemably élitist and devoid of democratic content.[40] His remarks on the subject strongly echo those of Lenin in *State and Revolution*, and can only be described as light years away from Togliatti's high regard for the institution. It is possible that, for Gramsci, working-class salvation would come about solely through an institution he described as thoroughly corrupt and bourgeois to the core of its being? The hallmark of democratic socialism is, of course, an unshakable adherence to the procedures of parliamentary government, which are deemed to be *neutral* in the class struggle. In Gramsci's view, the 'war of position' and the 'war of manœuvre', the strategy of patient permeation and subversion and that of frontal attack, are two forms of a single war—not mutually exclusive, but complementary approaches. It is true that Gramsci downgrades the war of manœuvre. Whereas once it was the whole story, it is now only 'partial';[41] but it is still essential to final victory. This point emerges from his discussion of military science, from which he draws his analogies:

> Even those military technicians whose minds are now fixed on the war of position, just as they were previously on that of manœuvre, certainly do not maintain that the latter must be expunged from military science; they merely maintain that, in wars among the more industrially and socially advanced States, it must be reduced to more of a tactical than a strategic function. . . . *The same reduction must take place in the art and science of politics*, at least in the case of the most advanced States.[42]

Thus, it is not a matter of choosing, once and for all, one strategy or the other. The 'war of position' must be the fundamental approach in advanced societies; possession of the 'inner fortifications' is the only decisive assurance of ultimate victory. But direct assault, while no longer the basic technique of revolutionary action, must not be ruled out, and the appropriateness of its use in a given situation will be dictated by circumstances. To be sure, the recourse to arms is always present in Gramsci's mind. In his words, 'every political struggle always has a military substratum'.[43] And elsewhere in his notebooks he declares: 'The decisive element of every situation is force, permanently organized and arranged of long standing . . . therefore the essential task is that of systematically attending to this force, patiently forming it, developing it, and rendering it more and more homogeneous, compact, and self-conscious'.[44] The 'military' aspect of the struggle becomes especially important when the proletariat has at last conquered the institutions of civil society and solidified a new counter-hegemony. At this point there remains the climactic attack on the state fortress: the 'revolution of the spirit' now gives way to the 'revolution of arms'. Gramsci never seemed to entertain the possibility of the bourgeoisie giving up without a last-ditch fight to the finish. This point is made clear in his notes on the 'crisis of authority',a situation where the dominant hegemony is disintegrating, where 'the great masses' are 'detached from the traditional ideologies', where their ties to the dominant modes of thought are ruptured.[45] This may result from purely external, or exogenous forces, such as a lost war, or from the conscious mobilization into political awareness of hitherto passive and repressed social groups. The purpose of the party's 'war of position' in civil society is to bring about precisely this 'crisis of authority': the ruling classes must be stripped of the spiritual prestige that has enabled them to rule with a large measure of popular consent; these regressive social groups must be left naked, bereft of their ideological robes. But do they then step aside peaceably and voluntarily? Not according to Gramsci. Rather they become ' "dominant", exercising coercive force alone, . . .'.[46] That is, in place of consensus we get 'coercion in forms less and less disguised and indirect . . .'.[47] To him, it was in the nature of the bourgeois state that, in any final confrontation, the armed apparatus of repression would inevitably supplant the ideological apparatus to occupy the dominant position in the structure of class power. In such a scenario, a typically reformist posture is not likely to prove effective, and Gramsci never even considered it. In his political discussions and lectures at Turi in 1930, he was unequivocal about his ultimate objectives (though some of his fellow prisoners obviously doubted his sincerity). According to Lisa's report he affirmed that 'the violent conquest of power requires the creation, by the Party of the proletariat, of an organization of a military type, which . . . is diffused in all the branches of the bourgeois state apparatus, and is capable of wounding and inflicting serious blows on it at the decisive moment of struggle'. In his *Quaderni* we find no clear-cut discussion of 'the decisive moment of struggle', but he does at one point refer favourably to 'the destruction of the State machine' and goes on to say that only 'abstract and schematic minds' would deny that, through such destruction, 'one comes to produce another stronger and better constructed one'.[48]

No matter how successful the proletariat was in dividing and demoralizing the coercive state machine, there still would remain a hard core of counter-revolutionary forces who could not be converted but only vanquished. Even the most popular revolution would not be unanimous. Gramsci's undoubted regard for the liberal values of free speech and discussion did not move him to deny that the ruling circles, their 'lackeys', and any other recalcitrants must be pummelled into accepting the new order. Just as the communist in bourgeois society is forced to respect property rights, whether he likes it or not, so the anti-communist must be coerced into obedience to basic revolutionary principles. Socialist transformation, to Gramsci, was no gentlemanly affair, carried out with meticulous concern for liberal constitutional principles. In sum, while he refused to follow Sorel in attributing a mythical and therapeutic content to violence, his theory did not shrink from it. The war of manœuvre is a crucial supplement to the war of position, and, contrary to what certain commentators believe,[49] it is not simply the conclusive act, the dotting of the 'i' of the revolutionary process. Gramsci suggests that physical confrontation and other militant tactics, while necessarily subordinate to the strategy of permeation inside the superstructure of bourgeois society, must always be kept in reserve, to be used as the situation demands.

It is not just Gramsci's downgrading of the 'war of movement' that encourages 'gradualist' interpretations of his prison legacy. His willingness to work for intermediate objectives, to strive for class alliances, to build consensus, and to adjust the revolutionary process to specific national practices have also played a part. Gramsci, it is argued (especially by those on the far Left), was so anxious to compromise, to work within the existing framework, that he lost sight of the need for revolutionary purity, for an unwavering commitment to a radical rupture with the past. And so he came to regard socialist transformation as a smooth and happy process, unmarred by severe dislocations and perfectly attuned to national traditions. This line of interpretation, with its presumption that flexibility equals revisionism, cannot withstand scrutiny. There is no greater paragon of revolutionary determination than Lenin, and he was the unparalleled master at adapting first principles to particular situations. In his eyes, Marxism was a guide, not a dogma. Strategy was to be formulated not by blindly pursuing what Marx and Engels had advocated in different situations but only by following their method of deriving programmes from the problem of the moment. All the injunctions that are presumed to reflect a lack of revolutionary resolve in Gramsci were prefigured by Lenin, and in him this flexibility is applauded as evidence of tactical brilliance. It was the hero of 1917 who first understood that the proletariat need not be the sole bearer of Marxist revolution, and that alliance with the peasantry could serve to give history a needed push. It was Lenin who argued, in *Two Tactics of Social Democracy*, that the cause of communism could be advanced, in certain historical conjunctures, by the institution of a liberal regime with proletarian support. And it was Lenin, of course, who showed that the path to revolution need not follow a universal pattern, valid for all countries. True, it was a Comintern assumption that all subsequent revolutions must essentially conform to the Bolshevik model. But Lenin himself was (in some moods) less rigid than is usually supposed and often stressed the important differences between Western Europe and Russia. For example, in defending the United Front strategy at the Third Congress of 1921, he pointed out the need to take account of Western conditions—so different from those of his homeland. The October Revolution, he insisted, did not constitute a lesson to be learned by rote.[50] Presumably, this is what Gramsci had in mind when he generously said: 'It seems to me that Lenin understood that a change was necessary from the war of manœuvre, applied victoriously in the East in 1917, to a war of position, which was the only possible form in the West. . .'.[51] But, it might be asked, did not Gramsci take this Leninist flexibility and pragmatism to unrevolutionary lengths? There is, I think, an anachronistic tendency to look at Gramsci through the lens of contemporary PCI behaviour and to ignore the very different context within which he thought and acted. His call for a parliamentary 'interlude' and a policy of proletarian alliances arose out of what he admitted to be novel and exceptional circumstances—the phenomenon of popular fascism, an exiled and decimated Communist Party. Gramsci's prison yard discussions and—to a lesser extent—his notes on revolutionary strategy were mainly concerned with the peculiar Italian situation. There is no real reason to assume that he would have approved of a similar strategy in the more favourable climate of post-war liberalism, wherein the PCI, because of its role in the Resistance, has enjoyed unprecedented prestige and an immensely sophisticated organizational structure. In any case the Party's drive for 'respectability' and its 'frantic, almost pathetic search for allies in every section of Italian life'[52] have little to do with the 'Modern Prince' of Gramsci's conception. Superficial similarities should not be allowed to blur fundamental differences. Gramsci may have been willing to cultivate instrumental alliances with lower-middle-class groups, but he certainly did not, like his successors, include industrialists and entrepreneurs in this category. The movement he envisaged, moreover, was to remain under the firm leadership of the proletariat; this was the true revolutionary class, to which allied groups must defer. Nowhere did he propose anything resembling Togliatti's 'national' Party, accepting labourers and proprietors as virtually equal partners. Nor is Gramsci's reluctant acceptance of a liberal-democratic *intermezzo* to be confused with Togliatti's impassioned defence of parliamentary government as an integral part of the socialist future. In fact, the line Gramsci took in the Turi discussions and in his notebooks was not *substantially* different from the line he adopted in 1924, when he was the Comintern's favourite Italian revolutionary:

What must be the political posture and tactics of our Party in the present situation? The situation is 'democratic' because the great labouring masses are disorganized, dispersed, and atomized into a confused multitude. . . . The essential task of our Party consists in the conquest of the majority of the labouring class; the phase we are passing through is not that of the direct struggle for power, but a preparatory phase of transition to the struggle for power, a phase, in short, of agitation, of propaganda, of organization.[53]

What moved Gramsci's super-militant prison comrades to denounce him as a social-democrat was not so much that his ideas had shifted to the Right, but that the Comintern policy had shifted mightily to the Left.

As I noted earlier, it is a common fallacy to conflate the

possible empirical consequences of a thinker's ideas with the ideas themselves. A Communist Party that follows Gramsci's instructions and immerses itself in present social reality *may* come to identify with that reality. Any radical movement that is careful to adapt its activity to the particular national culture *runs the risk* of becoming absorbed into that culture. The de-radicalization of European Marxist parties, like the SPD, bears witness to this possibility. Be that as it may, Gramsci made it abundantly clear, in his prison writings, that such an outcome was anathema to him; and he did this not just in his (let it be admitted) infrequent and allusive references to the need for violent tactics, but also in his discussions of the dialectic, in which he insists that revolution must be total, introducing radically new modes of thinking, feeling and behaving.

One aspect of Gramsci's criticism of Croce centres on the latter's manner of conceiving the moments of the dialectical process and the passage from one to the other. According to Gramsci, he misconstrues the mechanism of the Hegelian-Marxist dialectic; indeed, his conception amounts to a 'mutilation of Hegelianism and of the dialectic'.[54] Croce, it is argued, makes the same error for which Marx reproached Proudhon in a famous passage of the *The Poverty of Philosophy*, where the 'philosopher of praxis' accused the Frenchman of having misunderstood the meaning of the dialectic. Marx underlined the force of *negativity* in history, which for him was the nucleus of dialectical thought. Properly understood, the dialectic was a movement of opposition or passage from affirmation to negation to negation of the negation. Proudhon, on the other hand, had wrongly argued that the 'good side' of every historical moment was preserved in the dialectical antithesis. With explicit reference to Marx's critique, Gramsci attacks Croce for presupposing that 'the thesis must be "conserved" by the antithesis in order not to destroy the historical process . . .'.[55] This position, Gramsci writes, entails a disavowal of the force of negativity, which constitutes the backbone of the dialectic and of history. In historical reality, 'Every antithesis must necessarily pose itself as the radical antagonist to the thesis, to the point where it resolves to destroy and replace it completely'.[56] Again, 'In real history, the antithesis tends to destroy the thesis . . .'.[57] Genuine dialectical thought, then, considers the antithesis as the total negation of the thesis, which is demolished and not merely modified. Progress is discontinuous, for dialectical tension, when it reaches a certain point, precipitates a cataclysm. Interestingly enough, Gramsci brings his purely philosophical argument down to the level of practical politics. The idea that the antithesis conserves the 'good side' of the thesis, or alternatively, that the thesis comes to incorporate a part of the antithesis, is not simply a falsification of the dialectic. Worse, its political manifestation is the reformism, *à la* Bernstein,[58] which seeks to attenuate the dialectical clash between capitalism and socialism.[59] Historical analysis based on the 'degenerate and mutilated Hegelianism' of the Croces of this world, we are informed, is allied to 'a panicky fear of Jacobin movements, of every active intervention of the great popular masses as a factor of historical progress'.[60] By enervating the antithesis, Croce and Proudhon reduce 'the dialectic to a process of reformist evolution, "revolution-restoration", in which only the second term is valid, because it is a matter of continually patching up from without an organism that does not possess internally the proper conditions of health'. Reformist illusions notwithstanding, historical development has nothing to do with evolution; nor is it a 'sporting game, with its umpire and its pre-established rules to be loyally respected . . .'.[61]

In these reflections on the dialectic, Gramsci is repeating, in philosophical language, his youthful intransigence and contempt for reformist socialism. The proletariat is the antithesis, the innovative force; the thesis is the capitalist social order. The mature Gramsci certainly did repudiate the politics of *tanto peggio, tanto meglio* (the worse, the better), as flagrantly irresponsible: reforms were worth fighting for. What is more, he believed that revolutionary strategy must be intimately related to the historically defined circumstances of its operation, to the unique national configuration, and not simply represent a slavish imitation of the Soviet model, whose socio-cultural context was in many ways *sui generis*. But when people like Merli infer from this that Gramsci abandoned the idea of revolutionary rupture, they are grossly mistaken.[62]

Does the line of argument put forward here mean that various commentators are correct when they stress the theoretical distance between Gramsci and (what they deem to be) a corpulent, complacent PCI, whose only purpose is to gain a few more votes at each election? Must we agree with Lucio Colletti, when he declares: 'We should not allow either Amendola [see note 37 to this chapter] or anybody else to cover themselves with the name of Gramsci as they pursue their own—very different—aims'?[63] Must we conclude, with Jocteau, that a 'democratic' interpretation has no 'serious foundation either in the theoretical positions or in the strategies and political directives that Gramsci elaborated'?[64] The reader, I hope, will not accuse me of inconsistency if I fight shy of an affirmative answer to all these questions. In a certain measure, the PCI does distort Gramsci's legacy when it links his name to policies far more moderate and conciliatory than anything he ever advocated— indeed, similar to those he condemned. Still, the relationship between Gramsci's thought and the contemporary PCI is an intricate one; it cannot be convincingly maintained that there is *no* tie. In order to illustrate this point, I propose two distinctions rarely made in the literature on the subject: on the one hand, a distinction between the *letter* of Gramsci's directives and their *spirit*; on the other, between *reformism* and the PCI's 'democratic road to socialism'. It is now widely accepted, by cynics on both the Right and the Left, that the PCI has betrayed its Marxist-Leninist soul, its revolutionary heritage. In its search for a 'politics of unity', the Party, on this argument, now eschews any programme of major social and political change in the foreseeable future. Instead its paramount goals are maintaining electoral strength and projecting an image of responsibility. Consequently, the ultimate goal of socialism has been pushed so far into the background that it has vanished from sight. In its anxiety to meet the imperatives of new conditions, the PCI is moving along the familiar path once trodden by the German Socialist Party; it is shedding its revolutionary baggage and fast becoming a reformist party, interested in little more than piecemeal alterations to a system whose premises it now embraces. This is not the place for a lengthy discussion of the Italian Communist Party, but a few remarks would not be amiss. It should be pointed out, to begin with, that the structural reforms for which it fights are in no sense conceived as a means of *improving* capitalist society. According to its self-image, the PCI is putting forward intermediate objectives which foreshadow socialist solutions. These intermediate objectives, by expanding democratic control of political life, and by removing zones of activity from the criteria of profitableness, are allegedly designed to *hinder* capitalism's perpetuation, to sharpen and underline the conflict between the general interest and the interests of the monopolies. So the Party is not simply in the business of winning votes, but of mobilizing a wide variety of social forces around radical programmatic goals which contradict the inherent presuppositions of capitalism. To quote Giorgio Napolitano, the PCI's chief economic spokesman: 'What we are trying to do is to give ever newer and richer content to democracy—promoting an effective mass participation in the management of economic, social and political life, transforming economic and social structures, carrying out substantial changes in the power relationships between the classes'.[65] The point is to break through the logic of conventional politics and induce fundamental change through an alteration of attitudes and a mass mobilization of social pressure. Of course, the PCI has not yet effected any structural transformations, but the potential is there. Its behaviour *has* led to the erosion of the psychological and ideological barriers against its acceptance as a full and legitimate participant in the Italian political system. Indeed, it is no exaggeration to say that the PCI has become the 'natural' Party of the Italian intelligentsia. The Party, in brief, has gone some way towards creating the counter-hegemony of Gramsci's dreams. Whether or not its leaders are sincere in their socialist commitment is a matter of conjecture and, fortunately, not altogether relevant here. What is important is that they have *articulated* a plausible parliamentary strategy for the achievement of radical socialism, which is to be distinguished from social-democracy. And nothing in their actual policies clearly indicates a retreat from their avowed goals. It is worth keeping in mind, then, that when the Italian Communists appropriate Gramsci as a founder of their particular line, the line in question has a fair claim to be considered properly Marxist and (in a non-insurrectionary sense) revolutionary. The cynics have probably read too much into the Party's bourgeois demeanour and liberal-sounding rhetoric.

The second distinction that needs to be drawn is between what Gramsci *actually said*, which is in crucial respects divergent from PCI strategy, and the *spirit* that informed his entire approach. Gramsci, after 1929, attacked sectarianism, not the idea of revolution itself. He defined sectarianism as an inability to adjust theory to changing circumstances; rather, theories must respond to 'actual history, concrete existence'; they must be 'adapted to time and place, as if gushing from all the pores of the determinate society that needs to be transformed'.[66] The result would be a 'realistic politics' purged of 'every vague and purely ideological element'.[67] It is this realism—as opposed to moderation—that underlies his call for the Italian Communist Party to 'nationalize itself', to speak to the particular customs and aspirations of the Italian people. Now it may be that Gramsci's approach to socialism, with its intransigence and contempt for constitutional forms, would be counterproductive in the circumstances of modern Europe. To speculate about what Gramsci 'would have done' were he alive today is a futile exercise, for he would no longer be the same Gramsci. It can be said, however, that he had little time for doctrinal purity, especially in his prison years, and was quite prepared to override Marxist-Leninist traditions when he judged them inappropriate. In so far as its pragmatism is neither old-fashioned reformism nor rank opportunism, the PCI can plausibly claim to be following the *spirit*, if not the letter, of Gramsci' teachings. Furthermore, *some* Party attitudes and policies *undoubtedly* originate in his writings. In its healthy respect for the classical democratic values of free debate and popular participation, in its search for consensus and ideological supremacy, and in its abiding desire to 'complete' the Risorgimento and build a unified national culture, the PCI certainly echoes themes that were dear to Gramsci's heart (though they may be more consistent than he was in their adherence to these ideas). In its more subtle and measured forms, then, the PCI interpretation of Gramsci, while misleading, does possess a certain element of truth.

To conclude, the 'gradualist' interpretation of Gramsci, though not without foundation, is incompatible with his expressed views. And when this interpretation takes the form of equating his thoughts with social-democracy, it enters the realm of pure fantasy. Despite his pragmatism and concern for popular support, Gramsci never deviated from a belief in total revolution brought about in part through the intervention of armed force. While some of the currently fashionable doctrines of Eurocommunism do have a genuine basis in his ideas, he himself remained steadfastly committed to the very anti-parliamentarism and insurrectionism the Eurocommunists have repudiated. Why has Gramsci's position been distorted? Commentators to his Right have probably been motivated by a combination of opportunism and wishful thinking; those to his Left by absurd notions of revolutionary purity, usually based on a fetishistic concept of 'internationalism' and generally oblivious to the exigencies of historical reality. Yet again we see how Gramsci studies have been contaminated by contemporary political polemics.

CHAPTER 7

Evaluation and Conclusion

> Who has *really* attempted to follow up the explorations of Marx and Engels? I can only think of Gramsci.
>
> Louis Althusser, *For Marx*

As the above quotation suggests, Gramsci's harshest critics were impressed by his theoretical aims and achievements. But just how valid is his doctrine of hegemony and its surrounding theory, from both a scientific and ethical point of view? Earlier it was said that Gramsci's *Quaderni* provide innovative answers to three major questions which have troubled Marxism during the past half century or so. (1) How does one explain the survival of capitalism long after it should have passed into oblivion—why has the proletariat not developed the necessary class consciousness to make revolution in the advanced capitalist zones? (2) What strategy should be adopted by a Marxist party operating within a liberal democratic state, where the regime is firmly established and where the 'exploited' classes are more or less integrated into the system? (3) Why have actual socialist states failed so abysmally in their 'historically defined' task of achieving popular liberation? In what follows, some attempt will be made to assess Gramsci's proposed (or implicit) solutions to these problems. Accordingly, we shall—for purposes of discussion—divide his theory into three components, roughly corresponding to the above questions, and consider each one in turn. The Sardinian offers: (1) a *diagnosis*, or *analysis*, of modern capitalist society; (2) a *strategy* for overthrowing this society; and (3) a new *vision* or *concept* of Marxism—one bringing it more in line with the classical values of the liberal, humanist tradition. Because it raises so many fundamental theoretical and empirical issues, whose complexity is notorious, our evaluation of Gramsci's contribution can do little more than scratch the surface and indicate areas where further research or more extensive analysis might bear fruit. It is hoped that this unavoidable sacrifice of depth will be more than counterbalanced by the breadth and suggestiveness of the ensuing observations.

I. *Gramsci's Analysis*

Since it has been argued that Gramsci's concept of hegemony is solidly grounded in the Marxist proposition that the economic 'base' in some sense conditions or shapes all other social and cultural phenomena, it might be prudent to subject this core tenet of historical materialism to brief critical inspection. One logical objection (that base and superstructure are not conceptually distinct) has already been dismissed as irrelevant at best (see pages 118–9), but awesome difficulties remain. In searching for (strict or qualified) causal links between various spheres of social life, we assume that, in principle, these spheres can be delimited. But is such specification possible in practice? The range of phenomena on which a *natural* process depends is often very restricted and can easily be identified and isolated. We are usually interested in only a small number of properties of the examined natural process. In order to explain them and predict their future change, it suffices to take into account a limited number of other properties with which they usually stand in some relatively simple functional relationship. But in human society we deal with concrete totalities, not with abstract properties, and the boundary conditions of a given field of activity remain more or less vague. Closely related to this obstacle is the problem discussed by Blalock.[1] We could discover the precise relationships between the various spheres of social life only if changes in each sphere were to occur discretely, with a long enough interval between each change for the observer to note the temporal sequences involved. Unfortunately the real world does not operate so neatly. Historically, changes in both base and superstructure have occurred simultaneously and continuously, making it hard to isolate distinct orders of succession. To discover correlations, or 'elective affinities', is not sufficient, because a correlation, in itself, can tell us nothing about the direction of causation. What all these considerations point to is this: it is beyond the realm of possibility to conduct anything like a controlled experiment of the materialist hypothesis. This would be true even if the doctrine were rigorously formulated, and one searches in vain for such formulation in Gramsci's writings. Still, the apparent *methodological* impossibility of *proving* that some factor B in social life is a derivation of some other factor A does not render the relationship *logically* impossible. Nor does it mean that rational argument about such relationships is pointless. Let us avoid the empiricist fallacy of assuming that what cannot be properly observed and measured does not exist.

It would seem, then, that two inter-connected contentions embedded in Gramsci's doctrine of hegemony are not susceptible to conclusive proof or disproof: (1) the dominant ideas in capitalist society (e.g. conventional conceptions of democracy, rights, property, justice) arose out of the experience and exclusive needs of the bourgeois class, and (2) a new 'authentic' proletarian world-view is immanent in the changing system of production and 'implicit' in 'deviant' forms of working-class behaviour. Both these assertions presuppose the causal primacy of the economic factor. However, Gramsci's theory of hegemony involves two further claims, whose soundness or otherwise does not depend upon a prior assessment of historical materialism as an explanatory tool. The first is an analytic-explanatory one: that consensus over values and beliefs is the major source of cohesion in bourgeois society. The second claim is empirical: that existing capitalist societies do indeed exhibit consensual integration. Each of these will now be examined.

Broadly speaking, modern social thought has suggested two main types of answer to the Hobbesian question: why does social order exist? On the one hand, there is the school which adheres to a consensual model of industrial society (i.e. consensus theory); on the other, the school which focuses on conflict and value differentiation (i.e. conflict, or coercion, theory). We shall present these divergent perspectives in an abbreviated and somewhat exaggerated form in order to highlight their main themes. Consensus theory, associated with the Parsonian functionalist strand of thought, holds that the solution to the problem of order lies essentially in shared norms, values and beliefs. (Different writers stress one or another of these.) The first influential progenitor of the consensual model was Alexis de Tocqueville, who offered a succinct version of its essence in *Democracy in America*:

A society can exist only when a great number of men consider a great number of things from the same point of view; when they hold the same opinions upon many subjects, when the same occurrences suggest the same thoughts and impressions to their minds.[2]

While it is not denied that elements of coercion are present in the control system of every society, the function of such coercion is minimized. Obedience is viewed as a consequence of socialized commitment to the ongoing social set up.[3] Though its roots might be said to reach back to Hobbes's notion of the 'war of all against all', conflict, or coercion, theory was first put forward systematically by Marx. But it has also received much non-Marxist expression in modern sociology. Ralf Dahrendorf in his *Class and Class Conflict in Industrial Society* has perhaps been most explicit: 'Every society displays at every point dissensus and conflict; social conflict is ubiquitous . . . the distribution of authority . . . is the ultimate "cause" of the formation of conflict groups.'[4] Conflict is endemic in all systems which institutionalize stratification, because they presuppose differential access to scarce resources. It follows that power, not norms, is the key variable for explaining social order: men conform largely, if not wholly, because they are compelled to do so by those who monopolize the means of coercion. Non-compliance exposes one to physical punishment, deprivation of property, resources, rights, etc.

In the past two decades, attempts have been made to subject consensus and conflict theories to empirical testing. The merit of many of these studies, most of them done in the USA and Britain, is doubtful on methodological grounds.[5] In any case, belief systems (assuming they are conceptually distinct and separately identifiable from actual behaviour) do not surrender easily to empirical study and quantification. One very thorny problem intrinsic in the use of formal survey methods might be called linguistic, and arises from the artificiality of the procedure. Poorly educated people may not be able to grasp the meaning of the questions put to them. They may, in consequence, provide answers which do not really reflect their opinions or inclinations. On the other hand, middle-class respondents, because of their relative sophistication, will be much more familiar with the clichés and symbols embodied in the questions; they will readily understand which answer is socially acceptable and might reply accordingly. In addition, what is elicited in scientific investigation is a frozen entity or disposition, lacking the fluidity of its normal operation. Attitudes are complex things, incessantly modified by subtle and barely conscious considerations and subject to drastic change over time. Thus the responses elicited by even the most carefully designed questionnaires must be accepted with great caution. But even if it is granted that the investigator can ascertain people's beliefs, there remains the further difficulty of assessing the relationship between these beliefs and concrete action. Evidence suggests that the connection may be tenuous.[6] To the extent that this is true, the mere compilation of statistics about mass opinions runs the risk of becoming a rarefied proceeding of questionable relevance to the real world of social and political activity.

Clearly, no definitive solution to the Hobbesian problem of order emerges from the survey work available. Nevertheless, at least some of the empirical findings to date cannot be dismissed as unreliable or invalid. Taken as a whole, these results follow a definite pattern and shed light on the *nature* of mass beliefs (if not on their *significance* for social stability). And the characteristics which are discernible tend to substantiate Gramsci's description of 'contradictory consciousness'.

First, it is now undeniable that the beliefs of most men are inconsistent and often incoherent.[7] The textbook model of the rational democratic citizen, fully aware of and perfectly committed to the constituent ideas of the liberal *Weltanschauung*, finds little basis in reality. None the less, it is fairly clear that there exists, at least in Britain and the USA, widespread adhesion to certain symbols, values, and cognitions which are supportive of the existing system. According to the findings of Gabriel Almond and Sidney Verba, for instance, the 'democratic myth'—the belief that political decisions and outcomes are responsive to the claims of each and every citizen—is alive and well in both countries.[8] And while the extent of political equality seems to be *over*-estimated by the British populace, the magnitude of social and economic inequality appears to be *under*-estimated. W. G. Runciman's research into working-class feelings about their position in society points to a striking discrepancy between the degree of deprivation subjectively perceived and objective inequality. Because of their social isolation and perceptual limitations, many members of the more disadvantaged strata are quite simply unaware of how deprived they are in relation to other groups in the stratification hierarchy.[9] There is some reason to believe, moreover, that existing inequalities are considered legitimate. McKenzie and Silver, in their classic analysis of working-class conservatism in Britain, discovered that only four per cent of *manual workers* endorsed abolition of the monarchy, while only one in three favoured any change in the status of the House of Lords. Although it is arguable that the primary function of these institutions is to provide traditional legitimacy for their own subordination, members of the labouring class apparently regard them as valuable and integral parts of the British heritage.[10] Turning to the United States, we find evidence to suggest that the great majority of citizens really do accept the official myths about the opportunity structure. In a small mid-western industrial town, for example, 76 per cent of the respondents agreed that America is such a land of opportunity that anyone who works hard can go as far as he wants. (And 24 per cent of the sample was black!)[11] That British and American workers hold a benign image of their respective socio-political orders, at least on a general level, has also been documented in a number of other investigations.[12]

Yet there is also considerable survey evidence which indicates deviance from dominant ideological tenets. This deviance, however, rarely seems to consist of conscious rejection of established definitions; rather, it generally involves ignoring these definitions when specific actions or responses are called for. Dissensus mainly expresses itself either in actual behaviour in concrete situations, or in responses to specific questions about the application of general values and beliefs, or in responses that concern everyday life and material well-being.

To take one example, it is a common finding in research that industrial workers often endorse middle-class criticisms of the trade unions. A 1969 survey found that 67 per cent of trade union respondents subscribed to the statement that their leaders' activities constituted a 'threat to the prosperity of the country'.[13]

Other studies report like findings.[14] All the same, there is little evidence that workers wish to limit trade union power in *their own enterprises*[15] or that they are opposed to socially disruptive, illegal and even violent industrial action in furtherance of *their own particular demands*.

In reviewing much of the literature on delinquency, Hyman Rodman finds a similarly paradoxical situation. He concludes that because lower-class people often find dominant values, such as achievement orientation, irrelevant to their particular circumstances, they come to tolerate and eventually to evaluate favourably certain deviations from these values. But the result is not abandonment or even flouting of the middle-class ethos; it is, instead, what Rodman calls a 'stretched value system', with a low degree of commitment to all values, including the dominant ones.[16]

Drawing these survey results together, it would seem that the average man tends to have two levels of normative reference— the abstract and the situational.[17] On the former plane, he expresses a great deal of agreement with the dominant ideology; on the latter, he reveals not outright dissensus but a diminished level of commitment to the 'bourgeois' ethos, because it is often inapposite to the exigencies of his class position. Serious discontent and militant postures often come to the surface, but they are not accompanied by a realistic appraisal of alternative structures. Both the consensus and conflict schools stand partially refuted by the evidence.

Hence, despite his lack of familiarity with questionnaires and computers, Gramsci comprehended what appear to be the salient features of mass consciousness in those advanced capitalist societies where Communist Parties have made no inroads. To begin with, he understood that the average individual's belief system is internally contradictory; yet he also recognized the widespread, if somewhat equivocal, acceptance of perceptions and values favourable to the status quo. It is, of course, difficult to prove that this abstract adherence has substantive implications for action. As pointed out above, much research casts some doubt on the operational significance of the existing consensus; and no one yet has adequately specified either the conditions under which people's beliefs influence their responses or the forms these influences take. Gramsci himself saw that there was often inconsistency between expressed belief and action, that attachment to the dominant ideology was neither without qualification nor always incarnated in practice. In his schema, it will be recalled, the members of the subordinate classes come to accept the dominant network of beliefs as an abstract version of reality, but their life conditions weaken its binding force in the actual conduct of affairs. Still, it is reasonable to hypothesize, as did Gramsci, that any form of adherence, whether superficial or profoundly internalized, has consequences for behaviour, even if only to encourage ambivalence and confine deviant action within certain boundaries.[18]

Although the results of the existing survey studies are neither conclusive nor devoid of ambiguity, we must (tentatively) grant the substantial accuracy of Gramsci's depiction of 'contradictory consciousness'. Even in ostensibly consensual capitalist societies, the concrete behaviour and responses of the masses provide intimations, however vague, of an alternative worldview. While these intimations may not, *pace* Gramsci, indicate a proletarian ideology in embryo, they nevertheless constitute a popular base upon which such an ideology could be built. If the available evidence fails to support the more complacent theories of consensus, guided as they are by images of a genuinely happy, well-adjusted work force, it also shakes the foundations of those 'pessimistic' Marxist and neo-Marxist interpretations which view the Western worker as a 'one-dimensional' pseudo-being, the victim of a massive and virtually impenetrable 'false consciousness'. In assuming the absolute efficacy of the established universe of discourse and action, thinkers like Marcuse exaggerate the homogenity and tidiness of the system and thus overstate, perhaps, the insurmountability of the gulf between socialist thought and proletarian action.

It seems evident that Gramsci's conception of mass consciousness is more valid empirically than either the consensus or conflict models. It is also possible to demonstrate that Gramsci's conception rests on sounder theoretical underpinnings.

The weaknesses of consensus theory have been constantly reiterated by its many critics. The principal objection is twofold. First, the theory implicitly assumes an *independent convergence* in the outlooks of different classes: it fails to clarify the

connection between the distribution of power and the legitimation of values. The possibility that socialization is an *imposition*
of beliefs and values *de haut en bas* is not even considered. Second,
the theory uncritically accepts the doubtful premise that social
stratification, as we know it in the West, is both inevitable and
beneficial to all concerned. Thus any form of normative and
cognitive unity that promotes the stability of the system is
looked upon as inherently valuable and 'classless'. Consensus
theory, in other words, 'tends to become a metaphysical representation of the dominant ideological matrix';[19] it typically
considers neither the *origin* of common agreement nor the question of *who benefits* disproportionately from it. Gramsci, as a
Marxist, avoided this pitfall. His concept of hegemony refers to
a set of ideas which are dominant *as a consequence of a particular
structure of power*. To him, bourgeois hegemony was a legitimating
mask over the predatory nature of class domination. Whether
or not we *fully* agree with him on this point, it certainly *is*
inadequate to discuss consensus in isolation from the massive
inequalities of wealth and power that continue to plague most
Western societies.

The theoretical deficiencies of the conflict model are no less
fundamental than those of its rival. Most important, its conceptual apparatus is too rudimentary to cope with the complexity of the interaction among social, psychological, and
cultural factors. Lacking an adequate analysis of motivation, it
attempts to make do with a narrow and superficial utilitarianism
that sees men as impelled by rational calculations of personal
advantage. It is a prevailing view in modern psychology that
human behaviour is only very broadly controlled by genetic
models. Cultural patterns provide a blueprint for the organization of social and psychological processes, much as genetic
systems provide such a blueprint for the organization of organic
processes.[20] As Gramsci recognized, human behaviour, if it is to
have any effective form at all, must to a significant extent be
controlled by extrinsic cultural patterns. That is, men do not
define their interests 'objectively', or purely in terms of the
'factual' situation, but rather in terms of their perceptions,
evaluations, and goals—all of which are, in some measure,
independently variable and culturally determined. In addition
there is the *intuitive implausibility* of coercion theory. It is difficult

to see how force could be the *main* cause of social obedience over a lengthy period of time, especially in complex liberal societies where the use of coercive mechanisms is greatly circumscribed by custom and law. If (as psychological analysis and historical experience seem to indicate) men are by nature believing animals, incapable of shedding all the myths of existence, then they undoubtedly need to feel that they are governed not on the basis of mere material force but on the basis of moral principles. It is this deep need which gives the reigning symbols and doctrines of a society their powerful emotional appeal.

It might be objected, at this stage, that a third important line of attack on the problem of social order has been ignored in the preceding discussion—exchange theory.[21] While this theory, unlike its 'consensus' and 'conflict' counterparts, has not stood at the centre of the major debates in sociological thought, it has become increasingly fashionable in professional academic circles and merits some comment. Firmly rooted in utilitarian modes of theorizing, and obviously influenced by classical economic doctrines, the theory is based on the model of the market-place, with individuals conceived as entrepreneurs seeking to gain profit in interaction with others. Central to the theory's conceptual apparatus is cost-benefit analysis, focusing on material and psychological incentives as determinants of action. Social order emerges out of bargaining relationships between private actors engaging in the rational pursuit of self-interest. Men realize that they stand to maximize their interests through acceptance of a system of rules whose function is to specify the basis of social co-operation. Compliance, therefore, is achieved without recourse to coercion or appeal to cohesive values. It is essentially a matter of pragmatism. The theoretical shortcomings of this type of explanation should be apparent on a moment's reflection. Acts of exchange take place within a context that itself determines the bargaining power that different participants can wield, which distributes differentially the services they can offer and the resources they can employ. As a matter of fact, in most societies, the conditions under which actors compete are vastly unequal in the sense that some start with huge advantages derived from social position. Now exchange theory appears to assume precisely that which needs explanation: why do people agree to interact even though the existing bargaining situation puts them at a great disadvantage? Presumably because they either (a) regard the system as basically legitimate—the best of all possible worlds (the consensus solution) or (b) fear the consequences of non-conformity (the coercion solution)—or else experience some combination of the two motivations. Exchange theory can offer no explanation which avoids circularity. Why do people not opt out? Because they are receiving sufficient rewards. But how do we know that their rewards are sufficient? Because they do not drop out. [22] The fatal flaw of this theory is that it cannot account for the derivation of interests, which it simply takes as given. To explain all behaviour as stemming from 'self-interest' is to blur too many distinctions and to render the concept of interest empty of meaning.

It might well be argued that *all* the theories of social order discussed here exaggerate the rational, choosing element in compliance. Of course, it is an occupational hazard of intellectuals to assume that ordinary men would not act as they do unless they possessed goals or principles to govern their behaviour. But the ties that bind men to a community may have little to do with 'common value integration' or fear of sanctions or 'rational' calculation of self-interest; obedience may also stem from habit, from unreflecting common participation in established forms of activity.[23] Many men simply never enter into situations where the possibility of rejecting traditional patterns of behaviour actually arises. Consider the graphic, eloquent description of South Italian peasants by Carlo Levi, the anti-fascist novelist who, through a quaint peculiarity of Mussolini's legal system, was 'exiled' to a remote village in Basilicata:

They do not and cannot have what is called political awareness, because they are literally *pagani*, 'pagans', or countrymen, as distinguished from city-dwellers. The deities of the State and the City can find no worshippers here on the land, where the wolf and the ancient black boar reign supreme, where there is no wall between the world of men and the world of animals and spirits, between the leaves of the trees above and the roots below. They cannot have even an awareness of themselves as individuals, here where all things are held together by acting upon one another and each one is a power unto itself, working imperceptibly, where there is no barrier that cannot be broken down by magic. They live submerged in a world that rolls on independent of their will, where man is in no way separate from his sun, his beast, his malaria, where there can be neither happiness, as literary devotees of the land conceive it, nor hope, because these two are adjuncts of personality and here there is only the grim passivity of a sorrowful Nature.[24]

Ironically, unconscious conformity ('grim passivity') was a more important feature in the semi-developed Italy of Gramsci's time than in the advanced capitalist regimes of the present day, with their ubiquitous and universal systems of public education. No doubt, most of our everyday actions are not products of reflective mental activity, but habitual behaviour *is* rule governed, and most members of an integrated, literate society could make the implicit rule explicit if they were asked to justify themselves.

It must be stressed that Gramsci, in contrast to other advocates of consensus theory, was not making *universal* claims, applicable to all societies at all times. He well understood, for example, that 'grim passivity' constituted an important element of social order in pre-industrial societies, like Tsarist Russia or pre-Risorgimento Italy. He recognized, moreover, that value integration could dissolve, thus causing a 'crisis of authority', wherein force becomes the chief mechanism of social control.[25] (While it is by no means clear when his abstract category of 'organic crisis' applies to specific historical and social cases, contemporary Italy and perhaps France might be said to exemplify an early stage of just such a 'crisis'.) Yet, to his mind, such situations could never be *stable* in a modern industrial setting, where no regime could long endure without popular support and a unified cultural base. Gramsci may have underestimated the extent to which fear of economic deprivation or physical punishment could act as a functional alternative to consensus, but, as noted earlier, it is difficult to see how coercion (particularly in liberal societies) could provide a *long-range* solution to the problem of order. In the most 'stable' capitalist countries, social cohesion does seem to be (and probably has been) primarily dependent on shared beliefs and values, which present a formidable barrier to the penetration of revolutionary consciousness. But the next question is: *why* does consensus exist? Or, to be more specific, what causes people to endorse the essential features of the liberal status quo?

As has been observed, Gramsci found the answer to this question in the superstructure: owing to its subtle control over civil society—the mass media, the schools, the trade unions, and so on—the economically dominant bourgeois class has succeeded in persuading the masses to accept the legitimacy of their own subordination. If class struggle has been neutralized or rendered harmless, this is not due to the resolution of capitalism's inherent self-destructive tendencies. On the contrary, capitalism, for Gramsci, is an increasingly decadent system, rife with 'incurable structural contradictions' and utterly incapable of further developing the productive forces.[26] Whereas once it served a progressive historical function, capitalism is now an irredeemably 'unhealthy' system, which has fallen prey to 'speculators' and 'parasites'—'people who consume without producing'. Because of speculation, which has become a 'technical necessity' of the system, the productive process is more and more subject to panics, 'runs' and other irrational behaviour.[27] Nor can the system ultimately 'overcome the tendential law of the fall in the rate of profit'. 'Fordist' methods of intensification and rationalization of labour can provide a partial and temporary counter-tendency, but the dire economic consequences of the 'law' will assert themselves in the end.[28] The growth in state intervention (in the form of planning, investment, etc.)—a phenomenon remarked by Gramsci[29]—is also incapable of yielding more than short-term remedies for the intrinsic disorders of an economy founded on individual appropriation. Indeed, such intervention often functions to make matters worse, as in Italy, where the Fascist regime 'is creating new *rentiers*; i.e promoting the old forms of parasitic accumulation of savings and tending to create closed social formations [*quadri*]'.[30] By introducing a certain degreee of co-ordination and regulation, the bourgeois state can, *at best*, shore up the frail foundations of the monopoly capitalist edifice, not eliminate its structural defects.[31] In brief, Gramsci more or less accepted the conventional Marxist analysis of the 'laws of motion' of capitalist society (though, of course, he denied that capitalism would automatically *collapse* under the weight of its own contradictions). Now, if economic polarization is an unalterable fact of capitalist life, and if the system is rent by internal contradictions that prevent it from attaining its productive potential, then capitalism can survive only because the organs of civil society hide the regime's structural inadequacies behind a thick ideological veil. Gramsci's concept of hegemony rests on the assumption that the 'objective' conditions for the formation of revolutionary class consciousness are to a greater or lesser degree realized in contemporary capitalist society, and that what remains to be done is essentially the creation of the appropriate 'subjective' conditions through action at the cultural level.

This account of consensus as the product of cultural transmission *via* the agencies of the ideological superstructure doubtless captures a deal of the truth, but it hardly exhausts all the possibilities. The 'end of ideology' thesis, for example, argues that the logic of the industrial order, by increasing overall wealth, giving rise to the welfare state, encouraging occupational differentiation and enlarging the ranks of the white-collar strata, has rendered Marx's class polarization model obsolete. Thus, ideologies of the Left, which presuppose class struggle, are now irrelevant. The result is an end to 'apocalyptic thinking' and a growing convergence over general principles, reducing the area of social conflict and leaving room for technical disputes only.[32] Consensus is thus explained largely in terms of the changing *economic structure* of modern capitalism a system now deemed able to cope fully with the material aspirations of the workers. Such a diagnosis is not confined to defenders of the status quo. By way of accounting for the domestication of the workforce in the 'hell of the affluent society' Marcuse too has pointed to the equalization of life-styles and the general flattening out of the class structure. The startling technological efficiency of mass capitalist society, he maintains, has enabled it to conquer all centrifugal forces and kill the urge to resistance; the goods it produces lead people to believe they are living the 'good life', while on a deeper level, the very instinctual structure of the individual, his basic needs and psychological mechanisms, are moulded to suit the requirements of the productive apparatus. 'The products indoctrinate and manipulate'; they 'carry with them prescribed attitudes and habits, certain intellectual and emotional reactions' which bind men more or less pleasantly to the system. All possibilities of self-awareness and emancipation, concludes Marcuse, are closed off in a social order where 'false consciousness is immune against its falsehood'.[33] The immanent logic of technology consigns socialism to the attic. Marcuse's critique, it will be observed, presumes the literal falsity, or at least obsolescence, of Marx's analysis of capitalism as an inherently self-destructive system of production. For Marcuse, the real inculcation of the voluntary acceptance of capitalism is effected *within the productive process itself*, which induces habits of submission and diffuses an all-embracing consumer fetishism. The mass media, the schools, and all the other institutions of 'civil society' only serve to *reinforce* this antecedent process of conditioning.[34]

Both the optimism of the 'end of ideology' school and the pessimism of the Frankfurt school have come to seem dubious in the light of empirical inquiry and the actual events of the past decade or so. The evidence indicates that massive social inequalities *have* been maintained in Western society,[35] and that widespread discontent—however confused, directionless and muted—has *not* been eradicated. Capitalism, moreover, has betrayed definite structural failings during the past seven years of 'stagflation'; no one can any longer take for granted its capacity to shower us with an ever-increasing supply of material goods. Nevertheless, some part of the curiously similar analyses of these two schools must certainly be accepted. Although disparities in wealth, income, psychic satisfaction and access to facilities continue to be great, recent developments in the productive system and in the structure and composition of classes have definitely contributed to such stability as exists in the West. In this respect, three broad trends can be isolated.[36] First, an enormous increase in the total social product, along with the efforts of the trade union movement, have combined (especially since the last war) to assure for the working class a standard of living which by no means constitutes pauperization. While it is probably true that there has been no significant redistribution of wealth and income, and while *relative* deprivation is still very much with us, increasing affluence has indeed caused a merging in buying patterns and styles of life in general. Second, the stratification system itself has become more complex and differentiated. Marx expected the working class to become (a) more homogeneous because differences of skill and earnings would be reduced, if not obliterated, by the more extensive use of machinery; and (b) numerically stronger, because many members of the old middle class would sink to the condition of proletarians. Gramsci never seriously dissented from this view—which has been disproved by the force of events. The proportion of industrial workers within the population of advanced capitalist countries tends, in fact, to *decline* with the advance of technology. Meanwhile, a new intermediate stratum of administrative, technical and service personnel, often possessing a considerable degree of education, has emerged. Partly for reasons of status,[37] this stratum has thus far refused to align itself with the working class. Even within the category of industrial workers themselves, there has been no sign of 'homogenization'. On the contrary, we find 'élite' groups with special skills demanding special consideration and contracts to preserve their prized 'differentials'. All in all, society has *not* polarized around two great and antagonistic classes. Finally, the state has become so embedded in the economy proper—to the point of assuming co-ordinating, stabilizing and, to some extent, command functions—that we are now entitled to speak of a *neo*-capitalist type. The Keynsian 'revolution', by legitimating state regulation and a far-reaching extension of social services, gave capitalism a new source of vitality and regeneration.

Thus we confront a damaging shortcoming in Gramsci's diagnosis. His undoubted insights into the nature of popular consciousness and the socialization process were not founded on a rich knowledge of the economic base and its inherent dynamics. It has often been said that for the three founts of classical Marxism—British economics, French political thought, and German philosophy—Gramsci substituted two specifically Italian 'founts': Crocean philosophy and the politics of Machiavelli. In this substitution we see both the source of his originality and the limitations of his perspective. While his absorption of Machiavellian and Crocean ideas enabled him to form an accurate view of moral and psychological factors linking men to social orders, the absence of a serious economic analysis caused him to under-rate the productive possibilities and adaptive capacities of capitalism. Gramsci, it must be remembered, composed his notes when capitalism was suffering through the most agonizing phase of its history. Like all Marxists of his era, he simply *assumed* the decadence of capitalism as a productive system, and thus he never really escaped from what we might call the 'Bolshevik utopianism' of the twenties and thirties. For Gramsci capitalism was, in its pure form, an entrepreneurial system based on liberal *laissez-faire* principles. In consequence, he regarded any deviation from this 'ideal' model as a sign of either decay or arrested development. Neo-capitalism, with its large-scale productive units and political controls on economic life, was in his view only a degenerate variant of a once proud system. His simple-minded assumptions—'*laissez-faire* capitalism = healthy capitalism' and 'monopoly capitalism = stagnant capitalism'—prevented him from grasping the system's ability to develop technology and produce goods and services on an unprecedented scale. In other words, Gramsci did not realize the extent to which capitalism could 'purchase' consent, through satisfying the workers' material wants.

A less serious (but noteworthy) fault in Gramsci's analysis resides in his apparent inability to appreciate fully how the machinery of liberal democracy *itself* reinforces beliefs in the reality of citizen participation in government and in the rational basis of political decisions. As Edelman puts it:

To quiet resentments and doubts about particular political acts, reaffirm belief in the fundamental rationality and democratic character of the system, and thus fix conforming habits of future behaviour is demonstrably a key function of our persisting political institutions: elections, political discussions, legislatures, courts and administration. Each of them involves motor activity . . . that reinforces the impression of a political system designed to translate individual wants into public policy.[38]

This (not wholly false) impression of popular control is further strengthened by patriotic ceremonies, such as Presidential inaugurals, Independence Day parades, street festivals to celebrate the anniversary of the Queen's coronation, etc., which affirm the greatness, heroism and nobility of the nation. All these political rituals, mechanisms and symbols shape the perception of experience so as to still or minimize discontent—by influencing what people want, what they revere, what they fear and what they regard as possible. Although Gramsci did not entirely ignore such phenomena,[39] neither did he accord much weight to them.[40] Nor did he appear to realize that the *absence* of proletarian democracy and liberation in the East could foster acceptance of the established order in the West. Of course, Gramsci's imprisonment and premature death spared him the agony of coming to terms with the worst excesses of Stalinism— excesses which underlie the presently widespread belief that a drastic increase in state power carries with it more dangers to freedom than solutions for inequality. The extermination of the Kulaks, the Moscow trials, the Great Purge, the Nazi-Soviet pact, the concentration camps, the suppression of the Hungarian workers, the invasion of Czechoslovakia, the persistent Soviet contempt for civil liberties—all these make it difficult for an ordinary Western citizen to agree that, through social engineering, one can bring about a utopia of freedom and social concord. Alexander Herzen, in a dialogue over a hundred years ago, reproached a revolutionist in these terms: 'Do you truly wish to condemn all human beings alive today to the sad role of carytids . . . supporting a floor for others some day to dance on?'[41] All revolutions thus far made in the name of Marx are open to the same reproach: they would sacrifice the present mankind for a promised (and now largely ignored) tomorrow. In short, the alternatives to Western liberalism seem rather less than appealing; and while their evils may be exaggerated by lingering Cold War rhetoric, they are not simply an invention of the 'bourgeois' media.

Gramsci's analysis of advanced capitalist society, then, was provocative and insightful but also defective in crucial respects. In diverting Marxism from its standard conflict model, in perceiving the subtleties of mass consciousness, and in pointing to the profound effects of socialization into dominant cultural patterns, he made a significant contribution. The failure of the proletariat to carry out the historic mission proposed for it by the Marxist canon must indeed be explained, in large part, by ideological consensus—however tenuous or class-biased. All other explanations founder on theoretical and/or empirical grounds. However, his discussion of the *reasons for* this consensus is timebound and limited. What is needed here, it has been suggested, is a multi-dimensional approach, encompassing a broad range of factors. Much of Gramsci's discussion, moreover, presupposes the basic dependence of the superstructure on the economic infrastructure—a plausible enough idea but one which he nowhere defines with precision and which, for reasons already considered, is not amenable to anything like conclusive empirical testing.

II. *Gramsci's Proposed Strategy*

If Gramsci's precepts for making revolution rely on a diagnosis badly in need of emendation, then the effectiveness of the strategy itself is immediately called into question. Most important, he failed, as we have seen, to comprehend how the 'fundamental contradictions' of capitalism could be offset and neutralized by countervailing *structural* trends; the growing complexity of the division of labour, the expansion of the middle strata and increasing affluence all *in themselves* (and not just through the mediation of trade unions, the mass media and political parties) impede the development of revolutionary consciousness. In addition, the dismal political record of extant socialist states makes the conventional Marxist case against the 'empty formalism' of liberal representative democracy seem hollow and hypocritical. Given these considerations, the core feature of Gramsci's proposed strategy—the 'long march' through the institutions of civil society, in order to subvert and replace 'bourgeois hegemony'—would probably encounter some fierce resistance from its supposed beneficiaries. Nevertheless, the very contradictoriness of popular consciousness, even in the two great bastions of liberal civilization, could serve to facilitate the daunting task set for the 'Modern Prince'. In this respect, Gramsci gets a considerable boost from social-psychological research, conducted in the past quarter-century, on the problems of attitude change and attitude structure. It is a repeated finding that inconsistent or dissonant beliefs are frequently held in areas of people's lives distant from their daily concerns. When the salience or centrality of the psychological object is heightened, tremendous pressures are brought on individuals to force their heretofore inconsistent beliefs into harmony. Conversely, when opinions are held with low intensity, dissonance is often overlooked or tolerated with equanimity.[42] On this theory, consistency of ideological belief can be attained if people are 'politicized'—if they come to see issues in the socio-political world as increasingly central to their everyday lives. Of course, dissonance reduction can be attained by abandoning (or modifying) *either* of the inconsistent beliefs. If commitment to the socially dominant cognition or value is weak, then the quest for consonance may result in acceptance of the 'deviant' alternative.

Social-psychological research on dissonance seems to confirm what some may regard as intuitively obvious: systems of thought which contain some inner incoherence thereby contain *within themselves* the possibility of change. Nevertheless, we are dealing with some large 'ifs', and a sceptical observer might be excused for wondering whether the 'Modern Prince' (even assuming it had mass support) could provide a powerful enough institutional base for wholesale cultural transformation—especially as capitalism does seem to 'deliver the goods'. In countries where the mass parties of the Left have actually renounced Marxism (i.e. most advanced capitalist countries), the 'war of position' would have *no immediate institutional foundation at all.* And let us keep in mind: the struggle for hegemony involves not simply changing people's passing political opinions, but their entire way of conceiving the world and interpreting their common experience. At the heart of Gramsci's political thinking lies a paradox: a revolution must occur *before* the revolution; i.e. a fundamental transformation of the spirit of present-day society is a precondition for the proletarian seizure of power. But is it really possible, in the West, for a radical movement to establish its cultural and moral ascendancy prior to the acquisition of direct political power? And if civil society is *not* independently conquerable, the 'war of position' becomes a vacuous notion. Perhaps Poulantzas has a point when he says of the organs of civil society that 'their action is determined by the action of the State repressive apparatus' and that therefore 'the destruction of the ideological apparatus has its precondition in the destruction of the State repressive apparatus which maintains it'.[43] Althusser's disciple certainly exaggerates the power of the state, but he brings to light a crucial question: what is the nature of the relationship between the state (in the narrow sense) machine and the institutions of civil society—how intimate is the linkage? To what extent and in what ways can the mechanisms of cultural diffusion—the mass media, the schools, the universities—escape the restraints of the political apparatus? The answer will partly depend on how one conceptualizes the modern state. Is it, essentially, the guarantor of the socio-economic status quo or is it something of a neutral force, a mediator in the conflicts between groups and classes? To what degree do the economic 'powers-that-be' influence or condition state activity? Then there is a related problem: *in what measure* are the organs of the ideological superstructure themselves *controlled* by the economically dominant groups? Do not such groups own vast segments of the mass media, for example? In this sphere, at least, subversion is not likely to proceed very far. The general question is this: are there ineluctable constraints imposed by an established capitalist society which would defeat the hegemonic purposes of the revolutionary movement?

None of the above questions has ever received adequate treatment. While they are open to empirical inquiry, Marxists and anti-Marxists alike have usually remained content with *a priori* answers. The time has surely come for a more rigorous approach, based on a wide variety of concrete examples drawn from actual practice, past and present. It is not clear, however, whether empirical investigation of these issues could ever lead to *definitive* results; for such resolution would require us to develop objective, value-free criteria for distinguishing, say, a 'key' issue from a minor one, education from indoctrination, information from propaganda, and so on. But are not such distinctions, beyond a certain range of clear-cut cases, ultimately dependent upon prior notions of human 'needs' and 'interests'— notions which are irreducibly evaluative (and therefore essentially contested)? Within certain areas, one suspects, the *very description* of social phenomena must be value-laden, in the sense of presupposing a particular moral and political framework.

Gramsci's own (often implicit or half-formulated) answers to the aforementioned questions scarcely inspire much confidence in his strategic injunctions. Though not without reservations,[44] he by and large accepted the conventional Marxist assumptions about the generalized political and cultural power of the economically privileged. He conceded, moreover, that governments could mobilize the support of the mass media and other ideological instruments when faced with a serious threat.[45] In his favour, however, we could point to the present situations in France and Italy, where Marxist ideas *have* gone some way towards undermining 'bourgeois' hegemony. The universities, above all, have proved amenable to the siren calls of the Left, and the trade union movements in both countries are heavily impregnated with Marxist doctrine. In each country, furthermore, nearly half the electorate is willing to vote for radically socialist parties (though it barely needs saying that not all such voters adhere to even the main points of the Marxist creed). But even this evidence does not provide unambiguous support for Gramsci's strategy. To begin with, Communist and Socialist parties in France and Italy are operating within uniquely favourable conditions—hoary insurrectionary traditions, the dominant role of Marxists in the resistance movements against the Nazis, extreme inequalities, uneven and extraordinarily rapid industrialization—which make it difficult to draw general inferences. Second, in neither country has the dominant hegemony been truly subverted. Left-wing voting, it is often noted, does not necessarily reflect a rejection of the liberal capitalist order *as such*; the PCF or PCI voter, for example, may simply wish to register a protest against gross corruption and political immobilism—pathological traits to be sure but not necessarily endemic in, or distinctive of, capitalist regimes. It remains to be seen whether a Marxist definition of reality can become the guiding mode of thought in either France or Italy. Finally, it is far from obvious that further advances in Marxist cultural penetration would not be met by repression. Gramsci himself admitted that the ruling groups would increasingly resort to coercion as their ideological authority eroded (see pages 206–7). But if this is so, might not the whole counter-hegemonic project come to grief? When radical newspapers are closed, Marxist professors sacked and militant trade unionists arrested, the 'war of position' must perforce grind to a halt. In such an eventuality, Gramsci would counsel a shift to the 'war of movement', to general disruption and violent confrontations, but one wonders if this would save the day for the revolutionary legions. What if repression occurs well before the revolutionary party has managed to establish its hegemony? In this case, (a) it would be improper, on strict Gramscian principles, to seize power; and (b) the repressive solution need be neither draconic nor comprehensive—and might actually enjoy a fair degree of popularity. The upshot is this: especially if it is selective, intimidation, by stifling discussion, *could* succeed in preventing the revolutionary movement from establishing its hegemony within the confines of the present system. Whether this repressive reaction could *permanently* avert the spread of subversive ideas is another matter.

Turning now to the vexed question of revolutionary violence, we find that, once again, no firm conclusions are possible. Since Gramsci sanctioned the 'military' aspect of the struggle, he is open to two major criticisms. One rests on the familiar argument to the effect that in the revolutionary process, it is fatuous to posit a radical disjunction between ends and means; i.e. there is no escaping the intimate connection between the methods used to make the revolution and the character of the subsequent society. No doubt, violence does generate its own momentum, and history teaches us that violent revolutions tend to lapse into paranoia and barbarism. The weapons used on the old oppressors often become the weapons of a new form of oppression. On the other hand, history does furnish apparent counter-examples, the American Revolution to name but one. Violence, in any case, was a small part of Gramsci's strategy: assuming that the 'war of position' could actually be won, the deployment of force could be kept to a bare minimum. The second criticism is perhaps more damaging: in societies with established democratic traditions, no movement will succeed in attracting widespread adherence if it holds out the prospect of civil disorder and destruction of constitutional procedures. (Hence the mild-mannered rhetoric and behaviour of the Eurocommunists.) While this is probably true, it must be measured against a quite plausible counter-argument; to wit, when a revolutionary movement lays down its arms and aims for a peaceful transformation, it becomes especially vulnerable to the coercive apparatus of the State. What happened in Chile may not *refute* the *Via Italiana*, but it certainly leaves little room for confidence. Still, the initial point remains valid: traditional revolutionary bombast and activity is likely to prove counter-productive in the West. It must be stressed, at this juncture, that the commitment to insurrectionary violence was the least original and striking aspect of Gramsci's strategy. This commitment, it was argued in the last chapter, could be more or less dropped without violating the *spirit* of his thought.

All the above considerations assume that the 'Modern Prince' would genuinely *want* to overturn the capitalist order. Which brings us to another important objection to Gramsci's proposed strategy: he ignores the whole problem of 'deradicalization'. Can ideological militancy be sustained in the face of protracted struggle on the cultural and ideological front? As the party carves out areas of institutional power, will it not *pari passu* develop vested interests in the status quo? 'Deradicalization' denotes a subtle change in a movement's relation to the social milieu. Essentially, it settles down and adjusts itself to existence within the very order that it officially desires to overthrow and transform. This is not to say that the movement becomes opposed to all social change. Rather, it becomes 'reformist', inasmuch as it accepts the ongoing system and its institutionalized procedures as the framework for all political efforts. Robert Michels, in *Political Parties,* dealt with this phenomenon at some length, and his observations later became commonplace, if not axiomatic, in subsequent organizational analysis. He stressed the apparent inverse relationship between a radical movement's worldly success and the preservation of its radicalism. 'As the organization increases in size, the struggle for great principles becomes impossible', he stated baldly. There arise 'institutional needs' which act as major determinants of policy, supplementing and eventually displacing the manifest goals of the organization, and conferring on it a conservative character. These institutional needs are basically two. First, when a radical movement grows large and strong, it acquires a mass social constituency which it strives to increase. But the acquisition of a mass membership inevitably dilutes the movement's radicalism. To avoid alarming people who are not 'true believers', the pursuit of a policy based on strict principle is shunned. This tendency is reinforced by the parliamentary character of the political party, for '"Parliamentarism" signifies the aspiration for the greatest number of votes'. A modern political party is 'the methodical organization of the electoral masses', and therefore it must endeavour simultaneously to recruit members and to recruit votes. Here it finds 'its vital interests', for every decline in membership and every loss in voting strength diminishes its political prestige. Consequently, attention must be paid to *possible* adherents, which means an attentuation of doctrine.[46] But more important, a movement that grows strong and influential, says Michels, acquires a definite stake in the stability of the order in which the success has been won—a stake that is no less real for the fact that it goes unacknowledged. For bold revolutionary action can only endanger the position of a party that has achieved a mass membership, a bureaucracy, a full treasury and a network of financial interests. Such action would therefore threaten the livelihood of party leaders, sub-leaders and other employees, who become more concerned with their own narrow self-interest than with the cause itself. 'Thus, from a means, organization becomes an end', with interests peculiar to itself. As an inexorable result, the party 'becomes increasingly inert', 'loses its revolutionary impetus', and 'becomes sluggish'.[47] This, Michels assures us, is a 'universally applicable social law'.[48]

Were we to acknowledge this grandiose claim, then we would have to concede the bankruptcy of Gramsci's 'war of position'. No such acknowledgement is called for, however; for Michels does not even produce enough evidence to establish a general tendency, let alone a sociological law of any kind. His methodology has been attacked with devastating effect by Hands, who writes:

For a supposedly 'sociological' study, *Political Parties* contains surprisingly little hard empirical evidence. Michels's method can only be described as 'proof by anecdote': in the typical case, he simply outlines the tendency in question, suggests a rationale for it, and then gives a few disparate historical examples in support. What is lacking above all is any attempt at comprehensiveness, any indication of the frequency with which the phenomena in question occur.[49]

In other words, Michels makes no systematic attempt to gather and weigh the evidence. His generalizations do not grow out of the data; rather the data are simply appended to the generalizations as examples. Nevertheless, the various tendencies identified by him do have some historical basis and at least a superficial plausibility. 'Deradicalization' has been a definite empirical phenomenon. Even if we recoil from the methodological crudeness displayed by Michels, we can use his theory as a point of departure for a more systematic, empirically grounded approach. Any discussion of deradicalization will have to look at a number of variables: (1) the duration of struggle; (2) the party traditions; (3) the nature of the party organization; (4) the reaction of the existing powers within the community; (5) the international environment; (6) the character of the leadership. Moreover, the revised theory must be capable of drawing two important distinctions. The first is between *complete assimilation* into the established order and what Roth, in his study of the SPD in Wilhelmine Germany, calls '*negative integration*'; wherein a 'political system permits a hostile mass movement to exist legally but prevents it from gaining access to the centres of power'. A negatively integrated subculture, he rightly argues, 'constitutes at least a potential source of instability' and (hence) radical change.[50] The second distinction which needs to be recognized is between the *abandoment* of radicalism and the *necessary modification* of strategy or tactics under conditions of political isolation. As we saw in the previous chapter, for example, the 'Italian Road' ideology, despite surface appearances, cannot be equated with reformism.

To tie together the (exceedingly loose) strands of the foregoing arguments and considerations, it is impossible, in the absence of sufficient evidence, to decide whether the *Quaderni* succeed in providing a satisfactory strategy for the transition to socialism in the societies of Western capitalism. There is no doubt, however, that much of what Gramsci says is valuable. Above all, he is a source of both comfort and ideas to those Marxists who wish to combine revolutionary principles with prudence. If ends are not to become disembodied rituals, he maintained, then the strategy for attaining them must be constantly readapted to changing conditions. For those who treated the problem of revolutionary strategy as a matter of rigorous deduction from quasi-Biblical texts, Gramsci expressed nothing but contempt. And rightly so. Furthermore, even if the 'war of position' can never succeed, the idea that the spiritual transformation of the masses must *precede* the conquest of power furnishes the surest (indeed, the only) safeguard against the degeneration that often follows vanguard revolutions of the Jacobin variety. To put the point more emphatically, even if the 'war of position' turned out to be as futile as Don Quixote's bout with windmills, it would still be preferable to a Leninist *coup d'état*. Having said this, there is no denying that Gramsci's strategy is incomplete. For all their insights, the *Quaderni* do not contain a *fully articulated* theory of the superstructure. Certain crucial questions are left open or only partially answered. What elements of civil society are most important? In what precise ways can they be subverted? What are the relationships among the various elements and how do they tie in with the agencies of political society? Gramsci implies that there are no universal solutions to these questions. Maybe so, but the fact remains: it is incumbent upon any revolutionary who wishes to follow Gramsci's instructions to undertake a formidable task of analysis before any precise plans can be formulated or put into operation.

The present writer gets the uneasy feeling that, in this section, he has perhaps created more problems than he has solved. He prefers to think that he has *identified* and *cast some light on* a host of problems that need further study if Marxist debates on strategy are to avoid the depressing sterility that generally characterizes them.

III. *Gramsci's Vision*

It has been a main theme of this study that the libertarian, 'humanist' angle on Gramsci can be overdone. The 'ecumenical Gramsci' of the social-democrats is basically a myth. The essential structure of his thought and the core of his political commitment were Marxist and revolutionary—albeit innovative and flexible. Nevertheless, his originality and lack of dogmatism, his readiness to *absorb* liberal values, has justifiably encouraged many who wish to rescue Marxism from its professed disciples and set the doctrine firmly back in the humanitarian, Enlightenment tradition from which it emerged. The *Quaderni*, it is said, supply the ideological nucleus, however rudimentary, of an alternative type of communism, differing from the current brands in some essential points. The key to Gramsci's alternative, I believe, resides in his empirical cast of mind. It is his manner of thought, in other words, which underlies his relatively democratic conclusions. Let us elaborate on this contention.

Gramsci, we must remember, rebelled against the Marxist system builders, who were determined to fit the ebb and flow of concrete reality into a procrustean bed of abstract schemes and laws—none of which, he thought, could adequately embrace the variability and qualitative properties of social life. Notwithstanding his rejection of positivism, his *forma mentis* inclined him to a fascination for the concrete and a suspicion of all abstractions. He accepted the logical distinction, basic to scientific method, between 'data' drawn from the observable world, and the theoretical generalizations about such data. While we do not, in Gramsci's view, know social processes by 'observing' them from 'outside', neither is it the case that particular facts are purely the product of theory. Rather, the data of experience must provide the raw material for all theorizing, and theories should be modified or abandoned when the evidence so dictates. 'It is not reality which should be expected to conform to the abstract schema', but *vice-versa*.[51] To be sure, the *Prison Notebooks* are based on a close, comparative inquiry into the European past—especially the Italian past. Like Marx and Engels themselves, Gramsci thought that the nature of present social conflicts could be illuminated only through minute analysis of empirical materials. 'If one is unable to understand real individuals', he once declared, 'one has no hope of understanding what is universal and general.'[52] He never failed to bring his generalizations down to earth; for him the purpose of abstraction was to clear the ground for empirical study, not to render it unnecessary. Every theoretical solution must be tested by its applicability to the actual situation: '. . . every truth, even though it may be universal and capable of being expressed in an abstract formula of a mathematical kind . . . owes its efficacy to its being expressed in the language of concrete, particular situations; if it is not expressible in such particular terms, it is a byzantine and scholastic abstraction, good only for the amusement of phrasemongers'.[53] Gramsci's method works by means of cross reference within the flux and movement of the real world. It is necessary, according to his approach, to examine both the aims of conscious individuals and the circumstances in which they pursue their objectives. Historical reality is a pattern of forces for ever moving and changing equilibrium. Within this fluid situation the human will can exert influence through the exercise of choice and action. Because of this constantly shifting, unpredictable pattern of reality, abstractions—while a necessary component of cognition—must be applied cautiously and accepted tentatively. Herein lies the crucial justification for Gramsci's emphasis on an open and continuous dialogue with a broad range of ideas—a dialogue reflected in the extraordinary breadth of historical and philosophical culture so evident in his writings. As Joll points out, 'however much he reacted against them, Vico and Hegel, Sorel and Croce were in some ways as important for him as Marx and Lenin'; and this firm footing in the European intellectual tradition 'means that it is easier for the non-Marxist to conduct a dialogue with Gramsci than with any other Marxist writer of the twentieth century'.[54] Indeed, a substantial part of his work consists in the defence and illustration of formal logic,[55] classical culture, liberal education and disinterested inquiry.

The probing, tentative, empirically oriented character of Gramsci's Marxism received philosophical expression in his 'absolute historicism'. The essence of this view, it will be recalled, is that the 'rationality' of theoretical or philosophical systems is manifested solely in relation to the historical processes of which they are part. That is to say, the truth of ideas and propositions contained in any ideology or philosophy (Marxism included) can be established only on the testing ground of practice. Truth value is not determined by correspondence to some fixed standard, to an 'objective' reality beyond the reach of human volition. The stress is on empirical acceptance and effectiveness. 'Rational' conceptions of the world are those theoretical formulations that—because they meet human needs and aspirations—prevail historically and become the 'common sense' of an entire epoch. For Gramsci, then, the tenets of Marxism should not be reified into a closed system of scientific certainties and absolute truths.

As observed in Chapter 4, this philosophical position is fraught with political implications. If the vanguard party is not the repository of infallible scientific truth about man and history, then there can be no authoritative imposition of a pre-fixed schema on the inert masses. The political organization, states Gramsci, should be subordinate to the real (effectively expressed) wishes of the proletariat and should not be permitted to claim that it embodies those wishes by virtue of its own 'scientific' omniscience, no matter what the empirical masses actually think. Theory must be evolved in close relation with class praxis, developed in dialectical connection with the experience of the proletariat and always subject to its criticism. What he wanted, as we have seen, was a reciprocal relationship between the life activity of the masses and the theoretical/ practical activity of the party. Any other approach would isolate the party from the masses and stultify the creative process of revolution. It follows that a revolution is not proletarian and communist merely because it transfers power to people who proclaim themselves communists, or because it destroys the institutions of the old regime. Properly understood, a proletarian revolution is not a *coup d'état* enabling a self-appointed élite to inflict its will on society; it must be a mass process in which the people take power in their own name and not by means of an isolated political entity. If the party élite regards itself as the sole guardian of scientific truth, elaborated outside the actual consciousness of the proletariat, and if, further, this élite uses manipulative and demagogical means to seize power, prior to the spiritual reformation of the working classes, then it will degenerate into a privileged caste to which mass initiatives constitute not a source of vigour but a dangerous threat. 'The pathological manifestations of bureaucratic centralism', we are told, 'are due to a deficiency of initiative and responsibility at the base.'[56] Although Gramsci never *explicitly* directed these remarks against Lenin (for whom he always showed the greatest respect) or Stalin for that matter, their general implications are unmistakable.

Marxists and non-Marxists alike have expressed grave disquiet at Gramsci's identification of history and philosophy—which, they feel, saddles him with a debilitating relativism. From a Catholic perspective, Gramsci has been criticized for his failure to deal with the 'ultimate questions' of human existence or offer a firm basis for moral action. According to this interpretation, any theory which equates 'what is right' with 'what succeeds' is, in the final analysis, spiritually barren.[57] From within the Marxist camp, a new breed of Italian thinkers, following Della Volpe, fear that 'absolute historcism' undermines the essential scientific aspect of Marxism.[58] Althusser, of course, has put forward similar views.[59]

While Gramsci's 'immanentism' was certainly relativist in some sense, a few cautions are in order. In the first place, the Sardinian himself denied the imputation of relativism:

> To think of a philosophical affirmation as true in a particular historical epoch (i.e. as the necessary, inseparable expression of a particular historical activity, or praxis) but as superseded and 'nullified' [*vanificata*] in a subsequent epoch, without however falling into scepticism or moral and ideological relativism . . . is a somewhat arduous and difficult mental operation.[60]

Unless we view relativism as an univocal concept, this disclaimer is not without some validity. Gramsci, it must be said, nowhere espoused what is known as 'normative relativism', the extreme thesis which holds that 'right' means 'right for a given society', and that, therefore, it is wrong or inappropriate for people in one society to condemn, interfere with, etc., the values of another society. This (incoherent) thesis does *not* follow from Gramsci's belief that decisions as to good and evil and the meaning of the universe cannot have any objective or scientific foundation. Nor does it follow from his contention that a philosophical statement which is 'true' in a particular historical period can be nullified in a subsequent period, because it no longer expresses real developmental trends. Neither did Gramsci endorse the variant of relativism which claims (1) that there are no theory-independent objects of perception and understanding, and (2) that rules of logic and principles of reasoning are always internal to particular systems of thought and language. Another point is also worthy of mention. It is one thing to assert the universality and objective validity of certain moral values, beliefs and principles; it is quite another to present a conclusive or even convincing argument for such an assertion. *No one* has yet managed to demonstrate that fundamental disputes between rival systems of thought can be rationally resolved, and in the absence of such demonstration, the case for a kind of relativism survives.[61] But, in any event, Gramsci's relativism, apart from being limited in scope, was inconsistent; for many of his arguments and forms of expression are difficult to square with even the mildest form of relativism. Does a consistent relativist, for example, distinguish between

'false' and 'authentic' consciousness or demand a total reconstruction of society on the basis of his preferred principles or
extol the Communist Party as the ultimate referent of existence?
In the no doubt accurate words of Joll, 'Gramsci never resolved
the implicit conflict between the dogmatic certainty of the
Marxists and the historical relativity and subjectivity of
Croce'.[62] This conflict helps to explain the enduring tension
in his thought between a libertarian view of culture and the
doctrine of rigid discipline enforced by the Machiavellian party.
It might help to clarify matters if we make a distinction
(admittedly formal and artificial) between 'Gramsci the *intellectual*' and 'Gramsci the *politician*'. Whereas the former was a
sceptic, unwilling to proclaim the absolute validity of Marxist
insights and anxious to uphold the liberal value of free discussion, the latter was a 'true believer', prepared (it often
seemed) to resort to dictatorial methods in order to impose his
monolithic vision of life on a refractory reality. Gramsci, be it
noted, was a man beset by inner contradictions. While he
passionately defended democratic debate and intellectual integrity, neither of which could flourish in a climate of authoritarian imposition, the puritan fundamentalist in him sought for
a universality and tidiness which could not easily tolerate mass
vulgarity or the excesses of individualism. Yet, as this study has
argued, the logic and tenor of his thought banishes these undeniable authoritarian strains to the periphery. The *general
thrust* of his Marxism was open and democratic, with persuasion,
consent, free expression and popular participation occupying a
central place.

For those who wish to rid Marxism of its uncomfortable
association with doctrinaire élitism, Gramsci's contribution is
invaluable. One need only compare his thought with that of
other 'Western Marxists' to appreciate its merits in this respect.
Needless to say, the diverse variants of 'Western Marxism'
arose as a reaction against the vulgar reductionism of the
dialectical materialists. Any gains in sophistication, however,
have been purchased at the price of an intellectual arrogance
whose practical implications could only be—to borrow a phrase
from Labriola—'the pedagogy of the guillotine'.[63] Instead of
careful empirical analysis, we are presented with speculative
constructions, *a priori* conceptual schemes so top-heavy that

they tend to collapse upon contact with the surface of social life. The very *language* of Western Marxism has been cast in a specialized and inaccessible mould. Marx wished to develop concepts and categories clearer and closer to material reality than those of Hegel, and to present his work in as lucid a manner as possible. In contrast, Western Marxism, in part because of its divorce from any mass movement, has been caught up in a tangle of verbal complexity which turns theory into an esoteric and exclusive discipline. The cult of words has blotted out the living sense of things. Abstruse diction and inflated abstractions rule, with free-floating concepts and hypnotic formulae taking over from realistic social analysis. Perceived against the purity of grand theory, an insistence upon concreteness, precision, formal logic, and the complexity of reality appears as 'bourgeois empiricism' or worse. In its different forms, Western Marxism has fallen prey to the very 'spectre of abstractions' from which Marx himself tried to flee. Let us look briefly at three typical exemplars of modern Marxist thought in order to illustrate the connection (psychologically intelligible if not logical) between intellectual 'mandarinism' and political despotism.

Consider Lukács, who counsels us 'to leave empirical reality behind'.[64] Genuine knowledge, he announces, can only be generated from the standpoint of the 'totality', which cannot be constructed by accumulating mere facts. Only opportunists and revisionists, lacking rational insight, appeal to facts. If facts contradict the truth, so much the worse for the facts: the overall trend of historical development is more 'real' than the data of experience. Indeed, Marxism *à la* Lukács can survive the systematic disproof of every one of its empirical claims! Thus he declares:

Let us assume for the sake of argument that recent research had disproved once and for all every one of Marx's individual theses. Even if this were to be proved, every serious 'orthodox' Marxist would still be able to accept all such modern findings without reservation and hence dismiss all of Marx's theses *in toto*—without having to renounce his orthodoxy for a single moment.[65]

As Kolakowski rightly observes, 'Lukács' Marxism implies the abandonment of intellectual, logical, and empirical criteria of knowledge'.[66] How, then, do we know what is true? The truth can be revealed only from the perspective of the class whose revolutionary initiative is destined fundamentally to transform the whole of social life: i.e. the proletariat. Its privileged historical role entails the complete understanding of society; only it can apprehend history as a whole. Thus Truth (Marxism) is nothing but the theoretical awareness of the working class as it matures towards revolution. The proletariat, on this scheme, is the 'universal class', which—like Hegel's Spirit—embodies the full self-consciousness of history. But, as it happens, the proletarian class consciousness turns out to be an 'ideal-type'; it is not a matter of what the empirical working class *actually* thinks and feels, but what it *would* think and feel *if* it perfectly grasped its situation and understood its assigned world historical mission. Unfortunately, the chosen class, by itself, can never rise to true knowledge; and if the workers cannot see the light, then someone must see it for them and lead them to it. That someone is the communist party, which is hypostatized as the institutional will and consciousness of the class. The party embodies 'true' proletarian consciousness, which is independent of any *historically specific* manifestations of popular will and thought. The role of the working class is therefore 'not that of a concrete historical force, but that of a hitherto missing term in a geometrical proof'.[67] The political importance of Lukács's critique of 'empiricism' is here evident. One can never comprehend the totality of history and the 'real' interests of the masses if one confines oneself to the vulgar observation of actual workers. Nor should the party trouble itself over any empirical evidence which might seem to contradict its doctrine. For if the party by definition embraces the viewpoint of the proletariat, and if the proletariat is theoretically infallible by virtue of its social position and historical task, then the party is always right, notwithstanding any apparently contrary facts. Small wonder that Lukács always glorified the Soviet system, even during the darkest years of Stalin. Was not the Bolshevik Party the supreme fount and criterion of all truth?

Turning to Marcuse, we come across a similar doctrinal exclusiveness, but one devoid of links to either the proletariat or the party. The sovereign definers are not the leaders of the communist party, but some unspecified élite of Platonic guardians, capable of grasping the transcendental demands of rationality according to which the world should be judged and remodelled. The appeal is to an abstract 'reason' and 'authentic humanity'. But how do we know what these entail? Formal logic cannot help us at all, since it is unable to penetrate to the 'deeper' recesses of reality. Any reference to empirical data is rejected out of hand as a positivist folly, reflecting an uncritical worship of 'what exists'. In any case, the one-dimensional automatons who inhabit the affluent society cannot be expected to make any intellectual contribution to their own salvation; their expressed desires or aims are of no consequence in the formulation of political truth. Now, if those who appeal to empirical reality and conventional standards of rationality are dismissed as slaves to instrumental reason, to mystifying modes of thought, then we are left at the mercy of Marcuse and his followers. He (and others of the Frankfurt School) have developed a subjective interpretation of history and society, unconnected with publicly accessible bodies of knowledge or criteria of validity by which its assertions may be assessed. The 'critical theorist' sets himself up as the supreme judge of the irrationality of existing society, as the final arbiter of the 'real' needs of mankind, and as the sole authority on how these needs must be satisfied.

Marcuse does not hesitate to draw the obvious conclusions for political practice. In establishing the liberated society, those endowed with unmystified consciousness and higher wisdom must not permit indiscriminate tolerance of 'false words and wrong deeds'.[68] Freedom of expression is unjustifiable and 'repressive' if it perpetuates illusion—as determined by philosophers untainted by 'scientific-technological rationality'.

Next we look at Althusser's fusion of Marxism with structuralism. Structuralism in general aims to uncover the basic and universal systems of code lying beyond the empirical diversity of human societies. The world of structuralism is a world of sameness in its depths: all societies are constructed from a limited set of elements susceptible of combination in a limited number of ways. It is also a world of determinism, which eliminates the conscious activities of real life individuals and social groups from the scheme of explanation. Society is therefore discussed in terms of bloodless categories. Althusser's work represents a complete academization of Marxism: we are presented with a tireless elucidation of concepts, but one which rarely leaves the conceptual level to deal, as did Marx himself, with the historical *specificity* of social structures. The whole point, it seems, is to *insulate* Marxist theory from reality. Science, we are informed, cannot be bounded by 'external' criteria of truth, but creates its own 'scientificity' in its own 'theoretical practice'. Althusser rejects as empiricist the idea that concrete reality might form part of the raw material of 'theoretical practice', insisting instead that the production of knowledge takes place *'entirely in thought'*.[69] Immediate experience is a source of illusion not truth. The object of knowledge is situated within the realm of abstraction and has little to do with real, sensuous objects. Indeed, since for Althusser theory *is* a form of practice, the problem of the *relation* between theory and practice simply disappears, leaving only the problem of establishing correct theory. This problem is solved by taking a 'proletarian theoretical class position', which is not to be confused with what the proletariat *actually* believes; it is what Althusser thinks they *should* believe. Once again, the relationship between Marxist theory and the working class becomes one of exteriority; the former is—in effect—produced completely outside the latter, and must be imported into it. And so we come back to Lukács—except that Hegel has been replaced by Spinoza and Levi-Strauss and human subjectivity has been abolished. Since it is fatuous to assume 'that the "actors" of history are the authors of its text, the subjects of its production',[70] there can be little point in trying to *win men's minds* for a more just social order. (In fact, Althusser believes that the masses can *never* fully escape the phantasms of ideology.)[71] Moreover, if blood is spilt in the name of impersonal 'laws' or necessity, then there may be regret but no remorse, and the way is set for all obstacles to be crushed with ruthlessness. Despite its unrelenting intellectualism, 'theoretical practice' supplies a respectable 'scientific' justification for old-fashioned Stalinist intolerance.

The Marxist mandarins, it can be seen, exhibit little but contempt for empirical reality; within their respective frameworks, the working class remains a rather insubstantial entity, and the concern is with how the author would wish to define its 'interests', not with how its own members actually do so. Worse, the mandarins disdain *all* conventional rules of thought, whether empirical or formal. But once these shared principles are abandoned to the higher intuition of either the communist party or a new breed of philosopher-kings, intolerance and thought control become the order of the day, as the privileged few are no longer obliged to defend their opinions by invoking the common stock of logical rules and empirical procedures. Lurking behind the convoluted prose and the maze of neologisms is the despot's aversion for free and rational debate.

The authoritarian degeneration of Marxism in power, I would suggest, cannot be accounted for in terms of an unrealistic passion for absolute equality or perfect social harmony; after all, human goals, however unattainable, can always be (and always have been) modified in practice. The real origin of Marxist despotism is to be sought in the Leninist heresy which proclaims that the 'genuine' needs and desires of the workers can be discovered through rational speculation, without any reference to the workers' explicit wishes; and that, therefore, it is perfectly legitimate for an enlightened élite to impose its 'discoveries' on the benighted masses—by force of arms if necessary. According to this distorted view, to force human beings into the right pattern is no tyranny but liberation in the truest sense. The fault, in short, lies in a *dogmatic approach* to Marxist theory, not in the admirable values and ideals expressed by the theory. If this is accepted, then we can extract from the *Quaderni* a convincing (though implicit) explanation for the undeniable failure of all socialist states to establish the 'realm of freedom' envisaged by Marx and Engels. By the same token, we can detect the rough outline of an alternative doctrine, which holds open the possibility that Leninism-Stalinism was nothing else than a bastard version of the Marxist vision.

IV. *Final Remarks*

While the foregoing assessment has neither aimed nor claimed to be exhaustive, it has attempted to take a fresh look at the worth of Gramsci's theory—where does it supply valuable insights and ideas; where is it defective and in need of modification; where is it ambiguous and in need of more precision;

where are additional data required? To sum up my general argument, Gramsci's concept of hegemony constitutes the pivotal point for a theoretical enterprise which—for all its inadequacies—enriches Marxist doctrine, partly for the solutions it offers, partly for the approach it exemplifies and partly for the fields of investigation it opens up. On the level of empirical analysis, the *Quaderni* sketch out a novel framework of inquiry, specifying both the types of variables to be taken into account and a cluster of concepts to be employed. Not the least of Gramsci's contributions was his insistence, against the main currents of Marxist thought, on patient examination of the particular and the concrete. He had no terror of the commonplace: for him, a loaf of bread was a loaf of bread was a loaf of bread; there was no need to locate it within the 'totality' of experience or to search for the 'hidden structures' or 'dialectical laws' it manifested. Always wary of *a priori* constructions, he placed his faith in empirical actuality. Genuine knowledge was based on sense perception; it was not a purely logical or formal development of concepts. While socio-political analysis could not, in his opinion, meet the rigorous criteria of the natural sciences, it nevertheless involved the testing of all ideas against perceptible reality—through systematic observation of human behaviour. But Gramsci's most impressive contribution to Marxist analysis was to help shift its focus away from economics and natural science to the terrain of culture—to philosophy and the intellectuals, to popular psychology, and to the manifold agencies of socialization. It is in this province primarily that his thought benefited from his dialogue with previous thinkers— Croce and Machiavelli in particular. Largely because of Gramsci, Marxist views of culture now understand symbolic or ideological representations of a given historical situation as an integral and defining part of the situation. Moreover, since he depicted the communist millenium not as the assured culmination of history but as a difficult prize to be won through creative human action, he drew attention to the need for a comprehensive, systematic, long-range *political* strategy, based on a rigorous study of all superstructural phenomena. If the old reductionism—that everything is a predictable product of economic factors—no longer enjoys currency among Marxists, then much of the credit must go to Gramsci. In him we see the first signs of the hopeful disenchantment that characterizes present-day Marxism—a political passion matured by a sense of history as a complex, tragic process which guarantees nothing.

As regards strategy, Gramsci tried to free Marxism from its 'automatic breakdown' fantasies and demonstrate the necessity of a determined struggle to win the 'hearts and minds' of the masses. Here he revealed the democratic temperament which impelled him to set out the unfinished blueprint—whose implications he only half-perceived—of an alternative communism. Gramsci, like all revolutionaries, embodied the human hunger for absolutes, but he also embodied another, opposing basic urge—the urge to assert the autonomy of the individual. He was probably in contradiction with himself, understanding reality in its irreducible variety and multiplicity but longing for a unitary truth which would once and for all resolve the problems of human conduct. Yet it is not his fundamentalist desire (common to all Marxists) for a universal world formula which commands our attention; rather, it is his doctrinal flexibility and genuine feeling for democratic participation and debate which enable us to discern the embryo of a more humane form of Marxism.

Many people, even some of progressive inclination, have come to the conclusion that liberalism (i.e. a society where all men are equal only in law and rights) marks the extreme limit of human progress beyond which nothing is possible but a return backwards. They would agree with Machiavell's lament: 'Men commit the error of not knowing when to limit their hopes.' Others, however, would concur with Oscar Wilde, who once commented that 'A map of the world that does not include utopia is not worth even glancing at, for it leaves out the one country at which Humanity is always landing. . . . Progress is the realization of utopias.'[72] For most such people, Marxism—notwithstanding its Stalinist deformation—remains very much alive as a doctrine of hope and liberation. In Gramsci, they can find a genuine source of encouragement and inspiration. This, above all, makes him 'a true intellectual hero of our time'.[73]

Notes

Chapter 1

1. N. Bobbio, Preface to A. Davidson, *Antonio Gramsci: Towards an Intellectual Biography* (London, The Merlin Press, 1977), p. viii.
2. C. Boggs, *Gramsci's Marxism* (London, Pluto Press, 1976), p. 38.
3. N. Auciello, *Socialismo ed egemonia in Gramsci e Togliatti* (Bari, De Donato, 1974), p.121.
4. In a prison letter to his sister-in-law, Tania, Gramsci revealed a rather low opinion of his earlier work: 'In ten years of journalism, I produced enough words to fill fifteen to twenty volumes of four hundred pages each; however, they were written from day-to-day and should, I believe, have perished immediately afterwards.' (7 Sept. 1931), *LC*, pp. 136–7. False modesty perhaps; but before his arrest by the Fascist regime, Gramsci more than once refused proposals to gather a selection of his articles into a volume. This fact is disclosed in the aforementioned letter.
5. *Gramsci e il problema storico della democrazia* (Turin, Einaudi, 1973), pp. xxiii–xxiv.
6. 'Ritorno alla libertà', *Avanti!* (26 June 1919); *ON*, p. 252.
7. J. M. Cammett, *Antonio Gramsci and the Origins of Italian Communism* (Stanford University Press, 1967), pp. 205–6.
8. *CPC*, pp. 139–40.
9. *MS*, pp. 149–50.
10. All these interpretations will be considered in later chapters.
11. Quoted in E. Garin, 'Antonio Gramsci nella cultura italiana', *Studi gramsciani*: Atti del convegno tenuto a Roma nei giorni 11–13 gennaio 1958 (Rome, Editori Riuniti, 1958), p. 3.
12. *Antonio Gramsci: Life of a Revolutionary*, translated by T. Nairn (New York, Schocken Books, 1973), p. 236.
13. See, for example, letters of 9 Nov. 1931, 18 Jan. 1932 and 24 July 1933; *LC*, pp. 155, 160, 228.
14. Ibid., p. 201.
15. P. Togliatti, 'Il Leninismo nel pensiero e nell'azione di A. Gramsci', *Studi gramsciani*, pp. 15–19.
16. G. Amendola, 'Rileggendo Gramsci', *Prassi rivoluzionaria e storicismo in Gramsci, Critica marxista*—Quaderni, n. 3, 1967, pp. 21–2 (my emphasis).
17. For eternity, and, by extension, in a disinterested way.
18. Letter of 19 March 1927; *LC*, pp. 27–8.
19. Letter to Tania, 19 May 1930; *LC*, pp. 93–4. See, also, the following letters to his wife: 19 Nov. 1928, 15 Aug. 1932, 25 Jan. 1936. In *LC*, pp. 67, 200–1, 233.
20. *MS*, p. 199 (my emphasis).
21. 'The Identity of the History of Ideas', *Philosophy*, XLIII (April 1968), 87–8.
22. 'Meaning and Understanding in the History of Ideas', *History and Theory*, 8 (1969), p. 50.
23. Dunn, 'The Identity of the History of Ideas', pp. 98–9.
24. *Vico and Herder* (London, The Hogarth Press, 1976), p. xvi.

25. *PP*, p. 63.
26. *MS*, p. 239 (my emphasis).
27. (London, Longmans, 1963), I, ix.
28. S. Wolin, *Politics and Vision* (London, Allen & Unwin, 1961), p. 27.
29. Ibid., p. 26.

Chapter 2

1. For examples of rather hasty and superficial use of the concept by English writers, see E. Hobsbawm, *The Age of Capital* (London, Weidenfeld and Nicolson, 1975), pp. 249–50; P. Anderson, 'The Origins of the Present Crisis', in P. Anderson and R. Blackburn (eds.), *Towards Socialism* (Ithaca, N. Y., Cornell University Press, 1966), pp. 11–52; J. Saville, 'The Ideology of Labourism', in R. Benewick, et al. (eds.), *Knowledge and Belief in Politics* (London, Allen & Unwin, 1973), pp. 213–26; and R. Miliband, *The State in Capitalist Society* (London, Quartet Books, 1973), pp. 162–3.
2. *R*, p. 70.
3. Gramsci consistently uses the terms *'egemonia'* and *'direzione'* as synonyms.
4. It is worth noting the resemblance between the ascendant world-view in a hegemonic order and Hegel's concept of *Sittlichkeit*—the shared perceptions, conceptions and values embodied in community customs, laws and institutions. Of course, the 'class rule' element essential to Gramsci's conception is absent from Hegel's.
5. *I*, p. 9; *Mach.*, pp. 87, 130, 133, 150.
6. *Mach.*, p. 31.
7. *MS*, pp. 32, 39.
8. In a helpful discussion of the 'pre-history' of Gramsci's concept, Perry Anderson points out that 'hegemony' (understood in Lenin's sense) was an important political slogan in the Russian Social-Democratic movement from the late 1890s to 1917. It was pioneered, apparently, not by Lenin but by Plekhanov and Axelrod. After the events of 1905, however, the Mensheviks relinquished the slogan, declaring it to be obsolete since the bourgeois revolution was, in their view, now over in Russia. Strongly disagreeing with this interpretation, Lenin continued to call for the *gegemoniya* of the proletariat. Following the October Revolution, the term hegemony fell into relative disuse in the Bolshevik Party. Forged to describe the role of the working class in a revolutionary situation, it no longer had any actuality within the USSR. But the slogan of hegemony survived in the external documents of the Comintern, albeit still in the restricted pre-Gramscian sense. The proletariat's duty, it was proclaimed at the first two World Congresses, was to take a leading role in a system of alliances with other toiling masses, mainly the poor peasants. 'The Antinomies of Antonio Gramsci', *New Left Review*, 100 (Nov. 1976–Jan. 1977), 15–18.
9. (Rome, Editori Riuniti, 1972), p. 14.
10. *Mach.*, p. 103.
11. 'Il concetto di egemonia', *Prassi rivoluzionaria e storicismo in Gramsci*, *Critica marxista*—Quaderni n. 3, 1967, p. 78 (my emphasis).
12. See, for example, *Mach.*, pp. 31, 37, 46, 102, 132, 141, 150; *MS*, pp. 188, 201, 236, 249; *R*, pp. 70, 107, 157, 192; *PP*, pp. 19, 32, 164; and *I*, p. 9.
13. *R*, p. 70; *MS*, p. 188; *Mach.*, p. 88; *PP*, pp. 32, 164.
14. *LC*, p. 137.
15. *PP*, p. 164.
16. 'Civil society comprises the entire material interaction among individuals at a particular evolutionary stage of the productive forces.' *The German Ideology* in

Writings of the Young Marx on Philosophy and Society, edited and translated by L. D. Easton and K. H. Guddat (New York, Doubleday, 1967), pp. 468–9.

17. Marxism still lacks a *fully developed* superstructural analysis. In recent years, Louis Althusser has fastened on to the distinction between political and civil society (he talks about the 'Repressive State Apparatus' and the 'Ideological State Apparatuses') and attempted, without any obvious success, to develop it beyond Gramsci. See his 'Ideology and Ideological State Apparatuses' in *Lenin and Philosophy and Other Essays*, translated by B. Brewster (London, New Left Books, 1971), pp. 121–73. Unlike Gramsci, however, he denies that the ideological superstructure enjoys any autonomy from the system of state power. *In effect*, the distinction between political society and civil society is obliterated. On this point Althusser has been roundly criticized by Perry Anderson ('The Antinomies of Antonio Gramsci', 35–6) and Ralph Miliband (*Marxism and Politics*, Oxford University Press, 1977, pp. 54–7).

18. *PP*, p. 158.

19. *I*, p. 124.

20. See *Mach.*, p. 88, where he writes: 'Naturally all three powers [of the State] are also organs of political hegemony, but in different degrees: 1) Legislatures; 2) Judiciary; 3) Executive. It is to be noted how lapses in the administration of justice make an especially disastrous impression on the public.' See, also, ibid., p. 84.

21. *I*, p. 9.

22. *Mach.*, p. 87.

23. Ibid., p. 132.

24. *PP*, p. 72.

25. *Mach.*, p. 79.

26. F. de Felice, 'Una chiave di lettura in "Americanismo e fordismo"', *Rinascita—Il Contemporaneo*, 42 (27 Oct. 1972), 33; C. Buci-Glucksmann, *Gramsci e lo Stato*, translated from the French by C. Mancina and G. Saponaro (Rome, Editori Riuniti, 1976), pp. 97–115, 371–9; and Boggs, *Gramsci's Marxism*, pp. 46–7.

27. *Mach.*, p. 330.

28. See N. P. Mouzelis, *Organization and Bureaucracy* (London, 1969), pp. 81, 83 for a summary of Taylor's ideas.

29. *Mach.*, p. 317.

30. Ibid., p. 313.

31. Ibid., p. 317.

32. Ibid., pp. 327–8, 331–2.

33. H. Marcuse, *One-Dimensional Man* (London, Sphere Books, 1972), pp. 33–5.

34. *Mach.*, pp. 336–7. Given these remarks, it is difficult to see how Boggs can attribute the following projection to Gramsci: 'By reducing the workers to obedient automatons, rationalization would undermine creative and critical thinking and break down the impulse to resist exploitation.' *Gramsci's Marxism*, p. 47.

35. *Mach.*, pp. 337–8.

36. Easton and Guddat, *Writings of the Young Marx*, p. 438.

37. *Marx & Engels: Basic Writings on Politics and Philosophy*, edited by L. S. Feuer (New York, Doubleday, 1959), p. 26.

38. Easton and Guddat, *Writings of the Young Marx*, p. 434.

39. Feuer, *Marx & Engels: Basic Writings*, p. 18.

40. F. Engels, *The Condition of the Working Class in England* (London, 1892), p. 124.

41. *Karl Marx: Selected Writings in Sociology and Social Philosophy*, edited and translated by T. B. Bottomore and M. Rubel (Harmondsworth, Middlesex, Penguin Books, 1961), p. 194. Quotation taken from *The Poverty of Philosophy*.

42. Feuer, *Marx & Engels: Basic Writings*, p. 8.

43. V. I. Lenin, *What is to be Done?* (Moscow, Progress Publishers, 1967), p. 41.

44. *Collected Works* (London, Lawrence & Wishart, 1962), vol. 10, 32; vol. 16 (1963), 301–2. In this later passage he says: 'The very conditions of their lives make the workers capable of struggle and impel them to struggle.'

45. Cited in T. Cliff, *Rosa Luxemburg* (published as volumes 2 and 3 of *International Socialism*, 1959), p. 48.

46. 'The Proletarian Revolution and the Renegade Kautsky', in V. I. Lenin, *Selected Works* (London, Lawrence & Wishart, 1947), II, 372.

47. Gramsci was especially hard on trade unions: 'Trade unionism is . . . nothing but a form of capitalist society, not a potential overcoming of that society. It organizes workers not as producers but as wage earners, that is, as creatures of the capitalist regime of private property.' 'Sindacalismo e consigli' (8 Nov. 1919); *ON*, p. 45.

48. *Mach.*, pp. 59, 58–62, 83–5.

49. A. J. Carlyle, *A History of Mediaeval Political Theory in the West*; cited in P. H. Partridge, *Consent and Consensus* (London, Pall Mall Press, 1971), pp. 13–14.

50. John Locke, *Second Treatise of Civil Government*, § 122, in *Two Treatises of Government* (New York, The New American Library, 1965), p. 394.

51. J. Plamenatz, *Consent, Freedom, and Political Obligation* (London, Oxford University Press, 1968), Postscript, p. 170.

52. A. Gewirth, 'Political Justice' in R. B. Brandt, ed., *Social Justice* (Engelwood Cliffs, New Jersey, Prentice Hall, 1962), pp. 131, 137–8.

53. 'Centre and Periphery', in *The Logic of Personal Knowledge: Essays Presented to Michael Polanyi* (London, Routledge & Kegan Paul, 1961), pp. 117–30.

54. *I*, p. 9.

55. *Mach.*, p. 31. See, also, *MS*, p. 43, where Gramsci associates hegemony with 'active consent'. In *Mach.*, p. 79, he talks about how the ruling class 'manages to obtain the active consent of the ruled', but the word 'hegemony' does not actually appear in this passage.

56. 'Gramsci e l'egemonia del proletariato', *Studi Gramsciani*, p. 282.

57. *MS*, pp. 5–6.

58. Ibid., p. 6.

59. Ibid., p. 11.

60. When Gramsci speaks of the dominant ideology in modern capitalist society, he sometimes means that world-view which is specifically bourgeois—secular liberalism in all its variants. But in other places (e.g. the passages quoted above), he seems to refer to a broader conception: an amalgam or alliance of diverse traditional ideologies (especially religion) with that of the ruling class. However, some traditional beliefs, he observes, are so primitive as to possess only the most tenuous links with the 'official' world-view. In this connection, he discusses folklore. Yet this colourful mosaic of superstition and myth still serves the interests of the dominant groups, inasmuch as it narrows the mental perspective of the masses. See *LVN*, pp. 215–18.

61. *MS*, pp. 3–5, 25–6, 147–8. See, also, the exceptionally sketchy set of notes headed 'National Language and Grammar', *LVN*, pp. 197–211.

62. *MS*, p. 4.

63. *R*, pp. 71–2.

64. Ibid., pp. 85–6. Gramsci exhibits the Marxist tendency to exaggerate the achievements of the French Revolution and glorify its Jacobin heroes. For a more realistic assessment, see P. Ginsborg, 'Gramsci and the Era of Bourgeois Revolution in Italy', in J. A. Davis, ed., *Gramsci and Italy's Passive Revolution* (London, Croom Helm, 1979), pp. 54–5.

65. *R*, p. 72.

66. Ibid., p. 157.
67. Ibid., p. 106.
68. Ibid., pp. 70, 157.
69. Ibid., p. 100.
70. Ibid., p. 107.
71. Ibid., pp. 69–70, 83, 107; *Mach.*, p. 70.
72. *R.* p. 94.
73. Ibid., p. 70.
74. Ibid., pp. 71, 157. Gramsci also uses the rather ambiguous concept of 'passive revolution' in a slightly different sense, to refer to a 'molecular', gradual process of change which *does* result in a genuine shift in the locus of power. An example is the advance of the bourgeoisie in Restoration France after 1815. See *MS*, pp. 192–4. In both its senses, however, 'passive revolution' is, in Gramsci's phrase, ' "revolution" without "revolution" ' (*R*, p. 71), a series of transformations involving neither upheaval nor the active participation of the masses.
75. For a study of 'primitive rebellion' in various countries, see E. J. Hobsbawm, *Primitive Rebels* (New York, W. W. Norton, 1959).
76. *PP*, p. 14.
77. *R*, p. 71.
78. Ibid., p. 195.
79. It is not at all clear how the ancient Greek city-states would fit into Gramsci's typology. But to criticize him on the basis of historical evidence, as has often been done, is perhaps to misunderstand the nature of his enterprise. While he always upheld the virtues of empirical research, he was, I think, less interested in presenting accurate historical explanations than in developing concepts and models for historical and political inquiry. In any case his imprisonment prevented him from consulting most of the relevant sources.
80. *R*, p. 196.
81. *Mach.*, p. 129.
82. *R*, p. 9.
83. Reproduced in P. Togliatti, *La formazione del gruppo dirigente del partito comunista italiano* (Rome, Editori Riuniti, 1965), pp. 196–7.
84. See, for example, *CPC*, p. 64.
85. *Mach.*, pp. 62–3.
86. *Mach.*, pp. 66–7. Gramsci's extensive (and curious) use of military jargon and analogies perhaps stemmed from his admiration for Machiavelli (see Chapter 4), who employed military metaphors to describe and explain Florentine politics.
87. Ibid., p. 84.
88. Ibid., p. 88; *MS*, pp. 266–7.
89. *Mach.*, p. 42.
90. *MS*, pp. 130–1.
91. *R*, 70.
92. *Mach.*, p. 68.
93. Ibid.
94. *R*, p. 70.
95. *Mach.*, p. 68.
96. *Three Tactics, The Background in Marx* (New York, Monthly Review Press, 1963).
97. *MS*, p. 12.
98. G. Lichtheim, 'On the Interpretation of Marx's Thought', in N. Lobkowicz (ed.), *Marx and the Western World* (Indiana, Univ. of Notre Dame Press, 1967), pp. 14–15.
99. Easton and Guddat, *Writings of the Young Marx*, p. 368.
100. Feuer, *Marx & Engels: Basic Writings*, pp. 19–20.
101. K. Marx, *Capital*, translated by S. Moore and E. Aveling (London, Lawrence &

Wishart, 1974), I, p. 715. Marx also underlines the 'inevitability' theme in various 'prefaces' and 'afterwords' to *Capital* I. See, for example, ibid., pp. 20, 27.
102. Easton and Guddat, *Writings of the Young Marx*, p. 415.

Chapter 3

1. 'Gramsci e L'Ordine Nuovo'. *Quaderni di Giustizia e Libertà*, II (August 1933), 71–9.
2. Review in *Quaderni della Critica*, III (July 1947), 86–7. After reading the prison notebooks, however, Croce grew hostile to suggestions that Gramsci's thought was similar to his own. See 'Schede v. De Sanctis-Gramsci', *Lo spettatore italiano*, V (July 1952), 294–8.
3. See his 'Il pensiero di Gramsci e il marxismo sovietico', *Rassegna d'Italia*, III (July 1948), 779–85; and 'Gramsci tra Croce e Marx', *Il Ponte*, IV (May 1948), 428–38.
4. See his 'Un intellettuale tra Lenin e Croce', *Belfagor*, III (1948), 435–45.
5. Ibid., 436–7; and Morpurgo-Tagliabue, 'Il pensiero di Gramsci e il marxismo sovietico', 783.
6. Carocci, 'Un intellettuale tra Lenin e Croce', 436, 441.
7. 'Gramsci tra Croce e Marx', 429, 433, 435, 437. 'Il pensiero di Gramsci e il marxismo sovietico', 781–82.
8. See G. Carbone, 'Su alcuni commenti alle opere di A. Gramsci', *Società*, VII (March 1951), especially 146–9; and the Introduction written by Carlo Salinari and Mario Spinella for their reader of selections from Gramsci's works, *Antonio Gramsci: Antologia popolare degli scritti e delle lettere* (Rome, Editori Riuniti, 1957), especially pp. 10–11. In the meantime a rather extreme form of the 'Gramsci as Leninist' orthodoxy arose within certain Communist circles. It argued, in its more rigid formulations, that Gramsci was a faithful adherent of dialectical material-ism as defined by the official Soviet orthodoxy. See E. Sereni, 'Gramsci e la scienza d'avanguardia', *Società*, IV (March 1948), 3–30; and M. Aloisi, 'Gramsci, la scienza e la natura come storia', *Società*, VI (September 1950), 385–410. In the absence of textual support for their thesis, they assumed, implausibly, that since Gramsci, in his political practice, adopted the main categories of the Bolshevik approach, then it must follow that he also adopted the underlying Bolshevik world-view. Aloisi, who wrote his article after the publication of the first volume of the *Quaderni*, could only find one brief, ambiguous passage to prop up his argu-ment. In the passage in question (*MS*, p. 145) Gramsci criticizes Lukács for allegedly excluding nature from the dialectic. On this incredibly flimsy textual evidence, we are expected to accept the proposition that Gramsci's basic theo-retical viewpoint was essentially identical to that of Engels and Stalin! The 'Gramsci as Stalinist' thesis reached its culmination in C. Ottino's laborious and scholastic *Concetti fondamentali nella teoria di Antonio Gramsci* (Milan, Feltrinelli, 1956), one of whose central contentions was that Gramsci, as a good Leninist/ Stalinist, believed in the priority of matter over spirit. This 'dialectical materialist' interpretation was so tortured and sophistic, so much at odds with Gramsci's actual writings, and so obviously inspired by immediate political considerations, that no one any longer takes it seriously.
9. It did not, however, *literally* disappear during the 1950s; it simply became rather inconspicuous. In 1958 H. Stuart Hughes maintained, in the course of his study of modern European thought, that: 'In Gramsci's hands the doctrine [Marxism] returned to its idealist beginnings. It was in the consciousness of intellectuals alone, he recognized, that the great social ideas had their origins. They did not spring spontaneously from material conditions and economic relationships. They had an irreducible autonomy of their own.' 'Gramsci and Marxist Humanism',

Consciousness and Society (St. Albans, Paladin, 1974), p. 104. The PCI watch-dogs could not be bothered to take any notice of Hughes's brief (eight-page) discussion of Gramsci.

10. *Antonio Gramsci, La vita, il pensiero, l'azione* (Bari, Laterza, 1963).
11. Ibid., p. 195.
12. Ibid., p. 202.
13. Ibid., p. 223.
14. Ibid., p. 212.
15. Ibid., p. 216.
16. Ibid., p. 197.
17. For example, at the international conference of Gramsci scholars, held at Cagliari in 1967, the eminent Norberto Bobbio delivered a now famous paper which in all crucial respects supported the Tamburrano interpretation. For Gramsci, Bobbio wrote, 'the *ethico-political moment* . . . dominates the *economic* moment, through the recognition that the *active subject* of history creates *objectivity*, a recognition which permits the resolution of the *material conditions* into an *instrument* of action, and therefore the attainment of *the willed purpose*'. 'Gramsci e la concezione della società civile', in *Gramsci e la cultura contemporanea*, I (Rome, Editori Riuniti, 1969), 90. Throughout the 1960s the tendency to read Gramsci in an idealist key was particularly noticeable in the few Anglo-Saxon scholars who wrote about him. See, e.g., N. McInnes, 'Antonio Gramsci', *Survey*, n. 53 (October 1964), 3–15; A. Davidson, *Antonio Gramsci, the Man, his Ideas* (Sydney, *Australian Left Review*, 1968), ch. 2; and E. Genovese, 'On Antonio Gramsci', *Studies on the Left*, VII (March–April 1967), 83–107. Like Tamburrano (and Bobbio), none of these scholars went so far as to claim that Gramsci's 'voluntarist' approach was actually un-Marxist.
18. See, e.g., C. Reichers, *Antonio Gramsci: Marxismus in Italien* (Frankfurt, Europäische Verlanganstalt, 1970); and G. Marramao, 'Per una critica dell'ideologia di Gramsci', *Quaderni piacentini*, XI (March 1972), 74–92. A very early version of this far Left thesis was published in 1949 by O. Damen, who concluded that 'the disagreement between Gramsci-ism and Marxism is fundamental'. 'Premarxismo filosofico di Gramsci', *Prometeo*, III (August 1949), 605–12. *Prometeo* was the linear descendant of Amadeo Bordiga's *Il Soviet*, a communist newspaper that many years earlier expressed displeasure at Gramsci's alleged 'voluntarist' and 'idealist' tendencies.
19. Reichers, *Antonio Gramsci*, p. 243. It is perhaps superfluous to point out that the author uses 'democratic' in the pejorative 'bourgeois' sense.
20. Gramsci's critique of Bukharin is in *MS*, pp. 119–68; his critique of Croce, ibid., pp. 169–258. Bukharin's book was first published in Moscow in 1921, where it went through several editions. Gramsci probably read the French translation, published in 1927.
21. Stephen Cohen stresses this side of Bukharin's restatement of the orthodox tradition in *Bukharin and the Bolshevik Revolution* (New York, Vintage Books, 1975), ch. IV. Certainly, Bukharin did make some innovations in response to contemporary social theorists critical of Marx. In particular, the Bolshevik thinker was worried that Engels's understanding of the dialectic lumbered Marxism with a vaguely metaphysical explanation of movement, retaining 'the teleological flavour inevitably connected with the Hegelian formulation which rests on the *self-movement* of "Spirit"'. (Quotation from Bukharin, cited ibid., p. 115.) In positing a semi-mystical unfolding of the dialectic in history and nature, Engels seemed to be investing matter with what looked like covert spiritualization, and this bore embarrassing affinities to German idealist and romantic philosophy. Bukharin's desire to deny the charge that Marxism, through this concept of the

dialectic, embodied a hidden idealism led him forcefully to locate the 'real' source of dialectical motion in the conflict of forces, not in 'self-development'. (See the valuable discussion ibid., pp. 115–16.) Small wonder that more orthodox theorists, like Lenin, regarded his treatment of the dialectic as suspect, a weak point in an otherwise admirable effort to systematize the doctrine.

22. F. Engels, *The Dialectics of Nature* (Moscow, Progress Publishers, 1954), p. 266.
23. N. Bukharin, *Historical Materialism: a System of Sociology* (Ann Arbor, University of Michigan Press, 1969), p. 46.
24. MS, p. 120.
25. Ibid., pp. 155–6.
26. Ibid., p. 129.
27. Ibid., p. 131.
28. Ibid., p. 155.
29. Ibid., p. 138.
30. Ibid., p. 135.
31. Ibid., p. 80.
32. Ibid., p. 28.
33. Ibid., p. 23.
34. Ibid., p. 40.
35. Ibid., pp. 22–3.
36. In ibid., p. 47, for example, he claims that the *Theses* demonstrate the 'extent to which Marx had surpassed the philosophical position of vulgar materialism'. See, also, pp. 91 and 135.
37. Thesis I, in Bottomore and Rubel, *Karl Marx: Selected Writings*, p. 82.
38. *MS*, pp. 150–1.
39. Ibid., pp. 157–8.
40. Ibid., p. 91.
41. Even the later, more determinist and 'scientific' Marx did not abandon the essential points of the first Thesis on Feuerbach. For example, he writes in *Capital*: 'Labour is, in the first place, a process in which both man and Nature participate, and in which man of his own accord starts, regulates and controls the material reactions between himself and Nature. He opposes himself to Nature as one of her own forces, setting in motion . . . the natural forces of his body in order to appropriate Nature's productions in a form adapted to his own wants. By thus acting on the external world and changing it, he at the same time changes his own nature.' Vol. I, p. 173.
42. *MS*, pp. 160–1.
43. Ibid., p. 156.
44. Ibid., p. 157.
45. Ibid., pp. 55–6.
46. Ibid., p. 96.
47. *Mach.*, pp. 48–9.
48. *MS*, p. 97.
49. Ibid., p. 135. For another expression of his belief in the formal similarity between mechanistic Marxism and Christian metaphysics, see the letter of 1 December 1930, where he comments to Tatiana that 'many so-called theorists of historical materialism have fallen into a philosophical position resembling that of mediaeval theology, and have made a kind of "Unknown God" of the "economic structure" . . .'. *LC*, p. 106.
50. *MS*, pp. 236–7.
51. Ibid., pp. 230, 39–40.
52. Ibid., p. 238.
53. Ibid., p. 139. See pages 56 and 124–5 for similar remarks. It should be pointed out

that Gramsci, while denying that Marxism was a science in the strict sense, sometimes used the term 'science' in a broad sense, to encompass any study pursued through systematic thinking and orderly inquiry into a series of empirical facts. See, e.g., ibid., p. 136.

54. Ibid., p. 136; and *PP*, p. 162.
55. *MS*, p. 220.
56. *Mach.*, p. 38.
57. Ibid., p. 36; *MS*, p. 162.
58. *MS*, pp. 126–7; see *Mach.*, p. 34 as well.
59. *MS*, p. 134.
60. Ibid., p. 128.
61. Ibid., p. 125.
62. Ibid., p. 135.
63. Gramsci pours scorn on the *Popular Manual*'s treatment of the quantity-quality dialectic. The *Manual* completely ignores the human factor, instead 'contenting itself with simple word play about water changing its state (ice, liquid, gas) with changes in temperature, a purely mechanical fact determined by external agents (fire, sun, evaporation of carbonic acid, etc.)'. Bukharin does not realize that if one remains solely on the level of physical principles, 'one does not get out of the quantitative sphere except metaphorically'. Hence the transformation from quantity to quality becomes impossible. *MS*, p. 163.
64. Ibid., p.135.
65. *Mach.*, p. 36.
66. *MS*, pp. 125–6.
67. Ibid., p. 90.
68. Ibid., pp. 98–100.
69. Ibid., p. 127; *Mach.*, pp. 157–8.
70. *MS*, pp. 13–14.
71. Ibid., p. 126. I have taken this translation from the Hoare/Nowell-Smith edition of the *Prison Notebooks*, p. 428.
72. *MS*, p. 13.
73. Ibid., pp. 14–15, 19–20.
74. Letter to Tatiana (1 December 1930), *LC*, p. 106; *MS*, pp. 84–5, 223–5.
75 *Mach.*, p. 34; *MS*, pp. 125–7, 136–7.
76. *Logic as the Science of the Pure Concept*, translated by D. Ainslie (London, Macmillan, 1917), pp. 172–3. (Translation amended by J.F.)
77. *The Philosophy of Benedetto Croce* (London, Macmillan, 1917), p. 7 (my emphasis).
78. *Theory and History of Historiography*, translated by D. Ainslie (London, Harrap, 1921), p. 312.
79. Ibid.
80. Ibid., pp. 51–63.
81. See his *Storia del Regno di Napoli* (Bari, Laterza, 1925); *Storia d'Italia dal 1871 al 1915* (Bari, Laterza, 1928); *Storia dell'età barocca in Italia* (Bari, Laterza, 1929); *Storia d'Europa nel secolo decimonono* (Bari, Laterza, 1932); and *La storia come pensiero e come azione* (Bari, Laterza, 1938).
82. See *Logic as the Science of the Pure Concept*, pp. 310–30, for a discussion of the 'Identity of Philosophy and History'.
83. Croce, *Theory and History of Historiography*, p. 312.
84. *Consciousness and Society*, p. 201.
85. *Gramsci* (a collection of articles and addresses on Gramsci) (Florence, Parenti, 1955), p. 77.
86. *MS*, p. 199.
87. 17 August 1931, in *LC*, p. 132.

88. *Cultura e vita morale* (Bari, Laterza, 1955), pp. 34–7.
89. In 1910 Croce was named a Senator of the Realm. By 1911 he had become an implacable *opponent* of socialism.
90. For a discussion of this journal, and its influence on the teen-aged Gramsci, see Davidson, *Antonio Gramsci: Towards an Intellectual Biography*, pp. 50–3.
91. Ibid., pp. 57–61.
92. Published on 29 January 1916 in *Il Grido del Popolo*. The article is now reprinted in *SG*, pp. 22–6.
93. 'Audacia e Fede' in *Avanti!*; now reprinted in *SM*, p. 148.
94. 'I Moventi e Coppoletto' in *Avanti!* (19 April 1916); now reprinted in *SM*, pp. 118–19.
95. *Jean-Christophe* (Paris, Editions Michel, 1956), p. 221; cited in Davidson, *Antonio Gramsci: Towards an Intellectual Biography*, p. 101. In a few useful pages (99–103) Davidson considers the thought of Péguy and Rolland in relation to Gramsci's intellectual development.
96. The treatise is now contained in *SG*, pp. 73–89.
97. By 1918 Gentile seems to have supplanted Croce as Gramsci's preferred Italian thinker. The Palermitan, claimed Gramsci, was 'the Italian philosopher who has made the greatest contribution in the field of thought in recent years'. Impressed by Gentile's identification of thought and action, together with his radical affirmation of the freedom of the human will, Gramsci praised actualism as a doctrine that could 'enrich the literature of socialism'. 'Il socialismo e la filosofia attuale' in *Il Grido del Popolo*, 19 January 1918; cited in L. Paggi, *Antonio Gramsci e il moderno principe* (Rome, Editori Riuniti, 1970), p. 21. Gentile's influence on Gramsci, however, was neither profound nor lasting. In the *Quaderni*, Gramsci more or less ignores the man who became the official philosopher of Mussolini's regime, save to condemn, in a few sentences, 'the disordered crudeness of Gentile's thought' and his 'disreputable ideological opportunism'. *MS*, pp. 122–3.
98. This remark appears in a preface (to the selection of writings by Croce) which was not included in the *Scritti Giovanili* reprint. Cited in Cammet, *Antonio Gramsci and the Origins of Italian Communism*, p. 47.
99. *SG*, p. 78.
100. Ibid., pp. 84–5.
101. Davidson, *Antonio Gramsci: Towards an Intellectual Biography*, p. 89.
102. *SG*, pp. 150–1.
103. *MS*, pp. 76–7.
104. Ibid., p. 199.
105. 'Il partito e la rivoluzione', *Ordine Nuovo*, 27 December 1919; reprinted in *ON*, pp. 67–71. (Quotation on p. 68.) See, also, 'La conquista dello stato' (*Ordine Nuovo*, 2 July 1919), where Gramsci echoes a familiar Marxist theme: 'Capitalist concentration, determined by the mode of production, produces a corresponding concentration of labouring masses. It is in this fact that one must look for the source of all the theses of revolutionary Marxism, that one must look for the conditions of the new proletarian way of life, of the new communist order. . . .' This because social relations, political institutions, and 'man's spiritual awareness' are all rooted in the 'objective conditions for the production of material wealth'. But Gramsci adds that history is 'essentially unpredictable', thereby indicating that his opposition to evolutionary determinism remained undiminished. *ON*, pp. 13–16.
106. Davidson, *Antonio Gramsci: Towards an Intellectual Biography*, pp. 104–6.
107. As V. Gerratana has pointed out, '. . . in Italy, as well as on the international scale, the diffusion of Labriola's work remained only on the surface, and was not translated into real influence'. *Ricerche di storia del Marxismo* (Rome, Editori

Riuniti, 1972), p. 149.

108. A. Labriola, 'Historical Materialism' in *Essays on the Materialist Conception of History*, translated by C. H. Kerr (Chicago, Charles H. Kerr & Co., 1908), pp. 111, 108, 121.
109. Ibid., pp. 109–11.
110. Ibid., pp. 104, 120–4, 228.
111. Ibid., pp. 127, 135, 204.
112. A. Labriola, *Socialism and Philosophy*, translated by E. Untermann (St. Louis, Mo., Telos Press, 1980, p. 114.
113. 'Historical Materialism', p. 154.
114. For a discussion of this point and relevant references, see P. Piccone, 'Labriola and the Roots of Eurocommunism', *Berkeley Journal of Sociology*, XXII (Winter 1977–8), 37–9.
115. 'Historical Materialism', p. 190 (my emphasis).
116. See, e.g., ibid., pp. 112–13, 123, 152, 201.
117. Ibid., pp. 203, 122–3.
118. Piccone, 'Labriola and the Roots of Eurocommunism', 40.
119. 'In Memory of the *Communist Manifesto*' in *Essays on the Materialist Conception of History*, p. 17.
120. G. Marramao, *Marxismo e revisionismo in Italia* (Bari, De Donato, 1971), p. 117.
121. L. Faenza argues that Gramsci did indeed derive much of his vision from Labriola. 'Labriola e Gramsci', *Mondo operaio*, VII (4 December 1954), 15–17.
122. See, e.g., *MS*, pp. 79, 82.
123. Ibid., p. 200.
124. Ibid., pp. 80–1, 104–5, 119–20, 199.
125. Ibid., p. 199.
126. Ibid., p. 180.
127. Ibid., pp. 183, 190.
128. Ibid., pp. 179–80.
129. Ibid., pp. 201–2.
130. Ibid., p. 21.
131. Ibid., p. 199.
132. Ibid., p. 189.
133. Ibid., p. 190.
134. Ibid., pp. 191, 237.
135. Ibid., p. 204.
136. And yet Gramsci perceives a similarity between his two victims; for Croce, with his determination to classify all reality in terms of pure concepts, falls into a new kind of 'abstract and mechanical sociology', akin to that of Bukharin in its indifference to the 'petty' variations and contingencies of ordinary life that refuse to fit into rigid categories and schemes. Ibid., p. 188.
137. Ibid., pp. 43–4.
138. Ibid., pp. 216–17.
139. *PP*, p. 203.
140. *MS*, pp. 192, 189; Letter to Tania (9 May 1932), *LC*, pp. 186–8.
141. *MS*, pp. 241–2, 87.
142. *PP*, p. 63; *MS*, p. 93.
143. *MS*, p. 196.
144. Ibid., p. 191.
145. Ibid., p. 229.
146. *LC*, p. 193.
147. *MS*, p. 250.
148. Ibid., p. 221 (my emphasis).

149. *PP*, p. 26.
150. *MS*, pp. 174, 226, 247–50.
151. L. Salamini, 'Gramsci and Marxist Sociology of Knowledge', *Sociological Quarterly*, 15 (Summer 1974), 377; R. Orfei, *Antonio Gramsci, coscienza critica del marxismo* (San Casciano, Relazioni sociali, 1965), pp. 239–40. That the *Quaderni* texts in question express an essentially idealist ontology is also argued by Tamburrano in *Antonio Gramsci*, p. 213.
152. *MS*, p. 23.
153. Ibid., p. 55.
154. Ibid.
155. Ibid., p. 143.
156. Ibid., p. 142.
157. Ibid., p. 138.
158. Ibid., p. 142.
159. Ibid., p. 54.
160. Ibid., p. 142.
161. Ibid.
162. 'Karl Marx and the Classical Definition of Truth' in *Marxism and Beyond* (London, Paladin, 1971), p. 87.
163. *MS*, pp. 55–6.
164. Ibid., p. 153.
165. Ibid., p. 162.
166. Ibid., p. 55.
167. Ibid., pp. 141–2. (my emphasis).
168. Ibid., pp. 140, 53.
169. Ibid., p. 22 (my emphasis).
170. Ibid., p. 143 (my emphasis).
171. Croce, *Logic as the Science of the Pure Concept*, pp. 342–5.
172. *MS*, p. 41.
173. Ibid., p. 55.
174. Ibid., p. 161.
175. This example is borrowed from Andrea Calzolari, 'Structure and Superstructure in Gramsci', *Telos* (Spring 1969), pp. 39–40.
176. *I*, pp. 106–7.
177. *MS*, pp. 55–6. In an interesting passage Gramsci in effect accuses Lukács of precisely this 'nonsensical abstraction', because of the Hungarian's alleged attempt to reduce nature to human history alone. In order to avoid a 'dualism between nature and man', Gramsci thought, it is necessary to realize that 'human history must also be conceived as the history of nature'. Lukács, in an attempt to avoid materialism, 'has lapsed into the opposite error, into a form of idealism'. Like the metaphysical materialists, he is guilty of reductionism. *MS*, p. 145.
178. Ibid., p. 44.
179. Ibid., p. 144.
180. *Mach.*, p. 39.
181. L. Althusser and E. Balibar, *Reading Capital*, translated by B. Brewster (London, New Left Books, 1970), pp. 126–36.
182. Ibid., p. 126.
183. *MS*, p. 56 (my emphasis).
184. Ibid., p. 143.
185. *Logic as the Science of the Pure Concept*, pp. 334, 338, 339, 330.
186. *I*, pp. 46–7.
187. G. Lukács, *History and Class Consciousness*, translated by R. Livingstone (London, Merlin Press, 1971), pp. 7, 10–11.

188. Althusser, *Reading Capital*, p. 132.
189. *MS*, p. 43.
190. *MS*, pp. 27–8.
191. Ibid., p. 28.
192. Ibid., pp. 40–1.
193. Ibid., p. 40.
194. Ibid., pp. 129–30.
195. Ibid., p. 155. For other favourable references to Marx's *Preface*, see ibid., pp. 40, 44, 129–30, 154; *Mach.*, pp. 32, 43.
196. *MS*, p. 101.
197. *Mach.*, p. 45.
198. Ibid., p. 128.
199. For other passages expressing Gramsci's belief in the predominance of the economic base, see, e.g., *MS*, pp. 139, 161, 212, 233; *Mach.*, pp. 37, 82. In only one of these passages, however, does he explicitly or unambiguously accord primacy to the forces of production as such. Elsewhere, pre-eminence is attributed to 'the structure', the 'economic factor', the 'economy', 'economic phenomena' and 'material premises'. But it is always clear from the context that what Marx sometimes called the 'material powers of production' (i.e. productive forces) are *encompassed* by these terms.
200. *MS*, pp. 98–9.
201. *R*, p. 46.
202. *Selections from the Prison Notebooks*, p. 116. This passage was not included in the original Einaudi volumes.
203. *Mach.*, p. 37.
204. *MS*, p. 236.
205. Ibid., p. 97.
206. *Mach.*, p. 48.
207. Ibid., p. 37.
208. *PP*, p. 108. In *MS*, pp. 101–2 Gramsci discusses Machiavelli's concepts of *fortuna* and *virtù*, referring to them favourably as 'simple and profound intuitions'.
209. *Mach.*, pp. 42–3.
210. *MS*, pp. 29, 155, 256.
211. Ibid., p. 161.
212. H. B. Acton, 'The Materialist Conception of History', *Proceedings of The Aristotelian Society*, 1951–2; and 'Some Criticisms of Historical Materialism', *Proceedings of The Aristotelian Society*, Supplementary volume, 1970; Plamenatz, *Man and Society*, II, p. 274 ff.
213. In the *Grundrisse*, for example, Marx talks about how the capitalist economic system 'arises from the conscious wills and particular purposes of the individuals', yet is 'neither located in their consciousness nor subsumed under them as a whole'. Indeed the system appears to them as an 'objective relation, which arises spontaneously from nature. . . . Their own collisions with one another produce an *alien* social power standing above them. . . .' Cited in M. Evans, *Karl Marx* (London, Allen & Unwin, 1975), p. 57. On the non-Marxist side, E. Durkheim develops the concept of 'social facts', which are 'ways of acting, thinking and feeling, external to the individual, and endowed with a power of coercion, by reason of which they control him'. *The Rules of Sociological Method*, translated by S. Solovay and J. Mueller (Glencoe, Ill., Free Press, 1950), p. 3.
214. *MS*, p. 163.
215. 'History', he writes in his discussion of literary criticism, 'is a continuous process of self-consciousness and liberation'. *LVN*, p. 13.
216. *MS*, p. 40.

217. *Mach.*, p. 45.
218. *MS*, p. 35.
219. *Mach.*, pp. 39, 9–10, 13–15.
220. *MS*, p. 199.
221. Ibid., p. 232.
222. Ibid., pp. 217–18, 197.
223. Ibid., p. 5.
224. Ibid., p. 11.
225. Ibid., p. 87.
226. But Gramsci always retained admiration for Sorel. In the *Notebooks* he credits the Frenchman with genuine insight into 'present reality', though he also maintains that Sorel's political prescriptions have been 'surpassed'. See ibid., p. 243.
227. For an example of such confusion, see Reichers, *Antonio Gramsci*, p. 114, where Gramsci is accused of 'old-fashioned' utopianism.
228. *MS*, p. 80.
229. Ibid., p. 98.
230. *Mach.*, p. 39.
231. Bottomore and Rubel, *Karl Marx: Selected Writings*, p. 85.
232. In the few pages that Gramsci does devote to economic matters, he actually defends the theories of *Capital* from Croce's criticisms. See *MS*. pp. 208–15 in particular. But on Gramsci's interpretation, it is essential to note, acceptance of the 'tendential' laws enunciated in Marx's great work does not commit us to the prediction that capitalism will 'automatically' collapse.
233. Ibid., p. 158.
234. *History and Class Consciousness*, pp. 20, 177.
235. Ibid., p. xxiii.

Chapter 4

1. *I*, p. 3.
2. Ibid., p. 6.
3. Ibid., pp. 6–7.
4. Ibid., p. 6. What Gramsci seems to be suggesting here is that, in different social systems, activities 'weighted towards intellectual elaboration' might be differently distributed among the various occupational sectors of the population. Such an interpretation is justified by the following observation: '. . . the worker or proletarian, for example, is not specifically characterized by his manual or instrumental labour but by performing this labour in specific conditions and social relations . . .'.(Ibid.)
5. *R*, p. 100.
6. *I*, p. 3.
7. Ibid., p. 5.
8. Ibid., p. 9.
9. *R*, pp. 71, 104–5.
10. *Mach.*, p. 149.
11. *I*, p. 144.
12. *MS*, p. 35.
13. '. . . the whole system of superstructures can be conceived as distinctions within the realm of politics'. *Mach.*, p. 11. Gramsci's broad concept of politics corresponds to his broad, Hegelian definition of the state.
14. *Mach.*, p. 90.
15. Letter to Tatiana (7 Sept. 1931); *LC*, p. 138.
16. *Mach.*, p. 7.

17. Gramsci's view of Jacobinism was not always so favourable. In 1918 he wrote that 'Jacobinism was the substitution of one authoritarian regime for another', and went on to assert that the Russian Revolution could not be Jacobin because it was proletarian. 'Note sulla rivoluzione russa', *Il Grido del Popolo* (29 April 1917); reprinted in *SG*, p. 106. See, also, 'Due rivoluzioni', *L'Ordine Nuovo* (3 July 1920); reprinted in *ON*, p. 140.
18. *Mach.*, p. 3.
19. Ibid., pp. 5–6.
20. Ibid., p. 13.
21. Cited in A. Lisa, 'Discussione politica con Gramsci in carcere', *Rinascita* (12 Dec. 1964), p. 20.
22. See, for example, 'Lo strumento di lavoro', *L'Ordine Nuovo* (14 Feb. 1920), reprinted in *ON*, pp. 79–84; and 'Il consiglio di fabbrica', *L'Ordine Nuovo* (5 June 1920), reprinted in *ON*, p. 123.
23. *Mach.*, p. 22.
24. Ibid., p. 42.
25. The Lenin, at any rate, of *What is to be Done?*
26. *MS.* p. 13.
27. Feuer, *Marx & Engels: Basic Writings*, p. 20.
28. *PP*, p. 55. See also *Mach.*, p. 81: 'Ideas and opinions do not grow spontaneously in each individual brain: they have a centre of formation, of irradiation, of dissemination, of persuasion.'
29. *Mach.*, p. 5.
30. Ibid., pp. 77–9.
31. Ibid., pp. 45–6.
32. Ibid., pp. 147–8.
33. Ibid., pp. 8.
34. *MS*, p. 7.
35. Togliatti had received two degrees, one in law and another in letters and philosophy. Terracini also took a law degree, and went on to become one of the most distinguished legal minds in Italy. Tasca (like the others a graduate of Turin University) soon developed a reputation for meticulous scholarship.
36. A. Gramsci, 'Il programma dell'*Ordine Nuovo*', *L'Ordine Nuovo* (14 August 1920); *ON*, p. 146.
37. Before 1918, Gramsci tried hard to raise the intellectual level of the movement. Through lectures, seminars and study groups, he hoped to encourage habits of dispassionate study as well as an appreciation for great literature and philosophy. But his efforts were less than successful in a party firmly committed to the view that class consciousness came through struggle and not from reading books. On this, see A. Davidson, 'Gramsci and Lenin 1917–22', *Socialist Register*, edited by R. Miliband and J. Saville (London, The Merlin Press, 1974), pp. 126–8.
38. 'Il programma dell'*Ordine Nuovo*'; *ON*, p. 148.
39. 'Il programma dei commissari di reparto', unsigned, *L'Ordine Nuovo* (8 Nov. 1919); reprinted in *ON*, pp. 194–6.
40. Unsigned editorial, *L'Ordine Nuovo* (12 July 1919); *ON*, p. 447.
41. 'Sindacati e consigli', *L'Ordine Nuovo* (11 Oct. 1919); *ON*, p. 37.
42. 'Il programma dell'*Ordine Nuovo*'; *ON*, p. 150. These distinctions are also made in 'Il partito e la revoluzione', *L'Ordine Nuovo* (27 Dec. 1919), *ON*, p. 67; and 'Il consiglio di fabbrica', *ON*, pp. 123–4.
43. 'I gruppi comunisti', *L'Ordine Nuovo* (17 July 1920); *ON*, p. 140.
44. Ibid., p. 141. See, also, 'la conquista dello stato', *L'Ordine Nuovo* (12 July 1919); *ON*, pp. 14–15.
45. 'I gruppi comunisti'; *ON*, pp. 140–1.

46. 'Sindacalismo e consigli', *L'Ordine Nuovo* (8 Nov. 1919); *ON*, pp. 45–6.
47. 'Sindacati e consigli'; *ON*, p. 36.
48. Ibid., p. 38.
49. 'Il consiglio di fabbrica'; *ON*, p. 124.
50. 'Il programma dell'*Ordine Nuovo*'; *ON*, p. 152.
51. See Gramsci's article on the evolution and importance of the English shop steward committees in *Il Grido del Popolo*, 27 April 1918; cited in E. Soave, 'Appunti sulle origini teoriche e pratiche dei consigli di fabbrica a Torino', *Rivista storica del socialismo*, VII (Jan.–Apr. 1964), 3–4.
52. See, e.g., Togliatti, 'Il Leninismo nel pensiero e nell'azione di Antonio Gramsci', pp. 28–30. The more recent tendency of PCI theoreticians is to admit the importance of the consiliar thematic in Gramsci's intellectual development and frankly to dismiss it as something of a pre-Leninist embarrassment. See Gruppi, *Il concetto di egemonia in Gramsci*, p. 72.
53. See, e.g., R. Rossanda, 'Da Marx a Marx'; and L. Pintor, 'Il partito di tipo nuovo' in *Il Manifesto*, 4 (September 1969).
54. A. Davidson, 'The Varying Seasons of Gramscian Studies', *Political Studies*, XX (Dec. 1972), 461.
55. A. Caracciolo, 'Sulla questione partito-consigli di fabbrica nel pensiero di Gramsci', *Ragionamenti*, II (May–October 1957), 231.
56. A. Martinelli, 'In Defence of the Dialectic: Antonio Gramsci's Theory of Revolution', *Berkeley Journal of Sociology*, 13 (1968), 16 (my emphasis). For similar views in the recent English-language literature, see Davidson, *Antonio Gramsci: Towards an Intellectual Biography*, ch. 4; and Boggs, *Gramsci's Marxism*, pp. 118, 137.
57. See, for example, 'Il partito e la rivoluzione'; *ON*, p. 68.
58. Reprinted in *ON*, p. 122 (my emphasis).
59. 'Il partito comunista'; *ON*, p. 157.
60. 'Domenica rossa'; *ON*, pp. 163–7.
61. *ON*, pp. 67–71. The accusation of syndicalism was often levied at Gramsci by his opponents within the PSI. Despite the positive role he assigned to the party, his *Ordine Nuovo* theory did betray the influence of Sorel's idea that it was the task of the real producers not only to manage production but to organize the whole of social life. The society of the future, in other words, would take its pattern from the shop floor. Gramsci, for his part, denied the charge, belittling the vision of the syndicalists as 'only a utopia, a great castle of abstractions'. 'Sindacalismo e consigli'; *ON*, p. 48.
62. For a concise and detailed account of the Piedmont General Strike and its aftermath, see M. Clark, *Antonio Gramsci and the Revolution that Failed* (New Haven and London, Yale University Press, 1977), ch. 5.
63. The Internal Commissions were the executive committees of the factory councils.
64. Ibid., pp. 96–8.
65. *ON*, p. 118.
66. Ibid., p. 121.
67. The criticisms and solutions put forward in Gramsci's report were adumbrated in an earlier but much milder piece, 'Primo: rinnovare il partito', *L'Ordine Nuovo* (24–31 Jan. 1920); *ON*, pp. 389–92. Gramsci's disapproval of the Party's 'atrophy and lethargy' certainly antedated the April strike.
68. 'Il partito comunista'; *ON*, pp. 158, 161.
69. 'Superstizione e realtà', *L'Ordine Nuovo*; *ON*, p. 109.
70. For a straightforward and unmodified exposition of most of the pre-April themes, see, for example, 'Il consiglio di fabbrica', *ON*, pp. 123–7; and 'Il programma dell'*Ordine Nuovo*', *ON*, pp. 146–54. These articles were published on 5 June and 14 August respectively.

71. For a full, extremely well-documented discussion of the events, see Clark, *Antonio Gramsci*, chapters 8–9. A lively and detailed account is also provided by Gwyn Williams in *Proletarian Order: Antonio Gramsci, Factory Councils and the Origins of Italian Communism 1911–1921* (London, Pluto Press, 1975), pp. 242–76. The Williams book offers one of the lengthiest, most readable studies of Gramsci's ideas during the *Ordine Nuovo* period. The classic and perhaps fullest account of the September factory occupations is P. Spriano, *L'Occupazione delle fabbriche* (Turin, Einaudi, 1964); translated into English by Gwyn Williams, *The Occupation of the Factories* (London, Pluto Press, 1975).

72. 'Capacità politica', *Avanti!* (24 September 1920); *ON*, p. 170. This article was published a day before the referendum result was confirmed, but the result was a foregone conclusion.

73. See, e.g., the report called 'Trade Union Theses', which Gramsci, along with Tasca, presented to the Second Congress of the PCI in 1922. Reprinted in *SF*, pp. 499–518.

74. 'Il destino di Matteotti', *Lo Stato operaio* (28 Aug. 1924); reprinted in *Antonio Gramsci: Scritti politici*, edited by P. Spriano (Rome, Editori Riuniti, 1973), III, 93–4.

75. 'La volontà delle masse', *L'Unità* (24 June 1925); reprinted ibid., 140.

76. There is some doubt about Gramsci's position. While many of his writings indicate that he accepted the idea of imminent revolution, a letter he wrote (from Vienna) to Terracini and Togliatti in February of 1924 suggests that his endorsement of the Bordiga line was merely tactical. (He was fearful of the growing strength of Tasca's right wing and therefore did not wish to divide the rest of the Party.) The letter is reproduced in Togliatti, *La formazione del gruppo dirigente del partito comunista italiano*, pp. 192–3.

77. *L'Unità* (17 Oct. 1925), cited by Tamburrano, *Antonio Gramsci*, p. 166.

78. For a discussion of this evidence, along with appropriate references, see Davidson, *Antonio Gramsci: Towards an Intellectual Biography*, pp. 239–40.

79. See, for example, Togliatti, 'Il Leninismo nel pensiero e nell'azione di Antonio Gramsci', pp. 15–35; and Gruppi, *Il concetto di egemonia in Gramsci*, ch. 5, especially p. 95.

80. Letter to Togliatti and Terracini (9 Feb. 1924) in Togliatti, *La formazione del gruppo dirigente del partito comunista italiano*, p. 195.

81. *Mach.*, p. 23.

82. Ibid., pp. 22–3.

83. *PP*, p. 11.

84. *Mach.*, p. 24.

85. Ibid.

86. Ibid., p. 79.

87. Ibid., p. 24.

88. Ibid.

89. Gramsci quotes the summary of the law of fixed proportions offered by Maffeo Pantaleoni in his *Principî di economia pura*: 'Bodies combine chemically only in fixed proportions, and any quantity of an element which is in excess of the quantity required for a combination with other elements, themselves present in the amounts as defined, remains *free*; if the quantity of an element is insufficient in relation to the quantities of the other elements present, the combination can only take place in proportion as the quantity of the element which is present in a *smaller quantity* than the others suffices.' (*Mach.*, p. 78.)

90. Ibid., pp. 77–8.

91. A. R. Buzzi, *La teoria politica di Gramsci*, translated from the French by S. Genovali (Florence, La Nuova Italia Editrice, 1973), p. 233.

92. *Mach.*, p. 78.
93. Ibid.
94. Ibid., p. 28.
95. *PP*, p. 60.
96. *Mach.*, pp. 20–1.
97. *MS*, p. 172.
98. *Mach.*, p. 28.
99. Ibid., p. 76.
100. Ibid., p. 158.
101. Ibid., p. 157.
102. Ibid., p. 76.
103. Ibid., p. 26.
104. Ibid.
105. 'La situazione italiana e i compiti del pci' (theses prepared by Gramsci and approved by the III Congress of the Italian Communist Party—the Lyons Congress—held in January of 1926), *CPC*, p. 506; 'La lotta contro la frazione e la discussione nel partito', *L'Unità* (10 June 1925); *CPC*, p. 220. The 'wreckers' referred to by Gramsci were Bordiga and his followers, who organized a dissident 'Left' faction within the Party in 1925. Supporters of Trotsky, they found themselves at odds with Comintern policy and clashed with Gramsci on questions of organization and strategy. For an informative discussion of this controversy, see Davidson, *Antonio Gramsci: Towards an Intellectual Biography*, pp. 204–31.
106. *Mach.*, p. 51; see, also, *PP*, p. 58.
107. *Mach.*, p. 77.
108. 'One Step Forward, Two Steps Back', *Collected Works*, vol. 7 (1961), 405 n.
109. *PP*, p. 57.
110. *Mach.*, p. 77; *MS*, p. 120.
111. *MS*, p. 26.
112. *PP*, p. 59.
113. *MS*, p. 18. See, also ibid., pp. 23, 25.
114. Ibid., p. 142.
115. Gramsci tends to use 'rational', 'real', and 'necessary' interchangeably. See *MS*, p. 41, where he says that a conception of the world 'becomes actual, lives historically (i.e. socially and no longer just in the brains of individuals) when it ceases to be arbitrary and becomes necessary-rational-real'.
116. Ibid., p. 48.
117. A distinction should be underlined here. Gramsci, so far as I can tell, never says that a given ideology is valid *because* the great majority of people accept it, that mass acceptance *creates* truth. Rather, he asserts that an ideology will win mass adhesion if it *corresponds to the needs* of a particular historical period. Truth is not immanent in the process of verification. In this respect, his position differs from that of the influential pragmatist philosopher, William James, who held that an hypothesis *becomes* true when we verify it; i.e. 'true' *means* 'confirmed'.
118. *MS*, p. 95.
119. Bottomore and Rubel, *Karl Marx: Selected Writings*, p. 82.
120. *MS*, p. 159.
121. *PP*, p. 57: '. . . the leadership given to the [Turin] movement was both creative and correct . . . [The] element of "spontaneity" was not neglected and even less despised. It was *educated*, directed, purged of extraneous contaminations; the aim was to bring it into line with modern theory [Marxism].'
122. *I*, p. 135.
123. *MS*, p. 17.
124. *I*, p. 7. Gramsci recognized how difficult it would be to develop intellectuals from

social groups that have traditionally lacked the requisite attitudes and opportunities for disciplined study and rigorous thought. Ibid., p. 117.
125. *MS*, p. 87.
126. 'Gramsci and Lenin 1917–1922', p. 141.

Chapter 5

1. It is not clear whether this absence was for the benefit of the prison censor or whether it reflected a profound dissatisfaction with the whole concept of proletarian dictatorship. It will be argued in this chapter that Gramsci certainly did not favour what we would generally call dictatorship. But a certain ambiguity surrounds the idea of dictatorship in Marxist literature. Sometimes it simply stands for class domination, not authoritarian government as it is conventionally understood. Lenin, for instance, was in the habit of referring to liberal democracy as the 'dictatorship of the bourgeoisie'. And in the course of an attack on the Russian Bolsheviks for setting up a dictatorial regime, Karl Kautsky contended that a Marxist dictatorship of the proletariat would not be a dictatorship in the literal sense of suspension of voting rights and rule by a single person or small group. It would be class rule by the proletariat and, as such, it would be majority rule according to generally accepted democratic procedures and with full protection of minorities. In the proletarian context, then, 'dictatorship' was to be understood as denoting not a form of government but rather 'a condition which must everywhere arise when the proletariat has conquered political power'. To prove that this was the Marx-Engels viewpoint, Kautsky cited Engels's preface to a twentieth anniversary edition of Marx's *The Civil War in France*, where he (Engels) held up the Paris Commune as the first example of the dictatorship of the proletariat. (*The Dictatorship of the Proletariat*, Ann Arbor, Univ. of Michigan Press, 1964, pp. 30, 43–4, 46.) If Marxist dictatorship is to be understood in the attenuated sense, as simply a matter of government by a working-class majority, then Gramsci obviously was for it.
2. *Gramsci*, p. 30.
3. Ibid., p. 46. Gramsci's posthumous role as the PCI's 'patron saint', along with the new post-war strategy, will receive fuller treatment in Chapter 6.
4. 'Il Leninismo nel pensiero e nell'azione di A. Gramsci', p. 34.
5. V. Crisafulli, 'Stato e società nel pensiero di Gramsci', *Società*, VII (1951), 589–609. For other orthodox Communist examples of the Togliatti line, see V. Gerratana, 'Una deformazione del pensiero di Gramsci', *L'Unità* (19 May 1957); R. Battaglia, 'Egemonia e dittatura del proletariato nella concezione di A. Gramsci', *L'Unità* (25 May 1957).
6. 'Egemonia, cultura, partito nel pensiero di Antonio Gramsci', *Rinascita —Il Contemporaneo*, no. 5. (29 January 1971), pp. 19–20. See, also, Gruppi, 'Il concetto di egemonia', *Prassi rivoluzionaria*, p. 88; and U. Cerroni, 'L "eresia" Leninista', *L'Unità* (22 April 1972). The new approach still insists on Gramsci's Leninism, but the latter emerges, in much of the recent Party literature, as little more than a concern for class alliances and other intermediate strategies and aims. See, e.g., P. Spriano, 'Gramsci e Lenin', *Rinascita* (15 May 1970), p. 28. In this logic-defying manner, the real Lenin vanishes, only to be magically reincarnated as an apostle of the 'Italian Road' ideology.
7. 'I nostri conti con la teoria della "rivoluzione senza rivoluzione" di Gramsci', *Giovane critica*, no. 17 (Autumn 1967), 61–70.
8. In *Pensiero politico e storiografia moderna* (Pisa, Nistri-Lischi, 1954), p. 256.
9. A. R. Buzzi, *La teoria politica di Gramsci*, p. 353; see, also, R. Mondolfo, 'Le antinomie di Gramsci', *Critica sociale*, no. 23 (15 December 1963), 629–34.

10. 'Totalitarismo e storicismo nel pensiero di Antonio Gramsci', pp. 239–40.
11. Ibid., p. 233.
12. *La teoria politica di Gramsci*, p. 352; for similar sentiments in the Italian literature on Gramsci, see N. Matteucci, *Antonio Gramsci e la filosofia della prassi* (Milano, Giuffré Editore, 1951), pp. 73, 77; R. Mondolfo, 'Le antinomie di Gramsci', and *Da Ardigò a Gramsci* (Milan, Nuova Accademia, 1962), p. 160; G. Mura, 'A. Gramsci tra storicismo e intellettualismo', *Civitas*, no. 11–12 (November–December 1966), 103–7; and M. Aladino, 'Due marxisti italiani (Rodolfo Mondolfo e Antonio Gramsci)', *Critica sociale*, no. 11 (1 June 1948), 256.
13. G. Lichtheim, *Marxism: a Historical and Critical Study* (London, Routledge & Kegan Paul, 1964), p. 368.
14. *Consciousness and Society*, p. 101.
15. Buzzi, *La teoria politica di Gramsci*, p. 316.
16. Ibid., p. 353.
17. 'Le antinomie di Gramsci', 634.
18. Mura, 'A. Gramsci tra storicismo e intellettualismo', 104, 107.
19. *Mach.*, p. 134.
20. Ibid., p. 147.
21. Ibid., p. 8.
22. Ibid., p. 151.
23. See, for example, ibid., p. 83; *PP*, pp. 65, 154; and *I*, p. 107.
24. *MS*, pp. 18–19.
25. 'Le antinomie di Gramsci', 632; Tamburrano, rather naïvely, defends Gramsci by claiming that this apparently illiberal passage concerns the realistic organization of academic and cultural research, not legal or police repression: 'Gramsci poses the problem not in relation to the political aspect of the question, but in relation to the practicality, efficiency and constructiveness of research' (*Antonio Gramsci*, p. 291). It is presumed that Gramsci, in the passage in question, was directing his attention primarily to flat-earth pseudo-scientists and other academic incompetents or crackpots who might hinder the accumulation of knowledge. But if this is all Gramsci had in mind, it is not clear why he would have bothered to discuss it, as the existing academic structure, with its battery of sanctions and its received opinions about intellectual quality, dealt with the problem well enough and could be expected to do so in future.
26. *MS*, p. 16.
27. See, e.g., Mondolfo, 'Le antinomie di Gramsci', 632–3; and M. Vajda, 'Gramsci, la filosofia e le masse', *Aut Aut*, no. 135 (May–June 1973), 55–7.
28. *Mach.*, p. 8.
29. *PP*, p. 166.
30. Ibid., p. 120.
31. See, for example, *Mach.*, pp. 134, 147.
32. A Popperian, following the model of the experimental sciences, would argue that if a theory fails to work properly in practice, this alone shows that something is wrong with the theory. Such is of course the case in the natural sciences where there is, potentially, general agreement that a given theory has been correctly applied, and where the criteria of the theory's refutation are more or less unambiguous. Political theories, especially those with normative content, usually elude such certainty. Nevertheless, the tendency to raise questions concerning the possible practical consequences of such theories *is* legitimate, *so long as we do not confuse these consequences with the theories themselves.*
33. *Mach.*, p. 134.
34. Cited by Peter Gay in the Introduction to his English translation of E. Cassirer, *The Question of Jean-Jacques Rousseau* (Indiana, 1963), p. 14.

35. It has been argued that Gramsci was—at least indirectly—influenced by Mosca, Pareto, and Michels, that he was willing to make use of *certain features* of their theories (the full implications of which he obviously rejected). See G. Galli, 'Gramsci e le teorie delle "elites"', *Gramsci e la cultura contemporanea*, vol. II, 201–16; and D. Confrancesco, 'Appunti su Gramsci e la teoria dell'elite', *Mondo operaio*, no. 8–9 (August–September 1968), 28–34. Gramsci discusses Michels at some length in *Mach.*, pp. 95–100.
36. The conditions of class society.
37. *Mach.*, p. 17.
38. *MS*, p. 17.
39. *PP*, p. 166.
40. *MS*, p. 18.
41. *Mach.*, p. 132. See, also, ibid., p. 94; *MS*, p. 75; and *I*, p. 155.
42. *MS*, p. 40.
43. Ibid., pp. 3–4; see, also, *I*, p. 112.
44. *MS*, p. 11. Gramsci is not here contradicting his contention that the Catholic religion has managed to create a solid unity among the various intellectual strata within the Church (*MS*, p. 7). But what has been established, he holds, is 'purely mechanical, an external unity, based particularly on the liturgy and on a worship of pomp and ceremony . . .'. There is no attempt to raise 'the population to a higher cultural life' (ibid., p. 88).
45. Ibid., p. 11 (my emphasis).
46. *Mach.*, p. 133.
47. 'Marinetti rivoluzionario?', *L'Ordine Nuovo* (5 Jan. 1921); reprinted in *SF*, pp. 20–2.
48. But by 1921, one could plausibly argue, Gramsci had already entered into the 'later' or 'mature' phase of his thought, which received fuller, if fragmentary, elaboration in the *Quaderni*. Nevertheless, given his intellectual journey of development from an early idealism through the factory council thematic to a modified Leninism, indiscriminate quotation without regard for the historical context can be quite misleading. Two defenders of Gramsci, Massimo Salvadori ('Politica, potere e cultura nel pensiero di Gramsci', *Rivista di storia contemporanea*, no. 1, January 1972, 6–30) and Maria Macciocchi (*Per Gramsci*, Bologna, il Mulino, 1974, pp. 244–54) engage in the dubious practice of supporting an anti-authoritarian interpretation of Gramsci with textual evidence from his youthful writings. His multifarious opponents are not likely to be impressed by such a defence, since they base their position on the 'post-factory council' Gramsci. Still these early articles are worth noting, if only because they point to—what I consider—an element of continuity in his thought and indicate that his libertarian propensities had a long period of gestation. It is undeniable that the young Gramsci conducted what Salvadori calls a *'serrata battaglia'* against authoritarianism of all kinds. In one article, he refers to discussion as a 'fusion of souls and wills' whereby 'the individual elements of truth, which each person may bring, must be synthesized in the complex truth. . . . In order for this to happen, in order that the discussion be exhaustive and sincere, the greatest tolerance is necessary. . .' (reprinted in *SG*, p. 137). This is consonant with another piece, where he informs us that truth 'must never be presented in a dogmatic, absolute form, as already matured and perfected' (*SG*, p. 261). Elsewhere, he sees a continuity between liberalism and socialism on the level of custom and method: 'Liberalism, in so far as it is custom, is an intellectual and historical presupposition of socialism' (ibid., p. 225).
49. *LVN*, pp. 6, 11–13; *LC*, pp. 125, 205.
50. *MS*, pp. 26–7.

51. Ibid., pp. 157–8.
52. Ibid., p. 21. Gramsci here uses 'science' in the broad sense.
53. See, e.g., *Mach.*, p. 148, where he pours scorn on 'the blind and unilateral fanaticism of "party" . . .'; and *MS*, p. 93, where he writes that the philosophy of praxis 'is a philosophy freed (or which seeks to free itself) from every unilateral and fanatical ideological element, . . .'.
54. *Mach.*, p. 113.
55. Ibid., p. 158.
56. Ibid., p. 18. Which leaders did our author have in mind? The text does not specify, but Trotsky would seem to be a prime target. For in another section of the *Quaderni*, the Russian's 'over-resolute' attempt to rationalize and discipline the Soviet productive process is explicitly attacked for being founded on 'external and mechanical' coercion as opposed to the worker's own initiative. Such a policy 'was destined necessarily to end up in a form of Bonapartism'. Ibid., pp. 329–31.
57. 'Politica, potere e cultura nel pensiero di Gramsci', pp. 27–8.
58. Astonishing as it may sound to contemporary radicals, Gramsci actually defended the pedagogical worth of Greek and Latin (see, *I*, pp. 109–10). Steeped in the values of western civilization, Gramsci wanted the new culture to display 'the mass character of the Protestant Reformation and of the French Enlightenment' as well as 'the classical character of the cultures of Ancient Greece and the Italian Renaissance . . .' (*MS*, pp. 199–200). The paraphernalia of 'high' culture weighed heavily in Gramsci's outlook, perhaps more heavily than he cared to admit.
59. *Mach.*, pp. 19–20. See, also, *PP*, p. 67, where he claims that the dangers of 'discontinuity' are greater than those of 'hyper-bureaucracy'.
60. For a seminal critique, see G. Duncan and S. Lukes, 'The New Democracy', *Political Studies*, XI (June 1963), 156–77.
61. *Mach.*, p. 126.
62. Ibid., pp. 81–2.
63. *PP*, p. 65.
64. For a useful discussion of Marx on this question, along with relevant references, see Evans, *Karl Marx*, pp. 162–3. See, also, Engels's short essay of 1872, 'On Authority', in Feuer, *Marx & Engels: Basic Writings*, pp. 481–5.
65. G. H. Sabine, *A History of Political Theory* (London, Holt, Rinehart and Winston, 1961), p. 923.
66. *PP*, pp. 57–8.
67. Compare the spirit of Gramsci's formulation to the following quotation from Marcuse: 'As long as they [the masses] are kept incapable of being autonomous, as long as they are indoctrinated and manipulated (down to their very instincts), their answer to this question [as to their true and false needs] cannot be taken as their own' (*One-Dimensional Man*, p. 20).
68. *MS*, p. 94.
69. Ibid., p. 38.
70. *Mach.*, p. 6. He refers, in this passage, to a projected (though ill-defined) study called *The Modern Prince*, which would, one presumes, deal with the nature and tasks of the revolutionary party.
71. *MS*, p. 18.
72. Ibid., p. 11.
73. Letter to Julca (1 Aug. 1932); *LC*, p. 199.

Chapter 6

1. *Mach.*, p. 68.
2. Ibid., p. 84.

3. Ibid., p. 68.
4. Ibid., p. 66.
5. Ibid., p. 161.
6. *PP*, p. 71.
7. *Mach.*, pp. 114–15. See, also, ibid., p. 36, where he savagely condemns those revolutionaries who object 'on principle to compromises' or alliances.
8. Lisa's report has been published in *Rinascita* (12 December 1964), pp. 17–21; the substantial correctness of his account is confirmed by another prisoner at Turi, Giovanni Lay; see his 'Colloqui con Gramsci nel carcere di Turi' in *Rinascita* (22 February 1965).
9. Unless otherwise indicated, all the quotations in this paragraph are from Lisa's report (pp. 18–19), not from Gramsci directly.
10. Gramsci's attitude to the lower middle classes had certainly changed since his *Ordine Nuovo* days, when he dismissed them as 'social rubbish and debris deposited by centuries of servility and the domination of the Italian nation by foreigners and priests'. The function of these classes could only be regressive: 'The petit and middle bourgeoisie is in fact the barrier of corrupt, dissolute, rotten humanity with which capitalism defends its economic and political power: a servile, abject humanity, a humanity of lackeys and cut-throats. . . .' 'Gli Avvenimenti del 2–3 dicembre', *Ordine Nuovo* (6–13 December 1919); reprinted in *ON*, pp. 61–7. When it came to picturesque invective, Gramsci had few equals.
11. In a letter of 28 March 1931 to his brother Carlo, Gramsci wrote: '. . . I've come into conflict with some other prisoners and been forced to break off personal relationships.' Quoted in Fiori, *Antonio Gramsci: Life of a Revolutionary*, p. 258. In a letter of 13 July 1931 to his sister-in-law, Gramsci remarked on his growing solitude. 'It is as if, every day, another thread tying me to the past breaks, and it becomes ever more impossible to knot these threads together again.' *Antonio Gramsci: Letters from Prison*, translated by L. Lawner (New York, Harper and Row, 1973), p. 201.
12. At least one Left-wing critic, however, sees the reformist rot beginning to set in as early as 1924; see, S. Sechi, 'Gramsci a Turi', *Rinascita sarda* (1–15 October 1966).
13. 'Il partito comunista', *Ordine Nuovo* (4 Sept. 1920), now reprinted in *ON*, pp. 154–8.
14. For an example of such an erroneous approach, see S. Tarrow, *Peasant Communism in Southern Italy* (London, Yale Univ. Press, 1967), Chapter 5.
15. Tamburrano, *Antonio Gramsci*, pp. 173–6.
16. Ibid., pp. 284–97.
17. 'Fasi di sviluppo del pensiero politico di Gramsci', in A. Caracciolo and G. Scalia (eds.), *La città futura* (Milan, Feltrinelli, 1959), pp. 131–2. Tamburrano makes the same point in *Antonio Gramsci*, pp. 257–8.
18. See, for example, A. Giolitti, *Riforma e rivoluzione* (Turin, Einaudi, 1957).
19. *Antonio Gramsci*, pp. 260–1, 267.
20. Ibid., p. 267.
21. Pietro Nenni was an indefatigable Socialist Party activist and leader, whose political career spanned half a century. 'Nennian' was used as a term of abuse by Tamburrano's critics on the Left.
22. T. Perlini, *Gramsci e il Gramscismo* (Milan, CELUC, 1974), p. 55.
23. 'I nostri conti con la teoria della "rivoluzione senza rivoluzione" in Gramsci.'
24. Ibid., p. 70.
25. See, for example, Perlini, *Gramsci e il Gramscismo*, pp. 36–66; Marramao, 'Per una critica dell'ideologia di Gramsci'; Reichers, *Antonio Gramsci*; and L. Cortesi, 'Un convegno su Gramsci', *Rivista storica del socialismo*, 30 (Jan.–April 1967), 159–73.
26. *Gramsci e il Gramscismo*, p. 46.

27. Ibid., p. 61.

28. P. Togliatti, *La via italiana al socialismo* (Rome, Editori Riuniti, 1964), p. 197.

29. From a speech delivered in April 1944 to the recently liberated people of Naples. Reprinted in *Rinascita* (29 August 1964), pp. 4–5.

30. See *Sul movimento operaio internazionale* (Rome, Editori Riuniti, 1964), pp. 343–4.

31. For an especially disconcerting example of this, see his *Partito comunista italiano* (Rome, Editori Riuniti, 1961), p. 70, where he says: 'The advance towards socialism cannot and will not occur in our country in a manner that is different from the way it has occurred in the Soviet Union and elsewhere.'

32. See Enrico Berlinguer, *La proposta comunista* (Turin, Einaudi, 1975), where references to Lenin are conspicuous by their absence.

33. *Statuto del PCI*, 1966 edition, p. 3.

34. Reprinted in *Rinascita* (29 August 1964), pp. 15–17. A curious 'dialectic' was discernible in Togliatti's statements about Gramsci. On the one hand, he insisted (as we observed in Chapter 1) on the historical specificity of Gramsci's thinking; on the other, he was always anxious to invoke Gramsci's posthumous authority for Party policies. A classic case, no doubt, of 'having it both ways'. While the communists wished to bask in the reflected glory of their dead hero (which meant lifting at least some of his ideas out of their particular context), they also wanted to forestall the possibility of anyone using his writings against them (which meant underlining the nexus between his ideas and their historical context).

35. See, for example, V. Gerratana's spirited attack on Giolitti's pamphlet (cited in note 18 to this chapter), an attack which set the tone for later Party theorizing on the relationship between dictatorship and hegemony. 'Una deformazione del pensiero di Gramsci e della politica del partito comunista', *l'Unità* (19 May 1957).

36. Natta, 'Egemonia, cultura, partito nel pensiero di Antonio Gramsci', p. 19.

37. *Rinascita-Il Contemporaneo* (14 April 1967), p. 4. The basic interpretation set out in this editorial is elaborated upon by Party leader, Giorgio Amendola, in 'Rileggendo Gramsci', *Prassi rivoluzionaria*, pp. 37–45.

38. F. Calamandrei, 'L'iniziativa politica del partito rivoluzionario da Lenin a Gramsci e Togliatti', *Critica marxista* (July–October 1967), 101.

39. The standard line on Gramsci's contemporary 'relevance' has not changed significantly in the past decade, though one can perhaps discern a slightly greater stress on the 'historical limits' of his prescriptions. Typical is the recent and concise formulation of Leonardo Paggi, a leading PCI theoretician, who states that Gramsci's theory, while it supplies no 'political recipe for today', nevertheless 'constitutes a critical point of reference', 'Dopo la sconfitta della rivoluzione in Occidente', *Rinascita* (4 February 1977), p. 14.

40. *Mach.*, pp. 59, 81–2, 159; *PP*, p. 158.

41. *Mach.*, p. 84.

42. Ibid., p. 66, my emphasis. Gramsci may be making this same point (about the continuing validity of the war of manœuvre) in a rather puzzling group of notes on 'The Concept of Passive Revolution'. Using the parallel of the Risorgimento, and likening it to an unidentified 'restoration' (the demise of Fascism?), he poses the following, rhetorical question: '. . . in the struggle Cavour-Mazzini, in which Cavour is the exponent of the passive revolution/war of position and Mazzini of popular initiative/war of manœuvre, are not both of them indispensable to precisely the same extent?' *Mach.*, p. 70.

43. Ibid., p. 63.

44. Ibid., pp. 49–50.

45. *PP*, p. 38.

46. Ibid.

47. *R*, p. 72.
48. *PP*, p. 188.
49. See, e.g., Jean-Marc Piotte, *La pensée politique de Gramsci* (Paris, Editions Anthropos, 1970), p. 169: 'The war of position must precede and prepare the way for the war of movement; it is necessary to deprive the ruling class of the direction of civil society before attacking its state power; it is necessary to count on the help and support of the popular masses before taking arms against the dominant class; the struggle for hegemony must prepare for the military struggle.' Piotte does capture a part of Gramsci's meaning. It is true that the proletariat must win the battle for cultural supremacy before launching a full-scale armed attack on the last bastion of bourgeois control: the state apparatus. Yet Gramsci provides no textual warrant for assuming that the way of movement is valid only *after* the war of position is won. The problem may be that Piotte and other commentators interpret the war of movement too narrowly, viewing it solely as full-blown armed struggle. Gramsci gets so carried away by his use of military concepts that he never spells out in any detail the content of their political counterparts. The war of movement is especially hazy. But it is a reasonable supposition that Gramsci would include under this heading less cataclysmic acts, such as mass strikes, sabotage, demonstrations, factory seizures, etc. Indeed, he does actually say, in one (unfortunately undeveloped) passage, that strikes are a form of the war of movement. *Mach.*, p. 62.
50. *Collected Works*, vol. 32, pp. 471–5.
51. *Mach.*, p. 68.
52. G. Galli and G. Mancini, 'Gramsci's Presence', *Government and Opposition*, 3 (Summer 1968), 334.
53. 'La crisi italiana', *Ordine Nuovo* (1 September 1924); reprinted in *Scritti Politici*, edited by P. Spriano, III, 104.
54. *MS*, p. 185.
55. Ibid.
56. Ibid., p. 221.
57. Ibid., p. 185.
58. It is worth pointing out that, around the turn of the century, Croce was the leading Italian revisionist, a position he staked out in his collection of essays entitled *Historical Materialism*.
59. See, in particular, *MS*, pp. 219–22.
60. Ibid., p. 184.
61. Ibid., p. 222.
62. In a short but cutting note, Gramsci explicitly criticizes Bernstein's evolutionist belief that 'the movement is everything, the final goal nothing', and yet Merli ascribes this very belief to Gramsci himself! See *PP*, pp. 190–1.
63. 'Antonio Gramsci and the Italian Revolution', *New Left Review*, 65 (Jan.–Feb. 1971), 94.
64. G. C. Jocteau, *Leggere Gramsci* (Milan, Feltrinelli, 1975), p. 74. Not all commentators who perceive a disjunction between Gramsci's thought and PCI strategy are unsympathetic to this strategy. Massimo Salvadori, for example, argues that the Party should—in the interests of truth and 'greater realism'—'settle its accounts' with its theoretical tradition and admit that its policies and ideas are 'qualitatively different from Gramsci's'. 'Gramsci and the PCI: Two Conceptions of Hegemony', in C. Mouffe (ed.), *Gramsci and Marxist Theory* (London, Routledge & Kegan Paul, 1979), pp. 256–7.
65. *The Italian Road to Socialism*, an interview by Eric Hobsbawm with Giorgio Napolitano of the Italian Communist Party (London, Lawrence Hill & Co., 1977), p. 29.

66. *R*, p. 90.
67. *Mach.*, p. 115.

Chapter 7

1. Hubert M. Blalock Jnr., 'Theory Building and Causal Inference', in H. M. Blalock Jnr. and A. B. Blalock (eds.), *Methodology in Social Research* (New York, McGraw-Hill, 1968), p. 163.
2. Translated by H. Reeve (New York, Century and Co., 1899), I, 398.
3. See T. Parsons and E. Shils, eds., *Towards a General Theory of Action* (Cambridge, Harvard University Press, 1951), p. 180 for a useful formulation of the theory.
4. (London, Routledge & Kegan Paul, 1959), pp. 162, 172.
5. For a critique of two such investigations, see my own 'Élites, Participation and the Democratic Creed', *Political Studies*, XXVIII (March 1979), 1–20.
6. For a summary of the social psychology literature on this subject (up to 1969), see A. W. Wicker, 'Attitudes *v.* Actions: the Relationship of Verbal and Overt Responses to Attitude Objects', *Journal of Social Issues*, 25 (1969), 41–78.
7. Perhaps the most sophisticated and convincing empirical study to arrive at this conclusion is P. E. Converse, 'The Nature of Belief Systems in Mass Publics', in D. E. Apter (ed.), *Ideology and Discontent* (London, Collier-Macmillan, 1964), pp. 206–61. See also G. D. Garson, 'Radical Issues in the History of the American Working Class', *Politics and Society*, 3 (Fall 1972), 25–32. Garson invents the term 'multiple consciousness' to describe the seemingly schizophrenic attitudes of his sample of US autoworkers. For similar conclusions about the cultural perspectives of British workers, see S. Hill, *The Dockers: Class and Tradition in London* (London, Heinemann, 1976); and T. Nichols and P. Armstrong, *Workers Divided* (Glasgow, Fontana, 1976), especially the chapter on 'Ideology and Inconsistency'. Hill portrays the social consciousness of dockworkers as 'inchoate' and 'inconsistent', 'based on a mixture of personal experience, some exposure to radical ideologies, and the conditioning effects of the dominant culture' (p. 202). Nichols and Armstrong, who departed from formal survey methods by conducting in-depth interviews, found that their sample of chemical workers held 'inchoate and conflicting views' on the legitimacy of established social and political arrangements (p. 19).
8. *The Civic Culture: Political Attitudes and Democracy in Five Nations* (Princeton University Press, 1963), p. 186.
9. *Relative Deprivation and Social Justice* (London, Routledge & Kegan Paul, 1966), pp. 170–226 *passim*.
10. R. McKenzie and A. Silver, *Angels in Marble: Working Class Conservatives in Urban England* (London, Heinemann, 1968), pp. 145–52.
11. J. H. Rytina et al., 'Income and Stratification Ideology: Beliefs about the American Opportunity Structure', *American Journal of Sociology* (Jan. 1970), 707–8.
12. See, e.g., T. Veness, *School Leavers: Their Aspirations and Expectations* (London, Methuen, 1962), p. 144; E. Nordlinger, *The Working Class Tories* (London, MacGibbon and Kee, 1967), pp. 179–83; E. Chinoy, *Automobile Workers and the American Dream* (New York, Random House, 1955), pp. 129–31. M. Mann, in *Consciousness and Action Among the Western Working Class* (London, Macmillan, 1973), refers to three studies employing the 'football team' analogy, in which workers are asked whether employers and workers are on the same side or on different sides. The overwhelming majority of British workers reply 'the same side'. See p. 35.
13. Reported in *The Sunday Times* (31 Aug. 1969), p. 2.
14. See, for example, J. Goldthorpe et al., *The Affluent Worker in the Class Structure* (Cambridge, The University Press, 1968), I, 112–13; I. C. Cannon, 'Ideology and

Occupational Community', *Sociology* (May 1967), 168; and S. Hill, *The Dockers*, p. 139.

15. Hill discovered that many dockworkers who agree that 'trade unions have too much power in this country' nevertheless want their own union to have *greater* influence in management. *The Dockers*, pp. 138–41.

16. 'The Lower-Class Value Stretch', *Social Forces* (Dec. 1963), 208–15. Chinoy uncovers a parallel phenomenon in his study of mid-western car-workers. For example, while the workers by no means deny the desirability of 'getting ahead' and individual economic success—a central tenet of the American Creed—most either redefine it to coincide with their own modest ambitions or else seek 'to relegate it to a lesser position in the hierarchy of values', in order—says Chinoy— to maintain self-esteem in the face of their own 'failure' to realize the 'American Dream'. *Automobile Workers and the American Dream*, pp. 124–7.

17. Frank Parkin uses these terms in *Class Inequality and Political Order* (London, Paladin, 1972), p. 95.

18. Our hypothesis is not disproved by the number of empirical studies which have found only a slight correlation between 'attitudes' and overt behaviour (see note 6 to this chapter). It is difficult to conceive how the multi-faceted relationship between beliefs (for purposes of exposition I shall make no distinction between beliefs and attitudes) and concrete action can be tested with anything resembling mathematical precision, no matter how refined the instruments of measurement, how sophisticated the delineation of concepts, or how complex the theoretical models. If one is searching for a *direct* link between various beliefs and behaviour, the problem of inference is likely to be insurmountable. It is difficult to devise methods whereby types of observable behaviour can be objectively estimated for the purpose of comparison with beliefs, themselves elastic complexes of ideas and sentiments. Our statements about political behaviour and ideological phenomena are not usually discrete and distinct enough to admit determinant application of formal logic to them; discovering contradictions or consistencies is a matter for judgement, not scientific accuracy. In any event, beliefs are simply one factor we use in our attempts to understand and predict behaviour. Other sources of influence contribute to variation in action—role requirements, legal sanctions, material satisfactions, and so on. Gramsci's concept of 'contradictory consciousness' is predicated upon the realization that situational or structural constraints can vitiate the causal impact of ideational factors. But even in such cases, beliefs may exert an *indirect* influence by shaping the definition of the situation, thus conditioning and limiting the range of possible responses. This rather intangible role of ideology has not been properly explored by social scientists, most of whom find it insufficiently quantifiable and researchable. That, however, does not make it futile to formulate propositions about, and adduce evidence for or against, this indirect role.

19. I. L. Horowitz, 'Consensus, Conflict, and Co-operation: a Sociological Inventory', *Social Forces* (Dec. 1962), 180.

20. For a useful discussion of these issues, see C. Geertz, 'Ideology as a Cultural System', in D. E. Apter (ed.), *Ideology and Discontent*, pp. 60–5.

21. For a rigorous formulation of the theory, see R. L. Curry and L. L. Wade, *A Theory of Political Exchange* (Englewood Cliffs, Prentice-Hall, 1968).

22. Peter Blau, an important proponent of exchange theory, tries to overcome this difficulty by explaining acceptance of *enduring* power inequalities in terms of mechanisms through which 'common values' are perpetuated, so that '. . . once superior power has been attained by furnishing services, it can be maintained without furnishing these same services'. *Exchange and Power in Social Life* (New York, Wiley, 1964), pp. 197, 208. But then the explanation of power differentials

(and social order) in terms of free exchange transactions becomes irrelevant to the *present*; it is at most relevant to that hypothetical moment in time when power differentials first emerged. The inclusion of 'a moral obligation inculcated by socializing agencies' (p. 212) gives the theory added plausibilty, but at the cost of contradicting the author's avowed intention: to explain power distributions in complex social structures by means of exchange theory.

23. C. J. Friedrich argues this point in *A New Belief in the Common Man* (New York, Little, Brown, 1942), p. 153 ff.
24. *Christ Stopped at Eboli*, trans. by F. Frenaye (New York, Farrar, Strauss and Co., 1947), pp. 77–8.
25. See Chapter 6, pages 206–7.
26. *Mach.*, p. 42.
27. *MS*, pp. 272–3.
28. *Mach.*, pp. 311–12; *MS*, pp. 212–15.
29. *Mach.*, pp. 311, 340–2.
30. Ibid., p. 323.
31. That large-scale state intervention marks a 'pathological' phase of capitalist development, one of rampant parasitism and productive stagnation or decline, is a theme Gramsci introduced as far back as 1920. See 'Lo strumento di lavoro', *L'Ordine Nuovo* (14 February 1920); *ON*, pp. 83–4. In this piece he describes how the expanding bureaucracy *itself* saps the strength of the economic system, by vastly increasing the amount of unproductive labour. Resources once devoted to investment are now used 'to satisfy the greed of the enormous multitude of agents, functionaries and idlers' employed or sustained by the rapidly growing state apparatus.
32. See, for example, D. Bell, *The End of Ideology* (The Free Press of Glencoe, Illinois, 1960), Epilogue; and C. Kerr, J. T. Dunlop, et al., *Industrialism and Industrial Man* (London, Heinemann, 1962).
33. H. Marcuse, *One-Dimensional Man*, pp. 23–4.
34. Ibid., p. 21.
35. For example, in England in 1946–7, 1% of the population still owned 50% of all private property, and all indications are that the proportion has changed very little since then. See T. Bottomore, *Classes in Modern Society* (London, Allen & Unwin, 1965), pp. 34–6, for a brief but illuminating discussion of various empirical studies. In addition, a large body of British people own little or next to nothing. In 1959–60, for example, 87.9% of British taxpayers owned 3.7% of total wealth. This and other relevant data are cited in Miliband, *The State in Capitalist Society*, pp. 25–6. Turning to the United States, the research of Gabriel Kolko indicates that between 1910 and 1959 the share in national income of the top income-tenth declined only slightly, and remains about 30%, while the shares of the two poorest income-tenths *declined sharply* (from 8.3% of national income to only 4%). And these figures exclude sources of real income, like expense accounts and capital gains, which benefit mainly the upper class and thus increase inequality. See Bottomore, *Classes in Modern Society*, p. 44.
36. For a useful discussion of these trends, along with their implications for Marxist sociology, see N. Birnbaum, 'The Crisis in Marxist Sociology', in *Toward a Critical Sociology* (New York, Oxford University Press, 1971), pp. 94–129.
37. Studies show that clerical employees, for example, tend to regard themselves as part of a command hierarchy, as 'belonging to management'. See A. Giddens, *The Class Structure of the Advanced Societies* (London, Hutchinson, 1973), pp. 179–83.
38. M. Edelman, *The Symbolic Uses of Politics* (Urbana, University of Illinois Press, 1964), p. 17.
39. As we pointed out in Chapter 2, Gramsci, in a couple of places, notes that liberal

political institutions act as organs of hegemony, but he neglects to develop, or spell out the implications of, these somewhat casual remarks. *Mach.*, pp. 84, 88. Also, in a few interesting but inconclusive paragraphs, he discusses, in Durkheimian fashion, the mobilizing effect of modes and actions of a collective character, such as elections and plebiscites. For instance, he observes that in the first truly popular Italian election—that of 1913—'there was a widespread, mystical conviction that all would be changed after the vote, that there would be a true and proper rebirth of social life'. *R*, pp. 112–13.

40. Gramsci's location of hegemony firmly within civil society has recently come under attack from Perry Anderson, who writes: 'The fundamental form of the Western parliamentary State . . . is itself the hub of the ideological apparatuses of capitalism. The ramified complexes of the cultural control-systems within civil society—radio, television, cinema, churches, newspapers, political parties—undoubtedly play a critical *complementary* role in assuring the stability of the class order of capital.' 'The Antinomies of Gramsci', p. 29.

41. Cited in Bell, *The End of Ideology*, p. 375.

42. For an excellent review of the massive research prior to 1962, see J. W. Brehm and A. R. Cohen, *Explorations in Cognitive Dissonance* (New York, Wiley, 1962). The seminal and classic statement of dissonance theory is L. Festinger, *A Theory of Cognitive Dissonance* (Stanford, Stanford University Press, 1957).

43. N. Poulantzas, 'The Problem of the Capitalist State', in R. Blackburn (ed.), *Ideology in Social Science* (London, Fontana, 1972), pp. 252–3.

44. While (according to Gramsci) the state is 'the organ of one particular group, destined to create favourable conditions for the latter's maximum expansion', this 'does not mean that the relationship of means to end can be easily determined or takes the form of a simple schema'. *Mach.*, p. 46; *Selections from the Prison Notebooks*, p. 116.

45. *PP*, p. 158.

46. *Political Parties*, translated by Eden and Cedar Paul (New York, Dover Publications, 1959), pp. 366–7.

47. Ibid., pp. 367–73.

48. Ibid., p. 389.

49. G. Hands, 'Roberto Michels and the Study of Political Parties', *British Journal of Political Science*, I (April 1971), 157.

50. Guenther Roth, *The Social Democrats in Imperial Germany* (Totowa, New Jersey, The Bedminster Press, 1963), p. 8.

51. *PP*, p. 59.

52. Letter to Giulia (19 Nov. 1928), in *LC*, p. 67.

53. *PP*, p. 63.

54. J. Joll, *Gramsci* (Glasgow, Fontana, 1977), p. 112.

55. Unlike most Marxists, Gramsci was actually at pains to defend formal logic: 'This abstract methodology, that is, formal logic, is despised by idealist philosophers but erroneously', for it is, like grammar, 'a necessary condition for the development of science itself.' *PP*, pp. 162–3.

56. *Mach.*, pp. 76–7.

57. See, e.g., Orfei, *Antonio Gramsci*.

58. See, e.g., M. Tronti, 'Alcune questioni intorno al marxismo di Gramsci', in *Studi gramsciani*, pp. 305–21.

59. *Reading Capital*, pp. 126–38.

60. *MS*, p. 133.

61. My discussion here is indebted to S. Lukes, 'Relativism: Cognitive and Moral', in *Essays in Social Theory* (London, Macmillan, 1977), pp. 154–74.

62. *Gramsci*, p. 32.

63. *Essays on the Materialist Conception of History*, p. 177.
64. *History and Class Consciousness*, p. 162.
65. Ibid., p. 1.
66. L. Kolakowski, *Main Currents of Marxism*, translated by P. S. Falla (Oxford, The Clarendon Press, 1978), III, p. 300.
67. G. Stedman-Jones, 'The Marxism of the Early Lukács', *New Left Review*, 70 (Nov.–Dec. 1971), 46.
68. H. Marcuse, R. P. Wolff and B. Moore Jnr., *Critique of Pure Tolerance* (London, Jonathan Cape, 1969), p. 102.
69. *Reading Capital*, p. 42.
70. Ibid., p. 139.
71. Ibid., p. 131.
72. Quoted in A. Carter, *The Political Theory of Anarchism* (London, Routledge & Kegan Paul, 1971), p. 83.
73. Joll, *Gramsci*, p. 15.

Select Bibliography

I. *Main Italian Editions of Gramsci's Works*

(a) *Opere di Antonio Gramsci* (Turin, Einaudi, 1947–72).
Vol. 1. *Lettere dal Carcere*, 1947. Revised edition 1965, edited by S. Caprioglio and E. Fubini.
Vol. 2. *Il materialismo storico e la filosofia di Benedetto Croce*, 1949.
Vol.3. *Gli intellettuali e l'organizzazione della cultura*, 1949.
Vol. 4. *Il Risorgimento*, 1949.
Vol. 5. *Note sul Machiavelli, sulla politica, e sullo stato moderno*, 1949.
Vol. 6. *Letteratura e vita nazionale*, 1950.
Vol. 7. *Passato e presente*, 1951.
Vol. 8. *Scritti giovanili, 1914–18*, 1958.
Vol. 9. *L'Ordine Nuovo, 1919–1920*, 1954.
Vol. 10. *Sotto la Mole, 1916–1920*, 1960.
Vol. 11. *Socialismo e fascismo. L'Ordine Nuovo, 1921–22*, 1967.
Vol. 12. *La costruzione del Partito comunista, 1923–26*, 1972.

(Volumes 2 to 7 comprise Gramsci's *Quaderni del Carcere*; volumes 8 to 12 are collections of his articles and other writings prior to his imprisonment.)

(b) *Quaderni del Carcere*, edited by Valentino Gerratana (4 volumes, Turin, Einaudi, 1975). This new edition, unlike the previous one, reproduces the notes in the order in which they were written, not according to topic headings. Volume 4 contains an impressive critical apparatus.

(c) *Quaderni del Carcere* (6 volumes, Rome, Editori Riuniti, 1971). Arranges the notes in the same way as the first Einaudi edition.

(d) *Scritti politici*, edited by P. Spriano (Rome, Editori Riuniti, 1967). This is an exhaustive collection of Gramsci's pre-prison writings. Republished in 1973 in 3 volumes.

II. *Main English Translations of Gramsci's Works*

(a) *Selections from the Prison Notebooks*, edited and translated by Q. Hoare and G. Nowell Smith (London, Lawrence & Wishart, 1971).

(b) *Selections from Political Writings, 1910–1920*, selected and edited by Q. Hoare and translated by J. Mathews (London, Lawrence & Wishart, 1977).

(c) *Selections from Political Writings, 1921–1926*, translated and edited by Q. Hoare (London, Lawrence & Wishart, 1978).

(d) *The New Edinburgh Review*, three Special Gramsci Numbers, edited by C. K. Maisals (1974). Contains a translation, by Hamish Henderson, of the 1947 edition of Gramsci's *Prison Letters*.

(e) *Letters from Prison*, selected, translated, and introduced by L. Lawner (New York, Harper and Row, 1973; London, Jonathan Cape, 1975).

III. *Collections of Articles on Gramsci*

(a) *Studi gramsciani*, Atti del Convegno tenuto a Roma nei giorni 11–13 gennaio 1958 (Rome, Editori Riuniti, 1959).

(b) *La Città futura, Saggi sulla figura e il pensiero di Antonio Gramsci*, edited by A. Caracciolo and G. Scalia (Milan, Feltrinelli, 1959).

(c) *Gramsci e la cultura contemporanea*, Atti del Convegno internazionale di studi gramsciani tenuto a Cagliari il 23–27 aprile 1967, Rome, Editori Riuniti; vol. I, *Relazioni* (1969), vol. II, *Comunicazioni* (1970). Includes a complete bibliography of works on Gramsci up until 1967.

(d) *Prassi rivoluzionaria e storicismo in Gramsci*, Quaderno n. 3 of *Critica marxista* (1967).

(e) *Politica e storia in Gramsci*, Atti del convegno internazionale di studi gramsciani: Firenze, 9–11 dicembre 1977 (Rome, Editori Riuniti, 1977).

IV. *Secondary Literature on Gramsci*

(I have included all books and articles cited in the text, along with a number of others I have found useful or original or provocative.)

Agazzi, E., 'Filosofia della prassi e filosofia dello spirito', in *La Città futura*, cited above.

Aladino, M., 'Due marxisti italiani (Rodolfo Mondolfo e Antonio Gramsci)', *Critica sociale*, II (1 June 1948).

Aloisi, M., 'Gramsci, la scienza e la natura come storia', *Società*, VI (Sept. 1950).

Althusser, L., 'Marxism is not a Historcism', in L. Althusser and E. Balibar, *Reading Capital*, translated by B. Brewster (London, New Left Books, 1970).

Amendola, G., 'Rileggendo Gramsci', in *Prassi rivoluzionaria*, cited above.

Anderson, P., 'The Antinomies of Antonio Gramsci', *New Left Review*, 100 (Nov. 1976–Jan. 1977).

Auciello, N., *Socialismo ed egemonia in Gramsci e Togliatti* (Bari, De Donato, 1974).

Badaloni, N., *Il marxismo di Gramsci* (Turin, Einaudi, 1975).

Battaglia, R., 'Egemonia e dittatura del proletariato nella concezione di A. Gramsci', *L'Unità* (25 May 1957).

Bausola, A., 'Sulla fondazione dello storicismo in A. Gramsci', *Rivista di filosofia neo-scolastica*, III (1966).

Bobbio, N., 'Gramsci e la concezione della società civile', in *Gramsci e la cultura contemporanea*, I, cited above.

——. 'Nota sulla dialettica in Gramsci', in *Studi gramsciani*, cited above.

Boggs, C., *Gramsci's Marxism* (London, Pluto Press, 1976).

Bonomi, G., 'La concezione gramsciana dello stato', *Problemi del socialismo*, 16–17 (July–Oct. 1973).

——, *Partito e rivoluzione in Gramsci* (Milan, Feltrinelli, 1973).

Broccoli, A., *A. Gramsci e l'educazione come egemonia* (Florence, La Nuova Italia, 1972).

Buci-Glucksmann, *Gramsci e lo Stato*, translated from the French by C. Mancina and G. Saponaro (Rome, Editori Riuniti, 1976).

Buzzi, A. R., *La teoria politica di Gramsci*, translated from the French by S. Genovali (Florence, La Nuova Italia Editrice, 1973).

Calamandrei, F., 'L'iniziativa politica del partito rivoluzionario da Lenin a Gramsci e Togliatti', *Critica marxista* (July–Oct. 1967).

Calosso, U., 'Gramsci e L'Ordine Nuovo', *Quaderni di Giustizia e Libertà*, II (Aug. 1933).

Calzolari, A., 'Structure and Superstructure in Gramsci', *Telos* (Spring 1969).

Camberei, S., 'Il concetto di egemonia nel pensiero di Gramsci', in *Studi gramsciani*, cited above.

Cammett, J. M., *Antonio Gramsci and the Origins of Italian Communism* (Stanford University Press, 1967).

Caracciolo, A., 'Sulla questione partito—consigli di fabbrica nel pensiero di Gramsci', *Ragionamenti*, II (May–Oct. 1957).

Carbone, G., 'I libri del carcere di Antonio Gramsci', *Movimento operaio*, 4 (July–Aug. 1952).

——, 'Su alcuni commenti alle opere di A. Gramsci', *Società*, VII (March 1951).

Carocci, G., 'Un intellettuale tra Lenin e Croce', *Belfagor*, III (1948).

Cerroni, U., 'L' "eresia" Leninista', *L'Unità* (22 April 1972).

——, 'Per una teoria del partito politico', *Critica marxista* (Sept.–Dec. 1963).

Clark, M., *Antonio Gramsci and the Revolution that Failed* (New Haven and London, Yale University Press, 1977).

Colletti, L., 'Antonio Gramsci and the Italian Revolution', *New Left Review*, 65 (Jan.–Feb. 1971).

Confrancesco, D., 'Appunti su Gramsci e la teoria dell'elite', *Mondo operaio*, 8–9 (Aug.–Sept. 1968).

Cortesi, L., 'Un convegno su Gramsci', *Rivista storica del socialismo*, 30 (Jan.–April 1967).

Crisafulli, V., 'Stato e società nel pensiero di Gramsci', *Società*, VII (1951).

Croce, B., Review of Gramsci's *Lettere Dal Carcere*, *Quaderni della Critica* III (July 1947).

Croce, B., 'Schede v. DeSanctis-Gramsci', *Lo spettatore italiano*, V (July 1952).

Damen, O., 'Premarxismo filosofico di Gramsci', *Prometeo*, III (Aug. 1949).

Davidson, A., *Antonio Gramsci, the Man, his Ideas* (Sydney, Australian Left Review, 1968).

——, *Antonio Gramsci: Towards an Intellectual Biography* (London, The Merlin Press, 1977).

——, 'Gramsci and Lenin 1917–22', in R. Miliband and J. Saville (eds.), *Socialist Register* (London, The Merlin Press, 1974).

——, 'The Varying Seasons of Gramscian Studies', *Political Studies*, XX (Dec. 1972).

De Felice, F., 'Una chiave di lettura in "Americanismo e fordismo"' *Rinascita—Il Contemporaneo*, 42 (27 Oct. 1972).

——, 'Rivoluzione passiva, fascismo, americanismo in Gramsci', in *Politica e Storia in Gramsci*, cited above.

Faenza, L., 'Labriola e Gramsci', *Mondo operaio*, VII (4 Dec. 1954).

Femia, J., 'The Gramsci Phenomenon: Some Reflections', *Political Studies*, XXVII (Sept. 1979).

——, 'Hegemony and Consciousness in the Thought of Antonio Gramsci', *Political Studies*, XXIII (March 1975).

——, 'Gramsci, the Via Italiana, and the Classical Marxist-Leninist Approach to Revolution', *Government and Opposition*, 14 (Winter 1979).

Finocchiaro, M. A., 'Gramsci's Crocean Marxism', *Telos*, 41 (Fall 1979).

Fiori, G., *Antonio Gramsci: Life of a Revolutionary*, translated by T. Nairn (New York, Schocken Books, 1973).

Galli, G. and Mancini, G., 'Gramsci's Presence', *Government and Opposition*, 3 (Summer 1968).

Galli, G., 'Gramsci e le teorie delle "élites"', *Gramsci e la cultura contemporanea*, vol. II, cited above.

Garin, E., 'La formazione di Gramsci e Croce', in *Prassi rivoluzionaria*, cited above.

——, 'Gramsci nella cultura italiana', in *Studi gramsciani*, cited above.

——, 'Politica e cultura in Gramsci: il problema degli intellettuali', in *Gramsci e la cultura contemporanea*, vol. I, cited above.

Garosci, A., 'Totalitarismo e storicismo nel pensiero di Antonio Gramsci', in *Pensiero politico e storiografia moderna* (Pisa, Nistri-Lischi, 1954).

Genovese. E.. 'On Antonio Gramsci'. *Studies on the Left*. VII (March–April 1967).

Gerratana, V., 'Al di qua e al di là di Gramsci', *Rinascita—Il Contemporaneo* (28 April 1972).

——, 'Una deformazione del pensiero di Gramsci e della politica del partito comunista, *L'Unità* (19 May 1957).

Ginsborg, P., 'Gramsci and the Era of Bourgeois Revolution in Italy', in J. A. Davis (ed.), *Gramsci and Italy's Passive Revolution* (London, Croom Helm, 1979).

Giolitti, A., *Riforma e rivoluzione* (Turin, Einaudi, 1957).

Gruppi, L., 'Il concetto di egemonia', in *Prassi rivoluzionaria*, cited above.

——, *Il concetto di egemonia in Gramsci* (Rome, Editori Riuniti, 1972).

——, 'I rapporti tra pensiero ed essere nella concezione di Gramsci', in *Studi gramsciani*, cited above.

Hobsbawm, E. J., 'The Great Gramsci', *New York Review of Books*, 21 (4 April 1974).

Hughes, H. S., 'Gramsci and Marxist Humanism', *Consciousness and Society* (St. Albans, Paladin, 1974), pp. 96–104.

Jocteau, G. C., Leggere Gramsci (Milan, Feltrinelli, 1975).

——, 'Sul concetto di egemonia in Gramsci e Togliatti', *Rivista di storia contemporanea* (1973).

Joll, J., *Gramsci* (Glasgow, Fontana, 1977).

Karabel, J., 'Revolutionary Contradictions: Antonio Gramsci and the Problem of Intellectuals', *Politics and Society*, 6 (1976).

Kolakowski, L., 'Antonio Gramsci: Communist Revisionism', in *Main Currents of Marxism* (Oxford, The Clarendon Press, 1978), vol. III, translated by P. S. Falla.

Lay, G., 'Colloqui con Gramsci nel carcere di Turi', *Rinascita* (22 Feb. 1965).

Lichtheim, G., *Marxism: a Historical and Critical Study* (London, Routlege & Kegan Paul, 1964), pp. 367–70.

Lisa, A., 'Discussione politica con Gramsci in carcere', *Rinascita* (12 Dec. 1964).

Luperini, C., 'La metodologia del marxismo nel pensiero di Gramsci', in *Studi gramsciani*, cited above.

Macciocchi, M., *Per Gramsci* (Bologna, Il Mulino, 1974).

Magri, L., 'Problemi della teoria marxista del partito rivoluzionario', *Critica marxista*, I (Sept.–Dec. 1963).

Marek, F., 'Gramsci e la concezione marxista della storia', in *Gramsci e la cultura contemporanea*, vol. II, cited above.

Markovic, M., 'L'unità di filosofia e politica in Gramsci', in *Gramsci e la cultura contemporanea*, vol. II, cited above.

Marramao, G., 'Per una critica dell'ideologia di Gramsci', *Quaderni piacentini*, XI (March 1972).

Martinelli, A., 'In Defence of the Dialectic: Antonio Gramsci's Theory of Revolution', *Berkeley Journal of Sociology*, 13 (1968).

Matteucci, N., *Antonio Gramsci e la filosofia della prassi* (Milan, Giuffré Editore, 1951).

McInnes, N., 'Antonio Gramsci', *Survey*, N. 53 (Oct. 1964).

Merli, S., 'I nostri conti con la teoria della "rivoluzione senza rivoluzione" di Gramsci', *Giovane critica*, 17 (Autumn 1967).

Mondolfo, R., 'Le antinomie di Gramsci', *Critica sociale*, 23 (15 Dec. 1963).

——, *Da Ardigò a Gramsci* (Milan, Nuova Accademia, 1962).

Morpurgo-Tagliabue, G., 'Gramsci tra Croce e Marx', *Il Ponte*, IV (May 1948).

——, 'Il pensiero di Gramsci e il marxismo sovietico', *Rassegna d'Italia*, III (July 1948).

Mouffe, C., 'Hegemony and Ideology in Gramsci', in C. Mouffe (ed.), *Gramsci and Marxist Theory* (London, Routledge & Kegan Paul, 1979).

Mura, G., 'A Gramsci tra storicismo e intellettualismo', *Civitas*, 11–12 (Nov.–Dec. 1966).

Natta, A., 'Egemonia, cultura, partito nel pensiero di Antonio Gramsci', *Rinascita—Il Contemporaneo*, 5 (29 Jan. 1971).

——, Il partito politico nel "Quaderni del carcere"', in *Prassi rivoluzionaria*, cited above.

Nardone, G., *Il pensiero di Gramsci* (Bari, De Donato, 1971).

Orfei, R., *Antonio Gramsci, coscienza critica del marxismo* (San Casciano, Relazioni sociali, 1965).

Ottino, C., *Concetti fondamentali nella teoria di Antonio Gramsci* (Feltrinelli, Milan, 1956).

Paggi, L., *Antonio Gramsci e il moderno principe* (Rome, Editori Riuniti, 1970).

——, 'Dopo la sconfitta della rivoluzione in Occidente', *Rinascita* (4 Feb. 1977).

Paris, R., 'Il Gramsci di tutti', *Giovane critica* (Spring–Summer 1967).

Perlini, T., *Gramsci e il Gramscismo* (Milan, CELUC, 1974).

Piccone, P., 'Gramsci's Hegelian Marxism', *Political Theory*, 2 (Feb. 1974).

Pintor, L., 'Il partito di tipo nuovo', *Il Manifesto*, 4 (Sept. 1969).

Piotte, J., *La pensée politique de Gramsci* (Paris, Editions Anthropos, 1970).

Pizzorno, A., 'Sul metodo di Gramsci: dalla storiografia alla scienza politica', in *Gramsci e la cultura contemporanea*, vol. II, cited above.

Portelli, H., *Gramcsi e il blocco storico*, translated from the French by M. Novella Pierini (Bari, Laterza, 1973).

Ragionieri, E., 'Gramsci e il dibattito teorico nel movimento operaio internazionale', in *Gramsci e la cultura contemporanea*, vol. I, cited above.

Reichers, C., *Antonio Gramsci: Marxismus in Italien* (Frankfurt, Europäische Verlaganstalt, 1970).

Rossanda, R., 'Da Marx a Marx', *Il Manifesto*, 4 (Sept. 1969).

Rossi, P., 'Antonio Gramsci sulla scienza moderna', *Critica marxista*, 14 (March–April 1976).

Salamini, L., 'Gramsci and Marxist Sociology of Knowledge', *Sociological Quarterly*, 15 (Summer 1974).

Salinari, C. and Spinella, M., Introduction to their reader of selections from Gramsci's works, *Antonio Gramsci: Antologia popolare degli scritti e delle lettere* (Rome, Editori Riuniti, 1957).

Salvadori, M., *Gramsci e il problema storico della democrazia* (Turin, Einaudi, 1973).

——, 'Politica, potere e cultura nel pensiero di Gramsci', *Rivista di storia contemporanea* (Jan. 1972).

——, 'Gramsci and the PCI: Two Conceptions of Hegemony', in C. Mouffe (ed.), *Gramsci and Marxist Theory*, cited above.

Sechi, S., 'Gramsci a Turi', *Rinascita sarda* (1–15 Oct. 1966).

Sereni, E., 'Gramsci e la scienza d'avanguardia', *Società*, IV (1948).

Soave, E., 'Appunti sulle origini teoriche e pratiche dei consigli di fabbrica a Torino', *Rivista storica del socialismo*, VII (Jan.–April 1964).

Spriano, P., 'Gramsci e Lenin', *Rinascita* (15 May 1970).

——, *L'Occupazione delle fabbriche* (Turin, Einaudi, 1964). Translated into English by G. Williams, *The Occupation of the Factories* (London, Pluto Press, 1975).

Tamburrano, G., *Antonio Gramsci, La vita, il pensiero, l'azione* (Bari, Laterza, 1963).

——, 'Fasi di sviluppo del pensiero politico di Gramsci', in *La Città futura*, cited above.

——, 'Gramsci e l'egemonia del proletariato', *Studi gramsciani*, cited above.

Tarrow, S., *Peasant Communism in Southern Italy* (London, Yale Univ. Press, 1967), Chapter 5.

Texier, J., 'Gramsci, théoricien des superstructures', *La Pensée*, N. 139 (1968).

Togliatti, P., *La formazione del gruppo dirigente del partito comunista italiano* (Rome, Editori Riuniti, 1965).

——, *Gramsci* (Florence, Parenti, 1955). A collection of articles and addresses on Gramsci.

——, 'Il Leninismo nel pensiero e nell'azione di A. Gramsci', in *Studi gramsciani*, cited above.

Tronti, M., 'Alcune questioni intorno al marxismo di Gramsci', in *Studi gramsciani*, cited above.

——, 'Tra materialismo dialettico e filosofia della prassi: Gramsci e Labriola'. *La Città futura*, cited above.

Vacca, G., 'La "quistione politica degli intellettuali" e la teoria marxista dello Stato nel pensiero di Gramsci', in *Politica e storia in Gramsci*, cited above.

Vajda, M., 'Gramsci, la filosofia e le masse', *Aut Aut* (May–June 1973).

Williams, G., 'The Concept of Egemonia in the Thought of Antonio Gramsci', *Journal of the History of Ideas*, XXI (Oct.–Dec. 1960).

——, *Proletarian Order: Antonio Gramsci, Factory Councils and the Origins of Italian Communism 1911–1921* (London, Pluto Press, 1975).

V. *Other Works Cited*

Acton, H. B., 'The Materialist Conception of History', *Proceedings of the Aristotelian Society* (1951–2).

——. 'Some Criticisms of Historical Materialism', *Proceedings of the Aristotelian Society*, Supplementary Volume, 1970.

Almond, G. and Verba, S., *The Civic Culture: Political Attitudes and Democracy in Five Nations* (Princeton Univ. Press, 1963).

Althusser, L., 'Ideology and Ideological State Apparatuses' in *Lenin and Philosophy and Other Essays*, translated by B. Brewster (London, New Left Books, 1971).

——, and Balibar, E., *Reading Capital*, translated by B. Brewster (London, New Left Books, 1970).

Anderson, P., 'The Origins of the Present Crisis', in P. Anderson and R. Blackburn (eds.), *Towards Socialism* (Ithaca, N.Y., Cornell Univ. Press. 1966).

Bell, D., *The End of Ideology* (Glencoe, Ill., Free Press, 1960), Epilogue.

Berlin, I., *Vico and Herder* (London, The Hogarth Press, 1976).

Berlinguer, E., *La proposta comunista* (Turin, Einaudi, 1975).

Birnbaum, N., 'The Crisis in Marxist Sociology' in *Towards a Critical*

Sociology (New York, Oxford Univ. Press, 1971).

Blalock, H. M., 'Theory Building and Causal Inference', in H. M. Blalock and A. B. Blalock (eds.), *Methodology in Social Research* (New York, McGraw-Hill, 1968).

Blau, P., *Exchange and Power in Social Life* (New York, Wiley, 1964).

Bottomore, T., *Classes in Modern Society* (London, Allen & Unwin, 1965).

Brehm, J. W. and Cohen, A. R., *Explorations in Cognitive Dissonance* (New York, Wiley, 1962).

Bukharin, N., *Historical Materialism: a System of Sociology* (Ann Arbor, University of Michigan Press, 1969).

Cannon, I. C., 'Ideology and Occupational Community', *Sociology* (May 1967).

Carr, H. Wildon, *The Philosophy of Benedetto Croce* (London, Macmillan, 1917).

Carter, A., *The Political Theory of Anarchism* (London, Routledge & Kegan Paul, 1971).

Cassirer, E., *The Question of Jean-Jacques Rousseau* (Indiana, 1963).

Chinoy, E., *Automobile Workers and the American Dream* (New York, Random House, 1955).

Cliff, T., *Rosa Luxemburg*. published as volumes 2 and 3 of *International Socialism* (1959).

Cohen, S., *Bukharin and the Bolshevik Revolution* (New York, Vintage Books, 1975).

Converse, P., 'The Nature of Belief Systems in Mass Publics', in D. Apter (ed.), *Ideology and Discontent* (London, Collier-Macmillan, 1964).

Croce, B., *Cultura e vita morale* (Bari, Laterza, 1955).

——, *Logic as the Science of the Pure Concept*, translated by D. Ainslie (London, Macmillan, 1917).

——, *La storia come pensiero e come azione* (Bari, Laterza, 1938).

——, *Storia dell'età barocca in Italia* (Bari, Laterza, 1929).

——, *Storia d'Europa nel secolo decimonono* (Bari, Laterza, 1932).

——, *Storia d'Italia dal 1871 al 1915* (Bari, Laterza, 1928).

——, *Storia del Regno di Napoli* (Bari, Laterza, 1925).

——, *Theory and History of Historiography*, translated by D. Ainslie (London, Harrap, 1921).

Curry, R. L. and Wade, L. L., *A Theory of Political Exchange* (Englewood Cliffs, N.J., Prentice-Hall, 1968).

Dahrendorf, R., *Class and Class Conflict in Industrial Society* (London, Routledge & Kegan Paul, 1959).

de Tocqueville, A., *Democracy in America*, translated by H. Reeve (New York, Century and Co., 1899), vol. I.

Duncan, G. and Lukes, S., 'The New Democracy', *Political Studies*, XI (June 1963).

Dunn, J., 'The Identity of the History of Ideas', *Philosophy*, XLIII (April 1968).

Durkheim, E., *The Rules of Sociological Method*, translated by S. Solovay and J. Mueller (Glencoe, Ill., Free Press, 1950).

Edelman, M., *The Symbolic Uses of Politics* (Urbana, Univ. of Illinois Press, 1964).

Engels, F., *The Condition of the Working Class in England* (London, 1892).

——, *The Dialectics of Nature* (Moscow, Progress Publishers, 1954).

Evans, M., *Karl Marx* (London, Allen & Unwin, 1975).

Femia, J. V., 'Élites, Participation and the Democratic Creed', *Political Studies*, XXVII (March 1979).

Festinger, L., *A Theory of Cognitive Dissonance* (Stanford University Press, 1957).

Friedrich, C. J., *A New Belief in the Common Man* (New York, Little, Brown, 1942).

Garson, G. D., 'Radical Issues in the History of the American Working Class', *Politics and Society*, 3 (Fall 1972).

Geertz, C., 'Ideology as a Cultural System', in D. Apter (ed.), *Ideology and Discontent*, cited above.

Gerratana, V., *Ricerche di storia del Marxismo* (Rome, Editori Riuniti, 1972).

Gewirth, A., 'Political Justice' in R. B. Brandt (ed.), *Social Justice* (Englewood Cliffs, N.J., Prentice-Hall, 1962).

Giddens, A., *The Class Structure of the Advanced Societies* (London, Hutchinson, 1973).

Goldthorpe, J., et al., *The Affluent Worker in the Class Structure* (Cambridge University Press, 1968), vol. I.

Hands, G., 'Roberto Michels and the Study of Political Parties', *British Journal of Political Science*, I (April 1971).

Hill, S., *The Dockers: Class and Tradition in London* (London, Heinemann, 1976).

Hobsbawm, E. J., *The Age of Capital* (London, Weidenfeld & Nicolson, 1975).

——, *Primitive Rebels* (New York, W. W. Norton, 1959).

Horowitz, I. L., 'Consensus, Conflict, and Co-operation: a Sociological Inventory', *Social Forces* (Dec. 1962).

Kautsky, K., *The Dictatorship of the Proletariat* (Ann Arbor, Univ. of Michigan Press, 1964).

Kerr, C., Dunlop, J. T., et al., *Industrialism and Industrial Man* (London, Heinemann, 1962).

Kolakowski, L., 'Karl Marx and the Classical Definition of Truth', in

Marxism and Beyond (London, Paladin, 1971).

Labriola, A., *Essays on the Materialist Conception of History*, translated by C. H. Kerr (Chicago, Charles H. Kerr & Co., 1908).

——, *Socialism and Philosophy*, translated by E. Untermann (St. Louis, Mo., Telos Press, 1980).

Lenin, V. I., *Collected Works* (London, Lawrence & Wishart, 1962), volumes 10, 16.

——, *What is to be Done?* (Moscow, Progress Publishers, 1967).

Levi, C., *Christ Stopped at Eboli*, translated by F. Frenaye (New York, Farrar, Strauss and Co., 1947).

Lichtheim, G., 'On the Interpretation of Marx's Thought', in N. Lobkowicz, (ed.), *Marx and the Western World* (Indiana, University of Notre Dame Press, 1967).

Locke, J., *Two Treatises of Civil Government* (New York, The New American Library, 1965).

Lukács, G., *History and Class Consciousness*, translated by R. Livingstone (London, Merlin Press, 1971).

Lukes, S., 'Relativism: Cognitive and Moral', in *Essays in Social Theory* (London, Macmillan, 1977).

Mann, M., *Consciousness and Action Among the Western Working Class* (London, Macmillan, 1973).

Marcuse, H., *One-Dimensional Man* (London, Sphere Books, 1972).

——, Wolff, R. P. and Moore, B., *Critique of Pure Tolerance* (London, Jonathan Cape, 1969).

Marramao, G., *Marxismo e revisionismo in Italia* (Bari, De Donato, 1971).

Marx and Engels: Basic Writings on Politics and Philosophy, edited by L. S. Feuer (New York, Doubleday, 1959).

Marx, K., *Capital*, vol. I, translated by S. Moore and E. Aveling (London, Lawrence & Wishart, 1974).

Karl Marx: Selected Writings in Sociology and Social Philosphy, edited and translated by T. B. Bottomore and M. Rubel (Harmondsworth, Middx., Penguin Books, 1961).

Writings of the Young Marx on Philosophy and Society, edited and translated by L. D. Easton and K. H. Guddat (New York, Doubleday, 1967).

McKenzie, R. and Silver, A., *Angels in Marble: Working Class Conservatives in Urban England* (London, Heinemann, 1968).

Michels, R., *Political Parties*, translated by E. and C. Paul (New York, Dover Publications, 1959).

Miliband, R., *Marxism and Politics* (Oxford University Press, 1977).

——, *The State in Capitalist Society* (London, Quartet Books, 1973).

Moore, S., *Three Tactics, the Background in Marx* (New York, Monthly

Review Press, 1963).

Mouzelis, N. P., *Organization and Bureaucracy* (London, Routledge & Kegan Paul, 1969).

Napolitano, G., *The Italian Road to Socialism*, an interview with E. Hobsbawm (London, Lawrence Hill & Co., 1977).

Nichols, T. and Armstrong, P., *Workers Divided* (Glasgow, Fontana, 1976).

Nordlinger, E., *The Working Class Tories* (London, MacGibbon and Kee, 1967).

Parkin, F., *Class Inequality and Political Order* (London, Paladin, 1972).

Parsons, T. and Shils, E., eds., *Towards a General Theory of Action* (Cambridge, Mass., Harvard University Press, 1951).

Partridge, P. H., *Consent and Consensus* (London, Pall Mall Press, 1971).

Piccone, P., 'Labriola and the Roots of Eurocommunism', *Berkeley Journal of Sociology*, XXII (Winter 1977–8).

Plamenatz, J., *Consent, Freedom, and Political Obligation* (London, Oxford University Press, 1968).

——, *Man and Society* (two volumes, London, Longmans, 1963).

Poulantzas, N., 'The Problem of the Capitalist State' in R. Blackburn (ed.), *Ideology in Social Science* (London, Fontana, 1972).

Rinascita (29 August 1964). Contains transcripts of some of Togliatti's most famous speeches.

Rodman, H., 'The Lower Class Value Stretch', *Social Forces* (Dec. 1963).

Rolland, R., *Jean-Christophe* (Paris, Editions Michel, 1956).

Roth, G., *The Social Democrats in Imperial Germany* (Totowa, N.J., The Bedminster Press, 1963).

Runciman, W. G., *Relative Deprivation and Social Justice* (London, Routledge & Kegan Paul, 1966).

Rytina, J. H., et al., 'Income and Stratification Ideology: Beliefs about the American Opportunity Structure', *American Journal of Sociology* (Jan. 1970).

Sabine, G. H., *A History of Political Theory* (London, Holt, Rinehart and Winston, 1961).

Saville, J., 'Ideology of Labourism', in R. Benewick, et al. (eds.), *Knowledge and Belief in Politics* (London, Allen & Unwin, 1973).

Shils, E., 'Centre and Periphery', in *The Logic of Personal Knowledge: Essays Presented to Michael Polanyi* (London, Routledge & Kegan Paul, 1961).

Skinner, Q., 'Meaning and Understanding in the History of Ideas', *History and Theory*, 8 (1969).

Sorel, G., *Reflections on Violence*, translated by T. E. Hulme (New York,

Collier, 1961).

Stedman-Jones, G., 'The Marxism of the Early Lukács', *New Left Review*, 70 (Nov.–Dec. 1971).

Togliatti, P., *Partito comunista italiano* (Rome, Editori Riuniti, 1961).

——, *Sul movimento operaio internazionale* (Rome, Editori Riuniti, 1964).

——, *La via italiana al socialismo* (Rome, Editori Riuniti, 1964).

Veness, T., *School Leavers: Their Aspirations and Expectations* (London, Methuen, 1962).

Wicker, A. W., 'Attitudes *v.* Actions: the Relationship of Verbal and Overt Responses to Attitude Objects', *Journal of Social Issues*, 25 (1969).

Wolin, S., *Politics and Vision* (London, Allen & Unwin, 1961).

Index